DARKNESS FALLING

Peter Walther is the author of a bestselling biography of Hans Fallada. He studied German and art history and gained his doctorate in 1995. He has worked as a curator for numerous literary exhibitions and co-founded the Literaturport website with Ulrich Janetzki. He heads the Brandenburg Literary Office in Potsdam with Hendrik Röder.

Peter Lewis read German at St Edmund Hall, Oxford and Albert-Ludwigs-Universität, Freiburg, before taking his doctorate and teaching at St Anne's College, Oxford. He still lives in Oxford, where he works as a writer and translator. His recent translations include Heinrich Gerlach's epic war novel *Breakout at Stalingrad* (published by Head of Zeus in 2018) and Gunnar Decker's *Hesse: The Wanderer and His Shadow*.

DARKNESS
FALLING

THE STRANGE DEATH OF
THE WEIMAR REPUBLIC,
1930—33

PETER WALTHER

Translated from the German by Peter Lewis

HEAD
of ZEUS

An Apollo Book

First published in Germany as *Fieber* in 2020 by Aufbau Verlag
This translation first published in the UK in 2021 by Head of Zeus Ltd
This paperback edition first published in 2022 by Head of Zeus Ltd,
part of Bloomsbury Publishing Plc

9 7 5 3 1 2 4 6 8

A catalogue record for this book is available from
the British Library.

The translation of this work was supported
by a grant from the Goethe-Institut.

ISBN (PB): 9781800242272
ISBN (E): 9781800242289

Typeset by Ben Cracknell Studios

Printed and bound in Great Britain by
CPI Group (UK) Ltd, Croydon CR0 4YY

Head of Zeus Ltd
5–8 Hardwick Street
London EC1R 4RG
WWW.HEADOFZEUS.COM

CONTENTS

'As if whipped on by unseen spirits, Time's horses of Helios bolt, dragging behind them the flimsy chariot of our destiny and all we can do, with grim determination, is grasp the reins and steer the wheels – now left and now right – to try and stop ourselves from smashing into the cliff face or plunging into the abyss. Who knows where we will end up?'

Goethe, *Egmont*, Act II

Timeline

1929

24 October Beginning of the global economic crisis. Along with the USA, the German Empire is hardest hit.

1930

March An attempt to reform the unemployment insurance fund brings about the collapse of the Grand Coalition between the SPD, Centre and three smaller parties.

30 March Reich President Paul von Hindenburg names Heinrich Brüning from the Catholic Centre Party as Chancellor. Brüning's administration governs with the tacit support of sections of the German Nationalists and the SPD.

15 July After failing to win support for a piece of draft legislation, Brüning dissolves parliament and calls new elections.

14 September In the parliamentary elections, the NSDAP increases its share of the vote from 2.6 to 18.3 per cent, becoming the second largest party in the Reichstag; the Communist KPD also gains an increased mandate (13.1 per cent).

25 September During a trial in Leipzig of National Socialist army officers accused of high treason, Hitler pledges to seek power solely through legal means ('Legality Oath').

19 October With the support of the SPD, Brüning defeats a parliamentary motion of no confidence brought against him.

1931

13 July The collapse of the Dresdner Bank and the Danat-Bank sparks a banking crisis in Germany.

9 August A plebiscite supported by the NSDAP, various right-wing parties and the KPD to dissolve the Prussian parliament fails to gain sufficient support.

12 September Anti-Semitic rioting erupts in Berlin (the 'Kurfürstendamm Pogrom').

11 October Formation of the anti-democratic 'Harzburg Front' alliance by the NSDAP, the German National Party (DNVP) and a right-wing ex-servicemen's association, the 'Stahlhelm'.

25 November During a house search by police, the 'Boxheim Papers' – plans for a violent seizure of power by the National Socialists – are discovered and made public.

16 December Formation of the left-wing 'Iron Front', an alliance between the 'Reichsbanner' organization, trade unions and workers' sporting associations.

1932

25 February Hitler is naturalized as a German citizen (a vital requirement for running in the 1932 presidential elections) after he is appointed as a delegate to the *Reichsrat* ('upper house' of the German parliament) for the Free State of Brunswick by its interior minister Dietrich Klagges, an NSDAP member.

10 April In the presidential election, Hindenburg secures victory over Hitler and Thälmann in the second round of voting and is returned as president.

13 April The SA and SS are proscribed by General Wilhelm Groener, who holds the portfolios of minister of the interior and defence minister.

24 April In regional elections in Prussia, the NSDAP increases its share of the vote from 1.84 to almost 37 per cent and becomes the strongest political force in the region; it also makes large gains in Bavaria, Württemberg, Saxony-Anhalt and Hamburg.

12 May Wilhelm Groener resigns as defence minister.

30 May Brüning is dismissed as Chancellor by President Hindenburg.

1 June Franz von Papen is appointed Chancellor, heading a presidential cabinet.

14 June A secret agreement results in a lifting of the ban on the SA and SS; widespread violent civil unrest mars campaigning for the upcoming parliamentary election.

9 July The Lausanne Conference of delegates from the UK, Germany and France ends with an agreement to suspend Germany's crippling war reparations payments.

10 July Violent clashes between the NSDAP, Reichsbanner and communists in the Silesian town of Ohlau (Oława).

17 July The 'Altona Bloody Sunday' sees pre-election violence reach a high point. A firefight involving members of the SA and SS, communists and the police leaves eighteen dead. A report concludes most of them were killed by police gunfire.

20 July In the so-called 'Prussian Coup' (*Preußenschlag*), the ruling SPD government of the state of Prussia is dissolved by emergency presidential decree; Papen is installed as Reich Commissar of Prussia.

31 July The NSDAP emerges from the parliamentary elections as the strongest party, with 37.4 per cent of the vote; the other big winners are the communists.

10 August In Potempa in Upper Silesia, SA stormtroopers carry out a brutal murder, beating a trade unionist to death in front of his mother; in the ensuing trial, Hitler expresses solidarity with the perpetrators.

13 August Hindenburg grants Hitler an audience; the Reich President refuses to name Hitler Chancellor.

12 September A vote of no confidence is passed against Papen's government, forcing Hindenburg to dissolve parliament once more.

3–7 November Communists and National Socialists form a tactical alliance in support of a strike on the Berlin transport network. The management and unions of the capital's transport authority are dominated by the socialist SPD.

6 November In the parliamentary elections, the NSDAP's vote share falls to 33.1 per cent though it remains the strongest party.

17 November Franz von Papen resigns but continues in office as head of a caretaker government.

2 December Army minister Kurt von Schleicher is appointed the new Chancellor, while retaining his defence portfolio; his attempts to form a 'third position' by building a coalition between the SPD, trade unions and more moderate elements of the NSDAP fail, nor does he succeed in splitting the NSDAP.

1933

4 January Secret meeting between Papen and Hitler at the house of the banker Baron Kurt von Schröder; Papen sounds out the possibility of forming a government with Hitler.

10 January Papen and Hitler meet at the villa of Joachim von Ribbentrop in Berlin-Dahlem.

15 January Following its losses in the parliamentary elections of the previous November, the NSDAP scores a symbolic victory when it wins control in regional elections held in the small state of Lippe.

18 January Further talks between Papen and Hitler in Ribbentrop's villa.

28 January Schleicher resigns after Hindenburg withdraws his support.

30 January Hitler is named Reich Chancellor; initially, Hitler's cabinet contains only two other National Socialists.

1 February President Hindenburg dissolves parliament.

4 February With Hindenburg's approval, Hitler issues the 'Ordinance for the Protection of the German People'; freedom of the press and the right to free assembly are curtailed.

22 February Fifty thousand members of the SA and the SS are appointed as armed 'auxiliary policemen'.

27 February The Reichstag fire leads to nationwide repression of political opponents by the Nazis.

28 February The 'Decree of the Reich President for the Protection of the People and State' is issued, revoking a range of basic civil liberties and legalizing 'protective detention'.

5 March New elections to the Reichstag and the Prussian regional parliament, the last multiparty election in pre-war Germany: even though all other parties are massively hampered in their campaigning, the National Socialists and the German Nationalists still only secure a slim majority across the country.

8 March Communist Party members are disbarred from sitting in parliament; the Nazis enact 'co-ordination' measures (*Gleichschaltung*) imposing central control over all state assemblies throughout Germany.

21 March Joseph Goebbels marks the inauguration of the newly elected Reichstag by staging the 'Day of Potsdam', a ceremony designed to symbolize the alliance of the old Kingdom of Prussia with the new National Socialist movement; the first Nazi concentration camp is built at Oranienburg near Berlin.

23 March The 'Enabling Act', giving Hitler sweeping executive powers, in the presence of armed SA and SS units; only the SPD delegates in the Reichstag vote against the act.

The Straight Shooter

Heinrich Brüning

1

The little wooden house on Carpenter Street in Norwich, Vermont, painted rust-red, lies just a few hundred metres from the Connecticut River. Broad fields spread out to the east; to the north and west the property is bordered by woodland. To the south, however, there is a view of the small town. The main attraction in Norwich is the General Store.

The old man who purchased the house and garden with a down payment of $25,000 thirteen years ago takes great pleasure in seeing the trees grow taller year on year. Come the autumn, he gazes out of the wide windows of the house and watches the flocks of birds gathering for their annual migration. Occasionally his life companion, Claire Nix, who is thirty-three years his junior, will read to him from the works of Alexander von Humboldt or Annette von Droste-Hülshoff. Or they sit together listening to Haydn's 'Emperor' quartet or Schubert's *Winterreise*. The little property is guarded by Puli, the Hungarian sheepdog.[1]

The German newspapers and magazines are always a few days old by the time they arrive, but the news bulletins they pick up direct from Bonn on the radio are up to date. For many years now, the old man has been following the short-wave broadcasts. Konrad

Adenauer's 'mayoralty', as he is wont to rather disrespectfully call his former political rival's tenure as German Chancellor, is by now long over, and even his old friend Heinrich Lübke is no longer President of the federal republic. On the other hand, Walter Ulbricht, whose high-pitched voice he can still vividly recall from back then, continues to rule the roost in East Germany.

If he turns the dial on his radio and changes frequency, he can hear 'Honky Tonk Women' by the Rolling Stones or Marvin Gaye's 'I Heard It Through the Grapevine'. It is 30 March 1970. Four decades to the day after he took office, the former Chancellor of Germany Heinrich Brüning dies in faraway Vermont. According to the records of the Norwich municipal archives,[2] the household and personal effects he leaves in his estate amount to $540, while his unpublished papers are valued at one hundred dollars.

As the figure of the wanderer in Schubert's *Winterreise* sings: '*I came here as a stranger, / A stranger I depart.*'

2

'Well done, this is your handiwork. You've got your man into office.'[3] With these words, Theodor Wolff, editor-in-chief of the *Berliner Tageblatt*, congratulates General Kurt von Schleicher on the evening of 30 March 1930, after Heinrich Brüning's swearing-in as Chancellor of the Reich. Three days earlier, Brüning was sitting in his favourite restaurant, the Weinhaus Rheingold, with a group of friends from the Centre Party.[4]

This restaurant, on Potsdamer Straße, is divided into fourteen separate rooms. As if it were one large theme park, each room is inspired by a particular era or cultural milieu. The Bar Americain is designed as a space for the general public, while the home-grown clientele prefers the Kaisersaal ('Imperial Room'), where customers rub shoulders with busts of Charlemagne, Holy Roman Emperor Otto I, Friedrich Barbarossa and Wilhelm I.

The decor is opulent – mahogany, onyx marble and ebony – the cuisine refined. Up to 4,000 guests can be accommodated in the Weinhaus Rheingold, though the excessive luxury of the place stands in rather unsettling contrast to the surrounding area's distinct lack of exclusivity. This cavernous restaurant is also popular with the leaders of other parties, for instance the National Socialists. Whenever the 'chief' is in Berlin and party funds will allow it, he stays at the Kaiserhof and invites his confederates to the Rheingold in the evening, where he holds court in the company of his pretty niece Geli, alongside Hess, Göring, Amann and Goebbels.

The topic of the evening among Brüning's little circle of regulars is the fall of Müller's cabinet. It's a source of general wonder that the Social Democrat (SPD) government even lasted as long as it did. Brüning's take on the demise of his predecessor's administration is that Chancellor Hermann Müller had been 'slowly tortured to death by his own party'.[5] The SPD had for too long been forced to swallow all manner of unpalatable policies, the last straw being the Chancellor's pet project, the 'Armoured Cruiser A'. What was it that the Social Democrats had proclaimed on their posters during the general election campaign of 1928? 'Feed Children – Don't Build Cruisers!' Whereupon they'd duly gone ahead and approved construction of the vessel.

That same evening in Wilhelmstraße, the heart of the government district, President Hindenburg's secretary of state Otto Meissner tries, initially without success, to contact Brüning. Eventually, a messenger tracks down the group in the Rheingold, just ten minutes away, and a note is passed to Brüning from his old friend from student days and fellow centre-right politician Gottfried Treviranus, asking him to come to the Reich President's palace the following morning at nine o'clock. Everyone around the table knows what's afoot: it falls to Joseph Wirth, who has already borne the burden of the office that is now about to be bestowed upon his party colleague, to spell it out: 'It's your turn to take the helm, Heinrich.'[6]

3

The entry in the baptismal register at the church of St Ludger in Münster in November 1885 records the name of Heinrich Aloysius Maria Elisabeth Brüning, but in the family the boy is known simply as Harry. Heinrich is the youngest of six children, though three of his siblings die in childhood. He has no early memories of his father, the owner of a vinegar distillery and a wine store, as Heinrich was only eighteen months old when he passed away. Now his mother is left on her own with her three surviving children: Joseph, Heinrich's eleven-year-old brother; his sister Maria, aged six; and Heinrich.[7] When the boy goes out with his mother in Münster, he enjoys turning cartwheels or somersaults out of sheer exuberance. Little Heinrich also likes to press his ear up against telegraph poles and declaim messages that he wants broadcast all around the globe.[8] His hometown has been an episcopal see for the past eleven centuries. Catholicism and the Prussian state – a deep sense of religious belonging and at the same time the idea that an individual's highest calling should be to 'serve the common good in freedom' – make a strong impression on the growing boy. Casting his critical eye on Brüning in 1930, Carl von Ossietsky called the new German Chancellor 'Father Filucius [an anti-Jesuit caricature created by the satirical illustrator Wilhelm Busch] with the Iron Cross, First Class, hanging from his rosary'[9] and described him as having a 'sharp-nosed face made of parchment'. Leaving aside the intentionally disparaging and wounding tone of these remarks, isn't it true to say that Brüning the politician has a rather Jesuitical, elitist and ascetic air about him? As Chancellor, he will take decisions from a lofty height that are driven 'purely by practical constraints' and won't allow himself to be distracted by 'the general clamour'. Then again, at times when the pressure of work is less, he is assailed by bouts of gloom.

The key features of his psychological make-up – a tendency

towards melancholy and depression – are traits that he has inherited. Yet certain childhood experiences appear to have reinforced this predisposition. From early on, short-sightedness forces the rather frail boy to wear glasses. At seven, Heinrich suffers a heart spasm as the result of an accident. He experiences severe coronary pain, his pulse starts to race, only then to stop altogether, and for several minutes he is brought to a halt by a shortness of breath and panic attacks. Up to the age of fifteen he has to avoid any physical exertion. This means that he is excluded from organized sports and from playing and careering around with his classmates, and so escapes into the world of books.

At the Paulinum grammar school, which he enters after primary school, he is among the top pupils. This is the oldest humanist educational institution in Germany, founded way back in the legendary mists of time, in 797. Joseph Frey, the headmaster during Brüning's time there, presides over a rigid regime: there is a blanket ban on pupils going into public houses, and visits to the town's theatre are only permitted in exceptional circumstances. In contrast, attendance at Mass twice a week in the Jesuit church is strictly monitored, as is going to confession every six weeks. Almost every year, Heinrich spends his summer holidays with friends of his mother who live in Elbeuf in Normandy. Here, he gets to know the language and the lifestyle of Germany's neighbours to the west, an experience that renders him impervious to the widespread hatred for the 'arch enemy'.

Heinrich is an avid reader of the Catholic newspaper that his mother takes at home,[10] comparing it with other papers and building up a small archive of stories. We may assume that he gave little cause for complaint during his schooldays at the Paulinum from the fact that the headmaster gives him as a parting gift a copy of Horace's *Odes*, with a personal handwritten dedication in Latin: *Iustum et tenacem propositi virum non civium ardor prava iubentium, non voltus instantis tyranni mente quatit solida* ('The man who is just and sticks to his purpose will not be shaken from his firm resolve by either the frenzy of his fellow citizens clamouring for what is wrong, nor by the face of a threatening tyrant') begins the headmaster's quotation from Horace, and with a rather uncanny clairvoyance Dr Frey ends his dedication with the sentence: 'If the world should break in pieces around him, the ruins would leave him undaunted!' (*Si fractus illabatur orbis, impavidum ferient ruinae*).[11]

4

The evening at Weinhaus Rheingold lasts longer than anticipated. Brüning has misgivings – not just political, but also as far as his health is concerned – about plunging headlong into the adventures that now await him. His party colleague, however, the former Chancellor Joseph Wirth, is made of sterner stuff and loses no time in putting himself forward as foreign minister. Brüning has a taxi summoned. Before, he often used to travel home on the S-Bahn, but since becoming director of the umbrella organization representing Christian trade unions he no longer feels that's compatible with his position. His lodgings are situated on the other side of the Tiergarten, in the Alt-Moabit district. There, he lives in two furnished rooms as the tenant of Frau Heidemann. Brüning has remained a bachelor, just like his brother, who, in his role as a missionary and priest, has travelled the world widely but now lives in the USA. His sister, likewise, has never started a family.

The apartment at 15 Kirchstraße is barely presentable. That's quite a disadvantage for the leader of a major party, the Catholic Centre Party, for in times such as these, when there's little more to be said in parliament, it has become customary to gather in private dwellings in the evenings in order to conduct political business. A confession that Brüning made to a friend in later life reveals just how firm his conviction must have been when young that he could plan out his whole political career, and how assiduously he'd tried to insulate himself against life's surprises. He told his friend that he'd made 'a mistake' in not getting married, but that he'd thought that 'anyone who dedicates his life to serving mankind and the common good ought not to give himself solely to another person or start a family'.[12]

If it had been down to his mother, he would have followed his brother into the priesthood. But during his studies in Munich and Strasbourg his field of interests broadens and he starts attending lectures on philosophy, history, German literature and political sciences. He reads Plato's *Politeia* in the original and becomes fascinated with ancient Sparta as the ideal model state. A Spartan, then, an aristocrat of the intellect: his fellow Strasbourg student Gottfried Treviranus recalls that he rarely heard him laugh out loud, but that he smiled a lot.[13] The concise philosophy and the musical education of the Dorians appeal to Brüning the student: 'They taught their laws, hymns and encomia – in other words jurisprudence, religion and history – through the act of singing.'[14] In the company of friends he attends organ recitals by Albert Schweitzer, and is a keen piano player himself. He reads Dostoyevsky, Baudelaire and Voltaire and translates Virgil into German verse. He is captivated by the work of the English writer Walter Pater, an aesthete in his own right, who was hailed by his pupil Oscar Wilde as the best English prose author of his day. For decades, a plan to write a book about Pater remains an unfulfilled ambition for Brüning; even when he becomes Chancellor, Pater's works are always within easy reach in his study.

Eventually, Brüning sits the exams to qualify as a university lecturer. But instead of taking up a teaching post, he turns to the study of economics, attending first the London School of Economics and then the University of Bonn. By the time he finally completes his higher education ten years later, writing his doctoral dissertation in 1915, the First World War is in full swing. The myopic Doctor of Political Economics is conscripted into the army, where he is quickly promoted to lieutenant and company commander and is awarded the Iron Cross, First Class for valour. A staff report written by one of his superiors says of Brüning: 'He was held in high esteem by his comrades, and was loved and respected by his subordinates. He was one of those rare individuals who have no enemies.'[15] Brüning's war experiences further help convince him to forego a career in academia and seek his future in politics. He gets involved in Catholic welfare programmes, where he finds himself working alongside the renowned urban pastor Carl Sonnenschein, whom Kurt Tucholsky once called the 'gypsy of welfare'.[16] He also becomes an adviser to the Prussian Minister for Welfare. In 1919 he is appointed director of the League of Christian Trade Unions and in 1924 is elected to the Reichstag as a member of the Centre Party. There he soon gains recognition for his sound knowledge of fiscal matters. Yet the confirmed bachelor's taciturn nature and seriousness, allied to the air of asceticism he exudes, ensures that his circle of friends remains small. And he himself does not seek approval. He has brought from his wartime service the yardstick by which he judges anyone he encounters: 'How would he react when under fire, or after the fighting has ended, or in the absence of any orders?'[17]

5

On the night of Thursday 27/Friday 28 March, after the evening at the Rheingold, Brüning gets only two hours' sleep. On the Friday morning, he makes his way through the rainy streets of Berlin to Wilhelmstraße. Passing the two guards at the door, he heads for the office of Dr Meissner, who announces his arrival to the President. Hindenburg isn't exactly thrilled to be charging the leader of the Catholic Centre Party with the task of forming a new government. He has never been able to shake off his old feeling of resentment, which he has harboured since the days of the 'cultural struggle' (*Kulturkampf*) between the Prussian state and the Roman Catholic

Church in the 1870s, that Catholics are an 'un-German' body of people directed by a foreign agency. And yet the man comes to him with the warmest of recommendations from General von Schleicher. If parliament is to continue to govern the country at all, it will need someone like Brüning: a conservative, but one who, as a trade unionist at the same time, will be able to reach an accommodation with the Social Democrats while also having the trust of the armed forces.

With his erect military bearing, the eighty-two-year-old victor of Tannenberg, who has long since become a living legend, greets the slightly built reserve lieutenant. Hindenburg has received no fewer than eleven honorary doctorates and is in addition a freeman of 172 towns in Germany.[18] In 1915, when he fought this battle, the most famous engagement of his career, he saved the Fatherland from Russian invasion. On the Western Front, the pride of the German army had already become bogged down in the trenches, and the first two years of the war had been 'bloodily frittered away' as Field Marshal Hindenburg was later to remark, and only in the east had progress been possible, as the Russians, who had already advanced deep into East Prussia, were routed and driven out of Germany. That same year, an effigy of the country's saviour was carved out of twenty-six tons of alder wood and erected directly in front of the Reichstag. This statue of 'Iron Hindenburg' is the largest wooden sculpture in the world, and in return for a donation to aid the war effort people can hammer nail after nail into him. Ultimately, he ends up looking less like a hero and more like a hedgehog.*

Two days after his meeting with the President, Brüning has drawn up his list of cabinet posts. At the swearing-in ceremony,

---

* 'Iron Hindenburg' was one of a number of *Nagelmänner* ('Nail Men'), large wooden sculptures created during the First World War in the German and Austro-Hungarian Empires for fundraising and propaganda purposes. For a varying tariff of donations, iron, silver or gilded nails could be driven into the figures and the proceeds used to aid the war effort. Iron crosses were also a popular motif. The Hindenburg statue was inaugurated on 4 September 1915. [Translator's note]

Hindenburg makes a pledge to the assembled ministers: 'I will stand by you, and you must stand by me.'[19] The new Chancellor moves into his quarters in Wilhelmstraße with a carpetbag, making do with a suite of just three rooms in the chancellor's palace.[20] The situation is anything but rosy. Parliament is at loggerheads, while the country is groaning under the strain of the financial crisis, which by now has even begun to affect the more prosperous regions. On Berlin's smartest street, the Kurfürstendamm, there's already a scheme in operation called 'Lunch by Instalments', which the newspaper *Deutsche Allgemeine Zeitung* describes as follows: 'People who find themselves in only temporary financial embarrassment are to be given the opportunity to have a good and cheap lunchtime meal at modest cost[21] ... The only condition is that customers must commit to eating at least seven meals within a space of a fortnight at the establishment, and for each of these they will only be required to pay a quarter of the price. The remainder of the cost is to be paid off in three monthly instalments.'

The Brüning cabinet is the seventh German administration to take office in the twelve years since the fall of the monarchy. It is the first that can no longer count on a stable majority within the parliament; as such, it's a government in a constant state of crisis. After his inauguration on the Sunday, Brüning comments: 'I am taking on a challenge that's already nine-tenths a lost cause!'[22] Three million unemployed, twenty thousand bankruptcies, more than three hundred banks forced to close their doors in the wake of the Wall Street Crash the previous year, the farming sector close to collapse, bloody clashes on the streets, loutish scenes inside the Reichstag, the country saddled with reparations payments until 1988, and leading the nation a man who says of himself that he has 'the uneasy feeling of being an outsider in most people's company': this is the dire situation facing Germany on 30 March 1930.[23]

The Dodgy Dealer

Erik Jan Hanussen

1

t's fair to say that Berlin in 1930 isn't lacking in attractions. During this year, almost 300,000 tourists visit the city. They include large numbers of Americans, British and French, who are drawn by the theatre and art scene and the permissive nightlife. They find life here very agreeable. 'Germany's First Negro Bar'[1] has set up shop in Lutherstraße opposite the Scala, the country's largest revue theatre. And among the more than one hundred bars and drinking clubs catering to homosexuals and lesbians, the Eldorado in Motzstraße has a special place. For it is here that you will sometimes find the head of Hitler's stormtroopers (the SA), Ernst Röhm, 'the little *Stabschef*, short, dumpy and energetic, his merry eyes glinting with pleasure and anticipation in his round, scarfaced bullet-head'.[2] A young Englishman described a trip to this bar with relatives who were visiting him from home: 'My Uncle Geordie was so innocent that he did not realise what was happening all round him, and was deeply shocked at finding a male organ beneath the chiffon dress of the "girl" sitting on his knee.'[3]

On the newsstands at Friedrichstraße railway station, titles such as the *Berliner Morgenpost*, *Vorwärts* and *Die Rote Fahne* vie

for space[4] with gay magazines such as *Die Freundschaft* or *Frauen Liebe*. The covers of these publications show boyishly slender, naked young women striking playfully coy poses or young men, likewise completely nude, engaged in sporting activities. There's no place on the front covers for anything genuinely shocking; such things are, however, very much in evidence in the small ads. It's there – thinly veiled as having a supposedly educational purpose – that you encounter practices verging on the unutterable. For example, there's an advertisement for the private papers of Dr Ernst Schertel, which, it is claimed, 'with their enormously rich stock of illustrations tell you more than an entire library'.[5] The author promises to enlighten his readers about all forms of 'Flagellation: involving whips, needles or knives'. Then there's the privately printed publication *Sexual Deviants* by retired Detective Superintendent Wilhelm Polzer: 'All manner of sexual perversions are presented here in a popular scientific way. Masseuses and prostitutes tell their stories quite openly.'

A book by one Dr Gitta even has literary pretensions. For two Marks and fifty pfennigs, 'a novel packed with high erotic tension' boasting the title *Der sonderbare Turnlehrer* ('The Strange Gymnastics Coach') awaits readers. Other publications have as their subject 'demonic women', 'the urge to expose oneself' and the problems of 'lesbian love' or of 'ardent desires unleashed'. The stories are invariably told 'with unparalleled frankness', and almost always reference is made to the 'numerous accompanying photographs and artistic plates'. This is a time of endless possibilities. Nor is good fortune the sole preserve of the beautiful and the wealthy; the 'genteel young ladies' who form the target readership of the magazine *Berliner Wochenschau* also deserve happiness: 'Only you know what torments you go through[6] as, day after day, you realize that your breasts don't have that lush fullness which the bosom of a truly beautiful woman should possess. So, waste no more of your precious time: write today requesting our absolutely free [...] brochure demonstrating our brand new technique for enhancing sagging or underdeveloped breasts.'

The prudishness of the former Wilhelmine era has been supplanted by a remarkably liberal atmosphere. Just a few years previously, the wearing of clothes of the opposite sex in public was seen as a criminal offence. In 1912, for example, a young man named Georg von Zobeltitz was arrested for 'causing a public nuisance' by appearing on the street dressed in women's couture that he had tailored himself. From an early age, Zobeltitz had shown an aptitude for female handicrafts. As an exposé in the *Berliner Tageblatt* explained, he was said to have 'learned to fashion his own clothing and hats with tremendous expertise'.[7] When it came to light at the police station in Weißensee that Zobeltitz had for a long while been undergoing treatment for transvestism at the clinic of Dr Magnus Hirschfeld, he was released without charge. He was subsequently issued with a 'transvestite's certificate' valid for his home region of Potsdam, which protected him from any further unpleasant run-ins. A few years later, with the opening of his private Institute for Sexual Science at the Villa Joachim in Berlin's Tiergarten in 1919, Hirschfeld established a place of refuge for people in distress and for the growing number of those interested in sexual reform.

2

After the First World War, a new form of journalism takes root in the German capital: the society pages. The general public eagerly snaps up news about the lives and general goings-on of the 'upper crust'. The bleaker the situation people find themselves in, the greater their appetite for press photos and reports of the excesses and supposedly carefree lifestyle of the rich. Almost every major newspaper has a society reporter on its staff. The uncrowned queen of the profession is Bella Fromm. She gets herself invited to all the receptions,[8] tea parties and banquets held by the diplomatic missions in the city and has access to the political elite. Yet she also maintains contact with the old courtly society of Berlin and Potsdam. She fronts charity functions and organizes fashion shows, as well as reporting on balls and sporting occasions. But her favourite line of work is political interviewing. Her columns in the *Vossische Zeitung* are often themselves masterpieces of diplomacy, for her readership, which extends to the highest echelons of society, keeps a very close eye on which matters are reported, and in what light, and on whose names appear. Even Hindenburg is known on occasion to read Bella Fromm's articles.

In this febrile period Berlin is also a fascinating posting for foreign journalists. One of those in the colony of American reporters in the city is Dorothy Thompson. The novelist Klaus Mann, who along with his sister Erika belongs to Thompson's circle of friends, describes her as a 'slender and shy girl'.[9] Since 1923 Dorothy Thompson has been trying, so far in vain, to get the leader of the National Socialist Workers' Party to grant her an interview.

Her British colleague Sefton Delmer, Berlin correspondent of the *Daily Express*, is already a step further along this same road. He has gained the confidence of leading figures in the SA, following them around in his little BMW[10] or accompanying them on planes when they go electioneering. In the process, he notices how members of Hitler's personal bodyguard are wont to produce photographs of their boyfriends from their wallets and pass them around, with observations like: 'Isn't he sweet?'[11] He can habitually be found shadowing SA chief Ernst Röhm, whom he calls a 'gay and expansive old gangster', or drinking coffee from 'pretty little Rosenthal cups'[12] in Joseph Goebbels's private apartment. The social gatherings he hosts himself are 'the only ones in Berlin at that time at which you found my new Nazi friends drinking and talking with Jews'.[13]

If one is to believe what one reads in the papers, the 'most popular man in Berlin' in the spring of 1930 is Joseph Weißenberg. Back in 1903, this son of a Catholic day labourer prophesied the abdication of Kaiser Wilhelm II 'in fifteen years' time' and in 1918 foretold the hyperinflation that hit Germany in 1923. After experiencing a vision of Christ, he gave up his job as a bricklayer and shortly afterwards founded his own church. Now he is developing a healing technique which promises successful results through a combination of the laying on of hands and administering white cheese to the afflicted person. By 1925, the ranks of his followers, or 'serious seekers', had already swollen to 20,000, and in an allusion to its leader's name the cult's house magazine was called *Der Weiße Berg* ('The White Mountain'). Not least, Weißenberg's popularity is based on the thirty-plus court cases he is embroiled in during his lifetime, which ensure that he is constantly in the public eye. In 1930, it is the case of fifteen-month-old Hildegard Hänsicke that has come to trial.[14] Her parents took the child to Weißenberg for the treatment of an eye infection. The master treated the child through the laying on of hands before sending her parents home with the recommendation that they place compresses containing curd cheese on little Hildegard's eyes twice weekly. The constant moistness meant that the inflammation never healed. The poor child's ordeal ended with the permanent loss of her sight.

In the Winter Gardens at Friedrichstraße Station, a young Silesian miner called Paul Diebel is appearing as the secular equivalent of the Bavarian stigmatic Therese of Konnersreuth. Sensational reporting in the press tempts a constant stream of spectators to come and see the show. 'Under the strictest of supervision,'[15] runs one of the newspaper articles, 'he managed, while sitting almost naked on a chair, to perform the "miracle" of weeping tears of blood. Some fifteen minutes into the performance, his eyes began to turn dark red, and shortly thereafter blood started to trickle from his eyes. After that, Diebel made a bloody cross appear on his chest, a process that only took a few seconds.' In another routine, the miner demonstrates how impervious he is to physical pain: 'He not only had numerous needles and slim blades pushed into his stomach and his lower arm without bleeding, he even went so far as to have sharpened bolts fired from a gun into his body. He then laid his hand on the table and instructed an assistant to hammer a thick nail through it. When the needle was pulled out,' the writer of the article marvelled, 'once again not a single drop of blood was visible in the wound.'

Berlin is a playground for charlatans and prophets, madmen and crooks. According to the playwright Carl Zuckmayer, the city resembled a 'very desirable woman':[16] 'We called her arrogant, snobbish, an arriviste, lacking in culture and vulgar to a degree. But secretly each of us looked upon her as the fulfilment of his heart's desire: to one person, she was a voluptuous creature, full-bosomed and dressed in lace undies, while another would see her as a slim gamine with pageboy's legs clad in black silk. Truly immoderate people saw both, while her reputation for cruelty prompted many to go on the attack.'

One such person stimulated by the 'reputation for cruelty' to move there and go on the offensive is the variety artist and one-time society reporter from Vienna, Hermann Steinschneider. He succeeds in no time in becoming the talk of the town. Whereas his showbusiness colleagues dish up conventional routines like 'fasting acts' – one such 'hunger artist' can be seen exhibiting himself day and night in a glass box to the public, on payment of an entrance fee, in an arcade off Friedrichstraße – in other words, while the competition turns abject distress into a profitable virtue, it is Steinschneider who makes a truly sensational splash. Acting as an impresario, he presents 'Omikron – the Living Gasometer'. That's the stage name of a young out-of-work artist called Fritz Jung, who, if one is to believe the emcee, can under hypnosis pump his stomach full of acetylene gas from a cylinder. Having done so, he lets Steinschneider insert two lengths of rubber tubing in his mouth, one of which leads to a table lamp while the other is hooked up to a gas oven. At the hypnotist's signal, 'Omikron' now releases the gas he has breathed in into the tubes, whereupon – to wild gasps of astonishment from the audience – the lamp lights up, while at the same time a girl assistant proceeds to cook fried eggs on the gas ring. What the onlookers don't know is that, prior to the performance, the young man has inserted a sponge saturated with benzine into his mouth.

Hermann Steinschneider, who by now has given himself the stage name Erik Jan Hanussen, commits his thoughts to paper at this time: 'In actual fact, there is no future, no time, no space![17] How's that? Well, if they really did exist, then they would have an end, a limit. But they don't, and consequently they only exist as mental constructs. [...] The individual is nothing but an abnormal form of creation. Human beings are like carcinomas on the abdomen of creation. They're certainly not its ideal exemplar. The whole of existence is a struggle, after all! If we were perfect beings, how could we possibly have stomach pains? What we see of the universe is just a small part. Yet our world is just a pustule on the backside of the cosmos.'

3

Hardly anything of what we think we know about Steinschneider's childhood is properly attested, since it derives in large measure from information supplied by him. And what does Hanussen have to say in the foreword of his autobiography about the reliability of his recollections? They are, he claims, 'the experiences of a person who always sailed pretty close to the wind where plausibility was concerned.'[18] Steinschneider is born in Ottakring near Vienna in 1889, the same year as Hitler. Around this time, his father Siegfried and mother Julie (née Kohn) are touring the Austro-Hungarian Empire, playing various engagements. In his memoirs, Hanussen described his father as an 'actor in a band of travelling players', and called his mother 'a poet'; she is in poor health for a long time and dies young. Even as a three-year-old, Hanussen claims to have experienced premonitions that saved the lives of two people in the city of Hermannstadt (now Sibiu in Romania). And, aged nine, he says he set a house on fire, just for the notoriety it would bring, but in the process managed to flush out the leader of a well-known gang of brigands, a man named Grasel. The historically attested Johann Georg Grasel, however, had been apprehended back in 1813, almost a century earlier, in Lower Austria.

Hermann, known by his friends as Harry, attends school first in Vienna, and later in the Moravian town of Boskowitz (now Boskovice). His father remarries after the death of Hermann's mother and they find themselves living once more back in Vienna, in the 16th District, hardly the most salubrious part of the city at that time. 'If anyone had business to attend to at night there,'[19] writes Hanussen, 'they took a machine gun out with them.' The fourteen-year-old falls in love with a soubrette of forty-five and attempts to elope abroad with her, but his father puts a stop to it. By way of consolation, the boy joins a theatre group who are playing in Moravia at the time, but switches to another company after a short while, before trying his luck as a solo entertainer. He soon finds himself at rock bottom. Half-starving, as he recounts in his picaresque autobiography, he spends a night sleeping in a chicken coop, where a peasant who is 'a cross between a jackal and a grizzly bear'[20] has given him shelter. His lot barely improves after he is engaged by a small theatre troupe who go around villages performing melodramas like *The Girl with the Flaming Eyes* or *Fraternal Strife and Hatred in the Count's Castle*. Hermann's job is to go door-to-door handing out flyers for the plays in the hope of receiving small tips in return; written on the flyers is the message: 'May Heaven bring you good fortune and honour / But please grant me a small favour.'

Business is bad, and so Hermann transfers to the 'circus department'. Taking with him all his worldly possessions, which, as he writes, would have fitted 'in a cigarette packet', he now sets off in the company of Mischko the one-eyed clown, Heinrich the giant, a grey horse called Regent and Sandor the pony on a tour of the countryside. He finds camaraderie and a livelihood of sorts among these travelling folk, and isn't ashamed of the cheap effects they use to entertain their audiences. At the same time, though, the highly intelligent young man remains an observer; he isn't completely absorbed into the circus environment, but instead learns how easy it can be to reinforce people's credulity. He has a few good experiences of solidarity among the have-nots, but many more negative ones of narrow-mindedness on the part of the haves. It may well be during this period that he develops his contempt for the public.

It is none of his circus colleagues, but, rather, the grey horse Regent that becomes his best friend. When Hanussen touches on this subject in his autobiography, his account abandons its customary, somewhat studied tone of forced jocularity: 'Regent, you fine grey beast, how I groomed and cared for you, and prepared your straw bed, and how happy we always were to see one another [...] And in return, how soft it was when, on those nights when it got too cold in the stables, you'd let me snuggle up to your warm horse's belly [...] Your chestnut brown eye, moist and shining, gazed deep into me, penetrating my very soul, and if anything was hurting me, you could feel it too, and when I was happy, so were you, and whenever [...] I swung myself up onto your trusty back, off we'd go, galloping hell for leather across the fields. Who could have followed us then, you and me, who could possibly have kept up with us and caught us?'[21]

4

The Beethoven Hall in the Berlin Philharmonia on Köthener Straße can seat up to 1,500 people. Like all Hanussen's performances, on this evening in March 1930, too, the majority of the audience are women. Although the piercing gaze of his steely-blue eyes, which comes across very effectively on the posters, loses some of its mesmeric power at a distance, the audience still hangs onto

Hanussen's every word as he addresses them. In the space of just a few sentences, he gets to the very heart of occultism: 'Is this what life is all about, then?'[22] Could the world – this vast cosmos with its untold millions of different phenomena – really have been created just so that Herr Müller or Schulze or Lehmann might be born, take a wife, produce five children with her, stand behind a shop counter for decades on end, scrape together a series of metal coins, and then finally lay down and die – and so vanish forever from the course of events? Is that the sum total of the point of creation? Don't we have some deeper connection to nature? Is it the case that there aren't any miracles anymore, or is it just that we're unable to grasp them, to be privy to them?'

And with another leading question, he creates a neat link to the first item on the programme, the 'Telepathic Mail'. Who, he asks, would dispute that a radio set, 'a crude device made of wires and wood, devised by the human brain and manufactured by human hands, is able to receive radio waves that have been transmitted from thousands of kilometres away? So why shouldn't the human brain itself, that most sophisticated of all Nature's instruments, have the capacity to pick up thought waves from the brains of others?'[23]

Even so, a few mocking voices still make themselves heard in the house. Unlike for Hanussen, though, everything is a novelty for those who come to witness his performances. So now he asks a random member of the audience to write down on a piece of paper the name of someone they know who is also present in the room. The sheet of paper is placed in an envelope. Now the audience member becomes the medium. Hanussen instructs the person in question to concentrate hard on the place in the auditorium where their acquaintance is sitting, and takes him or her by the hand. The mind reader and his medium dash up the centre aisle, and then begin to traverse the rows of seated people at a somewhat more leisurely pace. Barely thirty seconds have elapsed before Hanussen is standing in front of the person whose location he had to divine. The audience applauds wildly.

For his next trick, the magician searches for a needle hidden somewhere in the room, and to the audience's great astonishment finds it in the cigarette case of a teacher attending the show. He then goes on to correctly guess a subscriber's number chosen at random from the Athens phone book.[24] The performance is punctuated by repeated pauses, during which the clairvoyant's secretary collects slips of paper from the audience, on which they have written events and other pieces of information for him to divine. Now and then, the assistant pretends that he can't read the handwriting on the notes and poses various follow-up questions. Then he moves on. Hanussen cannot guess every last thing, but it is precisely this fallibility that raises the stock of what he does get right and the plausibility of his predictions.

The evening's programme is wide-ranging. It includes 'Muscle Reading' and the 'Needle Search', along with 'Graphology and Love', 'Television' and the 'Miracle of Konnersreuth'. The self-styled 'psychographologist' Hanussen claims to have appropriated the handwriting of around 5,000 famous people, and has the audience call out names to him: Napoleon, Hindenburg, Goethe, Edison and Beethoven. He causes a particular sensation when he starts to write the poet Rabindranath Tagore's signature in Brahmi script, and an Indian scholar in the audience, an eminent academic authority, loudly exclaims: 'Why, that's absolutely right!' His next turn causes the number of sceptics to dwindle still further. Hanussen asks the audience to pass him letters and examples of handwriting and then begins to tell them about the person who wrote them and in what circumstances. For example, after glancing briefly at a sheet of paper he's been handed, he announces: 'This was written by a man who died in the war after taking a bullet to the lungs.'[25]

In another part of the programme, Hanussen maintains that he can tell the profession of any random audience member. During the intermission, his secretary Erich Juhn has been busy asking discreet questions and now proceeds to give him secret signs: 'A judge [*Richter* in German] was indicated by Juhn straightening [*richten*] his tie, a lawyer by Juhn twisting his head in an allusion to the German term for 'shyster' [*Rechtsverdreher*, literally 'law twister'] and a doctor by a crossing [*kreuzen*] of the arms and legs as a play on the colloquial phrase meaning that 'it's a pain' [*es ist mir ein Kreuz*] dealing with medics. A poet was signalled by Juhn running his hand through his hair (a gesture for artistic professions in general), while civil servants were, appropriately enough, indicated by yawning.'[26]

In the whistle-blowing exposé that the secretary subsequently writes following an acrimonious split with his former employer, much of what the public takes to be truly inexplicable is unmasked as mere sleight of hand. In it, Erich Juhn reveals the true nature of the clairvoyance business: 'A genuine prophet is *seized* by an idea – he becomes a slave to it, his whole being is one with it, he's prepared to die for it. A charlatan, by contrast, *invents* an idea – he puts it to use and earns a livelihood from it.'[27] But Juhn was on a sticky wicket, and Hanussen continued to hold the whip hand. Or, to put it in the arch-persuader's own words: 'Anyone who claims to be showing people something miraculous will always have the advantage over someone who's trying to convince them that that miracle is impossible.'[28]

5

There's no one looking out for Hermann Steinschneider, a runaway half-orphan from an impoverished Jewish family of showmen. The freedom enjoyed by the young Steinschneider is the bleak liberty of the homeless drifter, and he has no choice but to take his fate in his own hands. At least he's bright – bright enough even not to let others see that he is. Wherever he goes, he's conscious of his superior intelligence. And he's a presentable-looking lad, too, having built up his physique through his friendship with Heinrich, who appeared on the same bill as him in the circus, as 'The World's

Strongest Man'. The young Steinschneider likes women, but he doesn't need them, and that's part of what makes him so attractive to them.

While his contemporaries at the grammar school in Vienna are agonizing over the works of Plato and Thucydides, or Cicero, Pliny and Seneca, Hermann is learning 'how to eat glass, ingest fire and gravel, swallow daggers, smash a table-top with his bare hands and hammer large nails through planks with his fist'.[29] And while his Viennese contemporaries are preparing for their school-leaving exams, Steinschneider is pursuing a markedly different educational path by becoming 'manager of Europe's largest electrically driven carousel'. In this instance, the so-called 'electric power' was supplied by four children, who were concealed behind a tarpaulin and who propelled the roundabout by pushing on the four arms of a wooden cross-brace: 'For every ten revolutions, they were given a free ride. That was our electricity,'[30] Steinschneider recalled.

Other scams see him travel as far afield as Athens and Constantinople. He returns from the latter destination on board the posh passenger liner SS *Baron Beck*. He manages to wangle himself a first-class ticket on this vessel for the passage to the Italian port of Brindisi by masquerading as the famous baritone Titta Ruffo and promising the captain he'll give a performance for the other passengers at the end of the voyage. Things progress at a rapid pace from there. Steinschneider becomes a lion tamer and circus artiste, does a moonlight flit with the evening's takings, writes couplets and performs his own comic songs. The year 1911 sees him working as a journalist on a popular newspaper in the city of Osijek in the Slavonia region of Croatia.[31] Back in Vienna, he subsequently joins the staff of a 'trick newspaper' sold at weddings. The people who produce this paper claim that it is highly reputable, with a wide circulation – though for the most part it consists of an unchanging content. Only a single page is reset with each reprinting; this contains a photograph of the couple who are intending to marry, along with a few lines of flattering text about the future bride and groom and their families. The editors charge an extortionate fee for this confection. As 'proof' of its genuineness, the wedding party receives fifteen copies of the newspaper – which in fact comprises its entire print run.

Steinschneider is a quick learner and adapts his business model. He becomes editor-in-chief of an 'illustrated weekly' in Vienna, which goes by the name of *Der Blitz* ('The Lightning Bolt'). This publication's stock-in-trade is either to air all the local scandals it can unearth concerning prostitution, corruption and homosexuality and raking in money from increased circulation, or, conversely, to refrain from exposing those involved and taking a corresponding fee for hushing things up. Under Steinschneider's aegis, this profitable idea is given a literary refinement. The new editor pens two works of fiction. First of all, he publishes the supposedly authentic *Memoirs of a Snake-Dancer*,[32] whose list of intimate contacts are reputed to include many of 'the elite of Berlin's financial and artistic worlds': 'We have proof of each and every one of the incidents described here, kept under lock and key in the safe in our editorial offices.'

He then sets about writing the sequel, *The Escapades of Major Quitsch*, which takes place at various locations in Vienna. The protagonists appear as real people in the city, with attributes that are ascribed to them in the novel. The editors of *Der Blitz* even offer a prize to any reader who can find these characters 'in real life'. In each of the novel's freshly written chapters, the author has his characters experience diverse adventures in the city's nightclubs, later expanding the settings to include department stores and the premises of cobblers, opticians and varnishers. Whether or not these locations are presented in the novel in a positive light depends on the willingness of the proprietors – whom the author personally sounds out before each new episode is written – to cough up.

During the First World War, Steinschneider is initially stationed in Olomouc,[33] where he publishes poems and stories in the local press. He organizes 'trench theatre, louse-racing contests, and games of tombola'[34] and appears for the first time as a mind reader. With the help of a friend who works in the military censor's office, he arranges for certain letters to be held back, and then uses the information in them to stage seances in the officers' mess where he 'prophesies' news from the home front, which the recipients of the letters then only get to hear about some three or four days later. In the Moravian town of Jeseník (Freiwaldau), he gives a performance with items on the programme such as 'Telepathic Kinedrama'[35] and 'Hypnotizing Fish'. In 1917 he self-publishes a pamphlet about mind reading. Steinschneider's earliest experiences with a divining rod also date from this period. Even while the war is still going on, in the spring of 1918, under the pseudonym Erik Jan Hanussen – having been forbidden from appearing as 'Sergeant Steinschneider' – he presents his first major show in front of an audience of 3,000 at the Vienna Konzerthaus. Archduchess Bianca and Archduke Leopold Salvator witness this performance from their private box. Part of the show involves four pins being hidden in the auditorium, which the magician locates with the help of a medium. Steinschneider had learned from his teacher Labéro that the best mediums were young women, while the least suitable were fat men. A committee of doctors oversees this experiment in telepathy, and it all goes according to plan.

This finally proves to be the big breakthrough; Hanussen's fame spreads throughout the army, and wrangling among the various military authorities is resolved to his advantage. He no longer has to return to the front, but instead is promoted to company commander of a 'Divining Rod Corps of the Austrian Army' (yes, such a unit really does exist in the bizarre world of the Austro-Hungarian Empire). There he is responsible for training soldiers in the art of using divining rods to locate underground watercourses. He has his own house with an office and the exclusive use of a coach and horses; he also acquires a tailor-made dress uniform with little divining rods shown on the silver collar tabs.

After the war, Hanussen is able to capitalize on his success. The year 1919 sees him appear in Vienna to a combined audience of almost 50,000 people in a series of sixteen sell-out engagements. Yet here, too, he soon oversteps the mark. He hypnotizes men and women and induces them to crawl around the auditorium on all fours, barking or miaowing like dogs and cats. This prompts the city authorities to issue a ban on hypnotism. However, the magician is briefly able to circumvent this prohibition with the inventive contention that the technique he employs is not hypnosis but, rather, a form of 'waking suggestion'. At the same time, Hanussen claims to have used hypnosis to cure a prominent Viennese industrialist of the fear that he will be asphyxiated every time he swallows. In Nuremberg, he bets the air transport authority 10,000 Marks that he will be able to carry out to the letter 'thought commands' issued to him from an aeroplane circling 500 metres overhead. Hanussen's next stunt was to supposedly convey from the aircraft his own 'suggestive orders' to a crowd below: 'This experiment was likewise a complete success.'[36]A tour takes the vaudeville artist to North Africa and the Middle East. In Port Said, he falls in love with the young daughter of the governor. For the first time, he later confides in his secretary, he feels a genuine attachment to a woman. An opportunity arises for them to be alone together and he unburdens himself about his feelings for her. She admits to feeling the same way about him, but something prevents him from taking advantage of her there and then, perhaps the suspicion that it wouldn't do him much good either to overstep this boundary. In any event, he gets cold feet and does a runner. The following weeks see him plunge headlong into a dizzying bout of self-indulgence.[37]

On his return, the magician Hanussen, by this time a celebrity, engages in a running feud with his main competitor in Vienna, Siegmund Breitbart, one of several of the 'World's Strongest Men' then doing the rounds of variety theatres.[38] Hanussen's plan is to expose his rival to ridicule by getting a 'weak woman' to imitate his supposed star turns. To this end, he engages an unemployed model, the eighteen-year-old Martha Kohn. She assumes the stage name 'Martha Farra' and appears henceforth as the 'Iron Queen', whose specialities include biting through chains and bending thick iron bars. Breitbart responds to this challenge by appearing at the 'Ronacher' cabaret lying on a bed of nails and letting himself be driven over by a car containing twelve occupants; he performs this stunt for charity, with all the money raised going to a sanatorium for lung diseases. Martha Farra's riposte is to have herself run over by a four-cylinder Steyr automobile 'with her back wholly unprotected'. Things continue in this vein for quite some time, with each performance being interrupted by hecklers and troublemakers hired by the opposition and fights erupting outside the venues. Eventually the Viennese police decide that the situation has got out of hand and ban Hanussen from the city for ten years.

This fails to dent his fame, however. Town halls are packed to the rafters whenever he tours Czechoslovakia or Germany. A guest appearance sees him and Martha Farra travel to New York. The Americans take things to the extreme by getting Hanussen to appear on the same bill as his arch-enemy Breitbart. Meanwhile, Martha Farra is said to have lifted a baby elephant in Times Square. Back in Europe, Hanussen is brought in as a consultant by the police to help them solve a number of spectacular criminal cases. When planning his tours, Hanussen has been assiduous in always trying to arrange a performance at the local police station, as a way of pre-empting any overzealous action on their part should he stand accused of fraud; in addition, local worthies are given free tickets to his shows. When the magician succeeds in helping to solve crimes, he exploits it for promotional purposes and when he isn't he hushes it up. In 1927, Hanussen supposedly causes a woman in the audience to feel pain by cracking a whip onstage. Not everyone is happy about this. It is well known that Hanussen takes a hard line with sceptics in his audiences, belittling them and making them a laughing stock. And if a mind-reading experiment goes wrong, he is apt to snap at the medium: 'You're no medium! Don't ever volunteer for these experiments again!'[39]

After a performance in the Bohemian town of Teplice, the clairvoyant is arrested for fraud and thrown in the county gaol. The ensuing trial, held in the Czech city of Litoměřice, is widely reported on throughout Europe, with witnesses appearing for and against Hanussen, and he himself giving a demonstration of his art in the courtroom. The case turns on nothing less than trying to find a legal way of determining whether supernatural powers really exist or not. Despite the fact that proceedings ultimately drag on for more than two years, it is apparent from an early stage that legal instruments are wholly unsuitable for providing a definitive answer to this question. The trial ends in May 1930 with the acquittal of the clairvoyant. 'Nothing is more merciless or cruel,'[40] he writes in his autobiography, 'than the public when they sense they have got the upper hand. And nothing is smaller and more timid than the public when you've got them tamed.'

6

Hanussen has come a long way by the time he fetches up in Berlin in 1930, the city he loves most 'of all cities in the world. Say what you will about the Prussians, I'm mightily fond of them [...] At least you know where you are with a Berliner. He's a complete vulgarian and the biggest gobshite on earth. But if he ever encounters someone with a bigger mouth, he pipes down and becomes quite biddable. The whole world's in Berlin – America and Nice, Port Said and Lvov – and that's why I love this city like no other.'[41] And Berlin loves Hanussen too: sell-out performances at the Alhambra, as well as in the Bach or Beethoven halls at the Philharmonia, in front of audiences of up to 2,000, often twice daily – a matinee and an evening show. He has spent a long time honing the details of his performances and testing their impact: during the clairvoyance part of his act, he puts on a black blindfold and lets the beads of the *kombolói*, a string of Eastern worry beads that he uses as a so-called 'hypnoscope', run through his fingers. Hanussen, who is only about 1.65 metres tall and stockily built, puts body and soul into the performance, going into a trance, shaking and twitching and then giving a violent start before slumping down motionless. Ultimately it seems as if the maestro is on the verge of collapse. Supported by his assistants, he is led from the stage, twice a night…

In the meantime, Hanussen has only been able to deal with the constant stampede of clients to his door with the help of two secretaries; he also has two cars and has bought himself a motor yacht, *Ursel IV*. Yet his meteoric rise, from bedding down for the night in a dog kennel to occupying a luxury suite at the Hotel Eden in the Budapester Straße in Berlin, has come at a price. He has entered into three marriages, all of which have foundered on his egomania and his sexual insatiability – his former secretary Juhn claims to have counted no fewer than thirty instances of adultery[42] in the two years they worked together. Hanussen's road to fame is paved with legal skirmishes, with accusations by rivals and former colleagues who believe that he has plagiarized them or impugned their professional integrity, as well as by clients who claim he has swindled them. Of course, in Berlin he is not without competitors in his line of work. But what sets him apart from his fellow magicians is that, in the question of whether magic is about deception or plausibility, he ups the ante by allowing sceptics a glimpse into his box of tricks. He goes on the offensive by laying himself open to supervision and inviting people to test the accuracy of his prophecies. In his books he even writes quite frankly about the methods he uses to manipulate the public, admittedly not failing to suggest there are certain things that are beyond even his ken.

These are fertile times for magic; after all, people are willing to try anything that might alleviate their hardship. The economic crisis hits all strata of society – salaried employees, workers and the self-employed in equal measure. In the wake of firms going bust, the number of suicides rapidly escalates. In October 1930 in Nuremberg, the case of a businessman and former naval captain by the name of Staufer caused a sensation. His killing spree started with the shooting of his wife: 'When, shortly thereafter, his twelve-year-old son came home from school, he shot him too. He then turned the gun on himself, inflicting a fatal wound. He died in hospital. At the root of this dreadful deed were the family's desperate economic straits.'[43]

'What is magic, though?'[44] asks Hanussen, and freely admits:

It's not about disabusing people's fond belief in the miraculous but rather reinforcing it. I can show how a combination of willpower, audacity, energy and impertinence will allow you to get two thousand people sitting in an auditorium eating out of your hand. What are the public? Dimwits, credulous fantasists, hysterics and a sprinkling of genuine unfortunates – but above all children, whose main worry is that no teacher, father figure, superior or friend will impress them sufficiently to allow themselves to place their complete trust in him. So how is it that people will invariably trust me, without reservation? Because I'm stronger than them, bolder, more energetic and strong-willed. Because they are children and I'm an adult.

And it's not long before Hanussen is playing in the big league.

The Pig-headed Proletarian

Ernst Thälmann

1

The sentence handed down by the Hamburg District Court to the married couple Johannes and Maria Magdalena in 1892 could hardly be called lenient: for receiving stolen goods to the value of fifty Reichsmarks, they are gaoled for two years. This hits their children – six-year-old Ernst and five-year-old Frieda – hard. They are separated and packed off to stay with family friends for the length of their prison sentence. After their release, the couple set their sights on moving up in the world: in 1895, the father opens a greengrocer's shop in a damp basement in the Eilbek district. From there, they move to an apartment on the Wandsbeker Chaussee. Through a combination of sheer hard graft and determination, the family achieves a modest degree of prosperity. A horse and cart are acquired to make deliveries, as well as to do removals, and they also run a coal merchant's business on the side. Every morning before school, Ernst goes down to the wholesale market with his father and then finishes his homework before lessons even begin.

His mother is described as short and plump. Ernst is utterly devoted to her; even the fundamental clash of worldviews that arises between the adolescent Ernst and his deeply devout mother doesn't overshadow his unconditional love for her. And yet it is his father who has a stronger influence on his character. According to a neighbour's account, this lanky man had a 'rather spiritual and soulful air' about him.[1] However, this disposition did not, it seems, preclude flashes of violent spontaneity: decades later, Ernst recalled that his father had a tendency to lash out at the slightest provocation.[2] Jan, as his father was called, was dismayed to see his only son, the heir to his hard-won business enterprise, turning into a bookworm. 'But what I was reading,' Ernst Thälmann was to write about his education from his imprisonment as a convict in the National Socialist penal system in 1935,

wasn't Marx and Engels or socialist literature, but rather Schiller, Kleist, Herder, Goethe and especially the history of the Germanic tribes and their battles, as well as the history of the Carolingian, Saxon, Frankish and Hohenstaufen emperors. The things that piqued my interest were the Viking period and the era of the Hanseatic League, and what truly captivated me were adventures like Klaus Störtebeker's swashbuckling life of piracy, and tales such as the legend of the Nibelungs, the life stories of Andreas Hofer and Archibald Douglas, and the Battle of the Teutoburg Forest.[3]

A life of hard physical labour is not without its consequences for the young Ernst. At the age of thirteen, he suffers a bout of rheumatism, and for a while is unable to move and has to be carried around on a stretcher.[4] His father rejects a teacher's recommendation that his son be allowed to go to grammar school and instead puts the fourteen-year-old to work in the family business. It's not that there's no money to send him to the school, it's simply that Thälmann senior doesn't recognize the value of education. Ernst suffers throughout his life from not having been given this chance to develop his intellectual faculties. He spends his adolescence shuttling between the Hopfenmarkt (the principal

marketplace in Hamburg), the railway goods stations, the coal yard, the harbour and the wharves. Working in his father's business, he witnesses at first hand the easy confidence with which the well-off make their purchases, while the working-class women, ashamed of their poverty, hang back. And he observes the silent hunger of the children.

Around this time, he undergoes a kind of epiphany, which he later reflects upon while locked up in his prison cell in Bautzen in 1944; at a school graduation party held by the Social Democratic Party at Easter in 1901, he is transported by the pathos-laden address given by one of the speakers: 'Your life is about to take a more serious turn, and as individuals you're nothing, but together and united you're everything. Follow the red flags of freedom, follow the shining banners of socialism!'[5] The sheer force of the speech resonates with him, and he calls to mind his own situation: 'I find myself thinking back to my work at the family home. Am I to fritter my life away there, fated never to get to know the world of men from another perspective, and to forever have a one-sided picture of the depths of the human soul? Am I simply to allow myself to be corrupted when, before very long, my father starts taking me with him down the pub every evening? [...] My thirst for knowledge has got to find room to develop somewhere.'

Ernst is not quite sixteen at this point – a few days before, he has been brutally thrashed by his father for the most trivial of reasons – when he comes to the sensible conclusion to leave the parental home. After a few nights at a hostel for the homeless, he is taken in by a seventy-eight-year-old widow, who is herself finding it hard to make ends meet. 'This example of selflessness, this act of great humanity she showed me, made a deep impression on me,' Thälmann recalled. 'Over these weeks, I often fell to thinking that a bourgeois person would never have offered and given me shelter.'[6] For many weeks he is plagued by hunger. Only when he finally gets a short-term job with a firm at the docks is he able to afford a hot meal again. He sees instances of solidarity among the proletariat but also realizes that there is a pecking order, and observes the arrogance with which the dock workers, who are in an organized trade union, look down on the non-organized workforce, and how they in turn look down on casual labourers. Ernst Thälmann joins the Social Democratic Party in May 1903. Wherever he finds himself employed from now on, he agitates for his workmates to join the transport workers' union. His jobs include driver's mate on a lorry delivering bottled beer and a stint in an industrial laundry.

In the autumn of 1907, Thälmann travels to the USA as a coal trimmer on board the largest passenger vessel in the world at that time, the luxury liner SS *Amerika*, and over the course of three trips gets to know New York. He is impressed by the comparatively good living conditions and the great technological advances there. He also works for a short spell on a farm. Back in Hamburg, he takes up a position as a driver for the Frauenlob laundry. Here, too, he immediately sets about recruiting union members.[7] One of those he convinces to join is the ironer Rosa Koch. The young girl is very taken with this imposing man, especially his drive and energy and his engagement for the benefit of others, and they become an item. 'I really used to love dancing,' she later reminisces, 'and Ernst would always smile at me as I whirled round in a circle with other comrades. I had a naturally sunny disposition, and everyone else felt happy too to be united in a common cause.'[8]

2

Ernst doesn't have a great deal of spare time to spend with Rosa during the early years of their relationship. He works fourteen- to sixteen-hour days: 'Up and down steps all day long right up to nightfall, dripping with sweat in summer, with my clothes completely soaked, and back up into the driver's seat again. That just about sums up the lot of the laundry driver – hardly an enviable one.'[9] Thus ran Thälmann's description in 1911 of a worker's average day, which for a while was also his own routine. He spends his evenings engaged in political activism, or studying Marx and Engels. In their writings, he believes he has found the answer to his questions about inequality and injustice in society. Thälmann is not some airy theorist; for him, even the act of thinking is something that must ultimately have a practical purpose. Politically, he is increasingly gravitating to the left of his party, and he is impatient when it comes to asserting the interests of the working class. He doesn't understand the party chiefs' willingness to compromise, referring to them as 'old women' and accusing them of only being concerned about their own positions. In August 1914, he is almost alone in his criticism of the wartime truce between political parties and the SPD's approval of war loans. In the meantime, he has gone back to live with his parents. When the wife of the doorman at the apartment block asks him why he isn't at the front yet, he tells her in no uncertain terms: 'So, you reckon I ought to volunteer, do you? Well, let me tell you I've no intention of joining up. I can't get myself worked up about this war. It's a war by the rich for the rich.'[10]

Soon after, Thälmann receives his call-up papers. Before he is conscripted, he and his fiancée marry. They've known one another for five years now, and if he fails to come home, at least Rosa will receive some meagre state assistance. After three months' basic training he is posted to the Western Front as an artilleryman, where, in between stays in hospital, he endures three and a half years of trench warfare at the front and behind the lines. On several occasions he narrowly escapes death, survives gas attacks and is awarded the Iron Cross (Second Class), the Hanseatic Cross and the Wounded Soldier's Decoration for his service. Yet there are also quiet spells; in the summer of 1918, Corporal Thälmann is stood down from the trenches and detailed to look after horses. Daily life at the front also involves football matches, evenings playing cards, drinking sessions and, as Thälmann records in his war journals, church parades. He gets into an argument with an officer who upbraids him for giving a French child something to eat. It's not a 'French brat', the corporal tells his superior, but a hungry child.[11]

While on home leave, Thälmann notices how the public mood is beginning to turn against the war. Unrest is brewing among the Social Democrats, too. In 1917, a large section of the left wing breaks away to form the Independent Social Democratic Party. The soldier on leave finds himself in sympathy with the new party's aims. On 9 November 1918, the day the Weimar Republic is proclaimed in Berlin, twice over, Thälmann notes in his diary: 'Two o'clock in the afternoon: deserted from the front with four comrades.'[12] Back in Hamburg, the demobbed corporal joins the Independent Social Democrats. In the interim, events have reached a new radical pitch. The Spartacists on the far left of his party want to exploit the momentum of the general disruption in order to nationalize the banks, dispossess factory bosses and large landowners and introduce a system of workers' councils along Soviet lines. In December 1918, this faction forms the German Communist Party (KPD).

For most Social Democrats, the stewardship of their own country counts for more than the international proletarian revolution. Ironically, therefore, they enter into an alliance with the only force capable of maintaining order in Germany – the Supreme Command of what was, until very recently, the Imperial Army. By this time, the situation in the capital has escalated still further. 'Anyone who stands in the way of the Socialist juggernaut', writes Rosa Luxemburg in the newspaper *Die Rote Fahne* ('The Red Flag'), 'will be left lying in the road with smashed limbs.'[13]

Although Rosa Luxemburg's attitude to violence is decidedly ambivalent,[14] in the prevailing febrile atmosphere it is this one statement of hers that gains public notoriety. Civil war, chaos, Red and White terror – very few people desire such things at this time. Luxemburg and Karl Liebknecht become the target of extreme right-wing forces. Her political agenda never gains much traction, and it is only her martyr's death* that sees her popularity soar. Over 100,000 Berliners follow her and Liebknecht's funeral cortège, though one of the coffins is empty. Five months later, after lock keepers retrieve Rosa Luxemburg's body from the Landwehrkanal, tens of thousands more people assemble for her actual interment.

Of course, it wasn't Social Democrats who assassinated Liebknecht and Luxemburg, but they are on the side of the repressive forces. The Social Democrats see the suppression of the unrest fomented by the far left in January 1919 as legitimate self-defence, whereas the communists regard it as an act of betrayal. In the years that follow, the two sides refuse to speak to one another. As late as 1930, Carl von Ossietzky writes: 'Anyone who suggests that the Social Democrats and the Communists might finally talk to one another without carrying a revolver in their pockets with the safety catch off still shouldn't expect the two sides to hand one another bouquets of roses.'[15]

3

Rosa Thälmann spent more than three years worrying about her husband and hoping for a normal life after the war. But now that he is back home once more, he spends his evenings at party meetings and his nights reading Marx, Engels and Lenin. She takes him to task, and he retorts that he could do without a wife who's discontented and has a go at him the minute he gets home. The revolutionary comes up with a solution: to stop Rosa feeling isolated, he asks his comrades to include her in campaigning work for the party 'so that she'll make my life easier'.[16] In November

---

* During the Berlin 'Spartacist Uprising' of January 1919 (named after the *Spartakusbund*, a left-wing revolutionary faction), Luxemburg and Liebknecht were captured, tortured and executed by Freikorps militias. Two junior officers were given paltry sentences at court-martial for these crimes. [Translator's note]

1919, their daughter Irma is born. There's not enough money coming in to buy wood and coal. When Rosa breastfeeds her daughter, she lights the gas cooker in the kitchen in order to warm herself on its small flame. While Thälmann gains recognition for his political work – he is elected chairman of the Hamburg Independent Social Democrats in May 1919 – his bourgeois professional life advances only very sluggishly. To begin with, he helps out in his father's business before starting work as a public relief worker in the Hamburg City Park. Eventually he manages to land a reasonably well-paid position in the city's employment exchange.

Meanwhile, the left wing of his party has affiliated itself to the Communist International, or Comintern, and merged with the KPD. Thälmann is a staunch supporter of this move; indeed, he was instrumental in pressing for it. Marxist theory is a real eye-opener for him. His lively intellect is at home here and his thirst for knowledge finds its 'room to develop'. However, it is a hermetically sealed room, and a kind of knowledge that renders him unreceptive to other truths, with its own special terminology, preconditioned ways of thinking and a neatly ordered view of history. As if certainties were just there for the taking along the way. But the real attraction of this self-contained image of the world is that it doesn't remain in the realms of analysis; instead it provides an entire toolbox with which to tackle the real and pressing problems of the present day. Thälmann confesses some self-doubt to his wife around this time: 'You have to admit, Rosa, that I often struggle to formulate my thoughts clearly. I just can't find the right words. And maybe it's also true that I'm simply not forward enough in speaking my mind.'[17]

Thälmann is radical in his impatience, but at the same time he is a pragmatist where power is concerned. He regards the feverish convulsions of the Weimar Republic, such as the attempted coups by the far right and far left, as a series of new opportunities to replace the hated parliamentary system with 'governance by councils of the proletariat'. In the spring of 1921, emissaries of the Communist International campaign for an uprising in the industrial region of central Germany: the Comintern operative Béla Kun comes up with the slogan: 'Every worker should defy the law and get hold of a weapon by whatever means he can.'[18] Looting, arson attacks, bombings and bank robberies prompt the government of Chancellor Friedrich Ebert to declare a state of emergency in Saxony and Hamburg. In response Thälmann calls for the shipyards in Hamburg to be occupied. Violent clashes with the police ensue.

Ultimately, the uprising fails due to a lack of support among the workers, both in Saxony and in Hamburg. The incident doesn't result in any really serious consequences for the local leader of the communists: he is forced to go underground for a short time and loses his job at the labour exchange. In the Hamburg State Parliament, or the 'talking shop'[19] as he calls it, he reiterates that 'as Communists, we will keep fighting until the current capitalist state is broken and the bourgeoisie has been overthrown'. He is never assailed by doubts about the wisdom of the directives coming from Moscow. June 1921 sees him travel to the Soviet Union for the first time to attend the Comintern Congress, where he personally gets to know Lenin and Trotsky. That same year, he becomes a full-time party official.

One early summer's night in June 1922, a hand grenade set on a timer explodes outside the Thälmanns' ground-floor flat. Just a week before the murder of the liberal foreign minister Walther Rathenau, the Hamburg Communist Party leader has also become the target of extreme right-wing assassins. Thälmann wasn't at home at the time, and his wife and child were sleeping in the back rooms and so escaped injury. By this stage, the right have been responsible for 350 political murders, and the left have carried out 220.[20] Meanwhile, hardship and desperation are increasing in the country day by day. After French forces occupy the Ruhr, the German currency collapses completely. In the summer of 1923 you can see 'postmen with great sacks full of banknotes slung over their shoulders, or pushing prams crammed with paper money'.[21] The government considers linking the value of the Reichsmark to coal or even potash rather than to the nation's far too meagre gold reserves.[22]

A coup is in the air. The only question is, who will be first to stage it? At the beginning of September 1923, the far right mobilizes hundreds of thousands of demonstrators to attend a 'German Day' rally in Nuremberg. Adolf Hitler, wearing a trench coat and carrying a walking stick, inspects the march past in the company of Göring, Ludendorff and others and calls for a 'national dictatorship'. At the same time the KPD, in collaboration with the Comintern, makes preparations for an uprising that is intended to act as a beacon for global revolution. But Thälmann of all people is sceptical about the timing of the overthrow.[23] Stalin is quoted in the pages of *Die Rote Fahne*: 'The coming revolution in Germany is the most significant global event of our times. Without question, the victory of the German proletariat will shift the centre of the world revolution from Moscow to Berlin.'[24] Several dozen military and civilian advisers travel from Soviet Russia to Germany, the country is divided up into six large 'Military/Political Regions', fighting units numbering one hundred proletarians apiece are assembled, at least on paper, and arms dumps and food supplies are laid down in preparation.

The energies of the two political extremes come within a whisker of focusing on the very same day: in Moscow, the date for the Comintern-led uprising is set for 9 November, while Hitler plans his Beer Hall Putsch for that same day. Up to 2.5 million Red Army troops are poised to support the German communists.[25] But Stalin realizes the weakness of the KPD and decides to let Hitler's supporters take the lead: 'it will be to our advantage if they attack first.'[26] So, the date for the uprising is first postponed by the KPD and then cancelled altogether.[27] However, in Hamburg things have already got underway, and a bloody insurrection ensues. Seventeen policemen and more than one hundred insurgents are killed before the rebellion is put down. Thälmann, who plays a leading role in the uprising under the code name 'Teddy', witnesses the failure of a revolution for the second time. Yet far from it harming his career in the party, in January 1924 he is elected acting leader of the KPD. His hard-line position at this time couldn't be clearer: 'I won't give a single inch. I refuse to work with scoundrels who want to destroy the party by advocating evolution rather than revolution.'[28] Comintern head Grigory Zinoviev describes the German communist leader as 'the German party's best and most valuable asset' and as the 'gold standard of the working class'.[29]

However, before long praise from Zinoviev is anything but a desirable calling card. In 1936, Stalin's former comrade-in-arms is executed. The two bullets that kill Zinoviev and the old Bolshevik Lev Kamenev are later surgically removed from their skulls.[30] The secret service chief Genrikh Yagoda keeps them in a glass case. These macabre relics don't seem to bring their successive owners much luck, though. Yagoda himself is summarily shot just four years later. The new owner of the glass display case is his successor Nikolai Yezhov. He, too, is executed two years thereafter. The glass case now comes into the possession of the new head of the secret police, Lavrenti Beria, who is likewise put to death, on the day before Christmas Eve in 1953.

4

Ernst Thälmann is Moscow's favourite son; his unswerving obedience to the Comintern – behind which, more or less, resides Stalin in person – stands him in good stead. But equally important for his position within the party is the fact that he convincingly embodies the workers' leader, be it at rallies, on posters or in the newspapers: 'He looked exactly like you'd imagine a Hamburg dock worker: broad-shouldered, ungainly in his movements, and with a good-natured proletarian face,'[31] remarked Margarete Buber-Neumann, the long-term partner of the party theoretician Heinz Neumann. By now, Thälmann also represents his party in the Reichstag. Especially in the early phase of their parliamentary activity, the communists maintain puerile rituals of self-exclusion: for instance, political officials of the KPD are prohibited from greeting Social Democrats or shaking their hands.[32] And when being sworn in as local councillors, communists are instructed to wear red gloves. In 1925, Thälmann is put forward by the KPD, whose chairmanship he has meanwhile assumed, as a token candidate to become the next President of the Reich. In the second ballot, almost two million people vote for him. This gesture comes at a cost, for instead of a republican candidate being elected, Field Marshal Paul Hindenburg, as the representative of the anti-republican 'Reichsblock', now determines the fate of the Weimar Republic for the next seven years.

'Teddy' becomes known throughout Germany as a result of the presidential election campaign. He is a controversial figure within his own party, with many fellow members taking a critical view of the cult that develops around him. A fellow communist, the activist and theorist Clara Zetkin, offers the following judgement: 'Rather ominously, it is starting to become apparent that Teddy, aside from being ignorant and theoretically untutored, has become completely caught up in self-delusion and a state of self-infatuation which borders on megalomania and that he is wholly lacking in any self-control.'[33] She levels the charge at Thälmann that he has allowed himself to be 'hoodwinked and led astray by scandalmongers, flatterers, gossips and intriguers of the basest kind'. Time and again, his critics also point to his failings as an orator. He keeps an audience of over 10,000 people who have assembled at an event at the Sportpalast in Berlin waiting for almost two hours: 'His closing address', a Comintern observer writes to Stalin, 'lasted for around 40 minutes and triggered an almost inconceivable wave of boredom among his audience. All enthusiasm evaporated. People left the rally in droves, something that has apparently never happened before. This was a serious and heavy blow for the party.'[34]

There is no sign of proletarian solidarity among the upper echelons of the KPD; instead, everyone is engaged in a grim struggle to secure the most influential posts. The key players attempt to queer each other's pitch by writing letters denouncing one another to the party leadership in Moscow. In an attempt to 'cut down' rivals, as the party jargon is wont to put it, 'wavering elements' are detected and a meticulous record kept of 'left- and right-leaning deviators from the party line'. These include rightist 'Brandlerists' (followers of the former KPD leader Heinrich Brandler), 'conciliators' and, on the left, the 'remnants of Luxemburgism'. Prompted by a phrase of Stalin's, Thälmann wages a campaign against the so-called 'archive rats': 'These are the kind of people who constantly go poking about in search of "documentary evidence" rather than considering the bigger picture of the living praxis of a revolutionary party.'[35]

In February 1928, in a secret memorandum, the Soviet leaders dictate the new general party line to the leadership of the KPD: as its key point, it is stipulated that the principal enemy of the workers' movement in Germany remains the Social Democratic Party.[36] However devastating adhering to this principle will prove to be as the National Socialists steadily gain in strength, it nonetheless has a deeper logic to it: while the Social Democrats are concerned to bring about a reconciliation of interests, the communist worldview feeds on an implacable resentment towards the bourgeois state. Any improvement in the current situation pushes the 'proletarian revolution' further into the distant future, whereas everything that exacerbates the crisis in society brings the moment of supposed salvation closer. Anyone who simply wants to improve the lot of the working class is classed as a 'conciliator' and is lost to the communist cause.

5

Not everyone in the Communist Party leadership goes along with the course that Stalin has dictated to the German comrades. Around this time, Thälmann comes under severe pressure. For months he has covered for his Hamburg friend John Wittorf, who has been siphoning off large sums from party funds for private ends. When the story goes public in 1928, his initial reaction is to play for time by offering to step aside from all his duties. In such situations, there's no room for pussyfooting. Two years before, Thälmann himself was the first to act when his predecessor as party chairperson was deposed for being an 'ultra-leftist'. Back then, he insisted that 'we carry on this serious ideological struggle until we have achieved the definitive political destruction of Comrade Ruth Fischer'.[37] Now it is he who is in the firing line of his comrades. Wilhelm Pieck states that, in his opinion, the Communist Party chairman 'is unfit to remain at the head of the party'.[38] And Hugo Eberlin adds: 'Comrade Thälmann, you'd be doing the workers' movement a great service if you were no longer part of it.'[39]

Thälmann is dismissed as chairman of the KPD by a unanimous vote of the central committee, and one motion proposes that he be expelled from the party altogether.[40] Exulting in his demise, the Berlin SPD newspaper *Der Abend* runs the headline: '"President" Thälmann Toppled! On the Run to Moscow. – Which Faction Will Take the Helm Now?'[41] Two days later Stalin, on holiday in Georgia at the time, learns of the decision – and summarily revokes it. After twenty-four days in the wilderness, Teddy is back in office, and the erstwhile rebels are frantically back-pedalling. He uses his regained power to settle old scores with his enemies, the 'conciliators' and 'rightists', who are now ousted from the party.

Generally speaking, the rank-and-file members, whose number also includes, since 1927, Thälmann's father Jan, aren't interested in the power struggles among the leadership. For them, the party is an anchor in turbulent times. But at the same time, the KPD is a major political enterprise directed and financed from Moscow by the Comintern, a body described by Clara Zetkin as a 'dead mechanism',[42] which 'swallows orders issued in Russian at one end, and spits them out in various languages at the other.' This is the source of money that pays for the appointment of 200 full-time party officials and funds twenty-seven newspapers.[43] Soviet trading companies such as Derup, Deroluft and Derunapht, with branches throughout the whole of Germany, are utilized to transfer money, information and propaganda material.[44]

The political empire of the German communists includes more than a dozen organizations like International Workers' Aid, the Revolutionary Trade Union Opposition, Red Aid, the Red Front Fighters' League and the German Communist Youth Organization. The party maintains a secret 'military-political apparatus', a workshop for forging passports, a party self-defence organization and a division dealing in 'stocks of arms and ammunition'. For a short while, there is even a small so-called 'T-Group' – where the 'T' stands for *Tscheka*, or 'security agency' – which is charged with eradicating traitors within the KPD's own ranks and carrying out the assassination of rival politicians. The group leader Felix Neumann's appearance on the witness stand at the 1925 'Cheka Trial' in Leipzig causes a sensation. Neumann claims to have tested dysentery, typhoid and cholera bacteria on a rabbit with a view to using them as biological weapons.[45] Within the party, the role of the 'T-Group' is known – in a telling blend of officialese and atavistic emotionality – as 'organized revenge'.[46]

While Rosa continues to live in Hamburg with their daughter Irma, Thälmann now spends most of his time in Berlin. He once explained their different roles quite unequivocally: 'Over the passage of time, with its shifting dynamic, the woman always remains grounded in the practical business of life, while the man is engaged with cerebral matters.'[47] Chiming with this attitude are the qualities he wants his daughter to display; he'd like Irma to be 'modest, quiet, loyal to her mother and well-behaved'.[48] But part of the reason he's no longer drawn back to Hamburg so often to be with his small family has to do with Martha. Since he entered parliament in 1924, Thälmann stays regularly with the Communist Party members Hans and Martha Kluczynski in Lützowstraße in Charlottenburg. Ernst and Martha strike up a close relationship. Quite understandably, this causes tension between Hans Kluczynski and his wife's lover.[49] When Thälmann comes calling, Hans frequently decamps to the family's summer house on the 'Havelblick' allotments in Gatow. The Kluczynskis' son Günther, though, gets on well with Teddy, calling their frequent guest 'Uncle'.

When the KPD leader plays Skat* with his comrades after his interminable speeches, delivered in a monotonous, staccato tone (on one occasion he prepares a presentation that is supposed to last for eight hours), it is not some propaganda stunt.[50] Instead of going to embassy receptions, he'd far rather sit with his comrades over beer and schnapps in his favourite pub in Mittelstraße near Friedrichstraße Station. Despite having spent a lifetime stressing the importance of education, he feels uneasy around intellectuals, and no doubt he has also often observed how flexible an acute mind is, and how readily it is prepared to adapt to new circumstances. At times of heightened tension, petty antipathies are liable to come to the surface in Thälmann. Looking at the hands of his speech writer Heinz Neumann one day, he blurts out: 'What pitifully thin wrists you have!'[51]

Conversely, the intellectuals in the party, over whom he has the advantage of a charismatic appeal to working men, make fun of their chairman. Whenever Thälmann delivers an unscripted speech, he frequently mixes his metaphors. Some of these howlers, whether real or apocryphal, have even been preserved for posterity:

---

* A three-handed trick-taking card game involving bidding. Devised in Thuringia around 1810, it is the most popular card game in Germany. [Translator's note]

'That's the last biscuit that broke the camel's back' or 'like a dead duck running into the sand' or 'the tram workers have got one foot in the grave and the other on the breadline'.[52] One of his gaffes that is frequently cited was his unfortunate rhetorical turn of phrase: 'You have to deal with women with the organs specially created for the purpose.'

As a result of their sectarian ideology, the communist officials cut themselves off from the kind of professional or even private contacts commonly fostered among politicians of all other parties. In the final years of the Weimar Republic the KPD is, by some margin, the strongest political force in Berlin, but across the rest of the country, there are three times more Social Democrats than communists. 'Left-wing social democracy,' Thälmann says in a speech at the KPD Conference held in the Berlin suburb of Wedding in June 1929, 'is not only our most powerful adversary within the working class, but also the principal driver of social fascism.'[53]

In staging this conference, the KPD's new Secretary for Agitation and Propaganda, Walter Ulbricht, models it for the first time on those held by their Soviet Russian comrades: 'Calls of "Bravo!", sustained bursts of applause. Conference gave Comrade Thälmann a standing ovation. The delegates rise as one man to sing the "Internationale". The youth delegation greets the first chairman of the party with three cheers of "Hail Moscow!"'[54] On 12 September 1930, two days before the National Socialists record a sevenfold increase in their support at the parliamentary elections, *Die Rote Fahne* carries an advertisement on its front page for an election rally at the Sportpalast: above a photograph of Ernst Thälmann is the banner headline: 'Today Our Leader [*Führer*] Speaks.'[55]

The Devoted Lover

Maud von Ossietzky

1

The Palmers have been living in India for generations. An unfinished portrait of 1785 shows the British officer William Palmer with his second wife, the Indian princess Bibi Faiz Bakhsh. Family legend has it that Palmer saved the pretty girl during a rebellion, fell in love with her at first sight and took her into his tent. She spoke Persian and wrote poetry.[1] Sitting on his mother's lap, at just a few months' old, William Palmer Jr also appears in the painting. Later on, as a merchant and banker in Hyderabad, he was to lay the foundations of the wealth that the Palmers soon began to take for granted. And it is there, in the capital of the princely state of the same name, that Maud Hester Lichfield-Woods, the great-granddaughter of the man who founded the family firm, comes into the world in 1888.

Although she rarely gets to see her father – the family's servants are tasked with looking after the children – the news of his sudden passing during a trip to far-off England still comes as a shock to the seven-year-old Maud. And how much more deeply must she have been affected when her mother – who, unable to get over her husband's death, deliberately drank 'water contaminated with typhus bacteria'[2] – also died the following year. The eight-year-old orphan is dispatched to a convent school, where the children are ordered to pray and to dust the large statues of saints. The nuns who run this school won't allow her to hang a picture of her mother above her bed. She remains here for eight months before being put on a ship sailing from Bombay to England, where she is taken in by a maternal aunt.

Hardly any less strict than her time in the Indian convent school is the Victorian education to which Maud is now subjected at the English girls' boarding school where she is sent.[3] As a way of training her to have the right inward bearing as well as the correct external posture, until the age of eighteen she is not permitted to sit in armchairs. The other girls are envious of her Indian looks and her long eyelashes. When her classmates suggest to her one day that she singe off her eyelashes, she goes along with it because she desperately wants to look like everyone else.[4] After boarding school, Maud completes her education by attending a finishing school in Paris for several months. She is barely eighteen years old when her aunt begins to press her to marry soon. But the young woman opts instead for her independence. At Speakers' Corner in Hyde Park she listens to the speeches of radical advocates of women's rights. Before long she is taking part in demonstrations and getting up on an upturned margarine crate to deliver spirited addresses calling for women to be given the vote. Rather than steer for the safe harbour of a marriage befitting her social status, she enrols as a trainee nurse at a hospital in Manchester. In the end, though, she finds she cannot stand being treated like a servant by wealthy patients and returns home.

Maud spends Christmas 1910 with a female friend in Hamburg. Her two-month stay there is a dizzying social round of more than a dozen private balls and countless tea parties. She learns to crochet, knit and sew, dabbles in wood engraving and takes singing lessons. Her visit ends with a trip around Germany and a brief excursion to Switzerland. Maud returns to see her friend in Hamburg a year later. This time, she busies herself giving English lessons. Her

pupils include not only people of her own age from upper-class Hamburg families but also young Japanese, French, Dutch and South Americans. Whenever she isn't instructing her students in English, she teaches them how to play bridge and whist. One day, one of her regulars asks her to meet him for coffee. She waits at the Dammtor-Palast Café for half an hour beyond the appointed time but finally loses patience and is about to leave when a shy young man appears and rather awkwardly apologizes for the absence of his friend, a doctor, who has been unavoidably detained by having to perform an urgent operation. He asks whether he might be permitted to sit at her table in his friend's place.

Maud notices how the young man's reticence evaporates as soon as he starts talking: 'He appeared transformed when he spoke, his words spilled forth urgently and lit up his face in a quite remarkable way.[5] Later on, Carl von Ossietzky confesses to never having dared speak to a young lady before because of his shyness. 'It seems he wanted to eagerly seize the chance opportunity that now presented itself. But he did so in a most unobtrusive, charming way, without showing off his extensive learning [...] His large blue eyes set beneath his smooth blond hair in a well-proportioned face, which by now had lost its earlier nervous pallor, looked at me openly and candidly.' Hereafter, they start seeing one another frequently. They talk about the suffragette movement in England and social injustices in Germany. They visit museums and exhibitions. Sometimes they will spend hours together walking along the banks of the River Elbe. Carl contributes articles to liberal newspapers, and his greatest wish is to one day become a writer. At present, he is still just a clerk at the land registry office, with no prospects of promotion, having twice failed his secondary school leaving exams.

The two of them have known one another for almost ten months when, at the beginning of October, Carl invites his young lady friend to a concert to celebrate his twenty-third birthday. Maud recalled: 'Never before had I felt such delight in "putting on my glad rags" for an evening out: I wore a black evening coat and a simple, wine-red dress that I'd brought with me from Paris. My beau turned up, quite unexpectedly, in a dinner jacket, which I later discovered he'd had specially made for the occasion. Neither of us even noticed what pieces were performed that evening: we were deaf to everything but the music of the spheres…[6] Over a glass of wine in a little wine bar on Rotenbaumchaussee they abandon the formal 'Sie' form of address they've been using up to now. They talk enthusiastically about their futures, and things they plan to do together, but the later the evening gets, the quieter Carl becomes. It takes a while for Maud to find out what's troubling him. Reluctantly, he tells her that, given how slowly his salary is likely to increase, he won't be able to get married for some twelve years. All Maud's objections that they could do as lots of other young people do and just start from scratch fall on deaf ears. And because she knows how proud he is, she is reluctant to reveal to him that her family's substantial wealth would guarantee them a life of ease. Carl is adamant: it'll be twelve years before he's in a position to raise the material wherewithal to marry. He can't possibly expect her to wait that long, and so in his view there's no alternative but for them to go their separate ways. That evening, they part without arranging to meet again.

2

Maud struggles to get over the break-up with Carl. The paths that she once trod with him in growing intimacy she now walks alone, week after week. On a rainy late afternoon in early December 1912, she is once again walking the sodden tracks around the Alster when it starts to rain heavily. 'All of a sudden, a figure appeared by my side and politely offered me an umbrella,'[7] Maud recalled. It's Carl, who confesses to having watched her the whole time during her solitary perambulations. They go into a pâtisserie, which looms up 'like a friendly island in the incessant downpour'. Now the onus is on Maud to show Carl a way in which the seemingly intractable problem of the twelve-year wait can be overcome. She suggests that he starts giving private tutorials to contribute to the family finances.

It doesn't take much to convince Carl. But it is only the following spring that he decides to take the next step. On one of their evening strolls around the shores of the Alster, he vaults the low fence of a front garden, picks a white rose and hands it to the astonished Maud as a sign of their engagement. The pair hardly have any time to enjoy the romantic scene, however, as a policeman suddenly materializes beside them as if from nowhere, with his pencil and notebook at the ready. Carl is the first to regain his composure and explains the reason for his transgression. Without a word, the officer puts away his pencil and notebook and leaves the young couple in peace.

On Christmas Eve, Maud is introduced to Carl's parents at their home. He buys her a small gift beforehand at the Christmas Market. He has a fondness for markets and fairgrounds his entire life. Carl's stepfather takes an instant shine to his fiancée, though his mother is more reserved. Yet the relationship has scarcely any time to blossom: Maud receives news from London announcing that the condition of her aunt's cancer means she doesn't have long to live. In a trice she is at her sickbed, and spends the next few months caring for the aunt who took the place of her parents, remaining at her side until she dies. 'Only now that you're absent do I realize how fortunate I was when you were still here with me,' writes Carl from Hamburg. After Maud's return, planning for the wedding can go ahead. They are to be married in England, at the house of a childhood friend of Maud's. The bride-to-be decides to travel there personally to oversee the arrangements. 'The weeks passed in a flurry of frantic activity. We spent every evening avidly looking through a pile of catalogues and brochures, with friends and acquaintances helping us pick things out.'[8]

By August 1913, the stage is finally set. Carl steps off the train at Victoria Station in London, rather unsteady on his feet and green around the gills after his Channel crossing. His family know nothing about the real reason for his trip, and he is fearful of his mother's reaction. The ceremony passes off as in a picture-book: in bright sunshine, the couple walk the short stretch to St Peter's Church in Thundersley, as local boys and girls shower them with rice. As a society event, the wedding is covered not in women's magazines and the local press but also in *The Times*. One report runs: 'The bride wore an ivory silk dress decorated with the family's antique lace. The only piece of jewellery she was wearing was a miniature set in pearls, which came from one of her forebears on her mother's side, General Palmer, the former secretary to William Hastings […] The wedding reception was held in Fairhaven, near Thundersley. Afterwards Mr and Mrs Ossietzky travelled on to London, with the Continent as their final destination.'[9]

Their honeymoon lasts a mere twelve days. Maud's old family doctor has lent them his car, complete with chauffeur, for the trip. The idea is for Carl to get to know his wife's homeland. In London they visit museums and galleries. Maud announces that she wants to introduce him to her family and so takes him to the National Gallery, where some twenty-five portraits of members of her family are hanging, dating back to the fifteenth century. 'If you want to see my ancestors,' Carl remarks, 'then we'll have to start looking somewhere in Poland, as I can't trace my family's history so accurately since they weren't exactly what you'd call settled.'[10] Back home in Hamburg, there's a rift with his mother; she can't forgive him for taking such a life-changing decision without first consulting her. They are only reconciled some months later. Even so, throughout her life Maud never manages to strike up a good relationship with her mother-in-law.

Meanwhile, Carl has broadened his journalistic activities, which he continues to pursue alongside his job at the land registry. Articles by him appear in *Das freie Volk* ('The Free People'), a socialist weekly edited and published in Berlin by Rudolf Breitscheid. He writes a commentary piece in which he criticizes as disproportionately harsh the sentence passed by a military court on two territorial soldiers who disobeyed the orders of a policeman while drunk. Ossietzky's objections are cogent, but are delivered with a vitriol that matches the intemperance of what he is criticizing. Does his uncompromising attitude perhaps have something to do with his own bitter experiences? Does Ossietzky have an axe to grind with this society, in which he has had to overcome major hurdles in order to develop his gifts and talents, because they don't fit the template of formal educational qualifications?

Prussian Minister of War Erich von Falkenhayn responds to Ossietzky's article by taking recourse to law. The publisher and the author are each fined 200 gold Marks, a sum which Maud pays without telling her husband, to save him from the thirty-day prison sentence he will have to serve if he defaults. Even so, he loses his job at the land registry office and so has no means of support for the present. In addition, Britain's entry into the First World War in August 1914 means that all Maud's assets there are frozen. Carl now starts giving lessons himself, as well as public lectures (for an entrance fee) on playwrights like Frank Wedekind, August Strindberg, George Bernard Shaw and Oscar Wilde. These soon gain a growing following. By now, he appears to have lost his shyness where young women are concerned. Maud believes she has good cause to confront a rival for his affections: 'If you don't mend your ways', she threatens the woman, 'I'll shoot you. I was a markswoman at college and I'm a good shot!'[11]

But in the first instance it is Carl, the avowed pacifist, who is forced to take up arms. In November 1915, he receives his call-up papers. When swearing allegiance to the flag, Protestant recruits are first required to come forward, followed by those of the Catholic faith. And finally the order is issued: 'Free thinkers, atheists, sectarians and the godless – step forward!'[12] Carl is the only person in this final category. He sees himself at a turning point in his mental and emotional development. He writes to Maud, who acts as a sounding board for his inner state: 'I had grown vain, vain about my intellect. But anyone who wants to get on in life can't possibly manage that on his intellect alone, he must have the capacity to be shaken by powerful internal conflicts. Maud, he continues, has become 'the midwife to this new period in my life': 'My dear little lamb, whom I've so often deceived, who bade you share the fate of a person who is so much more unstable than many, many others?'[13]

In the meantime, Maud is keeping her head above water by taking lessons for a dwindling number of English-language students, but mainly by teaching people how to play bridge. She doesn't hear from Carl for long stretches, also there is no news from her half-brother in England. She is tormented by the thought that they might end up facing one another in the trenches. In the spring of 1917, Carl is sent home for three months on sick leave. Then he's off once more and doesn't write for months. But in December 1918, 'on a bright and sunny morning',[14] he is suddenly standing there outside the door.

3

The days that follow are filled with ceaseless activity. Maud sees little of her husband, who has been elected to a soldiers' council and is busy giving lectures, drafting proclamations and writing pamphlets and articles. Using borrowed money he founds a printing press and begins to produce a newspaper in small print runs. He receives an offer from Berlin to work as the secretary of the German Peace Society. He accepts, and they have four weeks to complete the move from Hamburg to the capital of the Reich, where they find accommodation in a furnished back room in Leibnizstraße. And it's clear there's now a child on the way. The rent is high and Carl's income is meagre. After a lecture at the Peace Society, the women's rights activist Helene Stöcker enquires after Maud's welfare. When asked why his pregnant wife is faring so badly, Carl replies: 'In all honesty, we just don't have enough to eat.'[15] Helene Stöcker duly arranges for Maud to be moved to a Hostel for Mothers and Children in Uhlandstraße, where she can be properly looked after. In December, not long before Christmas, she gives birth to their daughter Rosalinde. The newborn baby remains in hospital for five months, after it turns out that the new apartment they have found is also riddled with damp.

Carl makes the following entry in the family diary on New Year's Day 1920: 'There are now three of us. A new life has resulted from our life together. Still very delicate and weak. But what we are we have passed on to her.'[16] And as if he had reason to apologize, he goes on: 'Dear Maudie, we've been through good and bad times. Seen beautiful and ugly things. And what we've learned over those years should be to the benefit of our child. I mean to work hard for you both, though. To make sure life is good for our little girl, and to heal your wounds and make you strong and healthy like before.' Carl tries to augment his slender earnings. He moves from the Peace Society to the League for Human Rights, and publishes articles in the *Berliner Volks-Zeitung*. The chief editor of the paper is Otto Nuschke, who after the war becomes deputy prime minister of the German Democratic Republic. Carl also writes for English publications such as the *New Statesman and Nation* and the *Observer*, with Maud helping him translate. By roundabout routes, he tries to find out what his boss, the publisher Otto Lehmann-Rüßbüldt, thinks about his abilities. The answer is crushing: 'Ossietzky will never be a writer!'[17] Lehmann-Rüßbüldt survives the Nazi years in exile, and after his return from abroad to West Germany in 1962 he is the first person to be awarded the Carl-von-Ossietzky Medal.*

---

* It was originally intended that the editor of the news magazine *Der Spiegel*, Rudolf Augstein, should receive the award, but he turned down the honour as he did not want his own imprisonment (he was gaoled in 1962 for publishing allegations of corruption against Federal defence minister Franz Josef Strauß) to be placed on a par with what Ossietzky suffered.

In Berlin, Maud takes part in the 'No More War' (*Nie Wieder Krieg*) events that are held every year in the Lustgarten on Museum Island. A photograph taken in 1921 shows her, Albert Einstein's wife Elsa and an American women's rights activist handing out leaflets from an open-topped car at the gathering. The following year an anti-war poem entitled *Drei Minuten Gehör* ('Three Minutes of Your Time') by Kurt Tucholsky is read: because effective PA systems do not yet exist, four orators around the concourse read the poem simultaneously. One of the speakers at the event is the diplomat and writer Count Harry Kessler. A plan is drawn up for all pacifist forces to be brought together within a single new political grouping, the Republican Party of Germany. In the general election to the Reichstag in 1924 Carl stands as a Republican candidate for the Potsdam constituency, but the party fails to gain enough votes to enter parliament and is dissolved soon after.

Through his political and journalistic activities, Carl von Ossietzky has succeeded in making a name for himself in Berlin within just a few years. In the meantime, he has also begun contributing to the magazine *Das Tage-Buch*, which was founded in 1920 with the help of the publisher Ernst Rowohlt. Its left-liberal stance makes it hardly any different from its principal competitor, *Die Weltbühne*, whose proprietor Siegfried Jacobsohn keeps jealous watch to ensure that none of his authors publish their works in both periodicals. In March 1926, Carl von Ossietzky is summoned to an interview with Jacobsohn at the publisher's house. 'We drove in the pouring rain to Witzleben Station,' Maud later recollected. 'Because the men had business to discuss and I wasn't invited, I stayed outside sheltering under a tree. I waited there for the rain to stop and for Carl to return.'[18] The upshot of the meeting is that Jacobsohn makes Ossietzky a permanent member of staff at the magazine. Henceforth he writes a weekly column for *Die Weltbühne*. But, barely a year later, Jacobsohn is dead. Kurt Tucholsky is appointed as his successor, but he values his independence too much and finds that the job of chief editor isn't to his liking. And so Ossietzky takes charge of the magazine. By October 1927, it is there for all to see in black and white, as the front page of *Die Weltbühne* carries the by-line: 'Edited by Carl v. Ossietzky in collaboration with Kurt Tucholsky.'[19]

4

Carl von Ossietzky's new position at *Die Weltbühne* furnishes the family with material security – his yearly salary is now 10,000 Reichsmarks – but at the same time exposes them to increased liability. On four occasions in 1927 and 1928, he finds himself facing, as the responsible publisher, fines or prison sentences.[20] 'Shady Goings-On in German Aviation' runs the headline of a story published in *Die Weltbühne* on 12 March 1929, which incurs the wrath of the army. In this piece, the aircraft manufacturer Walter Kreiser provides details of secret rearmament plans that are afoot in the aviation sector, which violate the provisions of the Versailles Peace Treaty. In August, criminal proceedings are initiated and shortly afterwards both the editorial offices of *Die Weltbühne* and the Ossietzkys' private apartment are raided by the police. However, the trial is delayed as, behind the scenes, the Foreign Ministry and the army wrangle over the question of which course of action would be more damaging: to ignore the exposé, or invite unwanted attention by trying to make an example of the magazine.

The threat of a criminal trial hangs over Ossietzky for almost two years. Meanwhile, the mood in the country at large deteriorates from month to month. A few days after the sensational victory of the National Socialists in the September 1930 poll, Ossietzky travels to Sweden to see Tucholsky. His return journey takes him through Denmark. He writes to Maud: 'I still have some business to attend to here in Copenhagen: various house-calls to make and some people I need to talk to. And some soundings about how the land lies should the magazine run into further difficulties.'[21] At New Year 1931, he notes in the family's commemorative book: 'I've no idea what lies in store. But we should expect plenty of bad things to happen.'[22] All along, the Foreign Ministry continues to block criminal proceedings against *Die Weltbühne*; two projected trial dates fall through, prompting Defence Minister Kurt von Schleicher to write to the foreign minister, urging him 'to do his utmost to resist and protect against acts of treachery.'[23]

In truth, the pacifist Ossietzky represents a minority position. There's little doubt that, for the majority of Germans, the unspoken watchword is the need to stick together to oppose the unreasonable demands of the Versailles Treaty. Pacifism is seen as treason, while extreme right-wing thugs are given free rein to commit acts of violence 'motivated by a noble and ardent love of country.'[24] It is an open secret that the German army, despite the former Allies' best efforts to monitor and control the situation, is seeking to undermine limitations on rearmament; indeed, it is even the subject of debate in parliament. And revelations about the clandestine cooperation that has been going on between the German army and the Soviet Red Army have been appearing in major foreign newspapers for some time. In spite of all this, the trial of Ossietzky and Kreiser opens in Leipzig on 17 November and is held in camera.

The trial rapidly becomes the test case that the army was aiming for, and as expected the justice system plays along. It comes as no surprise when the defendants are found guilty, on the flimsiest of evidence, of divulging military secrets and sentenced to eighteen months in prison. The objection that the article in *Die Weltbühne* contained nothing that wasn't already public knowledge is dismissed by the court on the grounds that, according to the case law promulgated by the Imperial Court of Justice, a 'secret' does not necessarily presume a 'state of secrecy.'[25] As part of its judgement, the court orders that 'Issue No. 11 of the *Die Weltbühne*, 1929, along with all the printing plates and formes used in its composition, are to be rendered unusable.'[26] Considering this verdict, Thomas Mann remarks: 'The gagging of public criticism ought to be the preserve of fascist dictatorships, where things that are expressed openly in a free society can only be passed on secretly and cravenly from mouth to mouth.'[27] And Ossietzky himself gets to the heart of the judgement in his own particular way: 'Political journalism isn't life assurance: risk constitutes its very best stimulus.'[28] Maud is proud of Carl and supports him in the consistency of his position. She tries her utmost to encourage him. But who can *she* lean on for support?

The Red Czar

Otto Braun

1

Otto Braun is more a man of action than of words. As a lifeguard, between the ages of fourteen and fifteen he saved no fewer than eight people from drowning.[1] Now he is supposed to prevent an entire country from sinking into chaos, violence and civil war. To many of his contemporaries he appears like a revenant of Bismarck. Since 1918, Braun has occupied a ministerial post in the Social Democrat-run government of Prussia. For almost twelve years, he has been prime minister of the largest region in the whole of Germany. This broad-shouldered, powerfully built man, who in the manner of many tall people walks with a slight stoop and whose round head already shows distinct signs of balding even in his forties, is not only reminiscent of Bismarck by virtue of his alert, grey-blue eyes: like the Iron Chancellor, he has a surprisingly high voice in relation to his commanding physical appearance. In small gatherings he tends to speak softly, generally in a somewhat disgruntled and gruff tone of voice. In such settings he succeeds in juggling various opposing interests, ideologies, temperaments, predilections and antipathies, as well as the vanities of his fellow players and colleagues – and then ends up making an autocratic decision anyhow. 'He was born into the wrong class,' one close observer remarks. 'He really ought to have been born an aristocrat.'[2]

He gains a reputation for loyalty among his colleagues, and in turn they treat him with a great deal of respect. But whenever Otto Braun appears in front of a large crowd, his charismatic aura – which in the committee room reduces many an experienced civil servant who is called upon to field his searching questions to a stuttering wreck – vanishes in one fell swoop. In mass meetings, he comes across like some pettifogging auditor who struggles to put forward anything but plodding arguments and who rarely shows any intuitive capacity to 'read the room'. He is proud of being 'pretty down-to-earth',[3] and conveys 'an impression of chilly reserve'. Braun is widely regarded as a 'crisis-proof prime minister'. He has recently turned sixty, and the pro-republican press hails him as a 'genuine leadership personality'[4] and as the 'very model of the German republican statesman'. Even the far-right *Deutsche Allgemeine Zeitung* sees Braun as 'a real fighter, worthy of the respect of even the most implacable political adversary'.[5]

Very few friends know anything about Braun's mental state at this time. In February 1932, he writes to one of them, the philosopher and SPD politician Karl Kautsky, in the following terms:

There are already signs that I'm beginning to come apart at the seams, something I have to hide from the outside world as far as I'm able. One cannot endure a life of stressful work and remain truly effective without taking time out and relaxing now and then among family and friends. I have neither. My children are dead and my poor wife has been partially paralysed for the last four and a half years, and has on occasion been gravely ill, with the result that for years my life has been circumscribed by my study, parliament, and the sick room. Yet that has really worn me down and dangerously depleted the store of physical energy that I brought with me to Berlin from my East Prussian home.[6]

Even so, many people in Germany, even Conservatives, would find themselves agreeing with what President Hindenburg's friend Elard von Oldenburg-Januschau said about the Prussian prime minister: 'Otto Braun's a solid chap; he knows what he wants. The rest of that lot in Berlin who are involved in politics are nothing but shitheads.'[7]

2

Braun's father is a shoemaker, but his order book doesn't look too healthy in the war winter of 1871. People need to economize and are putting off having their shoes repaired or buying new ones. The last harvest was poor, the war against France is harming trade and food prices have risen sharply. At least the family still has its own house in the centre of Königsberg; it is here that Otto Braun is born in January 1872. He is the family's second oldest son; eventually the head of the family Carl Otto Braun will have eight mouths to feed, not counting himself and his wife. Not long after, the family's fortunes start to decline. Otto Braun is just eight years old when they are forced to give up their home. After a series of moves, they finally find accommodation in a gloomy rear tenement flat in the Hinterer Roßgarten district of Königsberg, between the garrison headquarters and the Castle Lake. Otto's father, an 'embittered, withdrawn man thanks to the blows fate had dealt him', finds occasional jobs as a labourer, a railway brakeman and finally as a signalman; as for his mother, the daughter of a farm labourer, Otto pushes her away because of her 'overanxious solicitude'.[8]

This backyard tenement life offers little in the way of light, and, as soon as he can, Otto's elder brother flees this confinement. As the second-born, Otto takes his place looking after his younger siblings. The primary school that he attends has only five grades. The pupils learn to read and write, but religious instruction plays a big part in their education; as Otto later writes, this succeeds in 'thoroughly dispelling any belief in God for my entire life'.[9] When he reaches the upper grades, he is put in charge of supervising the younger children. A tall, strong boy, Otto possesses a natural authority. And he is quick-witted, too. The school principal teaches him chess, and before long he is beating his teacher. Otto leaves school at fourteen and finds himself an apprenticeship as a lithographer at a printer's.

One day there is a knock on the door of the Brauns' tenement flat, a man asking sixteen-year-old Otto if he can leave a newspaper with him for a neighbour whom Otto has never met. 'It was the *Arbeiter-Chronik* ['Workers' Chronicle'], published in Nuremberg,[10] which had been permitted to appear in the final years of the Anti-Socialist Laws. Because I was always interested in any reading matter, I immediately read the paper from cover to cover. And a whole new world opened up to me.'

The Social Democratic Party becomes a surrogate family for Otto Braun. He later recalled the clandestine political activity he became engaged in at this time: 'Before long we were holding meetings with a few like-minded workers and also the odd student in a cellar bar, and we founded a discussion group under the innocuous-sounding name of "The Kant Reading Club" (*Leseklub Kant*) in which, concealed from the eyes and ears of the police, we set about solving major ideological problems and worked our way from Kant through Hegel to Marx.'[11] The SPD bosses regard the endeavours of these younger party members as 'bourgeois nonsense'.[12] Braun, too, sees no intrinsic value in education except as a means to an end. He finishes his apprenticeship in the spring of 1890 and sets off on his travels. Without even taking his leave from home, he heads for the station. By chance, on the way there he runs into his father, goes for a beer with him and calmly informs him of his plans. Then he promptly boards a train bound for Berlin. But his real final destination is America.

His attempt to make this great leap fails, however. After a difficult few months in Berlin and Leipzig, a telegram from Königsberg reaches the itinerant apprentice. His father, the family's sole breadwinner, has fallen seriously ill. Without further ado, Braun returns to Königsberg. In the interim, the Anti-Socialist Laws have been repealed, and the Social Democratic Party's success at the polls has made its leaders optimistic that they might one day soon attain their goals. In March 1891, Friedrich Engels raises the prospect of bourgeois society being overthrown by 1898.[13] Over the ensuing decades, social democracy's horizons of expectation are characterized by such optimistic pronouncements. Twenty years later, for instance, Karl Kautsky was still predicting that the proletarian revolution would occur 'in all likelihood within the foreseeable future'.[14] Yet the manner in which this should be achieved was a contentious issue that deeply divided the party.

At this time, Otto Braun belongs to the radical Young Turks, who shun parliamentary methods and instead advocate a violent overthrow of the system. In 1891, he falls foul of the state prosecutor's office. He finds himself accused of slandering the state and insulting the monarchy. He receives free legal aid from a lawyer, Hugo Haase, who is not much older than him and is also the son of a shoemaker. Apart from that, though, the two do not have much in common. Haase, who comes from a Jewish household, is cheerful, open and amiable, a good orator and an intellectual, who has found his way to social democracy through conviction, especially his strong sense of justice. In contrast, Braun is unsociable and withdrawn. To have someone from the middle classes deliberately side with the oppressed is often greeted not with gratitude by Social Democrats but, rather, with scepticism, particularly since the people in question are generally intellectuals. To loud applause from those present, a delegate at the SPD conference in Munich in 1902 voices the opinion: 'All theoreticians should be locked up together until they've devoured one another.'[15] Hugo Haase has frequently been on the receiving end of this mistrust, but it has only spurred him on to prove himself and driven him to become more radical. Otto Braun, on the other hand, is gradually metamorphosing from a radical Young Turk into a pragmatic, who by no means recants his radical aims, but who is becoming more flexible in his choice of ways in which to realize them.

3

Emilie Podzus is by nature reserved, taciturn and introverted. She must really have had to steel herself to appear as a podium speaker at a party rally. It is here that Otto Braun gets to know her. They marry in 1894, with Hugo Haase as their witness. That same year, their son Erich is born, and soon after their daughter Erna. To the outside world Emilie cuts a rather inconspicuous figure; as the life partner of a husband who in later years occupies a succession of senior positions in the public domain, this rather dumpy woman with her broad, bespectacled face never subsequently appears in public. But as a friend of the family observes, at home she controls domestic affairs with an 'almost virago-like' fervour.

As Otto Braun ascends the party hierarchy, so the family's standard of living improves. In 1897, at the age of twenty-six, Otto is appointed Social Democratic Party chairman in East Prussia, and in 1902 he becomes a member of the Königsberg city council. He might almost be counted among the worthies of the East Prussian metropolis, were it not for the fact that the Social Democrats are still not part of the bourgeois establishment, plus the various political groupings still tend to isolate themselves from one another. Despite the Brauns living in a highly respectable middle-class neighbourhood, and Erich attending the local grammar school, Braun consistently declines any invitations from 'bourgeois circles'. During the years of repression, social democracy developed so to speak a parallel universe, with working-class people socializing among themselves in cycling clubs, choral societies, gymnastics and bowling clubs and education associations.

In 1903, Braun is arrested once more and charged with inciting high treason. He is placed in strict solitary confinement. While in prison, he suffers an attack of appendicitis, which remains untreated as he is denied medical treatment. During the trial the prosecution case collapses. This episode leaves Braun with a feeling of bitter resentment, as well as permanent damage to his health in the form of acute rheumatic pains and neuralgia that dog him for the rest of his life.[16]

Otto Braun finds the following sentence in the works of Kant: 'Nothing is divine except that which is rational.' He paraphrases this and adopts it as his personal maxim: 'Anything that's against nature is ungodly.'[17] For him, rationality is synonymous with naturalness, and this conviction leads him to underestimate the role played by irrationality in politics. Whenever Braun grows weary of political squabbling, he thinks about the joy he finds in nature. 'Even the most superficial observer,' he writes in an uncharacteristically lyrical paean of praise to his East Prussian homeland,

> finds his heart gladdened when walking across the north-eastern plains of our Fatherland. He passes lush meadows that are a riot of colour, alive with the industrious buzzing of bees; his path leads him through rippling cornfields, where the heavy ears of grain bend and sway, wave-like, in the light breeze; and his gaze roams in delight over the golden sea of an oilseed-rape or lupin field, and he contentedly breathes in the pure, fragrant air. Freed from all the shackles of society, and feeling at one with the glorious nature that surrounds him, he flings himself down into the shade of a tree by the woodland's edge.[18]

4

By 1905, when he assumes his first office on the national stage for the SPD, Braun is regarded within his party as being on the left wing. But what does that mean in practice for someone like him, who fundamentally distrusts all ideologies? He can encapsulate his life experience in the dictum: 'Even the weak find strength within a community.'[19] Solidarity has enabled the Social Democratic Party to gain a mass following, but the external pressure it has been put under for decades has also led to radicalization. In the meantime, the broad spectrum of views it encompasses – extremely hard to bring together under the auspices of a single party – ranges from the idea of using parliamentary means to break down bourgeois society to the strategy of violent revolution, as advocated by a radical minority around Rosa Luxemburg, Clara Zetkin and Karl Liebknecht.

Braun joins the national executive committee of the SPD in 1911. For the family, this entails moving from Königsberg to Berlin. His remit on the committee is to look after the party's finances; he also becomes a delegate in the Prussian regional parliament. Here, the SPD can muster just seven delegates. By contrast, the Conservatives boast no fewer than 152, despite the fact that only around half as many people voted for them as for the Social Democrats. The reason for this is the grotesquely unfair Prussian three-class franchise system, which gives an elector with a higher taxable income up to twenty times more votes than someone in the third class. In addition, it is an open ballot, in which people's voting behaviour is logged – an invitation to the large landowners to bring undue influence to bear on their tenant farmers and labourers.

Braun's maiden speech in the Prussian parliament lasts for three hours. He speaks on agricultural matters, but finds himself facing a parliamentary majority on the opposition benches who don't even attempt to take his views seriously. His criticism of state subsidies for cultivating rye are rebutted by a Conservative member on the grounds that, as a party functionary, he doesn't understand a thing about farming. As it turns out, the Conservative delegate's own professional expertise in this area is summed up in the following argument: 'Rye is, and will remain, a German crop. It is the most noble of all German arable crops.'[20] It is scenes like this that throw into sharp relief the impotence of the Social Democrats, and indeed this feeling develops into a general mood of depression within the SPD. After decades of struggle, they have become by far the strongest political force in Germany, and yet their influence on the course of events remains minimal. The party's sole achievement, as commentators within its own ranks wryly point out, has been the adoption by parliament of the Babies' Feeding Bottle Bill. This legislation, concerning the quality of feeding bottles and the impact this has on infants' digestive disorders, was indeed adopted onto the statute book by the Reichstag in November 1912.

5

At the outbreak of war in August 1914, it is unclear how the government will deal with the Social Democrats. Otto Braun's fear that a state of siege might be declared and the whole of the SPD leadership arrested is by no means unfounded, since plans to this effect have been in place since 1907. To ensure the safety of the party's funds and its leaders, Friedrich Ebert and Otto Braun travel to Switzerland, where they stay for several months under a cover address. On the way there, Braun can hardly be said to be imbued with war fever: he sees his fellow travellers, who for the most part greet the prospect of war with euphoria, 'lying dead on the grass with a bullet in the chest within a few weeks' … 'What insanity to visit death and destruction upon these peaceful towns!'[21]

On the other hand, Braun has very little sympathy for those who accuse their own government of waging a war of conquest and who are blind to nationalism in the enemy countries. For him, Karl Liebknecht is 'a vain, ambitious political poseur whose principal goal is his own renown and who treats the party merely as a pedestal to that end' and a 'jack of all trades driven by vanity and self-promotion'.[22]

The more futile and costly the battles become, the greater the weight carried by the arguments of those who want to sue for peace. Was it really just grandstanding on Liebknecht's part, was it metaphysics instead of politics to have voted against war loans in the Reichstag and so flouted the holiest commandment of the party, namely to maintain party discipline at all costs? Braun runs himself ragged trying to deal with the clashes between the two wings of the party, which often descend to the level of personal animus. After one furious verbal exchange, he suffers an acute attack of neuritis and is forced to spend five weeks laid up in bed. He is tormented by thoughts of suicide: 'I was racked with indescribable pain day and night, with the result that I was often very close to putting an end to all the misery. If only I hadn't had a wife and children.'[23]

His son Erich is the bright spot in Otto Braun's life. He lavishes on the boy all the attention and care that he never got from his own father. After his son finishes grammar school, he supports him as he begins studying medicine, though when war breaks out Erich interrupts his studies to enlist as a medical orderly. He takes part in the battles to repel a Russian invasion at the Masurian Lakes. Not long after, in February 1915, Otto Braun receives news from the field hospital in Bialla that his son has been killed. In his initial grief, he reaches for his loaded Browning revolver:

All the pain would be over and done with, and I could draw a line under a life that had been so abruptly robbed of any prospect of sunny, happy twilight years. Certainly, it would have been a cowardly thing to do [...] Plus, my life and my efforts have never been, and still aren't, simply to do with my family; they have also been in the service of the great socialist idea that has preoccupied me since I was a young boy. Even so [...] it would have been easy to replace me in the party, especially since my powers are now all but spent, and who else would miss me?[24]

What happened in the days that followed – wandering around the East Prussian war zone in search of Erich's grave, exhuming his dead son with his own bare hands and placing his body in a coffin, the difficulties of getting the coffin back to Berlin by train, the body going missing for several days, and finally the funeral in Friedenau – all this merges into one nightmarish blur. Time and again, Otto Braun is tempted to shoot himself. 'I often envy those people,' he notes, 'who in their simplicity of heart are still able to believe in life after death. For sure, they are living a lie, but at least it brings them some solace.'[25]

6

Meanwhile, the split in the party can no longer be prevented. On 7 April 1917, the same day on which Kaiser Wilhelm II, decades too late, announces a root-and-branch reform of the Prussian electoral system, the Independent Socialist Party is founded in Gotha. Its first chairman is Hugo Haase, the witness at Otto and Emilie Braun's wedding.

Following the secession of their left wing, the Social Democrats now confidently formulate their claim to become the party of government. But before long, it seems as though they are running to catch up with events. In November 1917, the Bolsheviks topple the provisional government in Petrograd and following an election stage a coup to seize power. The fact that they did not receive even half as many votes as the social democratic parties does not bother Lenin in the slightest.* He contends that the Soviets represent 'a higher form of democracy'. Braun's position on the events in Russia is clear: 'It must be stated openly and quite unequivocally', he writes in a leader article in *Vorwärts*, 'that we as Social Democrats repudiate in the strongest possible terms these violent methods of the Bolsheviks [...] Socialism cannot be built on bayonets and

---

* In the November 1917 elections for the Russian Constituent Assembly, the Bolsheviks received 23 per cent of the votes, while the combined vote for Social Democratic parties was 62 per cent.

machine guns. If it is to survive and thrive, it must be achieved in a democratic way.'[26] Braun is adamant that a 'thick, visible line should be drawn' between the Social Democrats and the Bolsheviks.

Revolution is in the air everywhere. And the war is still not at an end. Braun travels around the Baltic region, where he is astonished at how out of touch with reality officers of a Pan-German mindset are and at Baltic barons and German military governors who still pore over maps in cafés, carving up Poland and the Baltic lands among themselves. But then things happen at lightning speed: Supreme Headquarters, the centre of command of the German armed forces, orders an immediate ceasefire, a move that is accompanied by the widespread implementation of representative parliamentary democracy throughout Prussia and the rest of the empire. Prince Max von Baden becomes the new, and final, Chancellor of Imperial Germany, and Social Democrats participate in his administration in ministerial roles. However, the attempt to forestall a revolution from below by instituting top-down reforms falters in the chaos of the final weeks of the war. Those who wanted to pull the strings now find themselves dictated to by events. On the morning of 9 November 1918, a Social Democrat delegation presents itself to Chancellor Max von Baden, demanding that the emperor abdicate and that government be placed in the hands of the SPD. When Max von Baden responds by offering Friedrich Ebert the chancellorship, Ebert casts doubt on the legitimacy of this act. It is Otto Braun who, having followed this exchange from the back row of delegates, leans forward and whispers in his colleague's ear: 'Oh, what the hell… just say "yes"!'[27]

What a seething mass of people there are out on the streets! With the barrels of their rifles lowered and brandishing red flags, soldiers are parading elatedly through the city; it seems as if everyone is on the move, and the police hang back nervously. Braun sits in the party office of the SPD executive committee and hands out ration coupons for provisions, clothing and railway return tickets. There is a creeping sense of unease that things might spiral out of control. Heavily armed young men are everywhere. What's going to happen when night falls? For weeks now, wild bursts of gunfire have been erupting for the most trivial of reasons. Braun gradually grows into his role as the person responsible for the new order. Invoking his authority as 'Chairman of the SPD', he dispatches a regiment of Prussian fusiliers in an attempt to impound at least some of the weapons. Soon after, he embarks upon a new phase in his life as he is appointed minister of agriculture in the Prussian revolutionary government.

7

The new Prussian Minister for Agriculture, Estates and Forestry is somewhat apprehensive as he enters his place of work for the first time in November 1918. 'There they all were, standing in a conspiratorial huddle in the conference room,' he later wrote, looking back and recounting his first impressions, 'the heads of department, the privy counsellors, the private secretaries, the secret emissaries and the shorthand typists […] with hatred, hostility and distrustful curiosity written on their faces. Not one of them displayed even a glimmer of happiness or satisfaction, or indeed any emotion betraying the slightest sign of sympathy for the new regime or us, its representatives.'[28] How was he, the boy from the tenement block, supposed to behave around these courtly flunkies, 'whose highly polished uniform buttons reflected the majesty of the Crown'?[29] Even what form of address to use proved problematic. Should members of the Prussian revolutionary government be addressed as 'Your Excellency', or ought he to insist instead on the 'Moscow import "People's Commissioner"'?[30] Otto Braun opts for the perfectly civil form of address 'Herr Minister'. The civil servants set out to frustrate him. He is burdened with inconsequential tasks so that they can circumvent him in making important decisions: 'An old bureaucrats' trick: They tried drowning me in paperwork.'[31] He rises to the challenge, staying over at the ministry every night for the first few weeks, learning the filing system by heart, and creating a private filing department, which makes him far less dependent upon the old bureaucratic apparatus. He faces irritating provocations from all sides. On one occasion, the audit office even enquires what has become of the bald tyres from his official car. Braun replies: 'I had a pair of galoshes made from them.'[32]

He also encounters resistance from within his own ranks. Many Social Democrats still hold to August Bebel's old dictum that 'the Prussian spirit is the mortal enemy of all democracy'.[33] 'What's the point of a Prussian parliament when one for the whole of Germany is just about to convene?' asks the SPD politician Max Cohen. His colleague Otto Landsberg puts it even more drastically: 'If Germany is to live, then Prussia in the form it has taken hitherto must die!'[34] These reservations about Prussia are by no means based solely on ideology. After the end of the monarchy, there is an urgent need to rebalance Prussia's weight in relation to the other German provinces, yet, considering Prussia's sheer size and economic power, this is scarcely possible. In Berlin, two comparably large administrations coexist side by side yet also interleaved with one another. 'The empire was so to speak a guest of Prussia's in Berlin. It did not have its own executive or police force.'[35] Hugo Preuß, the father of the Weimar Constitution, correctly identifies the continuing existence of the Prussian state as the 'fundamental problem facing the future internal configuration of Germany'.[36]

Otto Braun's attitude is clear: 'The new, democratic Prussia should not be destroyed.'[37] In the first place, other problems are far more pressing. The far left is threatening to seize power in a coup. As Braun says when addressing an election rally in January 1919: 'Truly, we haven't fought against the dictatorship and violent tyranny of the Prussian Junkerdom only to saddle ourselves now with the same kind of minority rule by the Spartacists and their autonomous fellow-travellers.'[38] Otto Braun proposes that all the troublemakers be forcibly transported out of Berlin and put to work on land reclamation projects in the countryside. However, he finds himself unable to push this measure through.

Shortly afterwards, the right wing stages a coup, under the leadership of Wolfgang Kapp and General von Lüttwitz, the 'old military blowhard who meddles in politics',[39] as Braun refers to the military leader of the putsch. After this attempt to overthrow the government fails, Braun is made prime minister. The conservative newspaper *Kreuzzeitung* offers the opinion that Braun 'has become the de facto dictator of Prussia. Radicalism reigns supreme. Under this regime, we are experiencing the disintegration of the last vestiges of state order. There can be no doubt that Prussia is rushing pell-mell towards its destruction.'[40]

Those closest to him take a very different view of the prime minister: a colleague observes that Braun is 'adept at taking on board and accepting different opinions and at defusing difficult situations with his cheerful sense of humour'.[41] Nonetheless, Braun maintains tight control over meetings in the ministry in Wilhelmstraße, summarily curtailing discussions that get out of hand and insisting on having the last word in all key decisions. 'The whole apparatus can only function properly if I've got my hands firmly on the wheel',[42] he once warns his own party when it displays a keenness to return to opposition. Yet although he can wield power with a facility that few other Social Democrats possess, he is no power seeker. He doesn't love his office, rather it is a burden to him, which he has only taken on out of a sense of duty. When he is accused in the Prussian regional assembly of clinging on to office at all costs, he counters: 'If someone had the choice of becoming a director of a refuse collection company or a minister, I'd completely understand it if he opted for the former, because firstly he'd have twice the salary, and secondly he wouldn't have nearly as much disgusting filth to deal with as a cabinet minister.'[43]

8

Otto Braun maintains a friendship – albeit not always one without conflict – with President Friedrich Ebert, whose office is just a few steps away in Wilhelmstraße. But after Ebert's unexpected death in 1925, Hindenburg takes occupancy of the presidential palace. Hailing from the region east of the River Elbe, Hindenburg embodies everything that is anathema to Braun: he is a Junker and a militarist, and, as Chief of the General Staff when surrender became inevitable in 1918, he left a situation of chaos for the Social Democrats to clear up. He was also (along with fellow field marshal Erich Ludendorff), responsible for originating the 'stab in the back' myth – the insinuation that Germany's armed forces, undefeated on the battlefield, had been undermined and betrayed by the revolutionary masses.

Yet no sooner has the prime minister made a courtesy call at the President's palace after he takes office than a surprising closeness develops between the two men. In his address to the President, Braun makes a passing reference to the growing elk population in East Prussia, and immediately they have found a topic of mutual interest. Hindenburg doesn't regard Braun as some functionary, or a party stalwart, but, rather, as a 'natural governing type'.[44] 'My friends in Hanover told me that Otto Braun was a fanatical firebrand. But now I see that he's a perfectly reasonable person with whom you can talk about anything,'[45] Hindenburg is heard to say. And when there's talk one time of state subsidies for the monarchical 'Union Club' being axed, he states: 'It's outrageous the way Prussia is being governed! I cannot imagine that my friend Braun has any part in this.'[46]

This unlikely pairing is seized upon and played up in the press. Rumours of night-time drinking sessions involving the President and the Prussian prime minister even make it into American newspapers. But the Social Democrats, too, are positively surprised by the way in which the new President is discharging his office. 'I got the feeling', Prussian interior minister Carl Severing writes about Hindenburg, 'that he would genuinely try his utmost to perform his role unblinkered by class prejudice. He made a not-unsympathetic impression on me and my colleagues in the Prussian government.'[47] Over the course of the years, a relationship of trust, based on mutual respect and transcending their difference in age and their core philosophies, develops between Braun and Hindenburg. They also find they have a common interest in hunting. Braun grants the President a hunting licence covering the whole of the Schorfheide, just north of Berlin. From time to time, they consult one another about problems concerning hunting and forestry or the conservation of landscape and nature. And occasionally they meet one another while out hunting. Hindenburg is troubled by the growing number of day-trippers coming to the area by car, a view that Braun shares; they also both have an antipathy towards wild camping on the Schorfheide.

Over time, however, those around Hindenburg conspire to work against Braun. The relationship between the men grows markedly cooler from 1929 onwards, on political grounds. Braun has the Stahlhelm,* an anti-republican ex-servicemen's organization that is closely affiliated to extreme German nationalist groupings and of which Hindenburg is an honorary member, banned in Prussia. Time and again, peers of the 'old man' beat a path to the presidential palace to complain about this or that law. On one occasion, the Prussian Prince August Wilhelm is injured when a Nazi demonstration is broken up by the police, and Hindenburg confronts Braun about it: 'The democratic rubber truncheon', Braun informs him, 'cannot make any distinctions between class.'[48]

---

* Full name: *Stahlhelm, Bund der Frontsoldaten* ('Steel Helmet, The League of Frontline Soldiers'). This reactionary and avowedly anti-Semitic organization was founded in Magdeburg in 1918 in response to the attempted left-wing November Revolution of that year. By 1930, the *Stahlhelm* and its affiliates numbered around half a million members. [Translator's note]

'Well, the fact remains I've received a complaint,' Hindenburg persists, somewhat resignedly. Aides whisper in the President's ear that the Prussian prime minister has full jurisdiction in this matter. Hindenburg looks suspicious: 'So, are you telling me that Herr Braun can dispatch a couple of policemen across the street and have me arrested if he so chooses?'[49]

Braun loathes the intriguing, the poisonous tittle-tattle and the backroom deals of the political domain. For a long time, he has been plagued by illness: a weakness of the cardiac muscle and low blood pressure, accompanied by dizzy spells, are making his life a misery. Whenever he can get away, hunting becomes his place of refuge from politics. Newspaper commentators are fond of taking satirical sideswipes at this private passion of his: 'All this fuss over crises and resignations, / Is for the likes of you and me, / Prime Minister Braun is shooting elks, / We really should let him be.'[50] Repeatedly, attention is drawn to the mismatch between Braun's social-democratic convictions and hunting, which is widely regarded as a pursuit of the squirearchy. For all that, the PM's own private lifestyle is decidedly modest. Up to 1926, he and his wife live in a three-bedroom house in Friedenau, after which they move to a house in Zehlendorf, which likewise has only three bedrooms. His neighbours in Dessauer Straße are the President of the Reichsbank, Hjalmar Schacht, and the trade union leader Theodor Leipart. In the evenings, Braun can sometimes be spotted, in his shirtsleeves and a gardening apron and accompanied by his German shepherd dog, tending his wife's potato patch or pushing a wheelbarrow full of manure. Journalists who pry into his private life are given short shrift.

In 1927, doctors discover that Emilie has a brain haemorrhage, and for several days she is in a critical condition. Her recovery is slow, as she gradually regains the power of speech. However, her hands and feet are largely paralyzed. Day after day, for years on end, when Braun returns home to Zehlendorf from the city centre, he assists her with her walking. Once she can manage a few steps again, he buys a small car and builds in an extra step on the passenger's side, illuminated by a little lamp, to make it easier for her to climb in. He works from home in Zehlendorf as often as he can and has a messenger fetch ministerial papers from Wilhelmstraße. In the first years of her recuperation, Emilie cannot read, so every night Otto reads aloud to her what he's been working on that day. It is time for him to think about stepping down from the premiership. He buys a building plot in Ascona in Switzerland, where he plans to settle down with his wife once he has relinquished his onerous office of state.

The Nazi Monster

Graf von Helldorff

1

The inhabitants of number 16 Kurfürstendamm constitute a tolerant community loosely bound together by their common affluence. However, the noises that have been emerging of late from Hanussen's apartment are beyond the pale for even his neighbours, who are used to all kinds of excesses. The rooms of the famous clairvoyant resound with loud hissing and thumping sounds, while dull thuds on the floorboards, which occur in rapid succession, make the floor shake and send shockwaves up the entire height of the building. The source of all this rumbling and crashing about is a genuine attraction, a life-size 'electric horse'[1] that Hanussen has acquired for his consulting room. The din of this mechanical monstrosity can be heard throughout the entire front section of the apartment complex. But its owner's delight is short-lived; much to his annoyance, after numerous complaints from neighbours, the house management committee bans any further use of the machine on the premises.

Hanussen has taken Berlin by storm, he is raking in money from all sides and spending it with wanton abandon. Another toy, the luxury motor yacht *Ursel IV*,[2] has cost him 30,000 Marks. Meanwhile, it has become fashionable in Berlin's high society to

seek the advice of the famous clairvoyant; he finds himself besieged by mostly female clients wanting private consultations with him. But his services are much in demand, too, by people who suffer from migraines, back pain or rheumatism and hope that he may be able to provide a cure. Hanussen's success also attracts both the envious and the querulous, and he is forever facing charges of fraud. The artist needs to protect himself from false expectations, and so hires Alfons Sack, originally a star lawyer of the political right, who later represents clients such as the leader of the communist faction in the Reichstag, Ernst Torgler, and the writer Hans Fallada. Dr Sack draws up a set of general terms and conditions for Hanussen, which all of his clients are henceforth required to sign: 'The visit by the undersigned is merely a private consultation session, and as such is subject to a fee chargeable by Hanussen. This fee will vary according to the duration and the difficulty of the operations performed. In no sense should it be construed as payment for any practical benefit accruing from these experiments, nor is the slightest guarantee given as to the ultimate efficacy of these treatments.'[3]

When the magician isn't away on tour, his working day begins at around nine o'clock in his office. Until the evening, his main sustenance consists of coffee and cigarettes. On some days he will put on two performances, one in the late afternoon and the other in the evening, for a paying audience numbering in their thousands. After the evening show, he goes out for a bite to eat, as a rule in a Hungarian restaurant on the Ku'damm, before moving on to a dance hall.[4] By this stage, he has usually acquired a female escort, with whom he spends the rest of the night, first in a bar, then often in the Romanischer Café and finally in his flat.

Hanussen's income doesn't come solely from his clairvoyance, but also from marketing a wide range of products. Above all, his *komboloi* are a bestseller. An advertising leaflet hails the beads as a 'revelation for humanity'. They are claimed to be an effective remedy 'for insomnia, agoraphobia, disinclination to work, despondency, shyness, masturbation, nail-biting, a propensity to violence, irascibility, nervous fits, smoking, stuttering, neurotic aches and pains, general lassitude and unrequited love.'[5] Another top seller is his 'clairvoyance disc', which was recorded at a studio of the Columbia gramophone company in late 1931 and contained predictions for the coming year: 'Erik Jan Hanussen prophesies the future for Germany and the rest of the world.'[6] The record was marketed as 'a valuable historical document for private individuals, scholars and collectors alike'. In addition, Hanussen also advertises 'Eukutol 3', a hormonal beauty cream for men. By now, he has also succeeded in turning himself into a recognizable brand: he invariably has himself photographed in the classic pose of a psychic, magically lit from below and casting a long shadow. Emblazoned above this likeness, in flowing handwritten script, is his full signature: 'Erik Jan Hanussen'.

Around the same time, this former journalist also becomes active once more in the line of work he knows so well, starting his own weekly publication, which appears from November 1931 onwards under the title *Die andere Welt* ('The Other World'), with the ambiguous subtitle 'The Magazine of the Fantastic'. The stock-in-trade of this expensively designed magazine is primarily astrological and esoteric topics. These include a series of articles on divining rods ('Anyone can do divining') or teaching courses with titles like 'Become a Chiromancer in Five Minutes' or 'Will-power as Medicine'.[7] After just two issues, the publisher transforms this specialist occult weekly into a tabloid newspaper aimed at a mass-market readership. Hanussen now embarks on a new line of business, and quite a risky one at that, given the country's volatile situation: he starts producing 'political horoscopes'. The psychic looks behind the façades of the profession, fosters contacts with political players and middlemen and tries to pick up on political undercurrents so as to improve the accuracy of his prognoses.

Hanussen is concerned about backing the right horse and so proceeds very carefully. In October 1931, in a column in the *Kölner*

Volkszeitung ('Cologne People's Paper'), he predicts the imminent rise of a 'dictator from the radical socialist sphere'.[8] Yet radical socialism is being preached both by the communists and the National Socialists. Soon after, in his own paper *Die andere Welt*, he writes: 'An enduring political scene without Brüning is not in prospect. Brüning remains the coming man, and the right-wing parties and the centre will reach an accommodation.'[9] Before long, however, in December 1931, Hanussen nails his colours to the mast: 'The world is not going to become Bolshevist – on the contrary, it will be Fascist. Germany is about to be ruled by an iron fist, which in no time will impose an extraordinarily harsh dictatorship on the country. The dissolution of parliament is in the offing.'[10]

Gleaning political inside information is undoubtedly helpful, but in these tense times it's almost as important for Hanussen to secure political patronage. How fortunate for him that he can achieve both objectives with his invitations to weekend excursions on board his motor yacht. *Ursel IV* becomes popularly known as the 'Yacht of the Seven Deadly Sins', though it was almost certainly a journalist who coined this phrase. On board the yacht, this illustrious company is treated to all manner of distractions. Hanussen proves himself 'tireless in his devising of erotic games. He called this a festival of the Indian love goddess Saraswati, after the Aryan Shakti devotions performed by the deity Shiva. In sacred ecstasy they worshipped the lingam, the divine phallus.'[11] On one occasion, Hanussen even hypnotizes his lover and induces her to have an orgasm in front of his guests.

A frequent guest on these weekend excursions is Count Helldorff, a slender man with a narrow yet somewhat fleshy looking face, straight nose, slightly protruding ears and bright blue eyes. It's not clear when the count first joins the band of voluptuaries. The actress Maria Paudler is said to have introduced him to Hanussen's circle.[12] A few years later, the journalist Bruno Frei, editor-in-chief of a communist tabloid in Berlin and a close friend of Hanussen, writes from exile about the legendary cruises of *Ursel IV*. Even today, it is hard to determine which parts of Frei's descriptions are authentic and which he turned his lurid fantasy to fabricating in order to expose the clairvoyant and his entourage. One of Frei's claims concerns a fourteen-year-old Indian boy, Kabir, whom Hanussen is said to have taken on one of his pleasure cruises.[13] In order to have a pretext for punishing the boy, Helldorff allegedly accused Kabir of having indecently touched one of the women on board. The count had his victim tied to the mast and then subjected him to such a frenzy of whipping that he passed out. When Bruno Frei reports this incident a year after fleeing Germany, many people are prepared to believe it, since by then Count Helldorff, the erstwhile friend of the prominent magician, is the leader of the Berlin-Brandenburg Nazi stormtrooper (SA) division.

2

Whether the Helldorffs really are descendants of the robber-baron clan that wrought havoc in the Lusatia region at the beginning of the sixteenth century is not attested, though if true it would certainly chime well with the judgement passed by his contemporaries on Wolf-Heinrich Julius Otto Bernhard Fritz Hermann Ferdinand, Count von Helldorff (b. 1896). He is variously described as 'a chancer and mercenary of the worst kind, a drunken, vainglorious lout',[14] or a 'gay, devil-may-care soldier and gambler',[15] while others see in him a 'curious mix of daredevil mercenary and nonchalant aristocrat'.[16] Helldorff is born into a family of landed gentry. In his early years, he is privately schooled by a tutor, before going on to attend the Latin school in Merseburg and a private monastery school in Roßleben. On the outbreak of war in 1914 he enlists in Hussar Regiment No. 12 in Torgau. Count Helldorff arrives at the Western Front on the day of his eighteenth birthday. By March 1915 he has been promoted to lieutenant. Towards the end of that same year, a sexually transmitted disease forces him to take a three-month break from front-line duties. As the commander of a machine-gun detachment, the count sees service on the Eastern Front as well as in France. He distinguishes himself through acts of bravery and is decorated with the Iron Cross, First and Second Classes.

Like so many others whom the war has prevented from gaining a proper education and embarking on a career in the bourgeois world of commerce, Helldorff finds it hard reintegrating into civilian society. His qualifications – the suffering that he has witnessed and experienced, his courage and his sense of responsibility – count for little in post-war Germany. All he has left is something that no one can take away from him: the good fortune to have survived. In the various volunteer corps in which he serves after the end of the war, Helldorff can carry on as he did before – and is it not a rewarding and important task to save Germany from sliding into anarchy? In 1920, he takes part in the Kapp Putsch and when it fails he flees into exile in Italy for several months. On his return to Germany he marries Ingeborg von Wedel, the daughter of a distinguished landed Prussian family. Now, finally, a bourgeois career path seems to open up for Helldorff; he is helped in this by the fact that his father is a firm believer in passing on assets while he is still alive, and so makes over the family estate at Wolmirstedt to his son without further ado. This estate has extensive lands to its name, 854 hectares all told, in addition to a manor house.

However, images from his past seem to hold Helldorff in their thrall. Instead of settling down in this quiet spot and enjoying his good fortune – something denied to so many of his contemporaries – he feels drawn to politics. He reneges on his family and farming obligations and, out of sheer adventurism and idealism, joins the Stahlhelm. On the eve of the Beer Hall Putsch in 1923 he is in Munich, and speaks with some of the protagonists of the attempted coup, which collapses the following day. Helldorff, though, does not witness this failure at first hand, as he is already on his way back north. Yet he keeps in contact with those around Hitler. At the 'German Day' gathering in Halle in May 1924, he meets Ernst Röhm for the first time. Röhm makes such a powerful impression on him that he leaves the Stahlhelm and turns to the National Socialists: 'My position [...] is one of extreme nationalism and extreme socialism,' he claims at this time.[17] That same year, the count enters the Prussian parliament as a National Socialist. When Ernst Röhm once again finds himself a fugitive from justice, Helldorff harbours him in a hunting lodge on his estate. Röhm comes over to the manor house in the evenings and plays tunes from Wagner's *Siegfried* and *Die Meistersinger* on the grand piano in the music room.

Even for wealthy landowners, the 1920s are not an easy time economically, especially when, as with Helldorff, the lord of the manor's business acumen is not nearly as highly developed as his willingness to spend money in pursuit of hobbies befitting his social class and his political objectives. In 1928, Helldorff becomes a partner in a horseracing stables in Harzburg. His most successful horse is Narcis; in 1929 it brings in almost 44,000 Marks, and over 40,000 again the following year. Meanwhile, two sons and a daughter have swelled the family ranks at the manor house in Wolmirstedt; later, two more sons are born. Helldorff's wife shares her husband's anti-Semitic views. Invited to a reception at the US Embassy some years later, she holds forth on the 'corrupt Jews'. She also takes the opportunity to lecture the ambassador on 'the need of sterilising [*sic*.] all Negroes in the United States. If you do not do this, the Negroes will one day own the country.'[18] With his income failing to keep pace with the enormous outgoings that Helldorff's lifestyle entails, the growing family is forced to leave the estate in Wolmirstedt in 1928. Within a few short years, the family inheritance has been squandered. Yet the count has no intention of changing the way he lives. His debts only increase; by 1929 he owes his racehorse trainer alone some 230,000 Reichsmarks, and he can only use a portion of race winnings to repay what he owes as other creditors need to be paid. In the spring of 1930, Helldorff leases a property in the Hoppegarten district of Berlin, near the racecourse, for the racing season and defaults on the rent. A year later he is bankrupt and is forced to declare insolvency. At this point he sets his sights on politics once again.

3

The National Socialist district administration (*Gauleitung*) is situated on the fourth floor of a building on Hedemannstraße in Kreuzberg, which during the First World War housed the agency responsible for procuring raw materials for the war effort. In the offices where Walther Rathenau once worked, the NSDAP and the SA have commandeered a suite of twenty rooms to house the civil and military departments of the party's Berlin headquarters. The entrance is guarded round the clock by six stormtroopers. Every day when he enters the building, Gauleiter Joseph Goebbels passes the brass plaque commemorating the former foreign minister of the Reich, who was gunned down by right-wing extremists in 1922. Goebbels takes his macabre game with the history of the place to the extreme by siting his office in the very room, at the end of the corridor, where Walther Rathenau once worked; the only difference is that the room has in the meantime been divided by a wooden partition.[19]

When Goebbels first arrives in Berlin in 1926, the Nazi Party and the SA are a tiny band of individuals constantly squabbling among themselves, a little brown island in a sea of red. Aged twenty-nine, Goebbels's chief concern is to make his mark at all costs. 'Berlin needs stirring up!'[20] is what this doctor – with a Ph.D. in German – prescribes, and he immediately sets about putting this into action. He is constantly embroiled in libel suits. He claims that Hindenburg does 'what his Jewish and Marxist advisers instruct him to do',[21] and confides to his diary: 'The old goat should clear off, or at least not forever be standing in the way of the young generation.'[22] He also accuses the Prussian prime minister Otto Braun of having taken bribes from 'a Galician Jew'.[23] National Socialist rallies are deliberately held in the city's communist strongholds in order to provoke rioting, propaganda marches of the SA are routed through districts that are known to be communist-dominated, and SA drinking dens are intentionally sited as close as possible to bars favoured by communists. 'Marching forward across graves!' is the slogan Goebbels uses to launch his conquest of Berlin for National Socialism.[24]

There are also jointly organized 'debate sessions' with their political adversaries, which regularly descend into chaotic mass brawls, as happens in the Pharus Rooms in the working-class district of Wedding (often referred to as 'Red Wedding') in February 1927. Goebbels speaks on the theme of 'The Collapse of the Bourgeois Class State'. An eyewitness recalled what happened: 'Chairs were smashed to pieces, the legs were torn off tables and batteries of beer glasses and bottles were assembled and lined up on tables ready to be used as missiles [...] then glasses, bottles, table- and chair-legs suddenly began flying in all directions through the air.'[25] Right at the beginning of the meeting, the opposing factions take up strategic positions. At the back of the room, near the exit, SA men have occupied a gallery overlooking that part of the room where the communists have chosen to gather so as to be able to make a quick getaway if necessary. But in positioning themselves there, they have made themselves easy prey for the Nazis, who, as one of the stormtroopers later recalled with simple-minded pride, 'tipped cast-iron tables complete with their heavy marble tops [...] over the gallery onto the heads of the densely packed Reds' below.

Tensions exist not only between the Nazis and their political opponents, however, but also between the National Socialist party and its army of hired thugs. The stormtroopers of the SA are rarely older than their mid-twenties. In the drinking dens where they meet in Berlin, which number more than one hundred and are often set up in laundries that have gone bankrupt in the economic crisis, they form an unruly mob. Most of them are unemployed. These young men profess their camaraderie, which has evolved over many long evenings spent in an alcoholic haze, by calling one another by nicknames such as Klöten-Karl ('Bollocks Karl'), Fliegertüte ('Sick Bag'), Mollenkönig ('Beer King'), Gummibein ('Rubber Legs'), Lumpenstich ('Ragstabber'), Revolverschnauze ('Revolver Muzzle') or Schießmüller ('Trigger Happy'). Anyone who is homeless can find shelter in SA hostels, where weapons are also stored. Shooting practice and military drill are regularly conducted in the back yards of tenement blocks.[26]

Over time, it becomes harder to finance this private army. The National Socialists are in large part reliant upon their own resources, and industry supplies only a trickle of funds.[27] As a result the party's coffers are almost always empty, especially with the many election campaigns eating up money. The SA Quartermaster's Office earns some income through the sale of metal badges to affix to walking sticks and flagpoles or souvenir picture postcards of the Nuremberg rallies, and as a general rule Nazi stormtroopers also have to buy their own uniforms. Not least, funds are also generated by the public appearances of leading figures in the party, for instance in the Sportpalast. Given that it costs some 5,000 Marks to hire such venues, an entrance fee of one or two Marks is charged to hear speeches by Hitler or Frick, and these events tend to attract audiences of between 12 and 14,000 people.[28] What's left of the takings is sent to Munich, where the NSDAP leadership is based and where the cake is divided. Berlin only gets the crumbs.

Presently, voices of dissent make themselves heard in the Berlin SA. Only a pittance in the way of wages is paid for their operations during the day and at night-time, not to mention the extra burdens imposed during election campaigns, while legal aid for the rank-and-file stormtroopers, who often find themselves up in court for brutal acts of violence, is not assured. On the other hand, members of the SA can see the ritzy decor of Goebbels's offices and his grand official Mercedes. Under the leadership of retired police captain Walther Stennes, the SA summarily occupies the Gauleiter's offices on Hedemannstraße and renounces its allegiance to the party's district administration. Stormtroopers also go on the rampage outside Goebbels's private apartment on Reichskanzlerplatz.[29] Eventually Stennes and his men are placated by promises that things will improve.

However, it's not all about money and seats in the national parliament. The major gains made by the NSDAP in September 1930 place the prospect of the National Socialists taking power by legal means within the realms of possibility for the first time – an opportunity that Hitler is keen not to lose. Accordingly, he focuses his attention on pursuing legal tactics. In this scenario the SA, with its unconditional commitment to violence, is now a fly in the ointment.

Six months later Walther Stennes stages a second insurrection. Several hundred stormtroopers occupy the district administration offices on Hedemannstraße and get involved in scuffles with the SS men guarding the building. According to Stennes, the SA is fighting against the 'bourgeois-liberal tendencies' within the political leadership of the NSDAP. Stennes declares that Hitler has been deposed, and in response Hitler replaces the renegade with an acting successor. Now the situation becomes very confused. Fist fights break out between supporters of the two groups. When one of Stennes's men, Walter Bergmann, is arrested by a police riot squad loyal to Hitler, he pulls no punches in saying exactly what he thinks about two prominent anti-Stennes leaders of the SA (Paul Röhrbein and Karl Ernst): 'Take a look at these parasites on the Party, these toy boys, these fucking arse-bandits who have dragged the Party's reputation through the dirt. Just look at them, these queer bastards!'[30] In the end, the revolt peters out, and 500 SA members are expelled from the party.

It's time for a fresh start in the SA. In the wake of the Stennes revolt, a man who has been a unit commander (*Standartenführer*) in the Berlin SA since May comes to Goebbels's attention for the first time. 'Really quite passable,'[31] Goebbels notes in his diary, 'though nothing like the people Stennes had around him. A bit perfumed. Wonder if he's one of Röhm's lot? A 175-er?"* Goebbels will quickly learn that his concern that Count Helldorff might also be gay is unfounded, and before long they will be snatching the young women who flock around them from under one another's noses. Having failed in the bourgeois world, Helldorff – 'a devil-may-care soldier-cum-playboy' as the British journalist Sefton Delmer called him – is now making headway in his political career.[32] Barely two weeks after being invited to meet Goebbels for the first time, the count is appointed by his old comrade Ernst Röhm as head of the entire Berlin SA, albeit only provisionally for the time being. In order to be confirmed in his post, he must first earn his stripes.

---

* An allusion to Paragraph 175 of the Reich penal code, which proscribed homosexuality. [Translator's note]

The Dogged Newshound

Dorothy Thompson

1

To the Methodist preacher Peter Thompson from Lancaster in New York State it must have seemed like the wrath of God when his wife, soon after undergoing a botched abortion performed by his mother-in-law, contracts septicaemia and dies. For eight-year-old Dorothy, a sensitive, bright girl, the death of her mother sees her world fall apart. Her father subsequently remarries, but unfortunately Dorothy and her stepmother don't get along and so from the age of fourteen, in 1908, she is brought up by an aunt in Chicago. During her teacher training course at Syracuse University, Dorothy finds her interest increasingly drawn to economics and politics rather than grammar. Involving herself in the suffragette movement, she drafts numerous appeals and articles advocating the rights of women, and discovers her talent as a public speaker.

By 1920, twenty-six-year-old Dorothy is employed by the Curtis Publishing Company as a foreign correspondent in Vienna. Before long, she has such a fluent command of German that she is equally at home chatting to a janitor or discoursing with a university professor. She takes great pleasure in mimicking the various different accents she hears, readily switching between Viennese,

Munich Bavarian and the Berlin dialect. In Budapest, at the Hotel Ritz, she meets the writer Joseph Bard. Giving an account many years later about why she married him so soon after they first became acquainted, she writes: 'for beauty, through beauty, because of beauty.'[1] Bard introduces her to artistic circles in Budapest and Vienna. They enjoy a blissful time together. Dorothy remembers nights of pure ecstasy spent at the Grand Hotel in Vienna or in a 'small, blue-painted flat down an alleyway in a poor part of town', and recalls how Joseph once surprised her by turning up clutching a posy of lilies of the valley.

Joseph Bard believes he is born to be a poet and philosopher. Up to now, he has muddled through as an occasional journalist. Dorothy, too, is convinced of her husband's true vocation, and so uses her income to take the strain off him. She is successful, pretty, clever and at the same time reserved. As a woman in her chosen profession she is something of an anomaly, and it's not unknown at press conferences or receptions for the assembled dignitaries and the press corps to be addressed in the following manner: 'Excellency, Gentlemen, and Dorothy.'[2] Meanwhile, Joseph uses the latitude she has given him not to hone his poetical and philosophical talents but instead to indulge his tendency to be unfaithful. It is a painful and deeply wounding process of disillusionment that he inflicts on his wife, who has been brought up in an atmosphere of Methodist austerity and rectitude. He selects the objects of his dalliances from among their closest circle of acquaintances, and as if it weren't already humiliating enough for him to cheat on Dorothy with her friends, Joseph's pillow talk to his conquests focuses on her supposed shortcomings in the bedroom, and her 'unsatisfactoriness as a wife'.[3]

2

Dorothy's superiors at the Curtis Publishing Company are very happy with her work. Hardly any of the major names from the worlds of politics, business and culture have refused her requests for an interview. Her circle of friends and acquaintances includes the writer brothers Thomas and Heinrich Mann, the actress Tilla Durieux, Pamela Wedekind (wife of the famous playwright Frank Wedekind), the Feuchtwangers, Carl Zuckmayer and Alma Mahler-Werfel. Her interviews with, among others, Aristide Briand, Sigmund Freud, Leon Trotsky and Kemal Atatürk appear in the daily newspaper the *Public Ledger* in Philadelphia or in the New York *Evening Post*. In 1925 she is made head of the company's Central European office in Berlin. She soon feels at home in the German capital, moving into a flat on Händelallee right in the heart of the foreign press colony in the Tiergarten district and gathering around her a group of close friends who include her colleague from the *Public Ledger*, Hubert R. Knickerbocker.

By the time Dorothy comes to celebrate her thirty-fourth birthday in 1927, she has already put the experience of her first marriage behind her, at least outwardly, and can look to the future: 'I have in me the capacity to be deeply faithful to one man whom I love and who loves me. What I want is to build a life with him which shall have breadth, depth, creative quality, dignity, beauty and inner loyalty. If I do not find him I shall go it alone.'[4] The day before her birthday she attends the weekly afternoon tea given for the benefit of the press by Gustav Stresemann in the Foreign Ministry in Wilhelmstraße. Knickerbocker has brought along a guest, a tall man with a striking shock of red hair, a narrow, ravaged-looking skull, sharp features, small, piercing eyes and a nose that protrudes beak-like from a face whose contours are disfigured by scars.[5] Stresemann is running late, and so the peculiar-looking guest decides to while away the time with a jape. He approaches the press corps and offers to step in for the foreign minister so long as they are happy to confine their questioning to Franco-German relations.[6] Knickerbocker introduces his companion to Dorothy, though she has long since recognized him. He is Sinclair Lewis, the most famous and successful American novelist of the age. Without more ado, she invites him to her birthday party the following evening.

The distinguished group of guests who assemble in the apartment on Händelallee include Mihály Károlyi, the former Hungarian president who was exiled in 1919, and the Countess von Moltke, who has brought with her son Helmut James, Count von Moltke. The evening is a resounding success. Dorothy's housekeeper Hedwig is an outstanding cook, while the hostess herself is no mean connoisseur of French and German wines. Large quantities of drink are consumed, while the lively conversation alternates between French, English and German. As coffee is being served and the first guests are starting to drift away, Sinclair Lewis turns to Dorothy and announces: 'I have been looking for you for years. Will you marry me?'[7]

Dorothy doesn't know quite what to make of this, but Lewis is perfectly serious: 'I will buy us a house in Vermont […] looking down a valley.'[8] Not long after, there is an official breakfast at which Sinclair Lewis, as the guest of honour, is asked to say a few words. He rises to speak and surprises those present by asking: 'Dorothy, will you marry me?' And thereafter, at every function to which the renowned author is invited, he poses the same question. Yet just as Dorothy begins to find herself taking pleasure in his company, she learns that her ardent suitor is already married. Sinclair Lewis immediately cancels all his upcoming plans and heads back to the United States in order to file for divorce. On his return to Berlin he rents a flat in the Herkules-Haus, an apartment block on Lützowplatz, so as to continue to be close to Dorothy.

She is flattered by his attentions. But it isn't his less than handsome exterior that gives her pause for thought, for she has long since fallen for his sparkling wit, his sarcasm and his boyish demeanour. It is the ominous consequences of his lack of self-esteem that cause her to keep him at arm's length for the time being. Fame, money and the experience of being loved and admired as a writer have not managed to rid Sinclair Lewis of a deep-seated complex that has blighted him his entire life. Even in puberty, as he once confided to a friend, he suffered from a crippling anxiety that others might find him physically repellent, and consequently avoided all contact with girls, even though they were the object of all his dreams and fantasies. With a face pockmarked by acne and a generally frail constitution, he developed a sense of his own inadequacy that caused his outlook on the world to become increasingly sarcastic and melancholic. While investing all his erotic energy in his writing, he set about numbing his complex with alcohol, which only made the symptoms that lay at its root all the more acute.

It's not long before Dorothy uncovers the truth. One evening, she goes to the Herkules-Haus to pick him up for a reception. She is looking forward to the soirée, and has picked herself out a taffeta dress by Lanvin with an elegant evening cloak. She takes a taxi over to Lützowplatz. There she finds 'Hal', as she calls Sinclair Lewis, lying prone on the bed in his dressing gown. He smiles, 'dead to the world,'[9] and stares blankly at her with 'fishy, dead eyes'. All at once, Dorothy sees all her dreams vanishing in a puff of smoke: 'our house in the frosty New England country, the gay wanderings about the world, the baby I want from Hal.'[10] Her first impulse is to turn on her heel and leave there and then. But her 'heart cried out: this is my man, the one man, and he has come too late! Nothing left for me but to become brittle or to rot. All the time Hal was making love to me. […] I wished I could lift him up and carry him to a high hill, where wind would be blowing.'[11]

In the small hours, at around half past one, Sinclair Lewis gets hungry. When room service fails to respond, he gets up and staggers to the door: 'I shall bring you nice little sausage,'[12] he slurs, and reappears about an hour later with potato salad, sausages and a bottle of cognac. Later he seems to have a flash of insight: 'I know it's giving up spirits or giving up you. And I can't give up spirits. A man takes a drink, the drink takes another, and then the drink takes the man.' He returns to the topic over breakfast: 'I won't take another drink for two weeks,' he promises the woman he intends to marry. 'Or just beer. Tell me, can I drink beer?'[13]

3

In November 1927, Dorothy travels to Moscow with a group of journalists in order to report on everyday life in Soviet Russia ten years after the inception of the communist social experiment. She notices how most of her travelling companions are sympathetic to the Soviet system and have invested their hopes in it. On crossing the border, which is marked by a 'huge, glowing red star over the railroad track', they break into a rousing chorus of the 'Internationale'.[14] 'Now thank God we are safe in our own country, thank God!' they exclaim as they enter the 'Fatherland of the Global Proletariat'. At the time, it is fashionable to travel to the Soviet Union. The fledgling state is keen to welcome journalists from abroad and draw their attention to the undoubted progress that has been made in the country's economic development.

The trips are well organized; Dorothy is put up in a comfortable room in the Grand Hotel in Moscow and provided with her own personal 'secretary'. As the partner of the prominent 'progressive writer' Sinclair Lewis, who is also highly regarded in Soviet Russia, she is granted relative freedom of movement. She's not about to let herself be dazzled, however: 'In these ten years,' she writes in her book *The New Russia*, which appears the year after her fact-finding trip, 'urban Russia having destroyed, exiled or reduced to the most abject misery all representatives of that previous civilization, is without most bourgeoisie amenities.'[15]

Dorothy longs to see her lover: 'I see always your funny darling face,'[16] she writes to him. Sinclair Lewis comes to join her in Moscow, but leaves again after just a week and, alarmed by reports of terror and brutality, never publishes a word about his brief sojourn in the Soviet Union. When Dorothy returns to Berlin, they start making preparations for their wedding. Although they are frequently apart from one another, they stay in contact through letters. 'On serious and solitary consideration,' writes Sinclair Lewis, 'I consider you the darlingest person in the world.'[17] To which Dorothy replies: 'I intended, when I sat down here, overlooking the sea, to write you a bright and witty note, and all I can find to say is "Hal, Hal, I love you".'[18]

The couple hold their wedding in the full glare of publicity at the Savoy Chapel in London,[19] the only place in the diocese where divorcees are permitted to get married. In his speech at the reception, the bridegroom can't help but indulge his love of clowning. He addresses the wedding party 'as if they were jute merchants and he were reviewing the situation in the jute trade throughout the British Empire'.[20] His whimsical idea of buying an old caravan to spend their honeymoon in makes them the darlings of the press. Reports and pictures of this famous couple appear in many European and American newspapers.

The newlyweds find a property in Vermont – Twin Farms – which they purchase from their joint funds. Hubert R. Knickerbocker takes over Dorothy's position at the *Public Ledger* in Berlin. When Sinclair and Dorothy's son Michael is born in 1930, they seem close to achieving the happiness they have long dreamed of. Yet no sooner has Sinclair Lewis tied the knot with the woman he courted for so long than he starts dictating the rules of their relationship. He invites friends over, drinks to excess, suffers nervous breakdowns in the middle of the night and leaves her alone with their guests. They live for months on end holed up on the farm with 'not one enjoyable dinner party the whole winter; not one evening at the opera,'[21] Dorothy complains. And when they do venture out, if she's noticed at all, the woman to whom government ministers paid court in Berlin is now just seen as plain old 'Mrs Sinclair Lewis'.

Dorothy bridles at this lifestyle: 'Can't bear it. I *won't* bear it. I had rather go & work in someone's kitchen than lead this sort of life.' But then she tells herself that she's really of no importance, that she's married to a man of genius and that all she needs to do is to make him happy. One time she asks him to forego the pleasure of her company, as she has been invited to give a talk: 'You with your important little lectures,' he sneers. 'You with your brilliant people... You want to talk about foreign politics, which *I* am too ignorant to understand.'[22] He puts her down in front of guests, accusing her of serving bad food, and insults her friends. Even her close friendship with Hubert James von Moltke suffers from one of her husband's scenes. At times she sees her marriage to Sinclair Lewis as a trap that she walked into with her eyes open: 'He is like a vampire – he absorbs all my vitality, all my energy, all my beauty – I get incredibly dull.'[23]

Yet there is another side to her husband. During spells of remorse and sobriety, he can be loving and solicitous and supports her work with his contacts. It soon becomes apparent that they can't live either with or without one another. In the letters that they write to bridge the distance between them during their frequent solitary trips, they spare no words in reassuring one another of their love. Yet their marriage is broken. When Sinclair Lewis staggers drunk into her bedroom at Twin Farms, Dorothy complains to a friend that he smells of 'rotting weeds'.[24] She takes refuge in her work, and presently becomes as famous as a journalist as her husband is as a novelist.

The award of the Nobel Prize for Literature to Sinclair Lewis in 1930 brings them closer together once more. They travel together to Stockholm in December, where Lewis accepts the prize, and from there to Berlin, where they see in the New Year. Finally, in January 1931, they take a short vacation in the Thuringian Forest.

Back home in Vermont, however, things soon revert to the

way they were before. For a long time they have needed not only separate bedrooms but also their own living rooms. In November 1931 Dorothy sets off to Germany again for the winter months. Her son Michael is to be looked after by friends while she is gone. Finally, after years spent trying in vain, Dorothy has got what her colleagues in Berlin would give their eye teeth for: a firm date for an interview with Adolf Hitler.

The Gentleman Jockey

Franz von Papen

1

When asked by a journalist who the next Chancellor of the Reich will be, Kurt von Schleicher, clearly flattered at being seen in the role of kingmaker, replies: 'Ah, I've got something really special for you. You'll be amazed.'[1] Hitherto, Franz von Papen hasn't exactly been regarded as a front runner; even within his own party, the Centre Party, he is an outsider from the right-wing fringes. 'He was thought of as superficial, slapdash, false, ambitious, vain, devious, and an intriguer. He is, however, very self-assured, a trait that comes across as endearing and almost unconscious,' is the judgement of the French ambassador in Berlin, André François-Poncet.[2] Not a few people see Papen's self-confidence as being rooted in his narrow-mindedness. When, after the war, his party colleague Konrad Adenauer spoke about Papen's role, he admitted to always having granted him 'extenuating circumstances' in his judgement, 'due to his extreme parochialism'.[3] Papen has never made any secret of his belief in a divinely ordained order of things. In his view, his party, the Centre, which for a long time formed the heart of the Weimar coalition with the Social Democrats, needs to free itself from the 'socialist embrace' and, together with other

nationalistically minded forces, become a 'guardian and bastion of the legacy of the West within the Central European region.'[4]

Papen himself is proud of coming from an aristocratic family whose lineage goes back over a thousand years of history. According to ancient folklore, it was at the Papen manorial farmhouse that Henry the Fowler, Duke of Saxony, was supposedly fixing his birding nets (hence his common epithet) when a messenger came to offer him the crown of the Kingdom of East Francia in AD 919. His family were one of the 'Erbsälzer' of the town of Werl in North Rhine-Westphalia – a group of noble families who had since the Middle Ages been granted the exclusive and hereditary right to mine salt there. Yet when Franz is born there in 1879, the source has either long since been exhausted or has been compromised by the sinking of coal shafts and no more salt is extracted. In their struggle to retain their ancient privileges, the Papens know that they can count on the support of the *Ecclesia militans*, the Church Militant. Thus, alongside family tradition, the Catholic Church is the second crucial pillar on which Franz von Papen's self-assurance is founded. In later life his entire political agenda is geared to the pattern that he internalized in his childhood and youth. The class-based system of rulers and underlings, rich and poor, is willed by God. Mitigating against the most repugnant side effects of this system through patriarchal *noblesse oblige* comes just as naturally to him as stoutly resisting all those who question this natural order – the godless and those who despise tradition – which in Papen's eyes is the cornerstone of every civilization.

Franz is the middle of five children. 'Growing up with merry siblings, we were unremittingly happy,' he recalls in his memoirs.[5] His father, whom Papen describes as a 'simple, unpretentious country squire', was an officer in the wars of German unification, while his mother was the daughter of a cavalry captain. His father's social connections extend from his time as a student in Bonn, where he made the acquaintance of the Prussian crown prince and later emperor Wilhelm II, to the highest echelons of Berlin society.

As the second oldest son, Franz is destined for a military career, which happily coincides with a predisposition inherited from his father: his love of riding and horses. After attending the elementary church school in Werl, the eleven-year-old Franz is sent to the cadet school at Bensberg in 1891. This institution is located in the castle of the dukes of Berg, and its high-ceilinged rooms are unheated and bitterly cold in winter, while it's not uncommon to find the water in the washroom basins frozen solid in the mornings. Meals consist mostly of gruel with a slice of bread, with a piece of meat once a week. Discipline, obedience and application are required from the cadets.

At Easter 1895, the fifteen-year-old is promoted to NCO and transferred to the main Prussian Military Academy at Groß-Lichterfelde, which in those days is located just outside Berlin. Here, too, there is a premium on discipline. But at least the rigours of everyday life at the school still afford him opportunities to pursue his musical interests; he and a Prussian prince take violin lessons together. Papen shows himself to be one of the most ambitious of all the cadets and completes his academic and military education with flying colours.[6] He soon obtains a commission as a lieutenant and on the recommendation of the imperial court is enrolled in the Royal Corps of Pages. Resplendent in a bright crimson jacket decorated with silver braid, a lace jabot and white breeches, the young Papen and his comrades form a colourful guard of honour at numerous formal court occasions henceforth. He enjoys all the pomp and ceremony and the outward display of majesty at the old imperial palace on the banks of the Spree. Sometimes, when he can evade the eagle eye of the Chief Marshal of the Court, he manages to steal 'a brief waltz with a pretty princess in a hidden corner of one of the great staterooms'.[7] At royal gala dinners, the young ladies of the court slip the pageboys copious sweetmeats which, since this form of endearment has become a long-established custom, come wrapped in wax paper as a precaution.

Papen's formative years in Berlin come to an end in 1897,

when the young lieutenant is transferred to an Uhlan regiment in Düsseldorf, where he has the pleasure of daily contact with horses. At provincial racecourses throughout the Rhineland and Westphalia, amateur riders meet on Sundays and stage handicap races. Papen competes with great success as a 'gentleman jockey' – ladies are excluded from entering – in a number of races. Soon after, he has the good fortune to be seconded to the cavalry school in Hanover for two years. It is during this period that he and a friend venture for the first time into the Prussian motherland of the German Empire, which makes a great impression on him. By 1905, he is back in Düsseldorf, where, in his extended family circle, he meets Martha von Boch-Galhau, the daughter of an industrialist from the Saarland. They are married the same year. His wife's family has branches in Luxembourg, Belgium, France and England, and this broadens Papen's European outlook. When, in the years following the First World War, German conservatives form a common front against France, he is one of the few to advocate a policy of compromise with Germany's neighbour to the west.

Although his father-in-law speaks barely any German, he has a soft spot for the Prussian army and so pulls strings to help Papen train as an officer on the General Staff. The entrance qualifications are rigorous, with over a thousand applicants for just 150 places, but even more exacting is the training itself. In his three years at the War Academy in Berlin, he forms a close bond with two fellow officers, Kurt von Schleicher and Oskar von Hindenburg, son of the celebrated field marshal – friendships that will prove decisive for his political trajectory in later years. Papen is an anglophile who has married into a French family; moreover, he is Catholic and has a cultural hinterland, good manners and a facility with languages – the whole educational programme he has undergone has clearly borne fruit, but how much of what he has learned has truly ingrained itself on his psyche?

The training course at the War Academy lasts for two years, after which another winnowing takes place. In 1913, by order of

His Imperial Majesty's cabinet, he is appointed to the German General Staff. War clouds have been gathering over the past few years. Even within the Prussian General Staff, no one knows what turn events will take. Just six months later, Papen is surprised to be offered the post of German military attaché to Washington. While this is a low-level posting, given that the USA at this stage does not have a credible army, it is still a real feather in the cap for a young graduate of the War Academy. Before he leaves to take up the post, he is granted an audience by his father's old student friend Kaiser Wilhelm II: 'He was extremely gracious, and insisted I join him and his close family circle for breakfast.'[8] Papen takes to heart the advice with which the emperor sends him on his way: 'Learn to speak English well and study the country and its citizens, especially the mentality of the American people.' By this time Papen's family has been blessed with three children, two girls and a boy, and Martha is pregnant again. In view of these special circumstances, Papen goes on ahead alone in December 1913, and a family reunion is planned for the summer of 1914.

2

In 1913, the German Embassy in Washington is housed in an unprepossessing building on Massachusetts Avenue. The ground-floor rooms are occupied by the chancellery, the ambassador's residence is on the first floor, while another building to the rear, which can only be reached via a narrow walkway, is home to the German military attaché to the United States of America. This almost rustic-looking official residence nonetheless affords its occupants a rich social life. At Chevy Chase Country Club, Papen gets to know Franklin D. Roosevelt. On one occasion, in February 1914, he is even received by President Woodrow Wilson. However, this quiet life in the American capital does not suit him, and Papen soon becomes bored with Washington. As luck would have it, his area of competence also includes Mexico, where a revolution has just broken out. He feels drawn to witness events there at first hand. Mexico City is under threat of regular nightly attacks by the rebel leader Emiliano Zapata, which the army and police seem powerless to repel. The dashing military attaché duly places himself at the head of a volunteer fighting unit of diplomats, which, as Papen claims in his memoirs, 'easily beat off several attacks by the Zapatistas'.[9] At a reception for the Mexican president Victoriano Huerta, he then intervenes in the conflict between the USA and Mexico by attempting to persuade Huerta to stand down. He does not appear to be troubled when his efforts meet with no success.

On 1 August, news reaches him that war has broken out in Europe. There can now be no question of his family joining him. Papen manages, by a somewhat tortuous route, to make his way back to the neutral United States, where he sets up an office in New York. The fact that Germans form the single largest group of immigrants to the USA is hardly reflected at all in its public institutions and press. English-language daily and weekly newspapers and journals set the tone, and in political matters they tend to take the part of the former motherland. The British also control the transatlantic telegraph cable, leaving correspondents with scarcely any other means of gleaning information. As a result, it is not long before public opinion in the United States adopts the distorted picture being painted by British propaganda of the 'Hun' hordes in their *Pickelhauben*, from whom European civilization needs to be protected. The true horrors of the war are not enough for American newspapers, which are full of fabricated stories of alleged German war atrocities; these include accounts of soldiers cutting off children's hands and women's breasts or bayonetting babies, and of corpses being rendered down to tallow and then turned into nitroglycerine for the manufacture of explosives.[10]

While the British are intent upon preparing the ground for the swift entry of the United States into the war on the Allied side, it is Papen's role to exert influence on public opinion to try and prevent it from turning totally against Germany. At the same time, he attempts to halt or at least hamper the export of goods from the USA that are vital to the Allied war effort. Day after day, Germans or German-Americans come into his office in New York offering their help. One young man suggests blowing up the railway bridge that runs over the Welland Ship Canal from the United States to Canada, in order to slow down Canadian troop transports. Papen hands this adventure-seeker 500 dollars and 'friends in New York' supply him with explosives. But who are these friends of the German military attaché in the United States? 'The attempted sabotage,' Papen continues in his memoirs, 'failed because the target was heavily guarded.'[11] This bad experience does not deter him from organizing another bombing. This time, the plan is to destroy the Vanceboro Railway Bridge over the St Croix River; however, the exploding dynamite only causes superficial damage to the structure. In the summer of 1915, the attaché plans to disrupt troop transports on the Canadian Pacific Railway. To this end, he sets out to reconnoitre the area along the Canadian border. As a 'man he can trust implicitly', the German consulate in Chicago recommends he take along as his guide the 'German patriot' Albert Kaltschmidt. Kaltschmidt instantly offers to blow up munitions dumps into the bargain. But the Canadian secret service uncovers the plot even in the reconnaissance phase.

Papen now switches his activities to another area. He makes contact with Irish Republican separatists who conduct terrorist attacks against British forces and tries to smuggle weapons to India to arm the independence movement against the British Raj. Through a bogus firm that Papen purchases for the astronomical sum of $5 million ('The Bridgeport Projectile Company'), he also issues contracts to firms in the USA that produce machine tools, hydraulic presses and other equipment that is required for manufacturing munitions so as to tie up their capacity, as well as trying to siphon off the labour force for this sector by recruiting them for his sham factory. Bridgeport also ties up the Aetna Powder

Company's entire capacity for the production of gunpowder up to the end of 1915 by placing a huge order for five million pounds of propellant, though the principal effect of this is to saddle Papen with a major storage problem. He maintains in his memoirs: 'The plan was relatively simple.'[12] But wasn't the plan perhaps too simple; hadn't his efforts only resulted in him cranking up war production in the USA? To bankroll all his schemes, Papen draws on the considerable funds that German-Americans donate in public collections for the German Red Cross.

Quite how effective Papen's activities were in furthering German interests is never subject to a proper audit subsequently. But what is certain is that the American authorities do not remain unaware of them. Long before President Woodrow Wilson issues a directive in May 1915 authorizing surveillance of German Embassy staff, the US Secret Service has been keeping a watchful eye on all its employees and visitors. Everyone entering or leaving the building is photographed. Now federal agents also put a tail on the attaché himself. Papen has to learn the art of shaking off surveillance: 'We got into the habit,' he recalled, 'of going into one of the large department stores en masse, stepping into a lift, switching to another lift on various different floors, and travelling up and down in the elevators until not one of the passengers who had originally entered the lift with us was still there. Then we'd leave the store as quickly as we could through a different door.'[13]

Was Frank Burke, the head of a ten-man team detailed to watch the Germans, impressed by such manoeuvres?[14] On 24 July 1915, Dr Heinrich Albert, an employee of the Central Purchasing Company and also the German Embassy's commercial attaché responsible for financing Papen's espionage activities, boards the elevated train after a strenuous day's work in Lower Manhattan. The rocking motion of the 'El' makes him nod off and he awakes with a start at his destination, 50th Street Station, dashing off the train and only realizing at the station exit that he has left his briefcase behind on the seat. A woman who had been sitting next to him calls after him, but before he can get back to retrieve the briefcase, Burke, who has been following him the whole time, snatches it and makes off with it. Albert and Franz von Papen meet up in the German Club in Central Park West to discuss what has happened. They conclude that a common thief must have taken the case. The papers it contains have no great monetary value. And yet in the hope of getting it back, they decide to place a small newspaper ad offering a reward. On 27 July 1915, the following advertisement appears in the *New York Evening Telegram*: 'Lost: On Saturday. On 3.30 Harlem Elevated Train, at 50th Street Station, Brown Leather Bag, Containing Documents. Deliver to G. H. Hoffman, 5 E. 47th Street, Against $20 Reward.'

In the meantime, the briefcase has been examined by the US Secret Service and its contents found to be so explosive that they are immediately sent to President Wilson. To cover their involvement in the theft of the documents, the government authorities decide to pass on selected excerpts to a newspaper. Beginning on 15 August, for a whole week, the front page of the *New York World* and the following two-page spread carry a blow-by-blow account of the whole gamut of Papen's sabotage activities, gleefully recounting every last detail in daily instalments, including facsimile illustrations. Public outrage at the reckless way in which the Germans have been abusing their diplomatic immunity grows by the day. Papen is exposed, and is castigated in the press as a 'Master Spy'[15] and a 'Devil in a Top Hat' – somewhat exaggerated claims in view of the rather modest success of his endeavours. The whole sham company edifice, so painstakingly constructed around a series of frontmen, now comes crashing down.

Soon after, the British intelligence service also intercepts papers revealing that Papen has been poaching workers from industries in the United States that are vital to the war effort. One of the documents seized is a private letter from Papen to his wife, in which he talks about the 'idiotic Yankees'.[16] This proves the last straw for the US administration, which promptly declares the military attaché *persona non grata* for his 'unwanted military and naval activity'.[17] In Germany, the War Press Office advises: 'The German press should refrain from commenting on this matter until further notice, since mentioning it would in no way serve the interests of the official concerned.'[18] For all his ineptitude, it is also the general political climate that brings about Papen's downfall. It will still be two years before the US abandons its neutrality and enters the war on the side of the Allies. In his memoirs, Papen succinctly sums up the main reason for this: 'The debts the Western Powers incurred with the United States reached such a level that any US administration would have had a vested interest in ensuring that the debtor nations were victorious and so remained solvent.'[19] In December 1915 Papen sails back to Europe on board the SS *Noordam*. He has with him a steamer trunk containing receipts requiring clearance by the Prussian Chief Audit Office. On one of the sheets, an agent submits an invoice for the supply of false passports. Another countersigns a note confirming that he has been paid a sum of money for the attempted demolition of Vanceboro Bridge. Papen is confident that the documents are secure in his diplomatic bag. But when the ship puts in for inspection at Falmouth on the English Channel coast, British Naval Intelligence disregards Papen's diplomatic immunity and summarily impounds the trunk. The Foreign Office takes the opportunity to publish the seized documents in a White Paper, which the United States will subsequently adduce as evidence justifying its entry into the war. A final postscript to Papen's mission in the USA comes in 1916 – by which time he is already back in Europe – when a federal grand jury in the United States indicts him on a charge of plotting to blow up the bridge over the Welland Ship Canal. This charge remains in force right up to the time when the former military attaché is sworn in as the Chancellor of Germany in 1932.

3

Surprisingly, on his return to Germany in January 1916 Franz von Papen's carelessness and his many failures are not held against him. He is received by the Chief of the General Staff, the Chancellor Theodor von Bethmann-Hollweg and finally the Kaiser. To all of them, he gives an account of the public mood in the USA and warns them against provoking the Americans by engaging in unrestricted U-boat warfare in response to the British naval blockade. The emperor replies: 'You can be sure that the American people and their Congress will never let themselves be pushed into a war against us!'[20] Eventually, Papen gets to see his family again, meeting his youngest daughter Isabelle for the very first time. On the political stage, he is caught between two opposing factions, the proponents and opponents of all-out U-boat campaign. Before he has a chance to speak about his experiences in the USA at a press conference, he receives an order 'to report to the Western Front within the next twenty-four hours,'[21] where he is sent into action as a battalion commander in Infantry Reserve Regiment No. 93.

Papen continues to command this regiment in the grinding trench warfare around the Somme until June 1917, when he is transferred to head an operational unit in Mesopotamia fighting the rebellious Arab tribes led by T. E. Lawrence (Lawrence of Arabia). Among his Ottoman allies in the region he makes the acquaintance of a young Turkish officer called Mustafa Kemal Pasha, who is later granted the honorific title 'Atatürk' ('Father of the Turks') by the Turkish parliament. It is while Papen is in Palestine that he also meets Joachim von Ribbentrop for the first time.

Reports about the revolutionary mood gripping the homeland reach German forces stationed in the Near East in the late summer of 1918. To represent their interests, the enlisted men form soldiers' councils. While Papen takes the view that discipline can no longer be maintained in such circumstances, his superior officer supports the establishment of the councils. This causes a rift between them. Acting on an order from Field Marshal Hindenburg, General Staff Officer Papen's CO court-martials him for insubordination. But Papen escapes custody and begins his journey home by posing as a blind passenger to secure himself passage aboard a hospital ship ferrying wounded Allied soldiers to Italy. In the post-war confusion, he manages to make his way back to Germany through Italy and Switzerland without being recognized.

In early January 1919 he finds himself in Munich. 'An indescribable feeling of despair'[22] overwhelms him after a member of a soldiers' council tries to tear the epaulettes off his uniform tunic. He travels on to Kolberg, where Hindenburg has relocated the General Staff HQ for the present. Here, he turns himself in to the field marshal, who immediately waives the charge against him: 'Consider the matter closed.'[23] Officer Papen pens his letter of resignation: 'The world that I had known and loved belonged in the past. All the values I had upheld and for which we had served, fought and died had become irrelevant. The Empire and the Prussian monarchy, which we had thought of as everlasting, had been supplanted by a nebulous republic. The defeated nation lay in ruins, and an immense chaos seemed to drag everything down into the abyss.'[24]

4

All the same, Papen suffers no real hardship after he is demobilized. Financial support is forthcoming from his wife's family; his brother-in-law is the principal heir to the ceramics concern Villeroy & Boch. Papen leases a farmhouse at Merfeld near the town of Dülmen in Westphalia. The house is in an idyllic spot, surrounded by 400-year-old oaks. There is no running water or electricity, nor is the place served by a local railway connection or roads that are passable all year round. Now and then, isolated groups of revolutionaries from the nearby Ruhr Valley disrupt the rural peace, and are sent packing by the Merfeld farmers' militia, under the command of Papen. 'I thus experienced at close quarters something that far exceeded the worst things I'd seen on the battlefields of France: the sheer moral depravity of civil war.'[25] Farming and family aren't enough for Papen; he yearns to be active in the public sphere and so throws his hat into the ring for election to the Prussian regional parliament. Undoubtedly his closest affinity is with the German Nationalists, many of whom hanker after a return to the era of monarchy and sympathize with the aims of the attempted right-wing Kapp Putsch of 1920. But in 1921 Papen opts for the Centre instead, as this party has a far larger voter base in Westphalia than the Nationalists.

He succeeds at the first attempt in getting himself elected to the regional parliament on the list of the Westphalian Farmers' Association, but soon aligns himself with the Centre, since most of its members are disposed to reach an accommodation with the Republic. By the end of 1921, the party has hammered out a Grand Coalition with the Social Democrats and two smaller parties; this proves the only way of achieving that stability which preserves Germany as a whole from fragmenting during the period of rampant inflation and the chaos engendered by coup attempts from both the far left and the far right. Meanwhile, Papen keeps looking in the opposite direction; he is captivated by the idea of a Conservative alliance, transcending the party boundaries of the Centre and the German Nationalists. On many occasions he is even prepared to oppose his own party, as for instance in 1925, when he campaigns for Hindenburg as the presidential candidate of the right rather than his party's own candidate. After he is elected, Hindenburg sends Papen a personal letter of thanks for his support.

In an attempt to augment their influence within the Centre, the Conservatives make a bid to buy a stake in the Centre Party newspaper *Germania*. The Conservatives' intention is to counter the leaning of the paper, which has hitherto been on the side of the trade unions, with their 'own party line'.[26] The funding of this bid comes from large agricultural concerns in Silesia and the owners of heavy industry in the Rhineland. At this time, Papen is almost the only politician who is invited to the 'Business Evenings' that are held with captains of industry such as Edmund Stinnes, Fritz Thyssen, Ernst von Borsig and Fritz Springorum.[27]

Papen has managed to position himself as the trusted confederate of major landowning interests and heavy industry, plus he is also in favour with the President. He is a papal chamberlain and on good terms with the Papal Nuncio to Bavaria (and *de facto* to the German Empire), Eugenio Pacelli. In early 1928, he is even mooted as being the new defence minister, but his family connections to France and his policy of compromise are viewed with suspicion by the army. In his own party, however, he is seen as a snake in the grass,[28] and in the Prussian regional elections he is placed so far down the list of candidates that he fails to secure a seat. Forced into the political wilderness, Papen turns his attention once more to *Germania*. Financial support for the modernization of the paper comes from an industrialists' federation called the Society for the Preservation of Common Commercial Interests in the Rhineland and Westphalia. Something of a mouthful, this body is commonly referred to as the Long-Name League.

Thus equipped with fresh capital, Papen is able to extend his domineering influence over the central organ of the party. In addition, he receives a monthly remittance of 1,000 Reichsmarks from the press office of the Long-Name League. In return the expectation is that 'the gentleman and his press organ will promote our interests in as effective a way as possible in the manner indicated'.[29] Soon enough, though, his sponsors will learn more respect and adopt a less condescending tone towards their trustee. Papen has become something of a political heavyweight in recent years, despite the fact that he is scarcely known among the German public at large. Still without a parliamentary seat, he offers his services to his party colleague Heinrich Brüning shortly before the latter's appointment as Chancellor: 'I do not believe I am overselling myself when I tell you that you will find me to be an extremely hard-working and convivial colleague.'[30] His offer falls on deaf ears. News of Papen's dual-track approach, which implicitly ties his policy of compromise towards France and England to an outright rejection of the Soviet social model, has reached Moscow,[31] where the powers that be regard a possible German government with the Centre Party man at the helm as more dangerous than a cabinet led by Hitler.

5

By now, Papen has been living on his leased property in Merfeld for over a decade. He has had fallow moorland turned over to cultivation, and constructed many paths across his land. He has also succeeded in getting an electricity supply to his local community and a railway spur linking it to the nearby main line. This prominent citizen acts as an unsalaried mayor and is active in a riding club, teaching young people 'how to handle, look after and love horses'.[32] Yet in 1930 the family gives up the leasehold in Merfeld and moves to Wallerfangen. Here, in the Saarland, which has become part of French-mandated territory under the terms of the Versailles Treaty, his wife has inherited a country estate. Papen's enforced spell away from parliamentary activity gives him the opportunity to engage in other walks of life. For quite some time, he has been noticing 'signs of moral decline', which have met with 'only insufficient resistance' and which are even being promoted by a 'powerful press, with the backing of radio and film'. This decadence, he claims, is clearly evident 'in the domain of the performing arts, painting and sculpture as well as in the theatre. Among certain intellectual circles, it is considered aesthetically chic to cultivate a radical champagne socialism'.[33] Papen and his friends of all confessions from the German League for the Protection of

Western Civilization set their faces against this trend. Alongside representatives of the Catholic clergy and the official Protestant Church, the Chief Rabbi of Berlin is also present at its inaugural meeting in 1930.

The German League for the Protection of Western Civilization[34] is one of the enterprises funded by Papen's friend Kurt von Schleicher. Indeed, this longstanding connection has never been severed. Schleicher and Papen know one another from the time when they were both training to serve on the General Staff; other former comrades include Oskar von Hindenburg and Kurt von Hammerstein, Head of the 'Troop Office' of the Reichswehr – the name by which what was effectively the army's General Staff was known from 1919 onwards, after the victorious powers banned the Germans from having a General Staff in the Versailles Peace Treaty. As François-Poncet notes, Papen is 'to some extent the butt of the others' jokes; they rib him mercilessly, though he takes it all in good part. He is the favourite of the Field Marshal [Hindenburg]; his vivacity and cheerfulness help distract the old man, he flatters him with his deference and devotion, delights him with his brazenness and is in his eyes the very model of a gentleman.'[35]

In his memoirs, Papen poses the rhetorical question: 'Is political life any different to horsemanship, in as much as in both fields, one has simply, when faced with a difficult decision, to take one's courage in both hands and leap the obstacle?'[36] His contemporary Theodor Eschenburg comments on this analogy, noting that there is in fact an important difference between the two spheres; whereas the race jockey has to overcome obstacles in order to stay in contention, 'to those same ends, the statesman must often circumvent them.'[37] In a report to the Foreign Office about Papen, the British ambassador in Berlin, Horace Rumbold, comes to a similar conclusion: 'Not only did he take every political fence at a gallop, but he seemed to go out of his way to find fences that were not in his course.'[38]Papen has only a small circle of friends, and hardly anyone really rates him. To Count Harry Kessler, he appears like 'a grumpy billy goat trying to strike a dignified pose'.[39] A more balanced view comes from someone who later reported to him:

He had [...] all the characteristic traits of a trained General Staffer, a diplomat and nobleman of the old school, and a devout Roman Catholic. But in him these traits did not combine in happy harmony, but instead existed so to speak in separate adjoining compartments. Many people regarded him as devious, dishonest and irresponsible. Whenever I entered his study first thing in the morning to brief him on important, often very pressing, matters, I first had to try and determine which Papen I had sitting in front of me at the desk that day – the young cavalry officer, the diplomat, or the Catholic?[40] By contrast, the French ambassador in Berlin finds little to criticize in Papen: 'He is well educated [...], has impeccable manners; he is a man of the world, wealthy, a habitué of the German Gentlemen's Club and the Union Club – the Berlin counterparts of the Jockey-Club in Paris – and speaks fluent English and French. His family life is beyond reproach.'[41]

But will all this be enough?

The String-Puller

Kurt von Schleicher

1

Brandenburg an der Havel isn't exactly the gateway to the world, but at least the town can, since 1846, boast a railway connection. There is an express train to Berlin four times a day, and you're there in less than an hour. The town's population almost doubles in size during Germany's years of rapid industrial expansion. The growing significance of the place is now underlined militarily, too; in 1882, Prussian Infantry Regiment No. 35, including First Lieutenant Hermann von Schleicher, takes occupancy of its new barracks in Brandenburg. In that same year Kurt von Schleicher, the family's second child, comes into the world here. His father continues to pursue his military career, albeit with his zeal for soldiering somewhat diminished since he won the hand of Magdalene Heyn, the daughter of a wealthy East Prussian shipowner.

Kurt is earmarked by the family for a life in the army. At the tender age of twelve, he leaves the parental home and enters the cadet training academy at Plön in Holstein. Wrenched from the company of his siblings, at first he takes little pleasure in the square-bashing and the one-track education he undergoes at the cadet school. Before long, though, he settles in and becomes an instructor for the fresh intake of pupils. One of them later recalls: 'The cadet detailed to look after us was a strikingly handsome youth of a rather delicate, pale, almost feminine appearance.'[1] According to this same witness, Schleicher was characterized by 'an amiable keenness and skilful persuasiveness'.

Two years later, Schleicher transfers from Plön to the Main Cadet Institute (*Hauptkadettenanstalt*, or HKA) at Groß-Lichterfelde. He has only just turned eighteen when he joins the 3rd Prussian Foot Guards' Regiment stationed at Wrangelstraße near the Silesian Gate in Berlin. The young Guards officer quickly becomes known for his adeptness in juggling the strict demands of military service with the off-duty attractions that Berlin has to offer. As a devotee of the turf, on Sundays he finds himself drawn to the city's racecourses at Hoppegarten, Karlshorst and Grunewald. His reputation in the officers' mess, meanwhile, is that of an outgoing raconteur who is always game for a laugh and who, for all his quick-wittedness, has no side to him. Many friendships develop over the ten years that Schleicher serves in this unit, notably with Oskar von Hindenburg, the son of the future President, and Kurt von Hammerstein. There follows an education at the War Academy from 1910 onwards. Here, too, he is 'known and loved by all and sundry', a fact that clearly emerges from this rhyming testimony to him in the comic newspaper produced by fellow students when their year graduates: 'His laugh rings out incessantly / As clear as any bell. / But one time not a sound was heard, / For five full minutes not a word. / So we asked: Schleicher, aren't you well?'[2]

In the autumn of 1913, Schleicher, by now a captain, arrives at the Great General Staff, where he is assigned to the railway division. His commanding officer is Wilhelm Groener, with whom he soon develops an unusually intense and familiar bond, all the more uncommon in that several ranks separate the two men. Groener calls Schleicher 'the son I'd have liked to have', and this friendship remains firm over three decades in spite of all the upheavals and drastic tests of endurance it has to undergo. At the outbreak of

war, Schleicher is serving as a desk-bound adjutant in the General Quartermaster's Office – something of an ignominious posting in the eyes of many of his glory-seeking contemporaries. In this role, Schleicher's engaging manner stands him in good stead. Like a spider at the centre of a web, he sits in his office servicing the logistical requirements of the Supreme Army Command as well as solving the problems encountered by behind-the-lines services, Germany's allies or the civil authorities. He also gathers information and shares it with others for their mutual benefit.

He is called upon to perform much the same tasks in his next posting, to the newly formed War Department, again with Groener as his boss. Here his main concern is to maintain a steady supply of armaments, something which has come under threat from sporadic strikes and growing unrest on the home front. Schleicher is responsible for gathering intelligence and sounding out the situation, while Groener, in his general's uniform, spends his time around tables with Social Democrat negotiators and trade union representatives trying to hammer out wage agreements. Both men are viewed with suspicion by the General Staff for their unconventional approach, while complaints about their conduct also come from bodies representing the employers. Yet Schleicher is not entirely spared front-line duty. At the end of May 1917, he is dispatched to the Galician front, where he is later described as having displayed 'nerves of steel'[3] and 'an admirable sense of humour'. From there he returns to the General Staff after two months, decorated with the Knight's Cross with Swords of the Royal House Order of Hohenzollern.[4]

Around this time, one of his superiors in the Supreme Army Command notes that Schleicher is 'a law unto himself, a real one-off – he is marvellously clever, multi-talented and educated, plus he's very savvy and has the Berliner's characteristically blunt "gift of the gab"'.[5] At the same time, he adds the following caveat: 'Thus far, though, I haven't found him terribly likeable. In actual fact, he adopts really quite a presumptuous tone […] But there's no denying he's very capable.' A few months later, Schleicher's name crops up again in his superior's diary: 'I predict a great future for him, provided that smart mouth of his doesn't make him enemies.'[6] In the final days of the war in 1918, Groener takes over the position of General Quartermaster and appoints Schleicher as the head of a newly constituted political division.

2

Exactly who is in control in Germany on 9 November 1918? The monarchy has collapsed and the Kaiser has fled to neutral Holland. The war is lost, and millions of troops need to be repatriated to Germany in an orderly fashion. The jubilant spirit of 1914 is now just a distant memory, with the euphoria that was felt back then having come to nothing but chaos and an uncertain future. How long will there still be food left in the shops, who will pay the rent, and who will ensure that order is maintained on the streets? Max von Baden hands over the office of Reich Chancellor to Friedrich Ebert. The Social Democrats, who have been kept from power for decades, are now expected to wield it. The position they find themselves in is a paradoxical one, for all of a sudden the threat does not come from the right. Rather, it is the radical left, their own flesh and blood, who are trying to exploit the general state of mayhem in order to institute in Germany a Soviet system of workers' and soldiers' councils.

On 10 November, just a day after the Kaiser's abdication, General Wilhelm Groener telephones Friedrich Ebert on a confidential line. A week later he informs his wife: 'To the best of our ability, the Field Marshal [Hindenburg] and I want to support Ebert, whom I regard as a straightforward, honest and decent character, in order to prevent the cart from rolling further to the left [...] Let's hope to God that people's reason hasn't gone completely to the Devil and that good sense will soon prevail. If

Liebknecht and the radicals gain the upper hand in Berlin, civil war will be inevitable.'[7]

There are many occasions when Groener lets Kurt von Schleicher speak for him on the telephone. The key objective is always to stabilize the situation so as to save the country from falling apart and suffering an Allied occupation, and so that German troops can be brought home in an organized manner. When, on 23 December, rebel sailors from the People's Marine Division burst into the Reich Chancellery, seize Friedrich Ebert and rough up the Social Democrat politician Otto Wels, help is forthcoming from the Supreme Army Command. In this way, staunch monarchists like Groener and Schleicher make common cause with 'loyal socialists' to shore up the state that will soon become the Weimar Republic.

At the beginning of December 1918 Schleicher's political department draws up a set of guidelines on the confused situation for liaison officers operating in Berlin: 'The Army regards the Ebert administration as legal, according to the will of the German people. The Army has no truck, on the other hand, with Spartacists and other radical elements that block and hinder the government.'[8] Ultimately it is the newly formed volunteer units (*Freikorps*) which succeed in putting an end to the unrest. The fighting goes on until March 1919. In the east of Berlin, in the district of Lichtenberg, the *Freikorps*, stoked up by false reports of atrocities committed by the Spartacists, attack the armed rebel groups with particular brutality, resulting in the death of 1,200 people, including seventy-five on the government side.

In the autumn of 1919, Schleicher is summoned to the newly founded Defence Ministry, where he is to take over the running of an 'internal and military-political department'. He represents the army in the National Assembly, and later in the Reichstag, and is in constant contact with the heads of government. The victorious Allied powers are requiring that the Reichswehr – the very force that is now needed for the protection of the fledgling state – be cut to a quarter of its former strength, while the *Freikorps* are to be completely disbanded. When, in 1920, a section of the army under Kapp and Lüttwitz uses the simmering discontent among the ranks to stage a coup against the newly constituted Weimar Republic, the army leadership is split. Hans von Seeckt, the head of the *Truppenamt*, and Schleicher are worried that the new force will break apart if soldiers start exchanging fire. Seeckt takes sick leave and works in secret from home against the coup. Schleicher, too, considers the Kapp Putsch a piece of irresponsible political stupidity.[9] In the end, the attempted coup fails because workers hold a general strike and civil servants refuse to cooperate with the organizers of the uprising.

During this period, insurrections and attempted coups take place on a virtually yearly basis. In 1920 the anarchist Max Hoelz and his 'Red Guard' bring instability to the Vogtland region of southern Germany. In one of his pamphlets, Hoelz threatens that, if the Reichswehr marches in, he will 'set the whole city ablaze and slaughter all the members of the bourgeoisie, regardless of sex or age'.[10] Unrest also erupts in central Germany and there are a number of incidents along the new border with Poland. In the spring of the catastrophic year of 1923, the industrial Ruhr region is occupied by French troops, and in October members of the 'Black Reichswehr'* attempt a coup, followed soon after by the communists in Hamburg and by Hitler and Ludendorff's Beer Hall Putsch in Munich in November. The fear is that French forces might advance as far as Berlin. If this were to happen, Seeckt informs the American

---

* A clandestine paramilitary unit, formed in 1921 under the aegis of *Sondergruppe R* (the group of senior Reichswehr officers created by General Hans von Seeckt, which was tasked with circumventing the military restrictions imposed by the Versailles Treaty). The Black Reichswehr comprised 2,000 service personnel and 18,000 civilian reservists, who were secretly trained at a base in the garrison town of Küstrin in Brandenburg (now Kostrzyn in western Poland). The unit was deployed on acts of sabotage against the French military occupation of the Ruhr from 1923 onwards. In October of that same year, after the unit rebelled openly against the Weimar government's attempts to enforce the terms of the Treaty in the Ruhr by attempting to seize control of Küstrin, it was disbanded. [Translator's note]

ambassador, they would have to 'wade through a sea of blood'.[11] In the meantime, the banks and the German economy teeter on the brink of the abyss, as the exchange rate for a single US dollar soars to over four billion Reichsmarks. At this time, Schleicher is positively allergic to the term 'national', claiming he can no longer even bear to hear a word that has been misused so often to justify misguided plans that run counter to the country's best interests.[12]

In such circumstances, those in power are prepared to countenance anything that might bring stability. To the great surprise and displeasure of the Western powers, the two pariah states – Germany and Soviet Russia – meet at Rapallo in 1922 and strike a trade deal. A military component is later added to this, which the parties hope will be to their mutual advantage. While the Red Army will benefit from the Reichswehr's high level of tactical and technical expertise, the Germans, out of sight of the prying eyes of the Allies in the vast expanses of Russia, will be able to train in ways that circumvent the demilitarization provisions of the Versailles Peace Treaty. A school for chemical warfare is established near the city of Saratov on the Lower Volga, and outside Kazan the Kama 'fighting vehicle school' is set up to train future tank crews. Yet the most important of these secret facilities is the Lipetsk fighter-pilot school north of Voronezh.

An initial meeting between General von Seeckt and the Soviet negotiator Karel Radek takes place in 1922 in Schleicher's private apartment. However, it is still two years before the agreement bears fruit. It is essential that not a word of this reaches the outside world. Schleicher is the person charged with keeping it secret. By way of concealment, a 'commercial office' is created, with contacts to 'Moscow HQ'.[13] Meanwhile, the airfield at Lipetsk, with its simple grass landing strip, is expanded into a cutting-edge military facility, involving hangars, living quarters, administrative blocks, an officers' mess, a hospital, test beds and radio and telephone installations. Over the summer months, up to 140 Germans, who have all travelled to the Soviet Union on genuine passports but with false names and occupations, are working and living on the base. The wearing of uniforms is not permitted at Lipetsk.

The main difficulty comes in obtaining military equipment via overland routes without arousing the suspicions of the Allied monitoring authorities. While innocuous goods are shipped to Leningrad through the free port of Stettin, young officers sail across the Baltic in small boats smuggling explosive materials like aerial bombs and other munitions past the control points. In the other direction, the bodies of pilots killed in crashes at the test facility in Lipetsk are shipped back to Germany in crates marked 'Machine Parts' and are waved through customs checks by border officials who are in the know.[14]

From 1925 on, senior German army officers are present as observers at Red Army manoeuvres, in mufti to begin with in the guise of 'German communist workers' delegations', but later also in uniform. Conversely, Soviet officers are invited to participate in the clandestine training of the General Staff in Berlin. Through its military cooperation with the Russians, the Reichswehr also meets a quite different need: artillery rounds are in very short supply. Some 300,000 Soviet shells are imported illegally to Germany. When news of this leaks out, there is speculation that these munitions might also have been used in quelling civil unrest. The Social Democrats don't pass up the opportunity to distribute a pamphlet with the claim: 'German Workers Killed by Soviet Shells.'[15]

3

Having been promoted to colonel in the interim, Schleicher spends his time shuttling between his ministry in Bendlerstraße on the edge of the Tiergarten and the capital's political nerve centres, holding talks with parliamentary delegates at the Reichstag and with ministers in the Reich Chancellery or giving briefings at the presidential palace. For most politicians, it is *he* and not the defence minister who is the true face of the army. When, following the death of Friedrich Ebert, Field Marshal Paul von Hindenburg moves into the palace on Wilhelmstraße as the new President, Schleicher finds himself with a private channel of communication to the state's highest representative. For over twenty years, he has been friends with Oskar von Hindenburg, who is now (not without some string-pulling on Schleicher's part) acting as adjutant to his father.[16] Parliament is still functioning for now, but it won't be long before all power lies in the hands of the President.

As a bachelor, Schleicher is lodging in his widowed aunt's house in Matthäikirchstraße in the quiet, genteel suburb of Tiergarten. She has turned over several rooms to him. Since April 1918, Marie Güntel, a woman who comes from a tiny hamlet called Kremitten am Pregel in East Prussia, has been running his household. She looks after all the myriad domestic arrangements when Schleicher invites friends and colleagues round to enjoy his famously generous hospitality. An invitation from Schleicher is highly prized, unlike those to General von Seeckt's, where all that is usually on offer are beer and sandwiches.[17] At Easter 1929, Brüning is a guest at a breakfast gathering in Matthäikirchstraße when conversation turns to the idea of a future emergency government. Schleicher grants himself the luxury of riding out in the Tiergarten every morning, and he often takes this opportunity to discuss the first business of the day with fellow riders, such as the Head of the President's Office Otto Meissner, or Oskar von Hindenburg, or later even with Papen.

With his early-onset balding and his middle-aged spread – he refers self-deprecatingly to his paunch as his 'radiator grille' – Schleicher hardly corresponds to the classic image of the Prussian officer. François-Poncet provides a waspish thumbnail sketch: 'Bald, with a shaven head and a remarkably pallid, wan complexion; a mask of a face with two shining, piercing eyes. His features, which are swamped by an unappealing fleshiness, with narrow, barely visible lips, do him no favours.'[18] Nonetheless, women are said to find him attractive. The French ambassador is struck by

Schleicher's 'elegant hands'.[19] Others mention his charm, his sense of humour and his lively eyes. Unusually for a high-ranking officer of the Reichswehr, he often prefers not to wear his uniform for official functions. He is a keen and regular habitué of the opera and the concert hall. He can often be heard humming or whistling tunes from these performances for days afterwards. Schleicher doesn't even find it beneath his station to attend masked balls in fancy dress.[20] President Hindenburg, to whom such behaviour is naturally reported, finds Schleicher's predilections decidedly odd, but in common with many other things he doesn't understand, he puts this down to the changing times.

Schleicher is made a major general in 1929. On the evening of his promotion, he appears for the first time in public – at a well-attended reception – sporting the large red cuffs of a general and is instantly surrounded by a gaggle of young women like some opera singer or film star.[21] When, later that same year, a new defence minister is due to be appointed, Schleicher lobbies successfully for his father figure and friend Wilhelm Groener to be given the post. This tried and tested team, which is viewed with such suspicion by the right wing, is back in harness once more. Schleicher himself, with his curious hybrid status between the military and political world, is confirmed as 'Head of the Ministerial Office in the Defence Ministry' and is now a secretary of state. The public remains largely in the dark about precisely what role he plays in the power structure of the republic. Groener calls him his 'cardinal in political matters'.[22] Soon enough, though, their roles will be reversed.

4

For many years Dorothea, the daughter of Wilhelm Groener, has nurtured hopes of a future life with the confirmed bachelor Kurt von Schleicher. Groener would also be delighted to see his 'adopted son' become his son-in-law. But things turn out quite differently. For a start, in 1930 the defence minister, who has been widowed for four years, remarries. His bride is his former housekeeper, a young woman from Dresden by the name of Ruth Glück; Groener has to endure people repeatedly making the rather obvious witticism that he has 'struck it lucky' (*Glück gehabt*). However, the birth of a son shortly after the wedding develops into a scandal. Officers are only allowed to marry in any event with prior permission. The fact that the sixty-three-year-old minister failed to obtain leave to marry could perhaps be overlooked were it not for the more serious business of the 'premature' birth of a child. This private affair not only damages the defence minister as a role model, it also causes Groener's stock with the President to sink. In addition, it shakes Groener's own confidence, and so for the time being he delegates many of his official duties to his secretary of state. Groener is surprised to discover that becoming a father brings him a great sense of fulfilment in his advancing years. The defence minister can sometimes be spotted proudly pushing a pram containing his infant son across Friedrichstraße.[23] He writes to a friend: 'This new family idyll has had the effect of reinforcing my tendency to idleness, and has also heightened my indifference to all things political to such a degree that I simply offload onto Schleicher everything that lands on my desk.'[24]

Schleicher usually relaxes after a day filled with meetings in Bendlerstraße, correspondence and studying files, and appointments at the Chancellery, in parliament or at the presidential palace by going to the opera, the theatre, parties or receptions. One evening he visits the opera in the company of a couple he is friends with. When they sit down together after the performance, the general is in high spirits. Over and over, in youthful abandon, he treats them to renditions of the couplets he has just heard in Léhar's *Land des Lächelns* ('The Land of Smiles'): *Immer nur lächeln und immer vergnügt, / Immer zufrieden, so wie's immer sich fügt* ('Always smiling and always happy / And forever content, which is just as it should be').[25] And isn't that the very dictum he himself lives by? *Lächeln trotz Weh und tausend Schmerzen, / Doch wie's da drin aussieht, geht niemand was an* ('Smile through the pain and the sorrow you hide, / To keep from the world what you're feeling inside'). Schleicher himself has been married since the summer of 1931. Pushing fifty, he has chosen as his life partner not Dorothea Groener but his cousin's former wife Elisabeth von Schleicher, who is widely admired, even among the general's political opponents, for her friendly nature, her attractiveness and her intelligence. Along with Elisabeth's daughter Lonny, they move into a flat in Alsenstraße, within walking distance of the Reichstag. Marie Güntel, who this year celebrates her own fiftieth birthday even earlier than the general, continues to run the Schleicher household, which also includes two long-haired dachshunds.

In the opinion of the political scientist Theodor Eschenburg, Schleicher 'was able to interact with anyone and everyone, he had the psychological knack of getting on the emotional wavelength of the most diverse individuals. He also had a quick, albeit somewhat shallow, grasp of subject areas that were unfamiliar to him, and was a resourceful tactician and a virtuosic improviser. And for all his rumbustiousness, at root he had real emotional intelligence.' Eschenburg went on: 'He was never at a loss for an argument or a solution and had no qualms about correcting one error with another. He tended towards a rather imprecise mode of expression, partly as a negotiating tactic and partly because he hadn't thought through, or couldn't be bothered to think through, the subject under discussion sufficiently clearly. The facts he commanded, the agreements he reached and the arguments he put forward were often quite dazzling.'[26] Schleicher's negotiating skills also impress Hindenburg. But will his repertoire of elegantly formulated ambiguities, his waspish remarks delivered with a rhetorical flourish – in short, his political chicanery – cut any ice with Hitler?

The Destruction of New York

1

Almost all the important ministries are located on Wilhelmstraße. After every general election, a giant game of musical chairs begins. Except for in the Prussian State Ministry, that is, which has witnessed no such arrivals and departures for a long time now. Otto Braun has seen his neighbours come and go – all the various presidents and chancellors, foreign ministers, finance ministers, ministers of the interior, justice ministers and transport ministers. At the end of March 1930, Heinrich Brüning takes occupancy of the Reich Chancellery; this unlovely building, which has had an annex added to it, is somewhat reminiscent of a high-rise bunker. The Chancellor's study, the conference room and the offices are all situated in the new building, while the older part is home to the Chancellor's private quarters and the reception rooms.[1] Brüning loves fresh air and schedules al fresco cabinet meetings as often as he can in the garden behind the Chancellery.[2]

Immediately after taking office in the spring of 1930, the Catholic Brüning holds a discussion with the Social Democrat Otto Braun. The two men have had many dealings with one another over the past two difficult years, and a dispassionate view of political realities conditions both their outlooks. In Prussia, the Social Democrats are the main governing party, with the support of the Centre, whereas these roles are reversed in the country at large. The two parties need and value one another. Brüning says about Braun and his interior minister Carl Wilhelm Severing: 'Even in the heyday of the Prussian government in the nineteenth century, there will have been few ministers who were so tireless in working for the good of the state.'[3]

Brüning has only been in power for four months when, in July 1930, the Reichstag vetoes the first state of emergency that he declares. The Chancellor responds by dissolving parliament and calling new elections. In normal times, the rules of the constitution see to it that the mechanism of political compromise kicks in to ensure that certain groups trade off their respective interests and eventually come to a majority view. But for quite some time, the desire to reach an accord in the Reichstag has no longer been relevant, with the different political forces at daggers drawn with one another. A small clause in the constitution that is only intended for use in times of crisis is now invoked, investing all power in the President, Hindenburg. His right to veto emergency measures implemented by the Chancellor, and if need be to dissolve parliament, makes him an emperor in all but name. But is it really the weaknesses of the constitution that are driving Germany onwards to perdition, or isn't it, rather, the case that, in times of desperation and chaos, the various political protagonists will always try to find loopholes in the law, however tightly it has been drafted?

On 15 September 1930, the day of the election, the secretary of state in the Reich Chancellery, Hermann Pünder, sits by the radio from the evening of the polling to the early morning of the next day, following the results as they come in. A few days later he notes in his diary: 'The people have been shaken to the core by the restructuring that has gone on within Brüning's cabinet [...] Only the two extremes have emerged as winners, the Communists and

the National Socialists. The former have gained 75 seats while the latter now have an unprecedented 107 delegates. A quite appalling result!'[4] At the previous elections, the NSDAP couldn't even muster 3 per cent of the vote, and now all of a sudden they are the second largest political grouping in the Reichstag.

A feeling of helplessness becomes all-pervasive following this strong showing by the National Socialists. There is a general clamour for Hindenburg to include the SPD in government, with even the leadership of the Reichswehr, the League of German Industrialists and leading bankers making representations to Brüning; however, the President brusquely turns down their requests.[5] Brüning and Braun meet and 'sit together until late into the night' trying, as Braun later recalls, to agree a common strategy on how to deal with the Nazis, namely whether to put up a united front to combat them, or to involve them in the responsibilities of government 'while they are still too weak to assert their totalitarian claim to absolute power'.[6] Brüning is unable to decide on either course of action. For the Social Democrats, the tacit alliance with the Centrist national government is the lesser evil, but, as Braun admits to his friend, it is 'becoming increasingly difficult to steer a course around the many rocks in such a way as to ensure that Brüning's administration doesn't run aground and fall prey to the Nazi wreckers'.[7]

The communists, too, are giving cause for concern. Rumours of a coup swirl around in Berlin in the autumn of 1930: 'Quite by chance, while in conversation with someone who is close to the circle around Max Hölz, I heard that the Communists, or at least that particular group, have a detailed plan to stage a coup in Berlin in mid-November and seize control of government,' notes Count Harry Kessler in his diary.[8] 'Even the date has already been fixed. They wouldn't be so stupid as to stir up trouble again on the streets like they did in 1919, but instead, relying on sympathetic elements in the police and the army, they plan to do it in a hush-hush way, under cover of darkness. Berlin will wake up to find that it has a new government. By all accounts, they're confident it will succeed.'

In late September 1930, the trial of three Reichswehr officers from Ulm begins. At Schleicher's urging, Groener has brought proceedings against them for 'preparing an act of high treason'. They are accused of having distributed propaganda for the NSDAP. While in custody one of the officers, Richard Scheringer, converts to communism under the influence of his fellow prisoners. The KPD exploits the case to make political capital in parliament. Adolf Hitler is called as a witness during the trial. Under oath, he swears in a propagandistic testimony lasting two hours that the National Socialists would only seek to gain power by legal means. The three officers are sentenced to eighteen months in gaol. Scheringer, who was involved in the abortive Küstrin coup by the Black Reichswehr, eventually survives the Third Reich, joins the KPD in 1945 and shortly afterwards founds a people's cooperative farm in Bavaria. As a result of his political stance, he is detained by the West German authorities more than twenty times under various administrations. When he dies in 1986, an SED (*Sozialistische Einheitspartei Deutschlands*, 'German Socialist Unity Party') delegation, sent from East Germany by Erich Honecker, forms a guard of honour at his funeral and the writer Ernst Jünger lays a wreath with the inscription 'To Our Old Friend'.

'National Socialism is a feverish spasm of the German petty bourgeoisie in its death throes,'[9] notes Count Harry Kessler in his diary, 'but the toxins given off by its sickness have the capacity to poison Germany and Europe for decades to come. This class is beyond salvation; but in its dying agonies it is still able to visit enormous misery upon Europe.' On the day that parliament opens, 13 October 1930, SA stormtroopers smash the plate-glass windows of the large department stores on Leipziger Straße with shouts of *Deutschland erwache!* ('Wake Up, Germany!') and *Juda verrecke!* ('Death to the Jews!'). Foreign observers are outraged, so to assuage them Hitler gives an interview to *The Times* on 15 October 1930, in which he claims: 'I have nothing against decent Jews, but the moment Jews start associating themselves with Bolshevism [...] they must be regarded as enemies.'[10]

And what of Hitler's 'oath of legality'? 'I can assure you,' Hitler tells the court, 'that when the National Socialist movement triumphs in its struggle, then there will be a National Socialist Court of Justice too; November 1918 will be avenged, and heads will roll.'[11] At the same time, at a conference of Berlin Nazi Party leaders, Goebbels crows: 'The system will have to pay us to bring it down.'[12] Hermann Göring voices a very similar sentiment when he announces: 'We are fighting against this state and the current system because we want to eradicate it, root and branch, but – and this is for any police snoopers listening – we will do this by legal means.'[13] And does the leading Nazi ideologue Alfred Rosenberg really only mean it metaphorically when he issues the following prophecy for the day they seize power? 'The head of a prominent Jew will be impaled on every telegraph pole from Berlin to Munich.'[14]

2

In 1931, in several instalments, the supplement of the *Berliner Illustrierte Nachtausgabe* ('Berlin Illustrated Evening Edition') carries the transcript of a session in which Hanussen responds to questions concerning the future. To begin with, the clairvoyant is asked to describe preparations for a trip to New York in the year 2500, and the journey itself, and then to tell listeners what he can see happening in Australia from his vantage point in New York. The room is darkened and the magician put into a trance. He closes his eyes and sinks back in his chair. As he replies to the questions, he manipulates the beads on his *kombolói* with both hands: 'Where New York once stood, there is now sea. I don't know the date when it happened, but there was a terrible catastrophe. We have a book at home describing the destruction of this city. The whole city was submerged during this catastrophe. Everyone perished. Ships, people, houses… yes, the buildings collapsed like houses of cards.'[15] A little later on, Hanussen does give a precise date for the destruction of New York: the year 2000.[16] And what about Berlin – what will that city look like in 2500? 'It's not a city,' comes the seer's brusque reply, 'it's a country, stretching far and wide. Gardens. Happy people live here. Contented people…'[17] That has not yet come to pass in 1930, however. Anyone who casts an eye over the streets of Berlin at this time will find little in the way of happiness and contentment. Parliament is being dissolved with ever increasing frequency. The rapid succession of election campaigns is inflaming the political atmosphere and at the same time fuelling discontent with the parliamentary system. The level of aggression on the streets grows with every election. 'In every conversation you have, without exception, the atmosphere that hits you like a gust of plague-breath', writes the political commentator Leopold Schwarzschild, 'is a sixty-million-strong blend of concern, unease, exhaustion, hopelessness, repugnance, bitterness and hysteria. This mood, which has gone largely unreported and is hard to describe, is a scourge in its own right.'[18]

Anyone with anything to lose is keeping their head down at this time. Not Hanussen, though. The front mudguard of his luxury Italian car proudly displays the standard of the SA whenever he lends the vehicle to friends in the party. His secretary, his assistant, his chauffeur and his manager – every last one of them is a National Socialist. Hanussen buys the services of the SA by giving them funds to pay for boots, uniforms and food, as well as free tickets to his shows. In return, the stormtroopers protect his performances from troublemakers. Eventually, as a 'supporting member' of the SA, his secretary recalls, the magician takes to wearing the uniform of the Sturmabteilung himself now and then in the office or on the street.[19]

Hanussen is at the peak of his popularity and is busy making plans to found his own School of the Occult and a sanatorium called Castle Hanussen, which will open up a whole new field of operation for his faith-healing activities. As an important testimonial, he can point to the fact that the famous opera singer Richard Tauber, who suffers from rheumatoid arthritis, has reported experiencing a palpable alleviation of his symptoms after four sessions with the clairvoyant. Hanussen keeps surprising his public with a constant stream of new ideas. He has recently begun recording his seances on a dictation machine known as a parlograph. Over the course of seven evenings in October 1931, while in a state of trance he dictates onto forty-six wax phonograph cylinders a novel, which he plans to publish under the title *S.O.S.*

Those fascinated by Hanussen's art do not just include wealthy idlers with a weakness for the supernatural, or just Nazi Party members hoping to benefit from his celebrity and the influence he wields as the proprietor of a mass-circulation newspaper. The clairvoyant has also piqued the interest of certain sections of the left-wing intelligentsia. For instance, the dramatist Ernst Toller, one of the leading lights of the far-left coup that saw the brief establishment of a Soviet republic in Munich in the spring of 1919, gives Hanussen his seal of approval in November 1930: 'I must say I've taken a very close look at Hanussen, and he has achieved things that leave me in no doubt that I'm not dealing with a con artist.'[20]

Likewise, the celebrated novelist Alfred Döblin doesn't want to pass up the opportunity of a private audience with the famous maestro. But what Hanussen commits to his dictaphone in a ninety-minute session fails to convince him. And so they decide to hold a kind of 'song contest', in which they settle on a topic and each deliver a ten-minute talk on it. At the end, Döblin concedes: 'I must admit that you presented things much more vividly and dramatically than me.'[21] And the theme on which the two men spoke off the cuff? – 'Berlin Is Being Governed by A Pimp'.

3

In January 1931, Heinrich Brüning embarks on a tour around the east of Germany, with stops planned in East Prussia and Silesia. Shortly before he is due to set off, a package arrives from the neighbouring presidential palace. Hindenburg, who at first regards the Centrist politician with scepticism but who later comes to refer to him affectionately as 'little Brüning', has sent him the fur coat he wore on campaign in 1915, 'together with a long handwritten note in a tone of almost fatherly concern', enquiring whether the Chancellor was 'up to facing the rigours of the journey'.[22] In the event, the trip to the eastern regions is an utter failure. The calculation in government was that Brüning would be given a friendly welcome there, considering all the state aid that had been pumped eastward, including lines of cheap credit and reduced taxes. The exact opposite is the case. In Farther Pomerania, the government delegation is met with rioting organized by right-wing groups, and in some places is even pelted with rocks. An observer reports that Brüning 'didn't even bat an eyelid. After all, he loved these people. He saw that they were suffering and thought of himself as a doctor, who oughtn't to be alarmed, let alone annoyed, if the invalid happened to shout at him and attack him while in a fever.'[23] Things are at their worst in Breslau (Wrocław), with the Chancellor's motorcade having to inch its way through a crowd of 40,000 demonstrators to the city hall, where it is met with a hail of missiles. Brüning personally isn't in danger because, as he writes, 'experience has taught me that the first car is never the one that gets hit'.[24]

Brüning combines his sanguine disposition and a sense of duty with the skill of being able to keep several balls in play at once. Dorothy Thompson writes that Heinrich Brüning puts her in mind of an eighteenth-century cardinal-statesman: 'A high-bridged, sensitive nose. A finely cut mouth. The convex profile of obstinacy.

Quizzical, wise, humorous.'[25] For Thompson, he is 'a man who will hold on for ever'. In reference to his great tactical abilities, Brüning is said to 'use his tail like a fox to erase the tracks he leaves behind him.'[26]

But anyone in whom he places his trust can count implicitly on his loyalty. He is an avowed opponent of socialist ideas and can put forward sound arguments to back his position, yet as a Catholic trade union leader he is anything but unsocially minded. But in the current German political landscape, the Centrist Brüning now only has one ally left: the Social Democrats. Every morning at 6.30 sharp, the chief press officer of the SPD telephones Gottfried Treviranus, the cabinet member and personal friend of Brüning, to exchange information. Treviranus calls it their 'silent partnership with the SPD'.[27] Admittedly, General von Schleicher, who has ordered his intelligence agencies to bug all official telephone lines, is also listening in.

Generally speaking, Brüning has noticed some odd goings-on in the Reich Chancellery. Whenever he uses the telephone, another wall-mounted receiver makes a strange crackling noise. On one occasion, an unknown caller gets through to him on an unlisted number and proceeds to hurl abuse at him. On another he surprises two men who are trying to force the drawers of his desk. In the loft above the library, which is used as a space for secret talks, the sound of footsteps can sometimes be heard.[28] Those who are closest to Brüning start wondering whether the Chancellor might be seeing ghosts. And there are ample grounds for mistrust; in the world of Berlin politics, practically nothing remains secret for very long. Confidential matters discussed at the highest level are frequently known about the very same day by the spies of all the main parties, as well as the ambassadors of France, Great Britain and the USA.

In the two years of the Brüning administration, hardship has reached epidemic proportions and the political situation has become increasingly radicalized. A never-ending succession of emergency measures are designed to stabilize the budget and at the same time impress upon foreign powers that Germany will never be in a position to meet its crippling war reparations bill. In Berlin thousands of unemployed people are living under canvas or in makeshift shelters on the shores of the lakes in the Grunewald Forest.[29] In Hamburg, the city's social services department decides it can only now offer support to 'worthwhile elements of the population'[30] and no longer provide a safety net to 'asocial types, psychopaths and other inferiors'. Brüning is lambasted as the 'Hunger Chancellor' by the communists and subjected to scurrilous personal attacks by the National Socialists. Bella Fromm remarks how viciously Goebbels lays into the Chancellor in the Reichstag: 'I had to marvel at Dr Brüning's self-restraint. He listened to these diatribes with complete equanimity. Anyone else would have punched the furious little dwarf in his fat gob.'[31] But is there really no alternative to the policy of austerity, no other recipe but to 'let Germany work its way to freedom through hunger'?[32] The country has just become a signatory to the Young Plan, the prime objective of which is to prohibit any attempt to solve the crisis through government borrowing. The Social Democrats are keeping quiet because they fear new elections from which only the radicals will profit. Otherwise, Brüning's only friends are abroad, where his polite yet resolute demeanour has won him the respect and trust of his negotiating partners. Things look very different at home, however: 'I can't sit by and watch this anymore. Poor old Heinrich can't handle anything!'[33] an exasperated Schleicher tells the Prussian interior minister Carl Severing at a reception in the Soviet Embassy.

Serious doubts over whether Brüning is the right man for the job are also growing in the upper echelons of German heavy industry, notably in the Long-Name League and also the Ruhrlade, an exclusive circle of prominent industrialists in the Ruhr region. In 1931, Franz von Papen delivers a speech in which he openly calls for Brüning to make a clean break with the Social Democrats and to form an alliance with German Nationalists and the National

Socialists. 'For many years I'd had in mind the possibility,' Papen explained in a speech long after the war, 'of involving this National Socialist Workers' Party in the apparatus of government, together with a hard core of other well-meaning and nationalistically minded individuals – people who were true patriots, but with a social conscience – and having its leader Hitler play the junior role in this coalition, just to see whether and how it might be possible to govern alongside them.'[34]

The pressure on Brüning grows when major farming interests also join the clamour for the President to remove the Chancellor. They accuse him of 'Agrarian Bolshevism', because of his plan for the state to purchase debt-laden estates in eastern Germany for housing developments. Baskets full of letters of complaint are delivered to Wilhelmstraße, a 'welter of missives from the cream of German society'[35] as Hindenburg complains to Brüning, including one from the former monarch August of Saxony, who voices his concern that Brüning's policies will cause the price of timber to plummet and that 'I and other old families will be ruined as a result'. Brüning senses that his days in power are numbered.

4

On the evening of 12 September 1931, the square around the Memorial Church (*Gedächtniskirche*) in Berlin is filled with young men, who have travelled there from other parts of the city by tram, underground and overground (S-Bahn) train. Some of them are wearing 'brown waistcoats, so-called "climbing vests", others brown trousers, with a few sporting so-called "bear boots" and many of them blue berets'.[36] Also in evidence are 'symbols such as the crooked cross, the "Wolfsangel"* and the steel helmet'. Before long, around a thousand SA and Stahlhelm members have assembled there, mingling in small groups in civilian clothes among the passers-by. It is the first day of the Jewish New Year festival (Rosh Hashanah), which Goebbels intends to mark with a new campaign of persecution. Originally the gathering was planned as a demonstration by the unemployed, who were meant to whip up sentiment on the Kurfürstendamm against the Jews by shouting slogans like 'We're Starving!' and 'We Want Work!'. So-called 'hunger demonstrations' also form part of the propaganda repertoire of the communists.[37] Many Jewish shopkeepers have set up businesses on the Ku'damm, and nowhere else in the city is the contrast between the prosperity of a few and the misery of the masses so glaringly obvious as it is here.

In a leading article published as early as 1927 in his newspaper *Der Angriff* ('The Attack'), the pathological anti-Semite Goebbels sets out the form that such demonstrations should take:

Jews are strolling up and down the pavements, with blonde German girls on their arm. And if a working-class fellow should happen by chance to brush past one of these plump, well-fed sons of the desert race as he minces along in his patent-leather shoes, reeking of perfume, he will hiss disapprovingly at him like he's the master of this city and the other fellow, the proletarian, is nothing but his chattel and slave. You might wonder what on earth he's thinking of – doesn't it occur to him that he's only here under sufferance in his fancy get-up? Why doesn't he stay out there, in the Orient – indeed, how come he's here at all, offending against the splendour and the glory of the West by his

---

* The 'Wolfsangel' is an ancient runic symbol. Thought to be a stylized depiction of a wolf trap, the device consists of an inverted 'Z' on its side, with a short bar across the centre of the diagonal stroke. The symbol was adopted from an early period by the Nazi Party and in the Second World War was used by various SS units as a vehicle marking. [Translator's note]

very presence? Is it any wonder, then, if the working-class man takes matters into his own hands and presses his 'visiting card' into the Hebrew's face in no uncertain manner?[38]

But instead of the planned crowd of unemployed workers that Goebbels first envisaged demonstrating, now it's men from at least eighteen Berlin SA units who are here to hunt down Jews. One of the detachments present on the Ku'damm that evening is the 'Killer Unit' (*Mördersturm*) Number 33 from Charlottenburg: Count Helldorff is leading the action in conjunction with his deputy, Karl Ernst. Proceedings begin with slogans like 'Wake Up, Germany – Death to the Jews!', which are chanted by one rabble-rouser and then taken up by the rest of the bellowing mob. Then SA men start looking at people passing by, searching for anyone whose appearance suggests they might be of Jewish origin. A non-Jewish witness later describes in court how he found his path blocked by a group of forty to seventy threatening-looking individuals. He crossed the street, but another group cornered him there. Several SA men in civilian clothes, armed with knuckledusters, blackjacks and cudgels, started laying into him. When he resisted, they beat him up so badly that 'there wasn't a single place on my body that wasn't cut or bruised. My face was smashed to a pulp, my teeth were knocked loose, my feet were soaked in blood and my suit was spattered with bloodstains.'[39]

That same evening, dentist Hans Hecht and his mother were also walking down the Ku'damm when they hear the shout go up: 'Beat the Jews to death!' They sought 'refuge in the entrance to the Siegfried Levy department store.'[40] While they were looking at the window displays, five or so people from the crowd that was milling about there came up to them and called out something to the effect of 'Hey, we've got one here!' The witness Erika Hecht took to her heels, crying out 'Someone help!' but ran straight into a gang of fifty to sixty people who'd come charging towards them, yelling. She received '[…] a hefty blow to her temples, whereupon she pulled off her hat to reveal her blonde hair and so convince them she wasn't a Jew.' Further along the Ku'damm, SA men chanting slogans like 'Happy New Year!', 'Pack your bags, Sarah!', 'The synagogue's on fire!' and 'Bet you never dreamed we'd visit you today of all days!' burst into Café Reimann, which is known to be a favourite haunt of Jewish customers. They shoot out the windows and smash the marble-topped tables and the crockery. The pâtisserie's customers panic and flee for their lives. With cries of 'Death to the Jews!', 'Beat the Jews to death!', 'Die, you vermin, you dirty dog!', 'Shoot the Jewish dog dead!', 'You're a fucking Jew too!', 'Here's another of these little Jewish bastards!', and 'Wake up, Germany!', many of the café's guests are assaulted.[41] Almost all the businesses between Uhlandstraße and the Memorial Church pull down their shutters and metal grilles. Groups of SA men are also lying in wait outside the synagogue on Fasanenstraße, attacking worshippers as they leave the temple.

At the height of the disturbances, a green, four-seater Opel cabriolet cruises up and down the Ku'damm at walking pace. From the back seat, the leader of the Berlin SA, Count Helldorff, who is wearing a naval officer's cap trimmed with gold braid, issues instructions and eggs on his stormtroopers.[42] At the same time, instructions concerning the progress of the operation are handed to messengers on motorbikes.[43] Alongside Helldorff in the car is Karl Ernst. When the police impound the Opel after the rioting, they find inside a 'large leather whip, as used by the driver of a horse-drawn artillery limber'.[44] Passers-by are repelled by this naked display of violence. But there are also some voices heard dissenting against this general view: 'Why do those fat Jewesses go around so provocatively wearing furs and with bouquets in their lapels?', 'What business have Jews got walking round in top hats?', 'People are right to feel aggrieved: poverty on the one hand, and on the other these toffs done up to the nines.'[45]

The police only show up at around 20.45. They disperse the larger groups of rioters, who respond with the tried and tested tactic of immediately reforming into smaller groups and continuing to cause mayhem. There are complaints that the police officers have been too half-hearted in their intervention. Certainly it's true that, consistently, the only arrests made are of the foot soldiers, who are sentenced in hastily convened proceedings to anywhere between nine months and a year and nine months in gaol. Helldorff and Ernst go to ground for the time being. Nine days later, however, they hand themselves in to the Berlin public prosecutor and are remanded in custody. Goebbels is fearful that the SA leaders will be given long prison sentences if they are tried by the same judge who presided over the other cases and so requests a meeting with the Chancellor.

Brüning receives Goebbels two days before a sensitive occasion, the visit to Germany of the French prime minister Pierre Laval and his foreign minister Aristide Briand. This will be the first time since the Congress of Berlin in 1878 that a government delegation from Paris has visited the German capital. Because of their harsh stance towards Germany, the French aren't exactly popular guests. The journalist Bella Fromm is presented by her friend Briand to the French premier Laval: 'Laval's teeth, completely yellowed by nicotine, are like those of some predatory animal,'[46] she remarks. She doesn't find much to like about him: 'He looks a bit too shifty to me, like a gypsy.' Brüning is worried that the Nazis will use the visit as a golden opportunity to disrupt the talks between the Germans and the French through noisy and violent protests. When he visited Rome in the summer, he was himself harangued by Hitler supporters chanting: 'Down with the Jew Chancellor!'[47] So Brüning grants Goebbels an audience, and in return for his promise not to cause any trouble during the French state visit, the Chancellor agrees to a separate trial for the two SA leaders.

The National Socialists do indeed refrain from causing any disturbances during the state visit. Even so, the atmosphere is sombre. The two governments agree to form a joint economic commission, but there is no meeting of minds on the question of reparations. Aristide Briand is suffering from an illness that deprives him of sleep at night, leaving him struggling with chronic fatigue during the day. It's not uncommon to find him fast asleep sometimes during parliamentary meetings. In Berlin, the French also pay the Reich President a routine visit, during which he voices his concern for Briand: 'The journey must have been really exhausting for the old chap!' Hindenburg – who is almost fifteen years Briand's senior – tells the French ambassador André François-Poncet.[48] On the other hand, Prime Minister Laval, the son of a café proprietor, is disappointed not to find sauerkraut served at any of the state banquets. So, the day before the French delegation leaves Berlin, he orders his heart's desire at the hotel where they are staying, but it disagrees with him. 'Greatly troubled during the night by indigestion,' François-Poncet recalled, 'he got up, left the hotel and paced up and down Unter den Linden, much to the astonishment of the men guarding the door, who kept having to salute him as he walked by. This was not a good omen, I thought to myself, as his train pulled out of the station.'[49] The second trial resulting from the Kurfürstendamm riots begins at the end of October 1931. Helldorff and Ernst are represented by the attorneys Alfons Sack, Roland Freisler and Hans Frank and are each convicted by District Court III to six months' imprisonment and a fine of one hundred Reichsmarks for defamation. During the hearing, Helldorff claims he was only present to help calm the situation on the Ku'damm, and that 'Communist *agents provocateurs*' incited the riot in order to discredit the NSDAP. On appeal, Helldorff is acquitted on the charge of committing a breach of the peace. In his concluding remarks, he states: 'What took place on the Kurfürstendamm happened for ideological reasons, and was prompted by an ardent love of the Fatherland.'[50]

The only other sanction imposed on Helldorff and Ernst is to pay a fine of one hundred Reichsmarks apiece for having slandered two Jewish traders as 'banking Jews'. *Die Weltbühne* reports the case in just three acerbic lines: 'District Judge Ohnesorge: You have imposed a Hundred-Mark fine on Count Helldorff. We trust this won't jeopardize your future career in the Third Reich.'[51] At various different levels, people seem to be preparing for this new era, just like in Revolutionary France under absolutist rule, where the watchword was *Le préfet travaille pour le gouvernement de demain* – 'The Prefect [a regional administrator responsible for law and order] works for the government of tomorrow.'

While it is reasonable to assume that the majority of Germans disapprove of the conduct of members of the SA, there is also surreptitious support in some quarters, and not just among Nazi sympathizers. The upheaval seems to strike a chord especially with the young. In the short time between October and the end of November 1931, membership of the Berlin SA increases almost threefold.[52] Following the riots on the Kurfürstendamm, Count Helldorff is confirmed in his position as head of the *Sturmabteilung* in Berlin. He has successfully passed his baptism of fire.

Halma

1

On 24 November 1931, Dorothy Thompson has to wait over an hour upstairs in the foyer of the Kaiserhof Hotel before she spots Hitler hurrying past on the way to his suite of rooms, accompanied by his bodyguard. She has been trying for eight years to secure a meeting with him. Back then, in 1923, she had been working as a correspondent in Vienna. Hitler had fled after his abortive putsch. He was rumoured to be staying with Katharina Hanfstaengl, an acquaintance of Dorothy's. They had got to know one another at a suffragette rally in New York in 1916. Katharina was there visiting her son Ernst, who lived in the USA. Although her plan to meet Hitler in 1923 came to nothing, Dorothy's connection with the Hanfstaengls was to prove a stroke of luck: as an early supporter of Hitler and a participant in the Munich putsch, 'Putzi', as Ernst had always been known since childhood, rose through the ranks of the NSDAP to become the head of its foreign press bureau.

Dorothy grows weary of the long wait at the Kaiserhof. She is all set to go in to meet Hitler, but he receives an Italian journalist ahead of her. So she goes to seek out Putzi Hanfstaengl in his office. She has, of course, prepared thoroughly for her meeting.

At the beginning of the year, she and her friend Helmuth James von Moltke held an interview with Gregor Strasser and two other NSDAP leaders, and she has also read Hitler's *Mein Kampf*. Her verdict? – 'Eight hundred pages of Gothic script, pathetic gestures, inaccurate German and unlimited self-satisfaction.'[1] For the upcoming interview, she has been allowed three questions, which she has had to submit in writing twenty-four hours beforehand. In the event that Hitler comes to power, she wants to ask him the following questions: 'What will you do for the working masses of Germany? Will you abolish the constitution of the German Republic? What will you do for international disarmament, and how will you handle France?'

When she's finally shown through to see Hitler, she quickly realizes it's impossible to carry on a conversation with him: 'He speaks always as though he were addressing a mass meeting.'[2] Her interlocutor fails signally to impress her. She describes him as a man 'whose framework seems cartilaginous, without bones. He is inconsequent and voluble, ill-poised, insecure. He is the very prototype of the Little Man. A lock of lank hair falls over an insignificant and slightly retreating forehead. The back head is shallow. His face is broad in the cheek-bones. The nose is large, but badly shaped and without character. His movements are awkward, almost undignified and most un-martial. There is in his face no trace of any inner conflict or self-discipline.'[3]

Even so, Dorothy cannot deny that the man 'who owns an army' and 'who terrorises the streets', the 'future dictator of Germany', possesses a 'certain charm… But it is the soft, almost feminine charm of the Austrian! When he talks it is with a broad Austrian dialect. The eyes alone are notable. Dark grey and hyperthyroid – they have the peculiar shine which often distinguishes geniuses, alcoholics, and hysterics.'[4] When the American journalist tries sidestepping the agreed ground rules of the interview by interposing extra questions, 'then his eyes focus in some far corner of the room; a hysterical note creeps into his voice, which rises

sometimes almost to a scream. He gives the impression of a man in a trance. He bangs the table.'[5]

The actual hard-and-fast information that the interview yields is disappointingly scant. But at least Hitler gives a candid response to one of her questions: 'I will get into power legally, I will abolish this parliament and the Weimar constitution afterwards.'[6] Dorothy Thompson does not believe that it will come to that. She recognizes the anti-Semitic mania, without which the Nazis' entire party platform would collapse in on itself, but also sees that neither Hitler himself 'with his Slavic cheek-bones, his broad nose, his face that might serve as the very prototype of the "inferior Dinaric"'[7] nor Goebbels belong to that elite group of 'Aryans… the "Nordics"', and doubts whether the 'drummer-boy', as she calls Hitler, will ever win over the German people with these lies. But hasn't she herself read what Hitler wrote in *Mein Kampf*: 'the broad masses […] themselves often tell small lies in little matters but would be ashamed to resort to large-scale falsehoods. It would never come into their heads to fabricate colossal untruths, and they would not believe that others could have the impudence to distort the truth so infamously'?[8]

But even if this were to happen, wouldn't President Hindenburg still be there to steady the ship? Dorothy Thompson writes that he 'is an odd old man with a peculiar sense of duty and consistency. He actually believes that it is the duty of a president of a republic to protect the republic. He is just that old-fashioned. I even believe that as long as his country sorely needs him, Hindenburg will not die. Though […] he is not so good. Eighty-four is old, even for Hindenburg.'[9]

2

These are difficult years for the Ossietzkys. Maud Ossietzky finds that her husband's job at *Die Weltbühne* leaves little free time and space for them to enjoy together. She increasingly takes refuge in alcohol. Even when she and Carl first knew one another, she tried to combat the feelings of anxiety and panic attacks that had plagued her throughout her life by drinking.[10] Carl in turn buries himself ever deeper in his work as his wife loses her grip. Maud would have happily emigrated with her husband; she had Uruguay in mind. But there's no more talk of that now. After his conviction in the *Weltbühne* trial, a gaol sentence is looming. He decides not to evade incarceration, on the grounds that 'being locked up would be the most uncomfortable position for me',[11] and she supports him in this. 'One of life's few satisfactions is to maintain your principled position in the face of all the threats earthly powers can throw at you,' he writes in the family diary a few weeks before the start of his detention. He's chiefly concerned about Maud: 'You know I stand by you in everything you do, even if I'm often a bit taciturn and don't tell you how I feel. There will be a brighter future when we can laugh more easily than we do now. But I'll stick by you come what may. I'll be by your side to help you – my problem child! And then there's our little sprog to think about too, whom we must be kind to and who deserves the very best.'[12] Before he goes to prison, Carl transfers his daughter to a school in the Odenwald, to protect her from any potential hostility at her Berlin school. At the same time, this ensures that Rosalinde won't be left alone with her alcoholic mother.

According to Kurt Tucholsky, the action against *Die Weltbühne* was 'the generals' payback'.[13] Not least, the Reichswehr minister Wilhelm Groener and Kurt von Schleicher used it for a personal reckoning with the man of conviction Ossietzky, who had harshly criticized them on many previous occasions. Accordingly, the day he starts his gaol sentence, 10 May 1932, becomes a mass political demonstration, which requires a special dispensation since open-air gatherings have been banned since March of that year. The Berlin Deputy President of Police gives his word that, for ninety minutes from the appointed time when the rally is due to begin in a small copse near Tegel prison, no police will show their faces.[14] Writers and scientists such as Lion Feuchtwanger, Arnold Zweig, Erich Kästner, Alexander Roda Roda, Leonhard Frank, Ernst Toller, Max Schroeder and Albert Einstein assemble to provide a guard of honour for the convicted man.

Prison conditions in Tegel are tolerable. The governor regards it as something of an honour to have Ossietzky among his inmates. Carl wears civilian clothes and is permitted to read the *Berliner Tageblatt*, the *Vossische Zeitung*, the *8-Uhr Abendblatt* and *Die Weltbühne*. He writes to Maud, informing her that his cell is brightly lit and freshly painted and that the guards are friendly. He doesn't get tobacco; for a while he is allowed to smoke menthol cigarettes, but later he gets friends to send him chewing gum.[15] The prisoners in the cell next door are just as famous as him in their own way – the safecracking Sass brothers.

Rosalinde receives news of all the hullaballoo surrounding her father in far-off Heppenheim. Maud keeps her abreast of the latest developments by letter, albeit in very ungrammatical German: 'I'm sending you the *Weltspiegel* picture of him going to prison; he went through the gates to the sound of people cheering + shouting Hurrah for him. We've got a fine and good daddy – you've no idea how many nice and kind letters I've received from so many famous people.'[16] Their daughter is used to her mother's rather idiosyncratic way of writing and expressing herself. 'I am coming from India aged 8 and could hardly write my ABC,' Maud wrote to Rosalinde on one occasion, 'although I could speak English + French and had passed my high-school exams at 17, as you know not just from me but also from Daddy.' Later she recounts: 'Carl is to blame for the fact that I don't speak German perfectly, he never used to correct me and laughed when I got all tangled up...'[17] During his time in prison, her husband worries about Maud: 'Neither your letters nor the way you looked when you last came to visit truly set my mind at ease. You seem to me to be incredibly on edge. Don't you think you ought to do something about it?'[18]

3

After seven years, the Reich President's period of office comes to an end in the spring of 1932. In the meantime, Hindenburg has reached the age of eighty-four, and he is exhausted; if he were to successfully run again, he would be ninety-one by the time he stepped down. In the President's study, under glass in a plain wooden frame, there is a yellowing sheet of paper bearing the legend *Ora et labora* ('Pray and Work'). Hindenburg's father wrote it for him when he joined the cadet corps. One spring evening in 1859, the eleven-year-old Paul finds himself standing outside the gates of the cadet training school at Wahlstatt in Lower Silesia. Everything is unfamiliar to him: 'I bade […] my father farewell,'[19] Hindenburg writes in his memoirs. 'There were tears in my eyes, and I saw them drip down onto my "battledress". Then a thought suddenly shot through my head: "Dressed like this you mustn't be weak or cry!" And so I snapped out of my childish sorrow and mingled, not without some trepidation, with my new comrades.' The young Hindenburg spends the summers on his grandfather's estate at Neudeck in East Prussia. His grandfather tells him how, in the winter of 1806–7, he went to see Napoleon, who was encamped at nearby Finckenstein Castle, to seek exemption from war levies but was sent away with a flea in his ear.[20] The young Paul has never wanted to be anything other than an army officer. Just as others desire to learn how to read musical scores, he wants to be able to 'read' battles.

Another memento of the past that Hindenburg keeps in his study is the helmet he wore at the Battle of Königgrätz in 1866. The hole made by an Austrian bullet is clearly visible; it missed him by literally a hair's breadth. Early on, he ceased to wonder at his own cold-bloodedness; after all, how can one alter one's natural disposition?[21] It's now almost seventy years since he first came to Berlin. Thereafter he has enjoyed a meteoric rise, and he was always among the elite. According to his War Academy final report, he is 'an independent, spirited character of great ability'.[22] In 1870, he falls in love for the first time, with a young lady named Irmengard. His happiness is shattered in 1871 when his fiancée succumbs to an incurable disease.

Paul von Hindenburg doesn't get over the pain for many years. Yet he is as accustomed to life's cruelty as he is to the dangers of his chosen profession. 'When all is said and done, war is the normal state of affairs for a soldier, and besides I place myself in God's hands,'[23] he writes to his parents. When the Second German Empire is founded in 1871, he is present at the official ceremony in the Hall of Mirrors at Versailles. All due deference to Prussia, but Germany is the future. Within just a few years, he progresses from having been a student at the War Academy to being an instructor there. It takes eight years for him to pluck up the courage to embark on another affair of the heart. He courts Gertrud von Sperling, organizing a skating party and inviting her to attend a ball. Then he ventures to ask the mother of his intended for her daughter's hand in marriage: 'The best that I have to offer,' he writes, 'is my inexpressibly deep, genuine affection and the honest desire – should I be so lucky as to have her entrusted to me – to carry this precious jewel through life and to be a steadfast support to her in good times and bad.'[24] It turns out to be a happy marriage, and the first of their three children will be called Irmengard.

By now, Gertrud is long dead and his life has run its course; all that he has left now are his children and grandchildren, whom he keeps close, and his faith in God. In these crazy times, could it be this – the straightforwardness he so plausibly embodies – that makes him appealing to people? He reads the Bible every day and underlines various passages, seeking divine guidance in important matters. However complicated everyday life might be, in the end it's all about decisiveness. He has never had any truck with aesthetes or shilly-shallying about what's real or unreal. His favourite play is Schiller's *Wallenstein*: that's a proper drama to warm the cockles of his old soldier's heart, and he can appraise scenes like 'Army Encampment near Nuremberg' or 'Battlefield at Lützen' with an expert eye.[25] He still gets annoyed at how much time and effort he had to expend learning Latin and Greek, and how little practical application this knowledge had in his life. Seven years ago he moved into the presidential palace with his wolfhound Rolf. An avowed monarchist at the head of the German Republic!

A lot has changed in the interim. Covert surveillance vehicles disguised as delivery vans are parked in Wilhelmstraße, observing, photographing and logging every movement, and every visit a secretary of state or a minister makes to the Chancellor or the President. Now even Hindenburg is obliged to deliver campaign speeches and go on political tours. He doesn't like automobiles – 'Petrol ruins the character' – and yet he finds himself obliged to use them ever since he fell off his horse and is plagued by persistent knee pains.[26] His Mercedes limousine with the number plate 'A1–1' is instantly recognizable from a distance thanks to its extraordinarily tall roof.[27] Its bodywork has had to be specially made because the President refuses to remove his top hat inside the vehicle.[28] Hindenburg has grown quite jovial in his old age. On one occasion he is being driven through Hamburg in an open-topped car with the city's mayor sitting beside him. Everywhere they are greeted with thunderous applause and cheering, when all of a sudden there comes a jarring note: a group of people can be heard chanting, quite audibly: 'Mass murderer!' 'They must be insane!' stammers the mayor in embarrassment. Hindenburg reassures his host, telling him: 'Well, that's a matter of opinion.'[29]

Whenever he travels across the country by train, he is in the habit of waving to the brass band that materializes at every station to welcome him. One time, the schedule has put the stopping points at such short intervals that there's scarcely time for Hindenburg even to answer an urgent call of nature. The train pulls in, the music strikes up but there's no sign of Hindenburg. His valet has to knock several times on the door of the WC before the crowd gathered on the platform is rewarded with the sight of the President's familiar face appearing at the carriage window. However, as his entourage notice with horror, this hasty departure is not without its consequences: slowly, Hindenburg's trousers begin to slip over his knees and down to his shoes as he continues, in blissful ignorance, to wave at the choir of schoolchildren.[30] On another occasion, Hindenburg complains about the lack of respect shown by the young men of the SA. Increasingly hard of hearing, he only catches the 'Wake up!' part of their slogan *Deutschland erwache!* and thinks they are mocking his advancing years. The leader of the National Socialist movement touches the same raw nerve when he tactlessly announces: 'The Reich President is eighty-five, and I'm forty-three and feel as fit as a flea!'[31]

Physically, the years are taking their toll on Hindenburg, though his mental faculties remain unimpaired. It is still his aim to achieve a new stability in the country, preferably without involving the left wing and if need be without parliament, too. Despite the great popularity that he enjoys, there are still some black marks: for instance, wasn't the victory at the Battle of Tannenberg actually down to Ludendorff? And on 10 November 1918 – an unforgivable act in the eyes of many monarchists – didn't Hindenburg urgently advise Kaiser Wilhelm II to flee ignominiously to Holland? And don't the field marshal's much-lauded constancy and straightforwardness have their limits when it comes to protecting his own reputation? Hardly anyone in Germany batted an eyelid when, on the occasion of Hindenburg's eightieth birthday, industrialists and wealthy landowners clubbed together to buy back his grandfather's estate in Neudeck and present it to the old man as a gift. What was thought to be in poor taste, however, was for Hindenburg to immediately sign over the property to his son Oskar as a way of avoiding inheritance tax. And the use of agricultural subsidies, the so-called 'Eastern Aid' programme, to redevelop the estate has been a thoroughly shady business. 'All we have left is an old general, / As the last hope for our Republic,' Kurt

Tucholsky writes sarcastically in *Die Weltbühne*.[32] For Hindenburg and the way posterity will see him, there's not much more to be gained but a great deal to be lost.

4

It is only with great difficulty that Brüning can persuade the aged President to run for another term and manages to pull off the feat of getting the Social Democrats to back Hindenburg's re-election. Otto Braun argues in *Vorwärts*: 'A deep gulf in ideology and political understanding separates me from Herr von Hindenburg. Any yet human considerations, which unfortunately all too rarely count for anything in public life nowadays, have created a bridge across this divide. [...] I have got to know the Reich President as a man whose word one can rely upon, as a man of pure intent and calm judgement.'[33] Braun announces that he's going to vote for Hindenburg and exhorts the newspaper's readers: 'Follow my example, defeat Hitler, vote Hindenburg!' Prominent figures like the playwright Gerhard Hauptmann and the painter Max Liebermann also weigh in for Hindenburg. The main concern of the field marshal's followers is to thwart the rival candidate Hitler.

Unlike Thälmann, who stands no chance of winning, the National Socialist leader has a real prospect of victory. He fights the campaign using very modern methods; for instance, 50,000 gramophone records of Hitler's speeches are distributed. But Hindenburg's campaign team is also receptive to technical advances, deploying aeroplanes equipped with loudspeakers that have been specially fitted out by the Junkers aircraft company. These machines bombard Berlin from the air with campaign slogans. 'Swallow your pride or you'll get Hitler!'[34] Otto Braun tells his socialist comrades. Whatever politicians of the other parties choose to do or not to do, constantly lurking in the background is the spectre of National Socialism.

Hindenburg succeeds in winning re-election only in the second round of voting. The President blames his Chancellor for failing to assemble a majority from among the right-wing electorate. Goebbels rubs salt in the wound, taunting Hindenburg in the Reichstag for 'having clearly thrown in his lot with Social Democracy'[35] and for winning plaudits 'from the party of deserters'. The President rebuffs an acquaintance who congratulates him on his victory: 'Who elected me, though? The Socialists, the Catholics and the *Berliner Tageblatt*, that's who. My own people didn't vote for me.'[36] Brüning recalls: 'I got the feeling that he'd dropped me.'[37]

Schleicher has been negotiating with the Nazis since the previous year. Together with Ernst Röhm and Count Helldorff, he moots the idea of using the SA as an auxiliary army, in order to 'enlarge the Reichswehr with a militia'.[38] Couldn't this unit be used to augment the border force in the east? Or will the SA be neutralized by merging it with other militias like the 'Stahlhelm' and the 'Reichsbanner' within some 'Reich Youth Training Board'?[39] It is a strange role, not remotely provided for in the Republic's constitution, in which Schleicher now finds himself operating: as secretary of state in the Ministry of the Reichswehr and as a friend of Hindenburg's son, he has unrestricted access to the Reich President, and he often knows what's afoot well before Brüning. Sometimes the three of them – Brüning, Oskar von Hindenburg and Schleicher – 'will sit together over a bottle, arguing about how to implement the old man's wishes'.[40] Hardly any major decision in domestic politics happens without Schleicher's input. He is a kind of political back-seat driver.

In April 1932, he tries to set the course for the new administration. He is keen to place more weight on 'the right shoulder'[41] and so puts out feelers to the National Socialists. Schleicher justifies his strategy in this regard: 'Business knows full well why it votes the most awkward and voluble shareholders onto the Board.'[42] Indeed, ever since the NSDAP recorded its first major electoral successes, many have been toying with the thought of taming or wearing down the National Socialists by involving them in government. Even among the Social Democrats, there are 'powerful forces who would be quite happy to see the National Socialists in government in order that they might be brought down by the experience,'[43] reports the *Berliner Tageblatt*. In the meantime, Brüning refuses to expand his cabinet to include ministers from the ranks of the NSDAP; what he has in mind is reinstating the monarchy as a way out of the political crisis. But his star is on the wane.

'I must finally turn to the right, then,' Hindenburg is said to have told Brüning, with tears in his eyes and head in hands.[44] 'The newspapers and the people are clamouring for it. But you've always refused to do so.' Army Minister Wilhelm Groener puts a different slant on things: 'We want to reel in the Nazis without driving the SPD into opposition.'[45] Following a spate of bloody incidents, Schleicher's boss has imposed a ban on the SA and the SS, and defends his action in parliament. It is a lacklustre speech that the army minister delivers to the Reichstag, amid constant interruptions by NSDAP delegates.[46] Yet Groener's actions against the SA threaten to frustrate Schleicher's plan to steer the National Socialist movement 'towards responsibility and disciplined collaboration in running the state'.[47] After his performance in parliament, Groener's ministerial position becomes untenable. At the end of April and the beginning of May 1932, Schleicher meets with Hitler and the two quickly settle on a course of action. In return for the promise that the newly proscribed SA will be unbanned and parliament dissolved pending new elections, the National Socialists agree to tolerate a new cabinet that has shifted to the right. Goebbels notes triumphantly in his diary: 'Brüning should fall in the next few days.'[48]

Just as Schleicher had smoothed his path into the chancellorship, so he now engineers Brüning's downfall. On 2 May 1932, the two men hold a meeting that lasts four hours. Brüning does not regard Schleicher as an intriguer by nature, but as one of those people who are 'so wrapped up in confidential and hypothetical matters that they discount things that are obvious and enduring.'[49] He notes: 'A state cannot get back on its feet when, as is the case with us, two talented people simultaneously pursue their political agendas, one of them openly and overtly and the other in secret.'[50] Their meeting ends in a split. Some polite, formulaic pleasantries are exchanged. In parting, Brüning enquires how Schleicher's wife Elisabeth is doing, whereupon the general flinches, lowers his eyes and replies hesitantly: 'That's the really awkward thing: my wife keeps telling me that you're right and that I'm not always composed enough to make important decisions.'[51]

5

On 26 May 1932, the telephone rings at Papen's house in Wallerfangen on the Saar, and Kurt von Schleicher asks his old comrade to come and see him in Berlin. Two days later, on a Sunday morning, the two men are seated opposite one another in Bendlerstraße. They discuss the current political impasse, Brüning's refusal to appoint a more right-wing cabinet and ways to reform the Weimar constitution so as to circumvent parliament and disempower the Social Democrats, who are still the ruling party in Prussia. They then come on to the question of a possible successor to Brüning as Chancellor. Together, they run through several candidates. Finally, Schleicher asks Papen straight out whether he might not like to assume this office. Caught unawares, Papen at first dismisses the idea out of hand, whereupon Schleicher resorts to flattery: 'But I've already put your name forward to the old man – he'd be delighted at your appointment.'[52]

Papen requests some time to think it over. He visits his old friend Hans Humann in Neubabelsberg, the son of archaeologist Carl Humann, who discovered the site of ancient Pergamon in Asia Minor. They weigh up the pros and cons of Schleicher's offer: 'In a little sailing dinghy, as befitted my friend's passion for all things nautical, we were able to freely express our views in the idyllic peace and solitude of the Wannsee.'[53] Humann shares Papen's scepticism.

Armed with fresh arguments, Papen sets off on Monday morning for Bendlerstraße fully intending to turn Schleicher down. But by the time he takes his leave of the general, he has all but agreed once more. On the Tuesday morning, Papen holds a meeting with the leader of the Centre Party. Here he learns that Schleicher's offer has already done the rounds. Even the French ambassador André François-Poncet knows who is on the cards to succeed Brüning. Papen's party chairman makes it clear to him that, if he were to assume the chancellorship, he would face the opposition of his own party, so Papen promises to tell the President that he is declining the post. A quarter of an hour later he is standing in front of Hindenburg: 'As always he received me with fatherly kindness. "Now then, my dear Papen, will you help me out in these difficult circumstances?" he asked me in his sonorous voice.'[54] The following day, Franz von Papen is sworn in as the new Chancellor of the Reich. His list of ministers is already confirmed. Schleicher has arranged everything, including appointing himself as the new army minister.

The last few weeks have not done Heinrich Brüning any favours; he has been suffering from cardiac arrhythmia. On the same day he is dismissed, he leaves the Reich Chancellery and goes to visit friends in Paretzer Straße in Wilmersdorf.[55] There, the ex-Chancellor spends the evening playing board games like *Mensch, ärgere Dich nicht*[*] and Halma with his god-daughter.[56]

---

[*] *Mensch, ärgere Dich nicht* ('Don't get angry, man') is a popular German board game similar to Ludo for up to six players, which was devised in the early twentieth century. Like Halma, an American game from the 1880s, it is a game of strategy. [Translator's note]

The Coup

1

'Have you noticed how alike the National Socialists and the Communists are?'[1] Aristide Briand asks the journalist Bella Fromm. 'You only need listen to their speeches. The arguments are so similar that you have to wait till the end to see whether the audience gives straight-armed salutes or raises clenched fists.' Bella Fromm is one of those who hang around Wilhelmstraße in the hope of gleaning as much information as they can about current political affairs. The press aren't allowed to attend the Reich President's annual reception for the Diplomatic Corps. Disguised as a man, Fromm drives to the Kaiserhof Hotel, leaves her car there and wanders about the government district without being recognized. Because she knows the number plates of almost all the important diplomats' cars, she is able to put all the significant pieces of the puzzle together and – much to the annoyance of her colleagues on other newspapers – to file a rather vivid report of the event.[2]

When Hindenburg was elected President for the first time, Fromm wrote in her diary: 'I have a genuine admiration for this great soldier. But is he the man Germany needs right now? Isn't he too old? And too easily influenced?'[3] Soon after writing

this, she gets to meet him at a tea organized by the wife of Oskar von Hindenburg, the President's daughter-in-law: 'The young Hindenburgs aren't terribly likeable; they are stand-offish and snooty.'[4] However, the 'old gentleman' stops by for half an hour: 'The whole room fell silent when he came in. This was the first time I'd met him. Over six foot tall, and with close-cropped hair. He walked with some difficulty. He kissed the hands of all the ladies present, in the chivalrous manner of the old school.'[5]

Since early childhood, Bella Fromm has been used to hobnobbing with the great and the good. Her father, a wine merchant from Kitzingen in Lower Franconia, is a purveyor by appointment to the Bavarian royal household. Here, in the sun-kissed Main Valley, Bella grows up the daughter of a Jewish family that has already been resident in Franconia for more than seven generations. Occasionally, Prince Ludwig of Bavaria drops by and strolls with them around the family's old vineyards. She receives an education befitting her station as the daughter of well-to-do parents, first attending a school in Frankfurt and then a music conservatory in Hanover, where she learns the piano, organ and singing. No sooner has she come of age, in 1911, than she is married to a Berlin businessman, Max Israel. She gives birth to their daughter Gonny two years later.

For the sake of Max, a wealthy textile manufacturer, Bella leaves her Franconian homeland and moves to Berlin. But the marriage brings her no happiness, and Max cheats on her. She accuses her husband of 'having a love affair with Miss Lisa Abel, addressing her by the familiar "Du" form, and kissing and embracing her',[6] and files for divorce. The accusations against Max weigh so heavily with the court that it finds in favour of the plaintiff Bella and rules that there has been an irretrievable breakdown of the marriage. Three years later, in 1922, she marries again. But when, not long after, the period of rampant inflation brings the collapse of her second husband's business, and she also loses her family's inheritance, she is forced to earn her own living.

She first finds work as a local journalist on the *Grunewald Echo*, and as a sports reporter for both the *12-Uhr-Blatt* and the in-house magazine of the Rot-Weiß tennis club. But she is best known for the pieces she contributes to the *Berlin Börsen-Courier* and the two titles owned by the Ullstein publishing house, the *Berliner Zeitung* and the *Vossische Zeitung*. She describes her new situation: 'I attended the same parties as before, only now as a reporter.'[7] In the process, she makes some disturbing observations: 'The upper classes are moving closer to Hitler. They are closing their ears to his constant diatribes against the privileged classes and "polite society". My grandfather had a very apposite phrase for this kind of fickle person: "You'd spit in his eye and he'd ask you if it's raining."'[8]

Despite the uncouth behaviour of the SA, anti-Semitism is not yet a serious threat. Among the upper crust, it is addressed with little more than ironic innuendo. For instance, one day Bella Fromm encounters Crown Prince Wilhelm, who recounts how he once courted another attractive Jewish lady and wanted to ask her to come for a spin in his car. The lady declined, telling him: 'It would be just too ghastly if we were to have an accident and our bodies were unrecognizably mangled. Then I could easily be interred for all eternity in the Hohenzollern burial vault in Charlottenburg Cemetery, and I dare say you'd find the thought of being laid to rest at the Jewish Cemetery in Weißensee pretty unsettling too.'[9] Bella Fromm is firmly convinced that Hindenburg would never allow Hitler to become Reich Chancellor. It's rumoured that he once said to Otto Meissner, Head of the Presidential Office: 'What would I want with that brown-hatter?'[10]

2

Otto Braun's Prussia is the last bastion of Social Democracy in Germany. Yet the Red Czar's throne is under siege from all sides. 'Whoever controls Prussia also has control of Germany,'[11] claims

Franz Seldte, Federal Leader of the Stahlhelm organization, which together with the German Nationalists instigates a referendum on the dissolution of the Prussian parliament. This move has the support of the smaller parties and also the NSDAP. And at the eleventh hour, under pressure from Stalin, the communists also weigh in on the side of the right-wing enemies of the Republic. The Prussian government fights back, issuing the following statement to all newspapers that appear in Prussia just three days before the plebiscite: 'Anyone who wants a Soviet Prussia or a Fascist Prussia should go to the polls and vote "Yes" in the referendum.'[12] In August 1931, the plebiscite fails in its aim and the Prussian government remains in office. But it's merely a reprieve. 'I have the distinct feeling that the Brown pestilence is spreading! You can't seem to escape its disgusting presence wherever you go,'[13] writes Bella Fromm. At a lunchtime engagement, she remarks: 'The Grill Room at the "Kaiserhof" presented the interesting spectacle of Nazi leaders lounging about in comfortable chairs. Some of them even turned up in their hideous brown uniforms.' The lunch party includes the SA leader Ernst Röhm, Prince August Wilhelm of the House of Hohenzollern and his friend Count Helldorff.

The National Socialists are a young force; they are the parvenus among the political parties of the right, a splinter group that has suddenly come up in the world. Initially, no one knows if they will sink back into obscurity just as quickly. In any event, in times of growing despair, their wild mix of an agitprop group and a gang of thugs makes the traditional right wing look old-fashioned. Under their egocentric leader Alfred Hugenberg,* the Nationalists have distanced themselves even more from the Republic. Hugenberg may have the press at his command, but Hitler has increasingly

---

* Alfred Hugenberg (1865–1951) was a businessman who was closely associated with the Krupp armaments firm. In 1920, he entered the Reichstag as a member of the German National People's Party and in 1928 became its leader. Like other traditional conservatives, Hugenberg fatally miscalculated that he would be able to use Hitler and the NSDAP to further his own ambitions. [Translator's note]

captured the imagination of the young. The two join forces on just one occasion, in October 1931 at Bad Harzburg, but it's a half-hearted alliance, because Hitler has long since renounced any idea of sharing power.

The communists continue to be seen as more dangerous than the Nazis because they quite openly act as agents of a foreign power. 'I promise at all times to fight unceasingly for the Soviet Union and the victorious world revolution, and to always be a pioneer of irreconcilable class hatred within all proletarian mass organizations, trade unions and the workplace,'[14] runs the battle pledge of the proscribed communist Red Front Fighters' League. In the provinces, National Socialists are already drawing up plans to deal with the contingency of an attempted communist coup. One measure is the immediate establishment of concentration camps for political opponents. 'Resistance will as a matter of principle be punishable by death,' runs one of the provisions of the so-called 'Boxheim Papers'.[15] When these are made public in November 1931, the outrage is intense but short-lived.

The election campaign gets going in the spring. Voting for the Prussian regional parliament is held pretty much in parallel with the presidential election. During the campaign, Otto Braun falls ill with a serious bout of flu and a painful bilious attack; he keeps himself going with a combination of tablets and alcohol but struggles all the while with fainting fits. While delivering a speech at the Sportpalast in April 1932, he gets bogged down in details and repeatedly falters. In addition to his failing health, he's also facing an even more serious problem: 'I was supposed to instil the masses of people who attended huge public rallies with a confidence in victory that I myself did not possess.'[16] After the SPD's final election rally at the Lustgarten, Otto Braun suffers a circulatory collapse.

3

The outcome of the election on 24 April 1932 is as expected: the National Socialists increase their showing from less than 2 per cent at the last regional polls to 37 per cent of the votes cast, which now makes them the single largest party in Prussia as well as many other parts of the country. However, they are not in a position to nominate the state premier as they have not cleared the newly introduced hurdle of an absolute majority. Accordingly, the old administration remains in office, conducting business as before. The National Socialists have also become the strongest political party in Hesse, too, and have only just failed to achieve this in Bavaria, while in the Free State of Anhalt, a National Socialist becomes premier for the very first time. Even so, it's not the decisive breakthrough they'd hoped for, as Goebbels make clear when he summarizes the results: 'Something's got to happen now. We must gain power in the near future or all we'll end up doing is winning all the battles but losing the war.'[17] As for the Social Democrats, their election defeat presents them with a real headache; part of the SPD argues that the party should withdraw from the Prussian parliament and cede power to the NSDAP. 'I'm pretty much at the end of my tether,' Braun admits to a friend, 'and I'm longing for the day when I can step down from office.'[18] The situation in the regional assembly takes on an ever more carnivalesque atmosphere, with unemployed people thronging the public gallery in anticipation of free entertainment.[19]

In what is only the second session of the new parliament, proceedings begin with a regular brawl. Wilhelm Pieck of the KPD provokes the National Socialists with a speech accusing them of having presided over the mass murder of revolutionary workers; he baldly states that the Nazi ranks contain hundreds of murderers.[20] This sets the two factions at one another's throats. As National Socialists surge forward to attack him, Pieck is protected by a human shield of communist deputies. Chairs, tables, cast-iron inkwells, lamps and drawers are used as missiles, delegates pull one another's hair and try to throttle each other by tugging on their ties.[21] The NSDAP is clearly in the ascendancy. 'Blood was streaming down the faces of some Communist deputies, forming pools on the floor and a red track on the carpet leading from the debating chamber to the first-aid room,' runs the report of the fracas in the next day's *Vossische Zeitung*. Once the communists have been driven out of the parliament, the Nazis sing all four stanzas of the 'Horst Wessel Song'. Goebbels notes in his diary; '8 seriously injured from various parties. This was a shot across the bows. It's the only way to win respect.'[22]

Braun stays away from the next sitting of the Prussian assembly.[*] The NSDAP and the KPD both vote in favour of a motion requiring representatives of the state government to attend parliament. Leader of the NSDAP faction Wilhelm Kube argues: 'As long as these gentlemen keep drawing their considerable salaries in these straitened times, they should appear here.' Wilhelm Kasper of the KPD lends his support to this demand: 'Today, the Braun–Severing administration stands in the dock here, accused of having implemented the criminal policies that have hitherto been inflicted upon the working masses in Prussia.' Kube sums up this tactical consensus with military brevity: 'Along with the Communists and the German Nationalists, we say to the Braun cabinet: It's time to face your final roll-call!' Braun refuses point-blank: 'I've no wish to subject myself to the guttersnipe insults of hoodlums in a parliamentary assembly that now has all the decorum of a cheap dive.'[23]

Nothing seems capable now of stemming the rising tide of violence. Braun takes voluntary leave of absence, clears his room and places ongoing business in the hands of his deputy. Apathetically and for the most part bedridden, he follows the

---

[*] The next sitting took place on 2 June 1932.

dramatic events that unfold over the following weeks from his home in Zehlendorf.

4

Elections to the Reichstag are scheduled for the end of July 1932 – after the two rounds of the presidential election and the regional elections to the Prussian parliament, this is the fourth poll in quick succession. Up till now, one bloody incident has been followed by another. The rescinding of the ban on the SA, one of the first official acts Papen undertakes, sees the violence reach a new peak. As the *Vossische Zeitung* reports in June: 'The fact that this election campaign is exacerbating the already febrile situation is a story in itself.'[24]

Through the length and breadth of Germany, hundreds of thousands of mostly unemployed young men are involved in street fights between paramilitary units. The communists and the National Socialists are responsible for most of the brutal violence. The German Nationalists also maintain their own militia in the form of the Stahlhelm. A common aim unites these three groups: the abolition of the democratic 'system' in favour of an authoritarian state. Standing in opposition to them is the Reichsbanner Schwarz-Rot-Gold ('Reich Flag Black-Red-Gold') organization, whose members are mostly Social Democrats or supporters of the Catholic Centre Party and the Liberals. Its purpose is to 'fight against the Swastika and the Red Star'[25] and ensure the survival of the Weimar Republic.

But even the Republican side and its self-defence leagues, known variously as 'protection squads' or 'strike forces', soon abandons all restraint. The leadership of the Reichsbanner calls upon its fighting units to use 'steely resolve and an iron fist to smash the enemy'. They take to chanting the rhyming slogan: *Schlagt Hitler, den Gendarmen, samt Hauptmann Röhm, den Warmen!* ('Smash

Hitler, the village policeman, and Captain Röhm, the queer!').[26] The opposing groups are outwardly so similar that police officers are issued with pictures of uniforms to stop them constantly confusing the Reichsbanner's 'protection groups' with the SA.[27]

In the Silesian town of Ohlau (Oława), for once the violence is not instigated by the National Socialists. On Sunday 10 July, competitors who have come there to take part in a sports festival organized by the NSDAP are confronted by members of the Social Democrat self-defence league. The district authority's subsequent report of the incident relates what happened: 'As the first participants in the National Socialist Sports Day began to arrive in Ohlau, they were apparently pelted with stones by a large crowd of people wearing armbands bearing the insignia of the Eiserne Front ('Iron Front'), the Reichsbanner and the communists.'[28] The situation gets really out of hand when Reichsbanner reinforcements arrive from their clubhouse. The men start laying into the National Socialists with fence palings. Four Nazis sustain serious injuries and one man, who has already suffered a fractured skull, is thrown unconscious into the River Ohle; his body is later recovered from the water. The Reichsbanner men finally resort to using firearms, killing an SA stormtrooper with a shot to the head. On 14 July 1932 Papen gets the President to sign an emergency decree paving the way for the dissolution of the Prussian parliament. However, Papen believes that he does not as yet have sufficient pretexts for legitimizing such a move.

Soon after, on the rainy Sunday of 17 July, some 7,000 members of the SA march through the Hamburg district of Altona, a stronghold of the KPD. At around 4.30 in the afternoon, the propaganda march reaches the old city and turns into the densely built-up working-class quarter. Here, the first fist fights break out between the rival groups. Prior to the march, Antifascist Action, a successor organization to the banned Red Front Fighting League, has distributed leaflets calling for resistance. Police reinforcements arrive from Hamburg city centre, but they are unable to separate the two camps. The first shots now ring out; two SA men are killed by the communists. Precisely what happens during the next few minutes will become the subject of numerous court hearings spanning six decades.[29] The final death toll is eighteen; alongside the two SA men, sixteen innocent bystanders are also killed by stray police gunfire.[30] Ninety-one communists are arrested, of whom only four come from Altona; the remainder, all members of Antifascist Action, have travelled from Hamburg to attend the protest.

Events now unfold at breakneck speed. Papen exaggerates the significance of a meeting in the Prussian Interior Ministry involving socialist and communist deputies to claim it heralds the threat of an SPD–KPD alliance, and seizes the opportunity to win greater control over the Prussian police, who are still answerable to the Social Democrat regime. After the Reichswehr, the police are the most significant force for imposing law and order in Germany. The final disempowerment of the Prussian government passes off without a hitch on 20 July 1932. The foremost representatives of the administration are summoned to the Reich Chancellery and politely informed that they have been dismissed and that their duties will henceforth come under the remit of a Reich Commissar, since it appeared that security and public order could no longer be guaranteed in Prussia.

At a quarter to eleven that morning, privy councillor Willi Katerbitz rings the doorbell of the furloughed Prussian prime minister Otto Braun in Dessauer Straße and hands him a confidential letter bearing the official seal of the Reich Chancellery, from which it emerges that Papen is relieving him of his office as the acting premier of Prussia. Braun's first thought is to drive in a fit of fury to the Ministry of State, which makes for a brief moment of panic at the Reich Chancellery, where they are amazed at how smoothly everything has gone thus far. But Braun, who is not given to grand gestures, soon thinks better of this. That evening, his interior minister Carl Severing allows himself to be escorted from his office with words that later go down in history: 'I am only submitting to this under duress.'[31]

What the head of the Reichsbanner has to say when rumours of the impending 'Prussian Coup' first reach him sounds much more like fighting talk: 'We'll crush them like lice.'[32] So why have the ruling Social Democrats made it so easy for Papen? 'I saw Reichsbanner members in tears at that time,' the Social Democrat Reichstag delegate Otto Buchwitz later reports. 'And long-serving party officials threw their membership cards at us.'[33] Didn't Severing have command of 6,000 policemen in Berlin, 'fine, freshly recruited, well organized and well-trained police officers and administrators'?[34] Yet in the long run, what use would they be against the army? So couldn't a general strike have been called in alliance with the communists? First, in view of the horrendous prevailing unemployment situation, there were quite justified doubts about workers' willingness to go on strike. And secondly, as Carl Severing pointed out, 'it would have been positively childish to believe that the communists would have unconditionally put themselves at the service of the Weimar Coalition.'[35] When all was said and done, republican authority had already evaporated with the election result on 24 April, and it was only a matter of time before power changed hands.

The former Prussian government challenges Papen's actions in the Constitutional Court, since the grounds for the 'federal intervention' are highly spurious to say the least. The fact that the situation in Prussia escalated to the brink of civil war – in just over two months, eighty-three people have lost their lives in political clashes – was not down to a lack of will on the part of the Social Democrats to confront the violence on the streets, but principally to the central government's lifting of the proscription against the SA.[36] In October 1932, the Constitutional Court fails to reach a clear adjudication on this question. While upholding the basic legality of Papen's actions, it nonetheless rules that his dismissal of the Prussian administration was unlawful. As a result, two Prussian governments co-exist henceforth – the old 'sovereign government', which is powerless, and the 'commissariat government', which governs at Papen's behest.

'I must capture your head!' the artist Max Liebermann implores Otto Braun on numerous occasions. 'When I have the time' is the latter's stock response. Following the 'Prussian Coup', Liebermann rings up and comes straight to the point. 'It's a real scandal,' he announces in his broad Berlin accent, 'but at least you've got some time on your hands now, so you must sit for me. Plus I've had a commission from your minister of culture.' Braun duly goes to see Liebermann at his villa on the shores of the Wannsee. He is amazed at the physical sprightliness of the eighty-five-year-old artist as he darts back and forth between his easel and his sitter's stool: 'You know, Prime Minister, painting's a lot like making love; while you're at it you don't feel tired at all, but once it's over you're absolutely knackered!'[37]

His excursion to the Wannsee is a rare moment of relaxation and distraction for Braun. For a long time he's been hoping that he might be able to lay down the burden of responsibility. But there now ensues a bizarre epilogue to his time in government. He and his erstwhile ministers still hold weekly cabinet meetings, despite wielding virtually no authority any more. Papen does his utmost to thwart the work of the former cabinet. He sends the following memo to his staff: 'If requests of any kind are received from the old Prussian government, they should be handled in a thoroughly dilatory way.'[38]

In response to Braun's demand that appropriate rooms be made available to the Prussian government, he is assigned a single office in the Prussian Welfare Ministry, divided by flimsy cardboard partitions into three tiny rooms.[39] Over the coming months, this is the home of the cabinet office of the largest German state. Subsequently, even this space is denied them, so that the rightful government of Prussia is forced to meet in restaurants and pubs.[40] 'The Braun government died an unlovely – if sovereign – death, far from the limelight: a grim reminder of the party's impotence,' writes Carl von Ossietzky in *Die Weltbühne*.[41] In these dark days, Otto Braun leaves his house in Zehlendorf only on rare occasions. He doesn't need to step outside his front door to read the signs of the times. From his window, directly opposite, he can watch the comings and goings, day and night, at the *Sturmabteilung* barracks just across the street.[42]

Balls of Destiny

1

'There's a mood of oppressive excitement,' writes Siegfried Kracauer, who has been sent by the *Frankfurter Zeitung* to review one of Hanussen's shows, 'which just goes to prove beyond all doubt how people's expectations of miracles have been heightened by these crisis times. As if a miracle could solve the crisis! Still, many people clearly prefer waiting in the gloom for him to appear to coming up with a systematic plan to improve their lot – now that really would be the only genuine miracle.'[1] And who'd even be interested in 'systematically improving' his or her lot when there's this far simpler alternative? Hanussen has devised a new routine: he throws 'balls of destiny' into the audience. Anyone who catches one can keep it, and in addition is given Hanussen's autograph and the opportunity of a brief Q&A session with the magician. But it's even simpler still if you're given the gift of second sight yourself! All the information on this can be found in Hanussen's newspaper. Readers who have worked their way through an interview with Thomas Mann or an account of the magician's meeting with Gerhart Hauptmann will find on the inside pages an advertisement for a miracle plant from South America, which gives those who ingest it 'the talent for prophecy'.

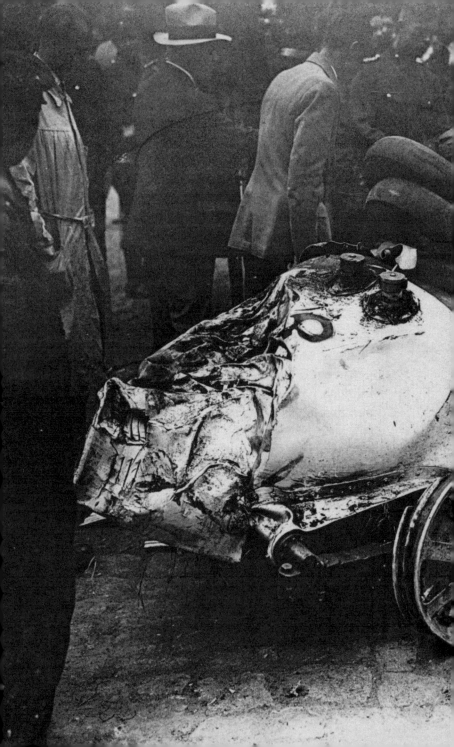

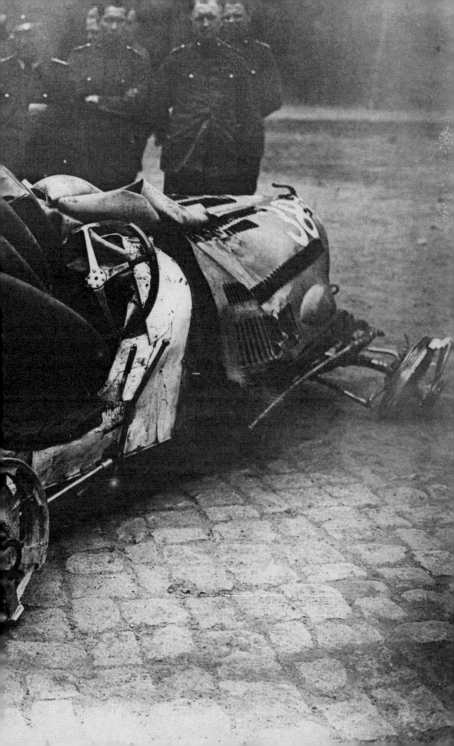

It contains the hallucinogen harmine.* Hanussen has tested it on a wide range of subjects, including a musician, a scientist and a career criminal with a long string of convictions. Finally, he puts himself in a trance by taking it.

A constant stream of new ideas for enthralling the public spurs the magician on. On the occasion of a reception for the press in the Grand Hotel Esplanade in May 1932, he stages a hunt for a hidden object with the help of a medium. Blindfolded, he leads an excited and intrigued crowd across Potsdamer Platz to a pharmacy. Here he locates the object he is looking for – a doll – in one of the many drawers behind the counter. The clairvoyant is omnipresent around this time. In a radio interview with Alfred Braun, he talks about the case of American aviator Charles Lindbergh's kidnapped son. But when, quite unbidden, Hanussen gives the legendary reporter Braun a tip that he should withdraw the investments he has in Liechtenstein, the broadcast is suddenly cut off. Wherever there are wagers being placed and people have gathered in large numbers – at major sporting events like the Six-Day Bicycle Race or horse-racing meets – you'll find Hanussen. The clairvoyant also appears at the trotting track at Hoppegarten and annoys the on-course bookies there by acting as a tipster; he also likes giving stock market tips and forecasting the outcome of motor races.

A motor race has been scheduled for 22 May 1932 on the AVUS.† Five days prior to this, Hanussen predicts that Count Lobkowicz is in great danger. The young Czech racing driver has, just a few weeks before, purchased a Bugatti T 54, a car consisting pretty much entirely of the engine. This eight-cylinder monster has a reputation for being difficult to control. When fuelled with petrol, the engine generates 300 horsepower, but if methanol is used instead this

---

* Harmine occurs naturally in various plants. One of these, *Psychotria viridis*, is the main constituent of *ayahuasca*, which is used in shamanistic rites by indigenous peoples of the Amazon Basin. [Translator's note]

† A section of public autobahn in Berlin, also used as a motor-racing circuit. [Translator's note]

can be boosted to 450 hp. In England the T 54 is known as 'The Widow-Maker'. 'Scanning the starting list and seeing the Count's name, I was immediately seized by a premonition of the terrible impending accident,'[2] Hanussen claims. He begs the chief press officer of the German Automobile Club to use some pretext or other to withdraw the count from the line-up. The stenographer's record of Hanussen's prophecy reads: 'Count Lobkowicz must drive carefully, as he is under the aspect of an accident.'[3] Unmoved by this, the twenty-five-year-old racing driver starts from last position on the grid. Just before the eight-kilometre mark, after Lobkowicz has battled his way up to fourth place, his car swerves violently while taking a curve and side-swipes a railway embankment at a speed of 200 kph. The driver is flung from the car onto the tracks and dies shortly after arrival at a hospital in Charlottenburg.

However, it's not just admiration that Hanussen garners for his clairvoyance; on the contrary, the communist newspaper *Welt am Abend* even accuses him of being complicit in the count's death. Lobkowicz, the article claims, learned of the prophecy and was unnerved by it. Naturally, it has not escaped the notice of the left wing that Hanussen has made common cause with the National Socialists. In the spring of 1932, the editor-in-chief of the paper *Berlin am Morgen*, Bruno Frei, takes up the cudgels against Hanussen's 'clairvoyance hoax'. Like the *Welt am Abend*, this tabloid is part of the communist media empire built up by Willi Münzenberg. These two titles, whose standard fare comprises sex scandals, suicides and political agitation, reach a far larger readership than the official party newspaper *Die Rote Fahne*, which is written in the dull newspeak of party apparatchiks. In his campaign, which he runs under the title 'A Charlatan Conquers Berlin', Frei adopts a deliberately insulting tone to try and goad Hanussen into litigation. Ammunition for his series of articles is supplied by Erich Juhn, the magician's former secretary, who is out for revenge. 'Hitler and Hanussen are a good fit,' Bruno Frei writes. 'But precisely because socialism is the product of a scientific outlook, it is duty-bound to fight against all forms of superstition and spiritualism. And against human stupidity and those who exploit it.'[4]

In the meantime, Hanussen is living it up on his motor yacht *Ursel IV*. On tour in the Netherlands and Denmark, he still finds time to stay in touch with the outside world by postcard. Even the philosopher Count Hermann von Keyserling, who runs a teaching academy known as the 'School of Wisdom' in Darmstadt, receives one such missive. The front of the postcard, which is produced by the 'Hanussen Printing and Publishing House', shows a 'Corner of the Sleeping Cabin' on board the yacht, furnished in the Biedermeier style; the reverse is decorated with a large stamp in red ink reading 'Posted from on board the Cabin Cruiser *Ursel IV*' and below this the legend: 'Owner: Erik Jan Hanussen'. There's just enough room for nine handwritten words of greeting and the signature 'E. J. Hanussen'.[5] The proud 'owner' of the vessel lives according to Goethe's dictum: *Nur die Lumpen sind bescheiden, / Brave freuen sich der Tat* ('Only nobodies are humble, / The bold take the bull by the horns'). By this stage, his fame has spread throughout Europe. He stays at the most exclusive hotels and fills auditoria. Things don't always go according to plan, though. In Copenhagen he struggles to hypnotize the Chief of Police and is eventually forced to admit defeat. And he is refused entry to Norway because the authorities there fear that hypnotism is injurious to health. His tour continues on to France, via Switzerland.

'Hanussen is the Cagliostro of the German Starvation Republic, the Rasputin of Hitler's Germany. The bubbling morass that pushed him to the surface, and onward to fame and fortune, also reveals the seething, red-hot crater of the social volcano. Pretty soon, it's going to blow,'[6] believes Bruno Frei, 'in a revolution whose glowing lava mass will bury the overstuffed palaces of a rotten society.' After Frei has long since been forced into exile, Hanussen will mock the 'notorious Dr Bruno Frei' as the author of a 'Bolshevist diatribe' against him. For the present, though, he takes seriously Frei's threat to 'settle his hash' and not to rest until 'Berlin has been cleansed of the last remnants of this clairvoyance filth'.[7] To safeguard against hecklers at his performances, Hanussen engages the services of the Charlottenburg SA-Sturm number 33, which has set up its HQ in the Zur Altstadt pub in Hebbelstraße. It was here that SA stormtroopers murdered twenty-two-year-old communist Otto Grüneberg in February 1931.[8]

It seems that 'Hanussen the Dane' has no fear of contact, at least not the same phobia as was said to afflict the Jew Steinschneider. In the building at Hedemannstraße, which the Nazi regional administration will presently use as their main site for interrogation and torture, the clairvoyant is observed passing over an envelope to Count Helldorff. All in all, Hanussen is rumoured to have lent the count, a notorious gambler with constant, heavy gaming debts, 150,000 Reichsmarks against IOUs. The count's adjutant Wilhelm Ohst also borrows money from Hanussen, as do his deputy Karl Ernst and even SA chief Ernst Röhm, who has an appointment every morning for a shave and trim with the magician's personal barber.[9] Hanussen reckons he has the entire leadership of the SA in his pocket. Through his weekly magazine, which eventually attains a print run of 140,000, Hanussen's involvement in politics is growing all the time. He correctly prophesies the result of the presidential elections in 1932 and in March of that year maps out 'Hitler's future while in a trance'.[10]

The clairvoyant espouses the National Socialist cause ever more frequently and unequivocally. 'The idea of National Socialism will grow and come to rule the world,'[11] his magazine proclaims at the beginning of December. A 'Death Horoscope for the Reichstag'[12] appears in the same place a fortnight later. And after the parliamentary elections in November 1932, Hanussen predicts that there will be an 'attempt to launch a politically motivated attack on a public building, or perhaps on a particular individual'.[13] This is followed in December by the following statement: 'We will acquire a leadership, comprising the newly reunified Nationalist tendencies, which will have to be categorized as an authoritarian regime of the strictest kind [...] The very existence of the Communist Party is threatened to an extraordinary degree by this strongly rightward-leaning government.'[14]

As things stand, though, all kinds of unpleasantness are threatened from this direction. In August 1932 Bruno Frei's *Berlin am Morgen* prints an exposé of 'Erik Jan Hanussen, or to give him his proper Jewish name, Hermann Steinschneider'.[15] To start with, things remain quiet in the Nazi press, but it's not long before the Goebbels-run paper *Der Angriff* picks up the story, describing Hanussen, alias Steinschneider, as 'a well-known Jew'.[16] Now things begin to get sticky for the magician. Through Count Helldorff's good offices he manages to get a retraction printed in the next day's *Angriff*: the paper maintains it has been informed by a 'well-placed source' that Hanussen 'is not a Jew'.[17]

Bruno Frei has the bit between his teeth, however, describing the clairvoyant as the 'descendant of Moravian rabbis [...] the nephew of Rabbi Daniel Prossnitz from Pressburg [Bratislava]'.[18] The muckraker-in-chief behind these revelations is Hanussen's former secretary Juhn, who was witness at his master's wedding ceremony at the synagogue in Rumburg. Juhn obtains a copy of a letter from the rabbinate formally confirming the marriage. On 12 January 1933, *Berlin am Morgen* reproduces on its front page a facsimile of this document, issued by the Rumburg Jewish Community. Beneath it, the paper has also reprinted, again in facsimile, the title page of the last edition of *Hanussens Bunter Wochenschau*, resplendent with a swastika and a photograph of Hitler.

Where the dispassionate reader is concerned, this slugging match in the press has undoubted entertainment value, but for Hanussen – coming as it does just weeks before the dawning of the Third Reich, which he has anticipated with such great enthusiasm – it is fraught with danger. In 1980 Bruno Frei voiced misgivings about what he had done: 'When I began hounding Hanussen, I was faced with a moral issue. Here was a drummer-boy for the

"Death to Jews!" brigade who was himself a Jew. Was it right to air this fact – especially considering I'm a Jew too? Was I justified in turning Hermann back into Herschmann? Should I have been providing succour to anti-Semitism? Wouldn't it have been better to keep quiet? Maybe I'd have held my peace if I'd had any inkling of the unspeakable horror to come, to which the daily battle-cry of the marching columns of Nazis was just the overture. If I'd known beforehand about Auschwitz, I would never have breathed a word about the Jew Hanussen.'[19]

2

For several months, Kurt von Schleicher's relationship with his old friend Franz von Papen remains untroubled, although there is little reason for complacency. At the Lausanne Conference, the new Chancellor is able to reap the fruit of the foreign policy for which Brüning did the spadework when he succeeds in getting the Allies to agree that Germany need no longer pay any further war reparations beyond a small outstanding sum. On the domestic front, however, the situation is nothing short of disastrous after the lifting of the ban on the SA and the removal of the Social Democrats from power in Prussia. Conditions in Berlin resemble those of a civil war. After the 'Prussian Coup' of 20 July 1932, fears are voiced that Papen might establish a military dictatorship in Germany. General von Schleicher goes on the radio for the very first time, passing comment that can be interpreted as an indirect criticism of Papen: 'If by a military dictatorship one means a regime that relies solely on the bayonets of the Reichswehr, then all I can say to that is that such a government would quickly run out of steam in the vacuum it created and would ultimately fail. In Germany, perhaps more so than in some other countries, any government must have the broad support of the masses.'[20]

At the Reichstag elections on 31 July the NSDAP emerges as by far the strongest party in the country. The communists also see an upswing in their vote. The Centre is squeezed by the political fringes, and, for the first time since 1890, the SPD finds itself in second place. In addition, the divided Liberals, the German Democratic Party and the German People's Party are all marginalized virtually into irrelevance by the extremes. In times of crisis, the concept of freedom is considered a 'first-world problem' for the well-off.

Following the July elections, parliament is in a state of paralysis once more. Schleicher now offers the leader of the National Socialists a role in government, but Hitler wants all or nothing.[21] All options are explored. Schleicher even goes so far as to lobby the President for Hitler to be installed as Reich Chancellor; his idea is to 'hem him around' with more moderate National Socialists. In parallel with this, Brüning and Gregor Strasser, the NSDAP's Head of Organization of the Reich, are engaged in negotiations to sound out possible conditions for a collaboration between the Catholic Centre and the National Socialists. Hadn't Dorothy Thompson also predicted 'that Hitler will be extinguished between two prelates [i.e. Hindenburg and Hugenberg]'?[22] When a date is finally set for a meeting between Hitler and Hindenburg, the leadership of the NSDAP believes it is on the cusp of legally taking power. Cabinet posts have already been assigned within the party, and the SA put on standby.

On 13 August 1932, Hindenburg receives the leader of the National Socialists. They have met one another once before, the previous year.[23] On learning where Hitler hailed from, the Reich President confused Braunau in Austria with a town of the same name in Bohemia, near which he had once been stationed. The man he thus disparagingly but incorrectly dubbed 'the Bohemian corporal' did not make a good impression on him. 'So, he wants to become Reich Chancellor, does he? Postmaster General at best, I'd say!' he tells Schleicher the day after their first encounter.[24] Yet now, barely a year later, Hitler is coming to speak to him on the same matter, as leader of the strongest political force in the country. He begins by assuring Hindenburg that he will abide by the constitution and never seize power illegally. Hindenburg, who is partially deaf, mishears him and thinks that Hitler has just threatened to stage a coup. He wags his plump forefinger admonishingly and growls 'Then I'll have to shoot you, Herr Hitler!'[25]

After little more than a quarter of an hour, the meeting is over; it ends in profound disappointment for the leader of the National Socialists.[26] His pretensions to power have been flatly rejected by Hindenburg. The minutes of the meeting that Secretary of State Otto Meissner drafts straight after are designed to put Hitler in a bad light. They stress that Hindenburg 'could not justify before God, before his conscience or before the Fatherland the transfer of the entire authority of government to a single party, especially not one that was so hostile to people who thought differently'.[27] The Reich President assures a friend that he could never 'allow Hitler to turn Germany into his guinea pig'.[28]

3

There's no let-up in the violence on the street. The following article appears in the *Völkischer Beobachter* of 6 August 1932: 'The product of a 14-year-long Bolshevist education system is the current breed of subhumans, which is capable of no improvement and which can only be prevented from committing further crimes by systematic extermination measures. [...] It must be established once and for all that there is a clear difference between weapons in National Socialist hands and weapons in the hands of Marxist criminals. People should be judged by their political stance, not by the acts they've committed. You can't combat these murderous vermin with legalistic hair-splitting.'[29]

Three days later the 'Directive Against Political Terror' comes into force, which is intended to stamp out 'the smouldering embers of civil war'. Anyone who commits a politically motivated act of murder must now reckon with the death penalty.[30] Hitler expressly approves this ruling, since it means the authorities 'can finally start eradicating murderous Red thuggery'. However, as an August issue of the *Völkischer Beobachter* explains: 'A National Socialist emergency decree would have gone about things quite differently […] by ordering the immediate arrest and sentencing of all Communist and Social Democratic party officials, smoking out the districts where these murderers live and detaining suspects and intellectual agitators in concentration camps.'[31]

The new decree comes into effect as of midnight on 10 August. An hour later, at one o'clock in the morning, a squad of SA stormtroopers assembles in the kitchen of the Lachmann guesthouse in the small Upper Silesian village of Potempa. They have come there from Broslawitz, where they are staying at an SA hostel. Community leader Lachmann entertains his visitors with beer, schnapps and cigarettes. Among the party is a butcher by the name of Golombek. The men are armed with five revolvers and a so-called *Scheintodpistole*.* The butcher is there to direct the gang to the homes of known communists in the area. Various names are bandied about; at the mention of one person, someone ventures the opinion that 'it'd be just fine if he didn't go on living for even another day; let's hang the flags at half-mast for that one'.[32]

The first port of call for the SA men is the house of Florian Schwinge, where they find the door locked. Disturbed by all the banging and crashing about, Anna Schwinge comes to the window. One of the SA men claims to be a friend of the man they're looking for. Anna smells a rat and goes to wake up her husband, then comes back to the window and asks the man she spoke to to step into the light. Butcher Golombek grows impatient and urges his comrade to shoot the woman through the window, but he refuses. When

---

* A *Scheintodpistole* (literally 'apparent-death pistol') was a three-barrelled, snub-nosed gun that, instead of firing a deadly projectile, discharged a shotgun-type cartridge filled with cayenne pepper and other irritants. A non-lethal weapon, it was used at close range and was designed to temporarily disable an assailant rather than kill him. [Translator's note]

they realize they're not going to get anywhere here, Golombek leads the stormtroopers to the house of the widow Pietrzuch; he's certain they'll 'get a result there'. The butcher instructs the men how to find their way down the hallway to the family's bedroom and then stands back, keeping himself hidden so he's not recognized. The Pietrzuchs's house is unlocked, and the SA men make their way through the hall to the bedroom, which they illuminate with their torches. There are two beds in the room; in one of them, the grown-up brothers Konrad and Alfons are asleep, while the other is occupied by their seventy-five-year-old mother.[33]

Marie Pietrzuch has been awoken by the noise outside in the hallway. When she asks what the intruders want, a revolver is shoved into her face and she's told, 'shut your mouth or you'll be shot'. Then the men go over to the other bed: 'Hands up – stand up, you Commie bastards!' Golombek directs proceedings from the shadows: 'Give the fat one a good kicking!' Konrad is dragged out of bed, while Alfons is knocked unconscious by a heavy blow to the temples. When he comes to, he hears the sound of blows raining down on human flesh. The stormtroopers are laying into Konrad; as his mother looks on, they stamp on his windpipe with the full force of their bootheels as he lies prone on the floor. Then they turn their attention to Alfons: 'Get the fuck out of here, you – up against the wall with you! Your turn's coming, we're going to shoot you too!' Meanwhile, the severely injured Konrad tries to save himself by shutting himself in a cupboard. One of the perpetrators pursues him, with Golombek close behind shouting, 'Shoot him, shoot him!' A bullet strikes Konrad in the upper arm. Then suddenly, the intruders are gone, as an order rings out for them to leave the house. Alfons listens as his brother emits an awful death rattle; moments later, he is dead. The post-mortem reveals that Konrad Pietrzuch's right carotid artery had been completely severed.[34]

The Potempa outrage causes a huge stir. Just three weeks later, a special court is convened in the Upper Silesian town of Beuthen. This is the first time that sentence is passed pursuant to the provisions of the new emergency directive – the decree that came into force a full hour before the crime took place. Five of the perpetrators are condemned to death. On the same day, a court hearing takes place in Brieg to pass judgement on those convicted of killing the two SA men in Ohlau; this crime, though, does not fall within the ambit of the new, more draconian act, and so only custodial sentences are handed down in this case.

No sooner have the death sentences for the Potempa murderers been announced than the National Socialist propaganda machine swings into action. Hitler, feeling humiliated after his audience with Reich President von Hindenburg, loses all patience with what he calls the 'government of the wealthy' and 'the cabinet of barons'. He dubs Papen a 'bloodhound' and sends a telegram to the Potempa perpetrators: 'My comrades! In light of this monstrous death sentence passed on you, I feel joined to you by a bond of unbreakable loyalty. From this moment on, securing your freedom is a matter of honour for us. And it will be our bounden duty to take the fight to a government under which such a thing was even possible!'[35] In a speech delivered not long after, he prophesies that, in a National Socialist Reich, five German men would never be brought to book for the death of one Pole.[36] Party ideologist Alfred Rosenberg emphasizes that a Nazi regime would spell the end of 'bourgeois justice', since National Socialism would judge people according to their 'ideology': 'For him [i.e. Hitler], one human soul is not on a par with all others, nor are all human beings equal; in his eyes, there is no "intrinsic natural justice"; his focus, rather, is on the strong German individual, and his sole commitment is to protecting this German, and all jurisprudence and community life, all political and economic endeavour is to be geared to this single aim.'[37] In September 1932, the death sentences handed down for the Potempa killing are commuted to life imprisonment, and just six months later all the perpetrators walk free.

4

'These years have robbed us of our Utopias,' laments Dorothy Thompson in her diary. 'We've seen them all realized and are disillusioned with all of them. Communism is a stupid rule of a mean-minded bureaucracy employing terror against every energetic and courageous individual, a contemptible glorification of the mass-man. Socialism is the rule of the *Bonzen** – entrenched bureaucracy mouthing noble formulas [...] Fascism is the rule of the top sergeant and the half-educated, national socialism is the sick affirming their health [...].'[38]

In August 1932, just after her article about her interview with Hitler has been published in book form in New York under the title *I Saw Hitler!*, Dorothy Thompson sails to Europe with Sinclair Lewis. With them on their voyage is the two-and-a-half-year-old Michael, who is in the care of a governess. Their destination is Vienna, where Dorothy has rented a house – Villa Sauerbrunn – in the hills above the city at the ski resort of Semmering. The building, as Sinclair Lewis ironically notes, resembles 'a cuckoo clock'.[39] No sooner have they arrived than the two of them go their separate ways. Dorothy's husband heads off to Italy; when he eventually returns to Vienna, he rents his own apartment so he can work and drink in peace. Dorothy meets friends, interviews politicians and fellow journalists and writes articles for newspapers. At Christmas, she organizes a grand party at the villa in Semmering. She invites her sister from the USA, writer and artist friends, princes and other prominent figures. The gathering, which is due to last ten days, turns into a disaster: dense fog and a clammy damp set in,

---

* *Bonzen* ('bigwigs'): a word (derived from Japanese *bozu*, a Buddhist priest) that gained popular currency in Germany and Austria in the 1920s and 1930s as a pejorative term for senior functionaries in the Social Democratic Party and the trade unions. Analogous with the disparaging usage 'union barons' in the contemporary British tabloid press. [Translator's note]

thwarting the plan to go skiing every day. Soon enough, in the prevailing atmosphere of boredom, the guests start to get on one another's nerves.

However, one unforgettable moment for Dorothy is her reacquaintance with Christa Winsloe, Baroness Hatvany. Ten years previously Dorothy's first husband, who was a friend of Baron Ladislas Hatvany, introduced the couple to one another. Now the baron wants to divorce Christa Winsloe and marry a twenty-year-old. His wife's name is currently on everyone's lips. A feature film entitled *Mädchen in Uniform* ('Girls in Uniform') has recently been on general release, based on her stage play *Gestern und Heute* ('Yesterday and Today'). Telling the story of a schoolgirl who has a crush on her female teacher and who tries to commit suicide when she is rebuffed, the film has been a hit not just in Germany but also internationally. Right now, Christa, who in the play dramatized her own experiences as a pupil at the Empress Augusta convent school in Potsdam, is working on a spin-off novel from the film.

Dorothy wrestles with her feelings towards Christa. 'Immediately I felt the strange, soft feeling… curious… of being at home, and at rest; an enveloping warmth and sweetness, like a drowsy bath. Only to be near her; to touch her when I went by. She has a quite simple, unconscious way of kissing the inside of one's arm.'[40] She frankly admits to herself: 'I love this woman.'[41] By now almost forty years old, Dorothy is all at sea where her emotions are concerned. Alluding to her earlier romantic entanglements with women, she confides to her diary: 'So it has happened to me again, after all these years.'[42]

The first time she had a lesbian affair, she was twenty, and the object of her affection seventeen years older, 'full-figured and womanly'. Later, in Berlin, she once more felt attracted to a female friend. However, she regrets not having confined this encounter to just a kiss on her 'soft, scented mouth'. 'One loves men differently, and the culmination of love for a man, with me, is very simple. Those forms of sapphic love were like making love to… being made love to… by an impotent man. One sickens. There's something weak in it and, even, ridiculous. *Mir auch passt es nicht. Ich bin doch heterosexuell.* [Anyway, it doesn't suit me, I *am* heterosexual.]'[43]

Her feelings for Christa Winsloe make her question her own self-image. She harbours an 'extraordinarily intense erotic feeling'[44] towards Christa but is uncertain whether it is in any way reciprocated. She tries to read the signs: 'The soft, quite natural kiss on my throat, the quite unconscious (seemingly) even open kiss on my breast, as she stood below me on the stairs – there were a dozen people around – "Goodbye", she said, "*Liebes*."'[45] Dorothy marvels at the white dress her beloved is wearing: 'some thin stuff, embroidered all over with small white beads.'[46] She is eager to translate Christa's novel, which she has only just started to write, and experiences 'this incredible feeling of sisterhood'.[47] Christa does not leave her in doubt for very long. One evening, when they are saying goodnight, they start kissing: 'she called me *Liebling* and said: "I will write to you & telephone, and you shall not get rid of me." And I felt full of beatitude.'[48]

She is 'happily married,' she writes in her diary, 'and yet wanting that curious tenderness, that pervading, warm tenderness'.[49] The fact that this clever and perceptive observer of foreign affairs does not appear to notice the glaring contradictions in her own self-analysis hints at the depth of her emotional confusion. During her stay in Semmering, she also falls in love with a man whom she has known for some while. They go walking in the woods, where, as she writes: 'he […] put both hands on my cheeks and we clung together. His mouth tasted deliciously of love, like the smell of semen, and I could have lain down with him right there in the woods then and there […] the old leap of the heart and womb were there, and we walked along, greatly shaken. But even then the sweet wistfulness remained […] the heart's reaching towards warmth.'[50]

Peace returns after she has seen off the last of her guests. Sinclair Lewis makes himself scarce for the duration of the house party – he speaks no French and barely any German and feels like a fish out of water around his wife's friends. Now, in what is quite a surprise for Dorothy, they begin to show affection for one another again: 'I stood a long time in his arms, loving his familiar feel and smell, rubbing my face on his face. "What are you going to do?" he said and I said: "First of all, take a bath." So he said: "Stop in on your way down." I stopped in in a dressing gown and nothing else and he said: "Come to my bed." So I did and it was awfully good. Especially good, with me just too tired to expect it to be and suddenly it was there and very wonderful.'[51] A few days later, she notes in her diary some advice an ice-skating instructor gives her: 'Gently, gently; no effort. You must let yourself be cartilage – above all let yourself go.' She laughs out loud and thinks to herself: 'That's the recipe for success in love & it's taken me twenty years to learn it. To be soft and receptive. All of grace & feminine beauty is in it.'[52]

Dorothy hasn't felt so close to her husband for a long time. She starts thinking it might be nice for them to have another child.[53] 'I am not sure that having a child, actually bearing a child isn't, for women, the only entirely satisfactory sexual experience. It is a kind of terrible ecstasy, accompanied by a feeling of great expansion and power, and terrific heightening of all impression and experience. The pain is secondary – as it is in the first embrace, when one strains that piercing agonizing blade to one. "No, no, beloved (fainting), do not go away. Stay! Stay!"'[54] Afterwards Dorothy sleeps all afternoon. As the evening draws in, little Michael comes into her room clutching a pile of books, climbs into bed with her and demands: 'Mammy wead!' [i.e. read]. 'I kissed the back of his neck and he smelled delicious, like a kitten.' So, is everything going to be alright now? 'I have been very, very happy,' writes Dorothy, 'And all the time, every moment, I have thought of Christa.'[55]

The Strike

1

On the evening following Hitler's meeting with Hindenburg on 13 August 1932, Kurt von Schleicher professes himself relieved: 'It was absolutely right not to appoint Hitler Chancellor.'[1] The general can see those whom he believed he could manipulate like puppets on a string beginning to free themselves from his control, but as usual he is a step ahead of them: if he can't manage to cut the Nazis down to size with his idea of 'wearing them down' by involving them in government, then it might still be possible to sow division in their ranks. At this stage, Hitler has not yet achieved absolute autocracy within the NSDAP. In addition to SA leader Ernst Röhm, Gregor Strasser also has a strong, independent profile within the 'movement'. Carl von Ossietzky, writing in *Die Weltbühne*, calls him a 'quiet intellectual'.[2] Strasser has been earmarked as Chancellor in the event that Hitler is elected Reich President. In the party's offices, a portrait of Strasser customarily hangs next to that of Hitler, and in north Germany in particular, there are 'Gregor Strasser Hostels' in several cities, while gramophone records with speeches by Gregor Strasser are widely distributed throughout the Reich. There's even an official party-approved biography of Gregor

Strasser. As the NSDAP's Head of Organization of the Reich, the equivalent of a parliamentary faction leader, he runs a tight ship. In 1932, Alfred Rosenberg writes: 'Adolf Hitler is unquestionably the leader of the party, but nowadays it is presided over by Gregor Strasser. Consider the parallels with Moscow: even during Lenin's lifetime, Stalin gained control of the party. In similar fashion, Gregor Strasser has done this with the NSDAP. And just as the party is growing into a position of power within the current state, so Strasser is consolidating his position as the heir to leadership.'[3]

Not that the Head of Organization of the Reich for the NSDAP isn't himself an anti-Semite, but the party's increased share of the vote is due less to Goebbels's virulent diatribes against the Jews than it is to the anti-capitalist slogans of the left wing of the party, as represented by Strasser. He talks about the 'right to work',[4] the 'legions of hardworking people' and the 'great anti-capitalist longing that has already taken hold of 95 per cent of our people'. Strasser is friendly with the philosopher Oswald Spengler, author of the seminal *Der Untergang des Abendlandes* ('The Decline of the West'), and he is a cultured man who reads the Greek and Roman classics in their original language. He also maintains extensive contacts with Social Democrat trade unionists, tends to favour conciliation and compromise and is regarded in the bourgeois press as a moderate. All of Schleicher's hopes of being able to split the NSDAP rest on Strasser. In an effort to come up with a new employment strategy, since the summer of 1932 representatives of diverse groups, ranging from Social Democrat trade unionists to the left wing of the NSDAP, have been meeting together in a working party that soon earns itself the popular name of *Die Querfront* ('The Third Way').[5] Under this motto, Schleicher tries over the next few months to find the basis for a politics that transcends the traditional parties, who constantly block one another in the existing power structure.

In the meantime, Papen has acquired a taste for governing; 'Little Franz has found his feet,'[6] observes Schleicher, not without disapproval. Papen has it in mind to dispense with parliamentary democracy altogether and to shuffle off the blame for this breach of the constitution onto Hindenburg. This idea doesn't entirely shock Schleicher, since the failure of the parties has led to a political impasse. In the 1932 elections, no fewer than thirty-eight parties seek a mandate and the voting slip is over half a metre long.[7] In the end, it all comes down to an absurd scramble over who can bring down the Weimar Republic first and still be left holding the reins of power: the National Socialists in a legal, spuriously democratic way or the forces around Papen and Schleicher through a violation of the constitution. The former want to exploit parliamentary democracy in order to manoeuvre themselves into a position where they can abolish it, while the latter wish to do away with it so as to prevent a one-party dictatorship. But Papen and Schleicher themselves differ in their aims by more than mere nuances. While Papen simply wants to revert to an autocratically ruled corporate state, Schleicher is seeking to forge an alliance between various different social groups, which will form the basis of a new administration. The watchword 'You can do everything with bayonets except sit on them',[8] or variants thereof, is one he now increasingly finds himself uttering.

2

On 30 August 1932, in the presence of the Reich Chancellor Franz von Papen, the communist chairwoman of the Reichstag by seniority, Clara Zetkin, declares the new parliament open; she is in poor health and her speech is interrupted by long pauses as she fights for breath. The strongest parliamentary group by quite some margin is the NSDAP. Almost all of the 130 National Socialist delegates have turned up in uniform, though their leadership has expressly instructed them not to disrupt proceedings. In return, the Catholic Centre Party has promised to vote for Hermann Göring as the new President of the Reichstag.

Distributed around the podium and the main debating chamber are five microphones, which pick up all the speeches and the heckling and transmit them via a cable from the Reichstag to the new 'House of Radio' in Charlottenburg. There, sound engineers operate a kind of dual record player. A cutting stylus that is remotely controlled by electromagnetic waves inscribes grooves of differing depths onto a wax disk. The matrices from which the final recordings are produced each hold four minutes' worth of broadcast sound.* So as not to miss a single sentence of the speeches, while the old matrix is still recording but nearing the end of the four-minute slot, the technicians always allow the new one to 'run in' for a few seconds.

Clara Zetkin has travelled to the opening of parliament from the Soviet Union, where she has been living for some time: 'The way to overcome economic crises is to stage a proletarian revolution,' she explains in her address. 'I hereby declare parliament open in fulfilment of my duty as "mother of the house" and in the hope that I shall in that same capacity, notwithstanding my current disability, one day have the good fortune of opening the first People's Congress of a Soviet Germany!'[9] Later, she hands over to the newly elected President of the Reichstag Hermann Göring, now the holder of the third most important political position in the country, who announces: 'This is the first time for many years that the Reichstag once again has a large, working nationalist majority.'[10]

Two weeks later, the newly elected parliament meets for its first and last regular session. Unsurprisingly, the communists propose a vote of no confidence in Reich Chancellor von Papen. But the truly sensational development is that no one opposes the motion. In order to pre-empt any vote on the motion, during a short recess Papen moves quickly to have a messenger bring him an order officially dissolving parliament. To the sound of booing

---

* Some of these recordings have been preserved for posterity. In 1945 they found their way to Great Britain, where they were re-recorded from the wax discs onto more modern media and stored in the BBC's Sound Archives.

and catcalls from his fellow parliamentarians, Papen strides to the government bench with the red folder tucked under his arm. But before he can address the house, Göring, flatly ignoring the Chancellor's request to speak, goes ahead with the no-confidence vote. The result, a devastating blow for Papen, reveals that he can count on the support of less than a tenth of the delegates – a humiliating defeat without precedent in the history of the German parliament.[11] But does this outcome mean that he even remains in office? Pandemonium reigns in the Reichstag.

Yet another round of elections now takes place. None of the previous ballots have brought any improvement, in fact quite the opposite. Growing hardship has seen tensions increase, and with them the tendency to radical solutions. The picture on the streets, in pubs and on demonstrations continues to be one of bloody set-tos between National Socialists and communists. Goebbels has called for a 'battle for Berlin'[12] and Heinz Neumann, editor-in-chief of *Die Rote Fahne*, coins the slogan: 'Smash the Fascists wherever you find them!' Not infrequently, the fighting between the SA and the communists becomes an end in itself. The punch-ups also attract teenage gangs of youths and girls ranging from fourteen to eighteen. These cliques have names like 'Tartar Blood', 'Gypsy Love', 'Red Oath', 'The Black Flags' and 'Egg Slime'. The boys style themselves 'bad lads', the girls call themselves 'clique cows', and they cultivate a distinctive look: 'Very popular among both male and female gang members are earrings and fantastical tattoos, some of which extend right down to their genitals.'[13]

These gangs have formed themselves into crime syndicates and have extensive connections to the world of pimping and prostitution. Their initiation rites include: 'performing coitus in public for a specified period, with the gang's enforcer timing proceedings on a stop-watch. Or engaging in masturbation, likewise in front of an assembled crowd [...] Quite often, the initiates are stripped naked, tied up and smeared with faeces and urine. And we'd best draw a veil over the "baptismal banquet" that the cliques lay on for would-be new members.'[14] For their dens, the juvenile delinquents mostly use attics, cellars or abandoned warehouses, where dime novels and the obligatory 'fucking sofa' are the most important furnishings.

These teenage gangs scarcely figure in the calculations of the rival political groups. The decisive factor in determining their interaction is the tactical guidelines issued by their respective party leaderships, which are ultimately designed to poach supporters from one another. For all the violence on the street, the National Socialists and the communists maintain flexible dealings with one another, in so far as their interests coincide. In April 1932, for instance, Thälmann proposes a 'far-reaching anti-fascist campaign', but in the very same speech, regarding the calling of strikes, he also decrees that 'it's absolutely necessary and also permitted for Nazis to be included on strike committees'.[15] The KPD, he goes on, must try and woo 'proletarian Nazis who have been led astray'. Conversely, the National Socialists are keen to win back 'fellow Germans indoctrinated by Moscow'.

At a KPD conference in October 1932, the new 'party line' is proclaimed: 'Communists and revolutionary workers must persuade the proletarian and working supporters of National Socialism to undertake joint action against income support being taken away and the Papen dictatorship. [...]'[16] At the same time, the trade-union branch of the NSDAP sees its first opportunity to 'win the trust of the working masses on a grand scale'.[17] By 30 October, collaboration has become a reality, as a 'Solidarity Committee' is convened, involving eight communists, four non-affiliated members and four National Socialists. They have been sent by the National Socialist Workplace Organization into the lion's den, Karl Liebknecht House on Bülowplatz, to draw up plans for a jointly organized strike on the Berlin transport system.[18]

3

Everyone suffers impositions at this time. Not just workers and private sector employees, public servants, too, are repeatedly forced to accept pay cuts in the face of the economic crisis. In the end, wage negotiations with the Berlin Transport Corporation come down to a matter of just two pfennigs. The pay cut that was originally proposed, of up to twenty-three pfennigs per hour, has been whittled down to this. The fact that a strike is still going ahead has a lot to do with the general mood in the country, with distrust of a political system that is incapable of surmounting the crisis, with contempt for the 'cabinet of barons', this 'crazy house' whose emergency decrees have created a world where wage cuts and 'cancelled shifts' are the norm, and with the widespread feeling that 'things can't go on like this'.[19] It is the communists who exploit this situation to the best advantage. Late in the day, Goebbels jumps on the bandwagon, recognizing the danger of losing face with the working class just before the elections.

The crisis comes to a head in the summer of 1932. Alongside the six million unemployed who can no longer be breadwinners for their families, a further three million are on short-time working and can barely make ends meet on what they earn. Over a third of the population is living on state handouts and the previous year's banking crisis and the catastrophic economic situation have brought the country's finances to the brink of collapse. In these circumstances, the new Chancellor Papen passes emergency legislation in June 1932 that slashes unemployment benefit by almost a quarter, cuts pension payments, welfare support and state benefits for war victims, while at the same time introducing a special crisis tax. These cutbacks are so swingeing that even the German Nationalist press baron Alfred Hugenberg tries to intercede with the Chancellor. Rents also see a drastic increase at this time, with many people being forcibly evicted from their homes.

The communists call for a rent strike: 'Food first, then rent!' is the slogan with which hard-pressed tenants fight their eviction. When apartments are cleared by the police, members of the newly unbanned SA and the still illegal Red Front Fighting League, often working hand-in-hand, respond by carrying the furniture straight back into the property. 'From every window, the united front of hardship displayed its flags,' wrote the *Arbeiter-Illustrierte-Zeitung*, 'emblazoned with the hammer and sickle, the three arrows of the Iron Front and even occasionally with the swastika.'[20]

The principal target of the strike for the communists is their arch-enemy the Social Democrats, whose great showpiece is the Berlin Transport Corporation (*Berliner Verkehrs Aktiengesellschaft*, BVG).[21] On 1 November 1932, during a speech by Ernst Thälmann at the Sportpalast, 200 uniformed BVG workers march into the auditorium in close formation, to wild applause.[22] A few days later Hitler speaks at the same venue, yet although the strike has already been decided upon, he does not mention it.

The original strike vote resulted in a clear majority for the action, but the Social Democrat-dominated general trade union federation complains that workers who are off sick or on holiday weren't counted and that the planned withdrawal of labour is therefore an illegal wildcat strike.[23] There is a lot at stake for both the blue- and white-collar workers of the BVG. If they are dismissed, they are threatened not only with long-term unemployment but also the loss of what are, in many cases, valuable pension contributions built up over many years.

Right from the outset, the driving force is revolutionary trade-union opposition on the part of the communists. The National Socialists are forced to perform a delicate balancing act. They are trying to avoid the appearance of acting in solidarity with their communist rivals while at the same time wanting to be perceived as representing the strikers' interests.

At six o'clock on the morning of 3 November, a Thursday, Berlin's transport network grinds to a halt; the only things still operating are the S-Bahn trains, which are run by the national railways (*Reichsbahn*). However, in normal times, these only carry a tenth of the total daily traffic. In the city centre, the pavements can barely hold the huge numbers of pedestrians attempting to get to their places of work on foot. The roads are clogged with bicycles and taxis and there are very few private cars. But for all the inconvenience, the public mood on the street is firmly on the side of the strikers. Goebbels 'keeps in touch with the Führer by telephone on an hourly basis'.[24] The demands of the 'Communist–National Socialist Strike Committee' are printed in the *Vossische Zeitung* as well as in the Nazi organ *Der Angriff*.

At 11.30, a meeting between Franz von Papen and his ministers begins. The strike at the BVG, which would normally be a matter of merely local concern, is item number two on the cabinet's agenda. The government regards it as a test of political strength by the KPD, which intends it to lead on to a general strike, and responds by banning *Die Rote Fahne*.

Around midday, the Social Democrat-dominated free trade unions signal their acceptance of the mediator's decision on the pay cut, thus rendering illegal the industrial action that has already gone ahead. Even distributing leaflets or handing out food to the strikers are now against the law. Yet despite the threat of sanctions, the strike remains solid.

On the Friday, the situation escalates when police clear Rudolf-Wilde-Platz in front of Schöneberg Town Hall, using live rounds and killing the SA platoon leader Kurt Reppich in the process. This incident stirs the Nazi propaganda machine into action. *Der Angriff*, employing a typical blend of pathos and outrage, reports: 'The blood of the man who had been shot stained the asphalt red. Passers-by looked with horror on the scene.'[25] The men of SA group 13 consecrate their standard as a 'blood flag' by dipping it in the dead man's blood: 'There they stand on the bare tarmac, with the flaming red fabric of a flag fluttering high above them. A flag on which there's no white background to be seen anymore. The whole thing is red, except for a black swastika. They dipped the flag in his blood and now stand there silently.' Someone who has no intention of remaining silent is Joseph Goebbels: 'This was an opportunity for us to show our true socialism,' he proclaims, 'when we threw our weight behind the disenfranchised men of the BVG, and when our comrade Reppich was gunned down by the police for this socialism.'[26] He also notes in his diary: 'In Schöneberg we carry the SA man Reppich, who was shot during the strike, to his grave. Four thousand men join the cortège. He is laid to rest like a prince. Aeroplanes towing swastika pennants draped with black crêpe circle over the cemetery, as if bidding their final farewells to the dead man. The SA men are deeply moved.'[27]

4

The Berlin Transport Corporation was founded in 1928 at the instigation of a city politician who gained his first experiences of municipal organization in the early days of the Soviet Union. As a prisoner of war from 1916 onwards in an internment camp north of Moscow, he learns Russian and translates for his comrades news about the political events that are unfolding in the country. The young man in question, a Social Democrat, joins the Bolsheviks in 1917 and in April 1918 is appointed as a People's Commissar for German Affairs by Josef Stalin.

After the outbreak of the November Revolution in Germany, there is nothing to keep him on the Volga any longer. In December 1918, he is one of three delegates of the Soviet regime present at the inaugural meeting of the Communist Party in Berlin. Under the assumed name of Ernst Friesland, he is right at the very heart of political events during this period. In 1921 he is engaged in planning a violent communist seizure of power in Germany. For a brief spell, 'Lenin's favourite' is promoted to General Secretary of the KPD. But by 1922, via the Independent Social Democrats, he eventually makes his way back in the SPD. From 1926 onwards he is the Berlin city councillor responsible for transport and assumes the chairmanship of the BVG board. However, it is only many years later, in 1948, that his name becomes known to a wider public: in a speech whose pathos, characteristic of the period, matches the gravity of the situation, he defends the Western sector of divided post-war Berlin against his erstwhile party comrades' attempts to wrest control of it (by imposing a blockade, which led to the Berlin Airlift). The key sentence in his speech was his urgent appeal: 'Peoples of the world, look upon this city!' In a letter of 1918 to Clara Zetkin, Lenin gave this assessment of the man who was later to become Mayor of Berlin, Ernst Reuter: 'Young Reuter is a brilliant and lucid thinker; the only thing is that he's a bit too independent in his thinking!'[28]

In April 1932 85 per cent of KPD members are unemployed, so their influence in most large companies is negligible.[29] But where the BVG is concerned it's a different story, and this has to do with events that took place when Ernst Reuter was in charge. Repeatedly at that time, the accusation was levelled that members of the BVG management had abused their positions for personal gain. Complaints were made, for instance, about inflated prices being paid for land during construction of the underground network, or about the horrendously high fees charged by arbitrators in the compulsory-purchase process. In most cases, it was leading Social Democrats who were the target of such accusations. The National Socialists and communists weren't about to leave this political ammunition unused. The epitome of the 'SPD *Bonze*' and 'class traitor' was one Fritz Brolat, who had trained as a locksmith but who rose to become the BVG's head of labour, with an annual income of 72,000 Reichsmarks – fully thirty times what an underground train driver earned in a year on average. There were rumblings about this even within the SPD's own ranks.

However, this growing political storm really breaks with full force when the affair of the Sklarek brothers comes to light in

October 1929. The Sklareks have, much to the detriment of the city, been bribing local politicians and civil servants left, right and centre. Yet the mud sticks first and foremost to the SPD. 'To find the real crooks, the true extortioners, bastards, cheats, twisters and murderers, all you need do is look at the Social-Fascist Party',[30] runs a piece in *Die Rote Fahne* under the headline: 'The System'. Of the two councillors from their own ranks who have taken bribes, the newspaper states: 'If there was a proletarian dictatorship in Germany, these two individuals would not only have been arrested long since, but also brought before an open people's tribunal and summarily shot.'[31]

For its part, Nazi propaganda makes much of the fact that the Sklareks were immigrants of Jewish origin, as were the protagonists of the so-called Kutisker–Barmat banking scandal some years before, in which prominent SPD politicians were similarly implicated. When the dust settles, the key fact to emerge from the accusations against the Social Democrat Fritz Brolat is that he accepted from the Sklareks a gift of six silk shirts to the value of 820 Reichsmarks.[32] To the court, such a sum is a mere bagatelle, but to a BVG train driver on the Berlin U-Bahn it represents half a year's wages.

5

The strikers continue to stand firm, in spite of the BVG issuing the first dismissal notices and, much to the dismay of those taking industrial action, managing to run several trams, especially on the high-traffic inner-city lines. Even so, hardly anyone boards them. Members of the SS overturn a lorry belonging to the Berlin Corporation's civil engineering department. This 'so impressed the communists present that a KPD campaign donations collector linked arms with a National Socialist tin-rattler and, to the delight of the assembled crowd, the two of them started swinging their collections boxes in unison, shouting "Donate to the election fund!"[33]

Two days before the November elections, the situation in the capital threatens to get out of hand. An attempt by the police to break up a gathering in the northern suburbs of Berlin is reported thus: 'When the police tried to disperse the crowd, they came under attack. Finding themselves in an increasingly difficult predicament, the officers opened fire with live rounds. Four demonstrators were hit by bullets and fell to the ground.'[34] One of the casualties is the communist Georg Horn. *Die Rote Fahne* comments: 'Once again, we Berlin Communists must lower our flags. [...] We have lost one of our best comrades.'[35]

On the Friday evening, Papen announces his intention of deploying the whole of the Berlin police force onto the streets and, in the event of them encountering resistance, of sanctioning them to use lethal force to get the transport system running again. That evening, he speaks on the radio on all German broadcast channels. He accuses Hitler of using the same propaganda methods as the radical left. But he identifies the real danger as being the political influence wielded by the communists: 'We will do everything within our power both intellectually and materially to counter this never-ending radicalization of our youth, this fomenting of class hatred, and this preparation for a proletarian revolution.'[36] Papen's determination to win this trial of strength even goes so far as deploying the Reichswehr should it become necessary – just one day before the election.

On Saturday, the BVG resumes operations, 'under the protection of the police, who are ready to shoot at the slightest provocation'.[37] Seventy communists, National Socialists and unaffiliated trade unionists hold an 'internal conference' to discuss the situation at the 'Freischütz' in Charlottenburg, a drinking den of the SA. However, by now the morale of the strikers is ebbing away, as many sense that they are fighting a losing battle. For the third day in succession, despite growing weariness, their communist comrades-in-arms once again go out on the streets, but the National Socialists quietly melt away. The brief marriage of convenience with the communists is at an end, because Hitler's aim is not to abolish the state but, rather, to take it over.

In the normal course of events, 653 KHz medium wave is the home of Radio Beromünster. However, on the Sunday of the elections this frequency has been hijacked by a communist pirate station. Germany 'lies in ruins after fourteen years of the Social Democrat regime', it claims, and calls upon members of the SA to vote communist. Between campaigning messages, it plays the 'Internationale'. The German Post Office's jamming service fails to find the location of the rogue broadcaster.[38] The communists' plan pays off come election day, as they emerge as the strongest political party in Berlin.

For the National Socialists, the election result of 6 November is a disaster. The murder at Potempa and the political manoeuvring during the Berlin transport strike appears ultimately to have scared off their voters. Two million fewer people vote for the National Socialists, who nonetheless remain the largest party in the Reichstag. At this juncture, Göring is said to have approached Schleicher 'with tears in his eyes'[39] and begged him for a ministerial position. Has the Nazis' spell been broken? Have they 'won all the battles but still lost the war'? The party coffers are exhausted and Hitler is sunk deep in depression – he even toys with the idea of withdrawing from active politics altogether.[40]

The BVG strike is a watershed moment; even the Social Democrats now begin to contemplate unconventional political configurations. In the SPD and the trade unions, cabinet lists with representatives from across a broad political spectrum are circulated – from the left wing of the NSDAP to the right wing of the Social Democrats. Strasser is slated as the next vice-chancellor, while the post of Chancellor is earmarked for Kurt von Schleicher. The aim is to sideline both Hitler and Papen when forming a government.

While Hindenburg would dearly love to retain Papen following the election results, the rest of the country has had enough of the 'gentleman jockey'. A leader in *Vorwärts* sums up the prevailing mood: 'Papen means war, a war of the government against the German people, 90 per cent of whom have roundly rejected Papen and Papen's policies. It is impossible to find a government that can work together peacefully with the majority of the people and their elected representatives. Instead, the talk is of a government of truce, with Herr von Schleicher at its head.'[41]

Yet the 'cabinet of barons' only finally comes to an end on 2 December 1932. On this day, Schleicher presents to his ministerial colleagues the outcome of a hypothetical 'war game' that he has tasked his friend and close collaborator Eugen Ott with mapping out.[42] After the unexpected collaboration between the National Socialists and the communists during the BVG strike, the question has arisen as to whether the army would even be able to keep control in a worst-case scenario. What if a general strike were to be called jointly by the parties of the far left and the far right, say? And how secure would the country's eastern and western borders be in the event of a civil war? Eugen Ott vividly describes to the cabinet the numerous 'difficulties that cannot be overcome by force of arms'.[43] Papen seeks to play down the danger, but by now almost none of his ministers fall in line with him. A few days later, he tenders his resignation to Hindenburg and proposes the minister for the Reichswehr as the next Chancellor. 'Then in God's name we must let Herr von Schleicher try his luck,'[44] is Hindenburg's resigned reply. Now it's Kurt von Schleicher's turn to step up to the plate.

Endgame

1

In the normal course of events, a dentist's chair is not a place for dialogue. Patients with their mouths agape are forced to listen to the dentist's anecdotes and are unable to offer much in the way of input, except to utter the occasional guttural sound or respond with a careful nod of the head. For the most part, the dentist's chit-chat is simply designed to distract patients from their anxieties. Yet in 1932, in the dental practice of Dr Elbrechter, nothing less than the political destiny of Germany is under discussion. The doctor's patients include Heinrich Brüning, Gottfried Treviranus, Gregor Strasser and Kurt von Schleicher. Elbrechter, who has had a practice in Berlin since 1926, used to live in Elberfeld in the Bergisches Land region of Westphalia. At that time the dentist, who has nationalist sympathies, was one of the circle around Gregor Strasser and his young adjutant Joseph Goebbels. In the mid-1920s these two men were busy trying to rebuild one of the many nationalist splinter groups, the NSDAP, after its proscription. Elbrechter is one of those members of his social class whose intellectual interests extend beyond his immediate profession and who cultivate political contacts. As a freelance contributor, he has

also been writing articles since 1923 for a small magazine entitled *Die Tat* ('Action').

A lot has happened since then. By now, Gregor Strasser is number two in what has since developed into the strongest political force in Germany, Goebbels is the NSDAP's Gauleiter for Berlin and *Die Tat*, under the leadership of its new editor-in-chief Hans Zehrer, has since 1928 grown to become the country's leading political magazine. It boasts as many subscribers as its two counterparts on the left of the political spectrum – *Das Tage-Buch* and *Die Weltbühne* – combined.[1] Mostly it is young men on the S-Bahn or the Berlin underground who can be seen with their noses buried in the journal. The lofty tone adopted by its contributors and their elitist self-confidence strike just the right note with this readership. Zehrer has turned *Die Tat* into a publication with a distinct political agenda and in so doing has managed to expand its circulation thirty times over. There are no sacred cows where *Die Tat* is concerned: the liberal system of government and the capitalist economic order are equally open to question. The enterprise is viewed with suspicion by its opponents: 'Does Herr Zehrer really believe,' writes Carl von Ossietzky in *Die Weltbühne*, 'that Hindenburg's signature was all it took to let socialism in through the legal front door?'[2]

From one issue to the next, the readers of *Die Tat* are encouraged to learn how to weigh up the state of chaos in which they find themselves forced to live, for it is Zehrer's considered opinion that only a deepening of the crisis will drive the supporters of the political extremes, the National Socialists and the communists, to coalesce into a third force: the 'new man'. The economic order of the Weimar Republic is dissected with a dispassionate, analytical eye, and a campaigning case is made for the nationalization of major industrial concerns. Commerce should once more be placed at the service of the state and the human being restored as the measure of all things. In pursuit of this, Zehrer maintains, party politics needs to be abolished in favour of a 'democratic dictatorship', a new state governed by authoritarian rule and organized according to class.

The system of free trade that has operated up until now should be replaced by the economic self-sufficiency of the empire. The economic and political essays that appear in *Die Tat* even attract attention in the Soviet Union, where they are submitted to Stalin in translation.

'Intellectually, these times are no longer comprehensible,' writes Hans Zehrer, 'so one is forced to simply observe and assimilate them.'³ When faced with repeated failed attempts to deal rationally with the crisis, Zehrer is not the only person to have consciously renounced the firm ground of a 'straightforward culture of reason'. Hitler and the Brownshirt hordes of the SA are despised as boorish and stupid, but as the foot soldiers who are going to cudgel a path through to a 'democratic dictatorship', Zehrer and many other proponents of the 'conservative revolution' are not inclined to question their right to exist. Will the crisis lead to the formation of a 'new state'? Such a question, and others in a similar vein, are the topics under discussion whenever the *Tat* inner circle get together in Dr Elbrechter's private apartment at Schaperstraße 29 in Wilmersdorf. Kurt von Schleicher has a high opinion of the young Zehrer, and supports him with a monthly subvention from the Ministry of the Army when, in the summer of 1932, Zehrer is appointed editor-in-chief of the magazine *Tägliche Rundschau*. For his part, Zehrer endorses Schleicher's plans to combine the might of the Reichswehr with the influence of the trade unions to create a 'national Socialism'. It is not long before he is seen as the mouthpiece of, and adviser to, the new Chancellor.

In a radio interview, Schleicher stresses that he had 'deep misgivings about taking on the chancellorship, because having the defence minister as Reich Chancellor smacks of a military dictatorship'. However, he went on, the Reichswehr was 'not there to protect outdated conditions of ownership'.⁴ In the main, the reaction of the press to the new Chancellor is an indulgent one of 'wait and see'. People are happy that the 'spectre of Papen'⁵ has been dispelled, or, as Count Harry Kessler puts it, 'regurgitated by the disgusted German people'. The Liberal Otto Nuschke writes in the *Berliner Volksstimme*: 'It is fortunate for our country that we have at least a few outstanding military figures who are political soldiers in the best sense.' Schleicher, Nuschke claims, is 'not just a man of extraordinary ability, but a constructive thinker too'.[6] And Carl Zuckmayer recalls: 'Most people – at least in Berlin – hoped that the efforts of Chancellor Kurt von Schleicher, the "socially-minded general", to create a broad front of trade unionists embracing both Right and Left would succeed. That would have taken the wind out of the sails of the extremists at both ends of the spectrum.'[7] The day after Schleicher takes office, Gregor Strasser agrees to join his cabinet as vice-chancellor. But just days later comes a rift with Hitler. Following a blazing row, Strasser resigns from all his posts within the NSDAP and goes off on holiday in South Tyrol for three weeks. In a letter to Hitler, Strasser writes: 'The violent confrontation with Marxism can and must not [...] be put at the centre of our domestic policy agenda. Rather, I believe the main challenge of our time is to create a broad, popular front of working people and to lead them towards the newly formed state. I regard the investing of all our hopes in a situation of chaos as the hour of destiny for our party as wrong, dangerous and counter to the interests of the whole of Germany.'[8]

At the Kaiserhof, Strasser's letter is the cause of great consternation. Hitler paces up and down his hotel room in the night, working himself up into apocalyptic fantasies. Would Strasser go ahead and join Schleicher's administration as vice-chancellor? Almost half the NSDAP members of parliament stood behind Strasser, including almost all of the Gauleiter.[9] Many of them fear that the party will suffer a further setback in the polls and are keen to finally reap the rewards of their struggle by taking up positions which promise to give them influence and a secure income. 'If the party disintegrates,' Hitler threatens his close circle of party chiefs, 'then within three minutes I'll put an end to it all with my revolver.'[10] Yet, in the event, Strasser fails to exploit the opportunity to rally his supporters behind him. Schleicher's calculation that he might be able to split the NSDAP has come to nought.

Nevertheless, the new Chancellor continues to negotiate with the unions, the Reichsbanner and the Stahlhelm. The key points at issue are ideas on how to defuse the crisis, job-creation schemes and the redistribution of agricultural land for new settlements and publicly funded infrastructure projects, such as the building of 'crossing-free motor-roads' (*kreuzungsfreie Kraftfahr-Straßen*), as the autobahns were originally known. To start with, positive signals come from the Christian trade unions and from the Social Democrat-dominated General German Trade Union Confederation, with Otto Braun talking about the 'grand coalition of the reasonable'. However, the left wing of the Social Democrats refuses point-blank to work with the general. Pressure is put first on the leadership of the Reichsbanner and then on the Trade Union Confederation to withdraw from the talks with Schleicher.[11] Since being ousted from power, in the country at large and then even in Prussia, the Social Democrats have become an increasingly radical talking shop. Their parliamentary group in the Reichstag calls for the nationalization of key industries and the introduction of a socialist-planned economy. Otto Braun complains that the party has 'in recent times allowed its agenda to be dictated more and more by Communist demagogues'.[12]

It is not just in the Prussian regional assembly, but in the Reichstag, too, that the opposing parties come to physical blows.[13] In the lobby of the Reichstag, a community deputy hurls a telephone at the head of a National Socialist, while spittoons, ashtrays and desk lids are used as missiles. No one invests any hope in the political parties any more.[14] Schleicher is now largely isolated, and while he keeps on talking to this or that individual, he has no inkling that much worse is to come: the spectre of Papen has returned.

2

Carl von Ossietzky is still in prison. When he and his future wife first got to know one another it was the elegant, charming and beautiful Maud who shored up the self-confidence of the young Carl. Later, the position is reversed, as Maud feels a great need for warmth and closeness.[15] As he becomes ever more absorbed in his work, she, with her desire for independence, finds she has no role in the marriage. Her overworked husband expects her to provide for him the refuge of hearth and home and is dismayed to find that she can no longer do so. There are times when he treats her like a child. From his cell in Moabit Gaol, he writes to his thirteen-year-old daughter Rosalinde: 'My dear baby, I don't know which of you is the greater baby – you or your mother. But in any event, I want you to make sure that your Mummy's eating properly and looking after her appearance.' He ends his letter with the plea: 'My dear children, you're not to worry about me, do you hear?'[16] Her mother, in turn, writes to Rosalinde: 'I'm full of woes + all this time without Daddy is killing me – it's five months already now. It seems to me like five years – I cry all the time, and on top of all that you're not here either.'[17] During his incarceration, a second charge is brought against Carl. Kurt Tucholsky has written in *Die Weltbühne* that 'Soldiers are murderers'. Carl appears before the court and speaks as though he has nothing to lose. That evening he returns to his cell and the charge is dropped. Friends step up to support him. On the occasion of his birthday in October 1932, the detainee receives a letter from Rudolf Arnheim, praising his editorial skills and his ability to sort the wheat from the chaff: 'Every morning the postbag of submissions is full of poems that go on about sunken-eyed whores and close with a preposterous vision of world revolution.'[18] The paper's editors send books to him in prison; at the beginning of September, for instance, he receives Lenin's *Socialism in One Country* and Ernst Jünger's *The Worker*.[19]

Ossietzky suffers mood swings but never loses his sense of humour. 'As for my exercise regime in here,' he says in a letter to Tucholsky, 'all I can say is that as soon as I'm released, I'm signing up with the Reichswehr as a PT instructor.'[20]

Bruno Frei, Hanussen's hostile shadow, writes about Ossietzky in the communist newspaper *Berlin am Morgen*: 'It's not Hindenburg's clemency but rather the power of the working class that will secure his release.'[21] Yet after more than six months, at Christmas 1932, it is indeed a political amnesty granted by Hindenburg that brings his incarceration to an end. The first thing the released prisoner does, even before driving home, is to buy cigarettes and cakes, which he sends to the prison for those of his former fellow inmates who are still locked up to enjoy with their Christmas meal. A party is laid on for him in the editorial offices of *Die Weltbühne*. His wife and daughter have come there to see him, too. As Alfred Polgar and Walter Mehring raise their glasses to him from an adjoining office, his own glass slips from his hand and shatters on the floor: 'It was only then that I noticed how his hands couldn't stop shaking,' Mehring reports, 'a knock-on effect of the emotional trauma he'd been through in prison.'[22] After almost twenty years, the family now take up residence in their own home for the first time, as opposed to renting. Ossietzky immediately throws himself back into work, while Maud continues to battle with her alcohol problems. For some time, Carl has felt himself attracted to a female colleague, the twenty-nine-year-old architect and journalist Gusti Hecht. Maud knows nothing about 'her husband's intimate friendship'[23] with Gusti, who works as a picture editor for the *Berliner Tageblatt* and the *Welt-Spiegel*. While Carl was still in prison, she sent him a book of short stories that she co-wrote. The title of the work is: *Must We Get Divorced Straight Away?*[24]

3

As 1932 draws to a close, it has been a year of ups and downs for Schleicher. After weeks of difficult exploratory talks and discussions in back rooms, scheming and dodgy dealings, one thing is abundantly clear: the string-puller is right back to square one. He can't drum up sufficient support, either with the assistance of the political parties or by trying to circumvent them. On the other hand, the triumphant onward march of the National Socialists has been halted. He feels sure that Hitler poses no further problem, nor his movement any significant political danger. Henceforth, the Chancellor now believes, he can rest easy on that score.[25] At the local elections in Thuringia in December, the National Socialists suffer losses of up to 40 per cent.[26] The following ditty appears in the satirical magazine *Simplicissimus*: 'There's one thing that's for sure, / We're very pleased to say / Herr Hitler's on the floor. / That Führer's had his day.'[27] The mood is much the same among the National Socialists themselves. Shortly before Christmas, Hitler writes to Winifred Wagner: 'I've given up all hope.' As soon as he's sure that everything is lost, he tells her, he means to 'end his life with a bullet'.[28] How much more secure, then, must Schleicher feel when he receives a telegram from Hindenburg at Christmas. 'My dear young friend! Thank you for giving me a peaceful, quiet Christmas, the quietest I have experienced during my time in office,' the old statesman writes. 'I'm delighted to tell you how deeply gratified I am at the way you are governing, my dear young friend!'[29] People are apt to be more magnanimous during the festive season, and it is in this spirit that Schleicher himself sends a telegram to his former regimental comrade and predecessor as Chancellor, Franz von Papen: 'All best wishes for '33 and my heartfelt thanks to the standard-bearer in decisive battles over the past year. Fondest regards to his dear little Franz and to his family, from Schleicher.'[30]

Schleicher, who still has feelers out all over the place, and who has got the army's intelligence service to bug phones and conduct surveillance on people's homes, nonetheless does not have the slightest inkling that his 'dear little Franz' has long since been pursuing his own agenda to try and make good the humiliating departure that his successor forced upon him. A golden opportunity comes Papen's way at the annual meeting of the German Gentlemen's Club on 13 December 1932, where he is to appear as the main guest speaker. After his address, he is approached by Baron von Schröder, a private banker in Cologne who belongs to an industrialists' circle named after its founder Wilhelm Keppler. While not representing the crème de la crème of German industry, this body is still a prestigious group of businessmen who have made it their aim to advise the National Socialists in economic matters. Kurt von Schröder proposes to Papen a meeting in his house with Hitler. Keppler brokers the meeting and instructs the host that Hitler 'doesn't drink any alcohol (only water, fruit juice and milk) and in addition has only eaten vegetarian food for the past year or two'.[31]

After his break in Italy, Strasser also reappears on the political stage in the New Year. He has a meeting with Brüning. Both men are in sombre mood; they know that Schleicher's sense of security is wholly misplaced. Hindenburg is receiving a growing number of complaints from industry about Schleicher's 'state-socialist experiments', while large landowners are concerned about the new cabinet's plan to build settlements in the countryside, which they denounce – as they did previously with Brüning – as 'agrarian bolshevism'. No less of a threat is posed by the ambition of Papen, whose influence on the President remains considerable. Following his resignation in November, he has not moved out of his official residence in the Ministry of the Interior, which means that he has access to the President at all times. Brüning begins to have dark forebodings about the year 1933. When he goes out walking on the morning of New Year's Day, he comes across the body of a waiter who has hanged himself in the doorway of a shed.[32]

Then again, maybe things will turn out all right after all. On the morning of 4 January 1933, Schleicher and his prospective vice-chancellor Gregor Strasser pay a call on the Reich President; this audience in the official residence of the head of state goes unnoticed by the press. Hindenburg is impressed by the Bavarian Strasser: 'The man cuts quite a different figure to that Hitler fellow, he's a different proposition altogether. I find Strasser far more congenial.'[33] On the same day, the meeting between Hitler and Papen that was arranged in such a clandestine manner takes place in Cologne. The dentist Elbrechter has got wind of the planned meeting from one of his patients and has dispatched a photographer to Cologne. A retired army captain, one of Strasser's circle, photographs the participants as they enter Baron von Schröder's villa. The next morning, news of the secret meeting in Cologne is the lead story in Hans Zehrer's *Tägliche Rundschau* and is the political sensation of the day. Will Papen, with Hitler's help, succeed in making a comeback as Chancellor? Schleicher's peaceful New Year is now comprehensively over. Elbrechter lays the photos out on his desk and remarks: 'Little Franz has betrayed you!'[34]

4

Why does Schleicher hesitate in appointing his favourite Strasser vice-chancellor? As André François-Poncet asks: 'Is he to be counted among those people who really shine in second place but who fail miserably in the top job?'[35] Has Schleicher switched sides too often? 'Schleicher's clever, but he's not loyal,' says Brüning, and the French ambassador observes: 'Driven by the desire to counter the misconceptions of the Left, he only succeeds in corroborating those of the Right. It was scarcely to be expected that he would ever win support from the Left. But now he's losing all the sympathy the Right once had for him.' When Schleicher takes his old friend Papen to task, Papen strenuously denies having gone behind his back. And yet the very next day, Papen obtains Hindenburg's approval for further secret negotiations with Hitler with a view to winning him round to a government under Papen's leadership. Even though he doesn't yet realize it, Schleicher's days in power are numbered. But Papen, too, has no idea of the true role he will play. For Hitler, his sole function is to open the door to power for him.

On 15 January 1933, elections are held for the regional parliament in the small province of Lippe. The entire constituency of those eligible to vote only numbers just over 100,000. For the National Socialists, whose popularity is on the wane, this couldn't be a more tailor-made opportunity to stage a turnaround in their fortunes. More than 48,000 of the party's pamphlets are delivered, loudspeaker vans tour the streets, canvassers go door-to-door, and a series of prominent National Socialists put in an appearance in the province – Hitler alone delivers seven speeches there in the space of eleven days. The historian Friedrich Meinicke referred to this 'sledgehammer and nut' approach as 'bombarding a village with heavy artillery'.[36] The ensuing victory of the National Socialists in a province with only as many constituents as a single city district of Berlin is puffed up by Goebbels's propaganda machine into a resounding victory for the party throughout the whole of Germany. Even more important than the effect that this symbolic triumph has on their opponents is the boost it gives to morale within their own ranks. Any hint of depression is now dispelled, and Hitler, with his self-confidence reinvigorated, lays claim once more to the chancellorship, and now hardly anyone thinks that he can be denied it.

Soon after, Papen and Hitler hold another meeting, this time in the villa of a mutual acquaintance: Joachim von Ribbentrop. A wine merchant by profession, Ribbentrop is urbane, a gifted linguist and a successful businessman. In 1919, while playing tennis, he gets to know Anneliese Henkell, the daughter of a sparkling wine producer, and they wed the following year. At first, he earns his living representing the Johnnie Walker and Henkell brands.

As the proprietor of an import and export business, in 1923 he commissions a famous Stuttgart architectural practice to design and build a villa for him in the Berlin suburb of Dahlem. The property includes parkland, a tennis court and a swimming pool. This solid and respectable modus vivendi is lent further kudos by the acquisition of an aristocratic title: the family styles itself '*von* Ribbentrop' when the thirty-two-year-old Joachim gets himself adopted by a distant relative from the nobility.

The Dahlem villa of the Ribbentrops is a favourite meeting place for Berlin high society, where the top names in business, politics and culture, including many Jews, come together for cocktail parties and bridge evenings. Whereas Papen's acquaintance with Ribbentrop goes back to the time they served together in Palestine during the war, Hitler and Ribbentrop have only known one another for six months. Ribbentrop, who for a long time showed no interest in politics, is captivated by Hitler's personality and goes to visit him at his home in Berchtesgaden, the Berghof on the Obersalzberg. Their meeting is arranged by an old regimental comrade-in-arms, Count Helldorff, who introduces Ribbentrop to the inner circle of the Nazi leadership in the summer of 1932. Eventually, Hitler and Papen end up meeting in Ribbentrop's villa on several occasions in January 1933, though they fail to come to any agreement. Papen is certain that the Reich President will never accept his interlocutor as Chancellor. Ribbentrop suggests letting the President's son Oskar von Hindenburg in on the act. His relationship with Schleicher has meantime cooled, after Schleicher threatened him: 'If you don't keep your fingers out of politics, I'll have you transferred to the remotest corner of East Prussia.'[37] On 22 January 1933 Oskar von Hindenburg and Otto Meissner, secretary of state in the Office of the Reich President, attend the opera on Unter den Linden in the company of their wives. The piece being performed is Wagner's *Liebesverbot*. Before the curtain rises for the second act, the two men slip away under the cover of darkness and hail a taxi. Halfway through their journey, they change taxis and keep going south through black ice and slush. When they arrive at Ribbentrop's villa in Dahlem, they find Hitler there, who asks the Reich President's son to join him for a private discussion in a separate room. Afterwards, a supper is laid on: hotpot and sparkling wine, served by waiters wearing white gloves. On the way back to the opera, Oskar von Hindenburg sighs: 'I'm afraid we're not going to be able to get round this Hitler chap.'[38]

What has happened to bring about this change of mind in Oskar von Hindenburg? After all, it was he who was originally lambasted by the right wing as 'Red Hindenburg'[39] for his fundamental opposition to a Hitler chancellorship. Has Hitler perhaps threatened to kick up a stink about the Eastern Aid scandal, and the misuse of public funds to develop the Hindenburg estate at Neudeck? Or did Hitler win him round with the promise of political patronage? Oskar von Hindenburg has his eye on becoming the Director-General of the German railways, an appointment that is out of the question without the support of a broad political majority. Furthermore, the property at Neudeck has proved to be a bottomless money pit, having required complete renovation. The estate is still saddled with debts amounting to 400,000 Reichsmarks.[40]

The pointlessness of all the cloak-and-dagger secrecy of the previous evening is revealed the next morning, when Schleicher telephones Otto Meissner and asks him if 'last night's hotpot was good'.[41] Schleicher has now finally got wise to what is going on, but it's too late. That same day, he seeks the President's authority to dissolve parliament for an indefinite period – this is the only way he could continue to remain in office as Chancellor. However, Hindenburg rejects his request with the offhand reply: 'I think not.'[42] Not long after, Papen goes to speak with Hindenburg and attempts to talk him round to the idea of Hitler as Chancellor of an emergency administration, but the President stands firm in his refusal. In the interim, it's becoming ever more unclear who is acting in whose interests. Papen, Ribbentrop and Oskar von Hindenburg are now pulling the strings. At first they try to persuade Hitler to bring the German Nationalist leader Hugenberg on board, then to convince the reluctant Hugenberg of the virtues of a 'Hitler solution', and finally to prevail upon the eighty-five-year-old President Hindenburg to accept Hitler as the Chancellor of an administration mainly made up of Conservatives.

The atmosphere is highly charged. As always before the formation of a new government, Hindenburg receives members of various parties and discusses with them possible ways out of the crisis. Greater than the fear of a Hitler cabinet is the marked aversion all of them express towards Papen being reappointed or to Schleicher's plans to disempower parliament for the foreseeable future. The old hope is voiced that, once burdened with the responsibility of government, Hitler will soon run out of steam. In the *Vossische Zeitung*, Schleicher is warned that if he tries to declare a state of emergency, he will 'instantly have the whole of the German people, from Hitler to Thälmann – albeit from very different perspectives – ranged against him'.[43] On 27 January, Schleicher approaches Hindenburg again: 'To save the Fatherland from tyranny and ruin, the only course that remains is one of self-defence enacted through extraordinary measures and the use of force. The SA, the SS and the KPD must be proscribed, and the most dangerous leaders of radical parties, principally Dr Goebbels, placed under arrest'.[44] Yet Hindenburg spurns any danger of a civil war. Even Schleicher's attitude is inconsistent: his main concern seems to be to prevent a government under the leadership of Papen rather than to stop Hitler – who after all does have the backing of twelve million voters – from becoming Chancellor.

Around midday on 28 January, the Chancellor informs his cabinet of the outcome of his discussion with the President, before walking across the snow-covered garden of the Reich Chancellery, without a coat or hat, to the building next door to request an audience with Hindenburg and submit the resignation en masse of his administration. Having done so, he returns to Otto Meissner's office and vents his spleen: 'The old man will be forced to reinstate me, me and my solution to things. Then we'll really show our teeth to that Brown scoundrel!'[45] That evening, Schleicher and General von Brednow attend the Press Ball in the ballroom at the Marmorhaus. They are the only occupants of the box reserved for the government of the day; none of the ministers have turned up. Schleicher orders champagne, leans against the railing and, smiling, gazes down at the 3,000 guests milling about below, who include the novelists Erich Kästner and Leonhard Frank, the playwright Carl Zuckmayer and the conductor Wilhelm Furtwängler.[46] When the radio news is broadcast at midnight, announcing that Schleicher's cabinet has resigned and that Papen has been tasked with forming a new administration, all eyes turn to the government box. The beams of the spotlights eventually pick out the two men sitting there alone. Schleicher fills his glass, walks over to the balustrade and announces loudly to the public: 'Ladies and gentlemen, your very good health!'[47]

5

So, does this really mean that all is now lost? On 26 January, Kurt von Hammerstein, Chief of the German Army Command, accompanied by General von dem Busche, expresses his deep misgivings to the Chancellor about Hitler being named Reich Chancellor. Hindenburg reassures the generals: 'My dear sirs, you surely can't imagine that I would call upon that Austrian corporal to become Reich Chancellor.'[48] Presently, as they observe matters taking a different course, senior Reichswehr officers hold a meeting with Schleicher in Bendlerstraße on the morning of 29 January. Hammerstein proposes mobilizing the Potsdam garrison, declaring a state of emergency, arresting Hitler and then reaching an accommodation with the SPD. Hammerstein declares that he no longer believes Hindenburg to be of sound mind. On the afternoon of that same Sunday, Hammerstein goes to see Hitler in the house of the Bechstein family (owners of the famous piano-making concern and generous financial backers of Hitler in the 1920s and early 1930s) and receives his reassurance that he will retain Schleicher as Minister of the Army in the event he is named Chancellor.[49] Yet by this time General von Blomberg, head of the German delegation at the disarmament talks in Geneva, has already been sent an urgent telegram summoning him back to Berlin to be sworn in by Hindenburg as the new Reichswehr minister.[50] Blomberg is Hitler's preferred candidate for the post, and, once he has been appointed, Schleicher will no longer be able to do anything.

When Werner von Blomberg arrives at Anhalter Station the next morning, he is met by Hammerstein's adjutant, who has been ordered to intercept him and bring him directly to see Schleicher at the Ministry for the Reichswehr. Also present at the station is Oskar von Hindenburg, who in turn has instructions to take Blomberg to see his father without delay. An argument breaks out. In this extraordinary situation, Blomberg decides not to heed the summons of his immediate superior, but instead that of the head of state. Soon afterwards, at around nine o'clock in the morning, the President swears him in as minister for the Reichswehr in an administration that does not yet exist. Oskar von Hindenburg advises Blomberg not to drive to his ministry in Bendlerstraße straight away, since he would run the risk of being arrested there.[51] Wild rumours of an imminent coup are doing the rounds.

Since the renovation of the Reich Chancellery went ahead, Otto Meissner has been living with his family in a furnished fourteen-bedroom house at number 17 Bendlerstraße. The property belongs to Erik Jan Hanussen. When they moved in, the new occupants had to drape the lampshades with cloths, as they were decorated inside with pornographic images that appeared when the light was switched on. The house bristles with listening devices.[52] It is here that Meissner is woken by a secretary at two o'clock on the morning of 30 January with the news that Schleicher intends to arrest him, the Reich President and his son Oskar. Oskar von Hindenburg's wife claims to have it on good authority that the 'old man' is to be carted off to East Prussia in a 'sealed cattle-truck'.[53] Word has long since spread of Hammerstein's threats to call a state of military emergency, and has also reached the ears of the Nazi leadership.

Count Helldorff immediately places the SS and the SA in Berlin on high alert.[54] Finally another rumour begins to circulate, that Schleicher, through two intermediaries who appeared at the Kaiserhof early that morning, has offered Hitler the opportunity to govern alongside him. An aircraft is allegedly standing by to fly Hindenburg back to Neudeck, and army units have already arrived at the estate to keep the President under house arrest.[55]

On Monday 30 January at 10.30 in the morning, the designated members of the new government gather at Franz von Papen's official residence in Wilhelmstraße. The hasty composition of the cabinet has resulted in chaos. Right up to the eleventh hour, not everyone is clear who is to become Chancellor – Hitler or Papen. Franz Seldte, the federal leader of the Stahlhelm organization, has been appointed labour minister, though no one has informed him of the time of the swearing-in ceremony. When Otto Meissner telephones him in the morning, he is still in bed and explains that he'll scarcely be in a position to appear on time. His deputy, Lieutenant Colonel Theodor Duesterberg, stands in for him. It is barely a year since Duesterberg stood as a Stahlhelm candidate in the election for Reich President and was decried by the Nazi press for his Jewish ancestry. It's essential nothing else goes wrong now. Hitler notices how reserved the lieutenant colonel is towards the National Socialists present, and so goes up to Duesterberg, the grandson of Abraham Selig, the head of the Jewish community council of Paderborn. He grasps his hand firmly and announces, in a voice full of emotion: 'I'm very sorry about the hateful insults levelled at you by my newspapers. I give you my word that this wasn't at my instigation.' Göring also extends his plump hand to Duesterberg and adds: 'It's vital we stand shoulder to shoulder now!'[56]

A more serious problem is posed, however, by the wayward Alfred Hugenberg, leader of the German National People's Party, who continues to rock the boat. With his money and his media influence, Hugenberg has taken control of the German Nationalists and led them on a course of strict opposition to the Republic. He claims to be the leader of the 'nationalist movement': 'We will become a bloc when the iron clamp of ideology joins us together and its firm embrace forces everything that is fluid and yielding to coalesce and coagulate into hard rock. Anyone who might hinder us from realizing our destiny must step aside or be melted down.'[57] Now, though, it's not all about the great overall strategy, but more about tactical details. It is only with great difficulty that Hitler is able to convince him that it would be sensible to dissolve the Reichstag again immediately after taking over government in order to prepare for new elections – the last for quite some time, as he has promised Hindenburg.

Suddenly, Seldte appears after all. Duesterberg, who has just been courted so assiduously by the Nazis, finds the official letter of appointment taken from his hands and torn up.[58] Seldte is handed the document meant for him. Meanwhile, Hindenburg has sent a message asking why the gentlemen have been keeping him waiting for quarter of an hour already. After twenty minutes have elapsed, the party leaders finally reach an agreement. 'Now we can go up at last!'[59] Göring urges. The men walk quickly up the flight of stairs leading to the reception hall, but when they enter the room is empty. Now it's their turn to wait for Hindenburg. The Reich President appears and gets the ceremony over and done with in no time. After reciting the oath and being sworn in, Hitler takes the floor, which is not in the script. In a short address, he stresses that he wants to return to normal parliamentary forms of government for the good of the Fatherland and its citizens.[60] Hindenburg dismisses the cabinet with the words: 'And now, gentlemen, forward with God!'[61]

A quarter of an hour later the car carrying Hitler leaves the Reich

Chancellery. The eight-cylinder Mercedes edges its way at walking pace through the cheering crowd that has assembled to hail the new Reich Chancellor. With tears running down his cheeks, Hitler basks in the ovations and shouts of 'Heil Hitler!' on the short drive to the Kaiserhof. 'We've done it! We've done it!,'[62] he sobs, over and over again. The NSDAP leadership is waiting for him at the hotel; at the south-western corner of the building, on the second floor, SA leader Ernst Röhm keeps an impatient lookout through his binoculars for Hitler's car. 'A few minutes later,' Goebbels reports, 'he is in the room with us. He says nothing and we too remain silent. But his eyes are wet with tears. Our time has come!'[63]

6

'Grandmother is dead!' runs a slogan of the SA.[64] Darkness has long since fallen when, at 7.30 p.m., a torchlit procession of 25,000 SA, SS and Stahlhelm paramilitaries sets off from Charlottenburger Chaussee and heads east, making for the Brandenburg Gate. Count Helldorff has mustered the whole of the Berlin SA and SS, along with some contingents from the surrounding Brandenburg region: 'Young men, nothing but young men, with fresh, boyish faces unsullied by downy beards, eager to be "on duty".'[65] At 8.15, the head of the procession reaches the Brandenburg Gate and Pariser Platz, where it swings right into Wilhelmstraße. The streets are thronged with the dark shapes of people, through which the long procession is moving like a glowing worm.

From the window of the luxury hotel she owns, Hedda Adlon surveys the scene:

Tight formations of men emerged from out of the darkness of the Tiergarten. Between these columns there were marching-bands, whose large drums lent the march its rhythm. There also came the sound of military airs and old Prussian marches.

When the bands came to cross the Pariser Platz, where the French Embassy was famously located, they broke off whatever tune they happened to be playing and, after a few beats of nothing but muffled drum rolls, struck up the provocative tune *Siegreich wollen wir Frankreich schlagen* ('We want to beat France triumphantly'). Many people in the crowd of onlookers lining the route were caught up in the euphoria and broke into sustained applause whenever this tune was played in front of the French Embassy.[66]

Ambassador François-Poncet watches the spectacle from his place of work: 'The men in their brown shirts and tall boots, marching in disciplined ranks and full-throatedly singing battle-songs in unison, exude an enormous enthusiasm and a dynamic power. The onlookers lining their route are swept up in the excitement.'[67]

The artist Max Liebermann, too, is gazing down out of the window of his house on Pariser Platz and encapsulates the scene in a comment that later becomes famous: 'I cannot possibly eat as much as I'd like to puke.'[68] From the Brandenburg Gate it takes the procession seven minutes to reach the old Reich Chancellery, where the old field marshal appears at a window in the north wing;[69] he normally retires to bed at seven o'clock, but today he stays up until midnight, waving to the cheering crowd. And then, as newspapers sympathetic to the Nazi cause report the next morning, 'the cheering swells to the force of a hurricane as, behind the darkened windows of the Reich Chancellery and surrounded by his ministers, Germany's new leader makes an appearance'.[70]

The mood is one of total euphoria. Hitler lavishes praise on Goebbels: 'This Doctor is a sorcerer – where did he get hold of all these torches at such short notice?'[71] And, turning to Papen, the new Reich Chancellor remarks: 'What an enormous task lies ahead of us, Herr von Papen. We must stick together come what may until our task is complete.'[72] The procession turns into Wilhelmplatz and passes the Kaiserhof, where Group Leader Count Helldorff takes the salute. 'Here was history in the making, not written on parchment but hammered down in the heavy, thousandfold marching step of the Brown battalions,' rhapsodizes the correspondent of the *Völkischer Beobachter* the next morning. 'German Berlin is on the march… the SA is on the march!… Berlin and Germany are ours!'[73] Hanussen weighs in with an open letter to Hitler:

> Herr Reich Chancellor! There is no such thing as coincidence! Just as surely as day follows night, some things are cast-iron certainties. The hundred thousand torches which yesterday illuminated your earnest face have not been alight only since that night. They have been glowing within millions of German hearts ever since the day when we realized: It will be Hitler! Herr Reich Chancellor! The torches of 30 January have finally lit the funeral pyres for Moscow and Versailles. They have burned to a cinder the shame felt by sixty million Germans – by everyone, that is, except for the last dregs of a corrupt gutter press. Dismayed, horrified and in a complete daze, the handful of unwashed, dandruff-ridden Soviet scribblers, who up until now have pretended to represent a section of German public opinion, find themselves staring into your face, and what they see bodes ill for them.[74]

A more sober appraisal is offered by a commentator in the *Vossische Zeitung*: 'When the facts contradict one another, you can't just force them to agree, but you can certainly use force to silence any contrary voices among the people. You can't do away with poverty, but you can certainly do away with freedom. Hardship can't be banned. Hunger can't be driven out, but the Jews can be. For the present, the constitution guards against the worst abuses of power but, to use a favourite term of Goebbels, the ties that secure it have worn "paper thin".'[75]

Red Circles

1

At the end of January 1933, a young unemployed jobbing bricklayer sets off on the long journey by foot from Leiden in the Netherlands to Berlin. For the past four years, he has been living off a pension that he has drawn upon since suffering a work-related injury – during a scuffle among apprentices, quicklime got into his eyes and robbed him of two-thirds of his sight. He takes almost three weeks to cover the entire route, which leads him via Cleve, Düsseldorf, Essen, Bochum, Dortmund, Braunschweig and Magdeburg. Sometimes a car will stop and pick him up. He's not the only person around this time who is trekking across Europe with little in the way of baggage or money. Communal hostels or the churches provide these people with a roof over their heads. On one occasion, he runs across a fellow traveller who greets him with the words: 'Hey there! Long live Moscow! Where's the nearest monastery round here?'[1]

He hitches a lift with a lorry for the final stretch from Potsdam to Berlin. He arrives in the city on 18 February 1933, a Saturday, and finds lodgings at a hostel on Fröbelstraße in the Prenzlauer Berg district. This isn't his first time in Berlin, so he knows where to go to get welfare handouts. In Gleimstraße, there's a communal

kitchen where he has lunch now and then. The jobbing bricklayer travels extensively around the city, mostly on foot. At his digs on Fröbelstraße, he's required to muck in on snow-clearing duties, so he switches to the men's hostel on Alexandrinenstraße, but then returns to Fröbelstraße. On the Tuesday, he joins the queue outside the welfare office and is given a meal voucher. At around 3 p.m. he goes to a cinema in the vicinity of Alexanderplatz, which is showing the film *Der Rebell* ('The Rebel'). On Thursday, he notices a poster on an advertising column for an election rally by the KPD that same evening, where Wilhelm Pieck is billed as the main speaker. He obtains a free ticket, but the event is cancelled before it begins.[2]

He has been in Berlin for a week now, and it's the afternoon of Saturday 25 February. The jobless brickie walks south from Alexanderplatz to Hermannplatz. In Liegnitzer Straße, he asks where he can buy 'those things for lighting stoves'. By the time he makes it to the Neukölln district, it's five o'clock and already getting dark. There, he spends thirty pfennigs on four packets of firelighters of a brand called 'Oldin – For the Houseproud Housewife' and some matches, clambers over a hedge and throws a burning firelighter through an open window of the Neukölln welfare office, which is housed in a wooden barracks on Mittelweg. He chucks two more lit firelighters onto the tarpaper roof. Without waiting to see what happens, he hurries to the nearest underground station and takes a train back to Alexanderplatz. At the town hall on the square, he notices an open window to a cellar, into which he drops a burning packet of firelighters before quickly making off in the direction of the City Palace.

By now it is 8 p.m. He climbs the left side of the palace's portico and gains access to the roof. There he gets rid of the last of the firelighters by dropping a lighted packet through an open skylight and hurries away, again without waiting to see the results of his handiwork. The following morning, a Sunday, Marinus van der Lubbe sets off on a long trek via Charlottenburg to the far outskirts of the city at Hennigsdorf, arriving there shortly after 6 p.m. He reports to the police in order to obtain shelter as a vagrant and, as the law requires, he is locked up in a cell at the station for the night. It is 26 February 1933.[3]

2

In January 1933, Eugen Hönig – who from November of that year will serve as the first president of the Reich Chamber of the Visual Arts and work to promote a 'German art' informed by 'eternal racial values' – accepts a commission from a prominent Jewish private client: a complete refit of the interior of a seven-room town house at Lietzenburger Straße 16 in Berlin's prestigious Westend district.[4] In truth, it's a bread-and-butter job for Hönig, the only challenging aspects being the tight deadlines, which are hedged around with punitive penalty clauses, and the client's numerous architectural and technical special requirements.

The job is completed in six weeks. The ceiling in the anteroom is magically lit so as to appear like the vault of heaven, and when the lights are turned down the stars emit a phosphorescent glow. The signs of the zodiac, lit from below, have been installed in the floor. One wall is occupied by a huge aquarium and a flowing fountain. Loudspeakers and film projectors have been placed at various strategic points. All the rooms are equipped with an electronic bugging system. Terraria house lizards and snakes, there is a large aviary full of birds and statues of the Buddha are set in niches with ghostly lighting. However, the centrepiece, the inner sanctum of this arcanum, is the consulting room. In it, a flight of steps leads up to a podium, on which stands the massive ebony desk of the master. Individual groups of chairs upholstered in leather are set round about at a distance calculated to inspire awe and respect. The rest of the room is taken up by a circular, rotating counter with a table top that is lit from below. In the centre of this, elevated on a throne-like seat, sits the master.[5] No question about it, Hanussen has gone all out for effect.

It would probably be a bit over the top to call the opening on the evening of 26 February 1933 of the 'Palace of the Occult', as the magician dubs his new residence, as a major social event for Berlin. But at least many of the city's movers and shakers – if not its absolute 'A' listers – have promised to attend. They include Prince Louis Ferdinand, Kaiser Wilhelm II's son, the actresses Maria Paudler and Anni Markart, the singer Willi Domgraf-Fassbaender and the writers Hans Possendorf and Hanns Heinz Ewers. The Grand Duchess Anastasia Romanova, the daughter of the last czar, attracts particular interest this evening. Unaccountably, she has somehow escaped the execution of the entire Russian royal family, which was personally ordered by Lenin. The Grand Duchess's existence first came to public attention in 1920, when she was admitted to a psychiatric clinic after attempting to commit suicide by drowning herself in the Landwehrkanal in Berlin. Strangely, Anastasia Romanova doesn't speak or understand Russian, but in view of the ordeal she and her family went through in her homeland, she can be sure of a sympathetic hearing.

Today, we know that the real Anastasia did indeed die a wretched death fifteen years earlier in Yekaterinburg. She wasn't killed by the bullets fired by the Bolshevik death squad, which lodged in her undergarments and the coins and other valuables that she had sewn into them. But then the Chekists set about her and her sisters with their bayonets. The execution turned into an orgy of butchery lasting twenty minutes. In the end, the twelve-year-old Czarevitch Alexei, the heir to the Russian throne, was killed by a shot through his ear as he lay moaning on the ground. In order to make the corpses unidentifiable, sulphuric acid was later poured onto the victims' faces. The woman who was fêted in Berlin as the daughter of the czar, on the other hand, was in fact called Franziska Schanzkowsky, a factory worker who had fetched up in the capital after leaving her native West Prussia. It is unclear whether she fell prey to her own delusion or was simply a fraudster, but in the event she survived until 1984, when she died in the USA.

That Sunday evening, the rooms of Hanussen's palace slowly fill with guests. Count Helldorff, the leader of the SA in Berlin and Brandenburg, only puts in an appearance late in the day; he is the only one in uniform. On the stroke of midnight, Hanussen gives demonstrations of his clairvoyance. Each of his guests is permitted to ask him one question. Franziska Schanzkowsky, the fake czar's daughter, has her identity as Anastasia Romanova confirmed by Hanussen. Count Helldorff passes the seer a note: he is keen to know the outcome of the election on 5 March. 'Germany will take great strides towards its resurrection,' prophesies Hanussen.[6]

'The parliamentary elections will result in an unprecedented triumph for populist ideology and an overwhelming majority of the German people for Hitler and his government. I see Germany once more at the head of the civilized nations of the world, I see its fields blossoming again and its workshops humming with activity [...] I see Hitler's victory and Germany's ascent once again to the sunlight.' Consciously or unconsciously, the clairvoyant's arm stiffens into the straight-armed Roman salute.[7] His guests, it is subsequently reported in Hanussen's newspaper, respond 'with an enthusiastic show of support for a nationalist Germany'.[8]

Hanussen now asks for a medium, but no one steps forward. Eventually he goes and seeks one out himself, lighting upon Maria Paudler, who is led up to the podium amid much protest. She is seated in the master's ebony chair, whose excessively high armrest is shaped like a magic circle, and is handed a glass of sparkling wine, which she quickly downs. By now, Hanussen has already begun to wave his hands directly in front of her face. 'I pulled my head back and closed my eyes for an instant,'[9] the actress later recalled,

> and then it started! All of a sudden, in a sing-song voice, he asked me if I could see red circles? Of course, a lot of

after-images flutter behind your lids when you close your eyes in a brightly lit room that has suddenly been plunged into darkness by some unseen hand... and then there were those extraordinary zodiac symbols all around me in this completely alien environment... and I also started to notice the effects of the glass of wine, which was still repeating on me... and so I replied 'Yes!'. But then, when he kept on asking in an ever more insistent way whether it might be flames I was seeing... flames from a large building... some unerring instinct told me that this scenario was going beyond the bounds of a mere parlour game...

Maria Paudler extricates herself by falling into a faint and sinking into the arms of Hanussen's secretary. By now, it is Monday morning.

3

On the morning of 27 February, at 7.45, Marinus van der Lubbe is released from police custody in Henningsdorf. He sets off for the city centre on foot, passing through Tegel and Wedding en route. On the way, he stops in Müllerstraße to buy another four packs of firelighters. At around 2 p.m., he is standing outside the Reichstag. He scouts out the building from every angle. In the hours that follow, the bricklayer takes another stroll around the centre of Berlin, first walking south to Potsdamer Platz, then down Leipziger Straße to Alexanderplatz. Finally returning to the Reichstag, he scrambles up onto a ledge running at head height to the right of the main flight of steps and makes it onto a balcony. A few minutes after 9 p.m. he kicks in the glass of a set of French windows that give onto the restaurant, where he sets fire to the first packet of firelighters and places it beneath a curtain.

At the same time, in the Sportpalast in Potsdamer Straße, the

Social Democrats are commemorating the fiftieth anniversary of Karl Marx's death. In fact, the actual date is still more than a fortnight hence, but owing to the forthcoming elections the event has been brought forward. On the flimsiest of pretexts, the police close down the meeting before it is due to end – a sly way of helping the National Socialists, and a fact of life to which all other parties have since grown accustomed. Meanwhile, in the Gentlemen's Club on Voßstraße, Paul von Hindenburg is attending a reception.[10] This evening, the 'pacesetters of misery', as Thomas Mann calls the denizens of this establishment, are hosting the annual gathering of former Imperial Household Cavalry officers. At peak strength, this association numbers some 5,000 members, who regard themselves as the country's conservative elite. The dinner has been organized by Vice-Chancellor Franz von Papen, a founder member of the club. From 9.30 on, news begins to circulate that a fire has broken out in the Reichstag. Hindenburg gets up and looks out of the window at the red glow cast by the burning cupola of the grand building that was designed by Paul Wallot. Swirls of smoke drift across to his vantage point. The field marshal does not seem unduly troubled. Papen accompanies him back to Wilhelmstraße and then has the chauffeur drive him on to the burning building.[11]

A crowd of morbid sightseers, along with journalists and politicians who have been alerted to what is happening, have already gathered at the scene. The thermometer stands at minus 4° Celsius. With only a few hundred metres to walk from his office on Unter den Linden, the first politician to arrive is the President of the Reichstag, Hermann Göring. Hitler is spending the evening at Goebbels's invitation at the Gauleiter's private apartment on Reichskanzlerplatz. They race 'at 100 kilometres per hour down the Charlottenburger Chaussee towards the scene of the crime'.[12] No sooner has he arrived there – by which time it is ten o'clock – than the Reich Chancellor turns to Sefton Delmer, the Berlin correspondent of the *Daily Express*, and later head of the Soldatensender Calais radio station,* and announces: 'You are now witnessing the beginning of a great new epoch in German history, Herr Delmer. This fire is the beginning.'[13] It has been quite some trajectory, from the high point of the Cannonade of Valmy† to the nadir of the Reichstag fire! But has the genie of revolutionary politics, which has held the world in thrall ever since the storming of the Bastille, now finally been put back in the bottle?

Between 9.30 and 9.45, Erik Jan Hanussen tries to contact the managing director of his publishing house by telephone. But he is no longer in the office. Instead, the editor-in-chief of two newspapers that are printed in the same building finally picks up the receiver. Hanussen enquires about the Reichstag fire and the possible perpetrator. He is told that there are unconfirmed reports about a band of communists being responsible for the arson attack. The editor adds that this is highly implausible, to which Hanussen responds indignantly, telling him he's certain it's a communist plot, the consequences of which will soon become clear.[14]

In the meantime, the gathering of people at the burning Reichstag continues to grow. A thousand rubbernecks have come to gawp, and the police cordon off the area. Among the crowd, 'silent for minutes on end and fearing the worst',[15] is Hans Kippenberger, head of the 'military-political apparatus' of the KPD. Hanussen's arch-enemy, the communist editor Bruno Frei, has also come to witness the spectacle: 'I was staring at the dome of the building,

---

* The Soldatensender Calais radio station was a misinformation broadcaster established in 1943 by Britain's Political Warfare Executive. It masqueraded as a transmitter of the German military broadcasting network. Sefton Delmer's extensive pre-war knowledge of Germany and German culture made him the ideal choice to conduct 'black ops' for Britain during the Second World War. Delmer described the work of the station in his second volume of memoirs, *Black Boomerang* (1962). [Translator's note]

† The military engagement at Valmy, which took place in northeastern France on 20 September 1792, was the first victory of the army of France in the Revolutionary Wars that followed the French Revolution. Fought against a combined Austro-Prussian force, it is often referred to as a 'cannonade' rather than a battle because it consisted primarily of an artillery bombardment. [Translator's note]

eerily lit from the inside, and in the process tripped over some black fire hoses.'[16] Several hundred firemen have been called out. Yet the fire engines that race to the scene don't stand a chance. In the main debating chamber, the seating is ablaze, and in this lofty space the chimneying effect of the fire generates temperatures of up to 1,000°C. When senior civil servant Rudolf Diels, who is presently set to become the first head of the Gestapo, turns up to report to Göring, he finds the Reich Chancellor beside himself with fury. 'Now I saw that his face was purple with agitation and with the heat. He shouted uncontrollably, as I had never seen him do before, as if he was going to burst: "There will be no mercy now. Anyone who stands in our way will be cut down. The German people will not tolerate leniency. Every communist official will be shot where he is found. All the communist deputies must be strung up this very night. Everybody in league with the communists must be arrested. There will be no longer be any protection either for Social Democrats or the "Reichsbanner".'[17] Another eyewitness, Joseph Goebbels, notes in his diary: 'Hitler is in a towering rage.'[18]

Almost the entire Nazi elite have gathered at the Reichstag. But where are the other politicians? Ernst Thälmann is chairing a clandestine meeting of the Politburo at a pub in Gudrunstraße in Lichtenberg that evening. Two days previously, he penned a lengthy report for the Comintern leadership in Moscow from his hideout: 'As we have now learned, before the next election Hitler is planning to drop another bombshell [...] SS men are going to carry out a supposed communist assassination attempt against Hitler, which will of course fail. On the one hand, this will foment the necessary pogrom atmosphere for a ban to be imposed, while on the other it will take votes from the Communist Party and ultimately, and above all, trigger an election landslide for the Nazis.'[19] On his way home from the meeting, Thälmann wonders why there are so many firemen in evidence.[20] He only learns about the Reichstag fire, which by then has also been reported on the radio, from Martha Kluczynski, whose house he arrives at just before midnight. His name is at the very top of the lists of communist officials who are to be placed under arrest. In the days that follow, he doesn't venture outside his lover's home in Lützowstraße.

Carl von Ossietzky spends that evening with friends at his girlfriend Gusti Hecht's flat huddled round the radio listening to the unfolding news of the Reichstag fire. His friends urge him not to return home but to get out of the country without delay. His rejoinder is that they won't be able to track him down that fast, since he hasn't put a name plaque up on his door at home.[21] He comes up with a whole string of other excuses. Out on the street, it's teeming with police and SA stormtroopers, and the newspapers are rushing out special editions. Back home, Maud greets him with the question: 'What are we going to do now?' 'First of all, get some sleep,' is Carl's reply. She urges him to flee, but he shakes his head: 'No, I'll just give it three days.'[22] Who knows, perhaps things won't be so bad after all? Ossietzky isn't in any hurry to relinquish everything he's worked for. How is he supposed to earn a living abroad? The family is heavily in debt, what with the redecoration of the apartment, the treatment costs for Maud's alcohol addiction and Rosalinde's school fees – even the generous remuneration he receives as editor-in-chief of *Die Weltbühne* can't cover all those outgoings.[23] The couple try in vain to get some sleep that night. Maud gets up and brews coffee, which they drink together in silence before going back to bed. At half past three in the morning there is a ring at the door. Two detectives produce their warrant cards and ask to see Carl von Ossietzky. They allow him enough time to wash and get dressed. Carl eats a slice of bread and butter without saying a word, drinks a cup of hastily brewed coffee and then takes his leave of Maud with the words: 'Chin up! I'll be back soon.'[24]

And where is Brüning? Since the end of January, he has been laid low with bronchitis at St Hedwig's Catholic Hospital in the Mitte district of the city. On 11 February, Kurt von Schleicher visits him; they talk for four hours, primarily about the events of the past few years and they get things straightened out as far as their personal relationship is concerned. On 16 February, Brüning, though still not fully recovered, flings himself back into the political arena. He is now only able to hold election hustings for the Centre Party under heavy police protection. After giving a speech in Karlsruhe, he is escorted from the venue by a police squad: 'I was put into a car, with police cars following. I heard shots ring out behind me; several young people from the Bavarian People's Party [the Bavarian branch of the Centre Party] lay dead or wounded on the street.'[25] In Breslau (Wrocław), his own constituency, 16,000 people listen to his speech in the Century Hall: 'So, are those of us who have served the Reich President, and who voted for him in February and April, now seen as outlaws, while those who opposed him, it would appear, have the right to oppress and abuse the Reich President's supporters?'[26] he asks, referring to the National Socialists' growing campaign of terror. On the evening of the Reichstag fire, the former Chancellor is speaking in Gelsenkirchen.

4

And what of Count Helldorff? Could his whereabouts be accounted for the whole time, as Göring later swears under oath? Or was he even instrumental in starting the fire? In the heated election atmosphere, speculation is rife from the word go about who was responsible. While Hitler affects to believe that it was a signal for a communist uprising – years later, apropos of nothing, he voices the conviction that Ernst Torgler, the leader of the KPD faction in the Reichstag, set the building alight[27] – many contemporary observers take the view that the Reichstag fire was staged by the National Socialists. Even high-ranking Nazi officials like Alfred Rosenberg aren't sure: 'I only hope that our people had nothing to do with it. That would be just the kind of stupid thing some of them are capable of.'[28] There is a joke that does the rounds at this time: 'Mummy, Mummy, the Reichstag's on fire!' – 'Eat, eat, my child!' (The German for 'Eat, eat' is *Ess, Ess* = 'SS').[29]

Although the exact sequence of events has been pieced together down to the last minute, the question of who might have been complicit in the crime remains open to this day. Even at the time, pieces of supposed evidence and photographs are manipulated by all sides. Witnesses are paid or threatened and documents are forged. While the National Socialists finger the communists Torgler, Dimitroff, Popoff and Taneff as the alleged arsonists on the basis of a set of circumstantial evidence that is full of holes, the communists attempt, from exile, to persuade world public opinion that Göring is guilty. In Paris, under the aegis of the publisher Willi Münzenberg, two so-called 'Brown Books' appear, which alongside verifiable facts also contain many fabrications, cleverly tailored so as to seem within the realms of the plausible. The editors' task is made easier by the fact that the Nazis' barbarism and unscrupulousness is already well attested in many instances. The German communists who have been driven into exile can also count on the credulity of prominent intellectuals and artists outside Germany. The 'Brown Books' reach a circulation of over a million and are translated into seventeen languages. One of the authors is Bruno Frei, who, as editor-in-chief of the *Berlin am Morgen*, has just been facing Hanussen in court in a libel action. The other contributors to the 'Brown Books' include Alexander Abusch, Albert Norden, Alfred Kantorowicz, Max Schroeder, Gustav Regler and Arthur Koestler.

A wide range of fates eventually befalls these collaborators on the 'Brown Books'. After the war, Abusch and Norden become SED party functionaries in the Stalinist German Democratic Republic, and Schroeder the first editor-in-chief of the state's literary publishing house Aufbau Verlag. Kantorowicz, Regler and Koestler, on the other hand, later turn into apostates from the communist cause; in 1940, from his exile in Britain, where he was to spend the rest of his life, Koestler publishes his bestselling novel *Darkness at Noon*, a powerful indictment of totalitarianism. Otto Katz is also involved as an anonymous author; under the cover name 'André Simon', Katz led a glamorous life as a Comintern agent in France, the USA and Mexico. After the Reichstag fire, he worms his way into the confidence of the van der Lubbe family and, using made-up quotations, falsely claims that the arsonist was a homosexual, because it suits the general tenor of the 'Brown Books' to taint him by association with the SA. After the war, Katz becomes the chief editor of *Rudé pravo*, the official newspaper of the Communist Party of Czechoslovakia, but falls victim during the Slánsky Trial to the anti-Semitic purges of the late Stalin era. He is executed in December 1952 and his ashes mixed with the salt and grit that is spread on the icy winter streets of Prague. In the aftermath of the show trials held in the Soviet Union during the late 1930s, Münzenberg himself, the 'Red Hugenberg' who was the driving force behind the 'Brown Books' enterprise, also begins to doubt the doctrinaire party line. In October 1940, his body is found in woodland near the village of Montagne in the South of France, with a noose around his neck.

The 'Brown Books' are so successful that their ripples are also felt in Leipzig. It is here, in September 1933, that the Reichstag fire trial opens. Immediately, a point of key concern is the whereabouts of Count Helldorff on the night in question. Did this 'degenerate and perverted aristocrat',[30] as the 'Brown Books' claim, take 'his catspaw' Marinus van der Lubbe into the Reich President's palace, from where he could have gained access to the Reichstag through an underground corridor? There is nothing to substantiate this allegation. After the war, Arthur Koestler recalled: 'But how could we make the naïve West believe such a fantastic story? [...] We had, in fact, not the faintest idea of the concrete circumstances. We had to rely on guesswork, on bluffing and on the intuitive knowledge of the methods and minds of our opposite numbers in totalitarian conspiracy.'[31] Helldorff himself attests that, on the night of the fire, he was in his office until around 7 p.m. Thereafter, he claims, he went out to dine with the staff leader of the SA Group Berlin–Brandenburg, Achim von Arnim, in the oyster restaurant Klinger on Rankestraße.[32] There, a telephone call informed them of the Reichstag fire. In American captivity in Bad Mondorf in 1945 with nothing more to gain, Göring is said to have assured Hindenburg's secretary of state Otto Meissner that he'd had nothing to do with the Reichstag fire. However, he went on, he didn't exclude the possibility that 'rogue elements […] possibly even the Berlin SA leaders Count Helldorff and Karl Ernst, were the plotters and instigators of the Reichstag fire and to this end had used van der Lubbe as their dupe.'[33] At the Nuremberg Trials, Göring asserts: 'I had no reason or motive for setting fire to the Reichstag.' He invokes an aesthetic argument: 'From the artistic point of view I did not at all regret that the assembly chamber was burned – I hoped to build a better one. But I did regret very much that I was forced to find a new meeting place for the Reichstag and, not being able to find one, I had to give up my Kroll Opera House, that is, the second State Opera House, for that purpose. The opera seemed to me much more important than the Reichstag.'[34]

Finale furioso

1

Even during the night of the Reichstag fire, arrests are made throughout Germany both of communists and KPD sympathizers and of Social Democrats and diehard supporters of the Weimar Republic. The detention lists, which have existed since November 1932, are not only sent to the police, but are also wired by the Wolff Telegraphic Bureau (WTB) to all its affiliated news agencies. As a result, even as dawn is breaking on 28 February, many journalists get to learn of their impending detention.[1] At eleven o'clock that morning, the Reich cabinet meets in Berlin, and is presented with the hastily drafted 'Presidential Decree Concerning Safeguarding the People and the State'. Göring, who days before made tens of thousands of SA, SS and Stahlhelm paramilitaries auxiliary police, invokes the spectre of communist acts of terrorism, such as bombings and other outrages aimed at crippling 'the electricity and transport networks'.[2] The assembled ministers of state, who for the most part are not National Socialists, promptly signal their assent to the measure, with just a handful of minor amendments.

At the end of the meeting, Hitler and Papen go to see Hindenburg. They give him a report about the previous day's events. The Reich

Chancellor points out the arsonist's communist background. During the previous year, he claims, three thousand hundredweight of explosives were stolen in Germany and have allegedly ended up in the hands of the communists.[3] The two men both urge the Reich President to approve the emergency legislation, which he duly does that same evening. At a stroke, as has happened so many times before in the Weimar Republic, this sets aside people's most basic civil rights. At a rally in Frankfurt two days before the elections, on 3 March, Göring sets the future direction of travel: 'The measures I'm planning to institute won't be hampered by any legalistic reservations or bureaucracy. My job isn't to administer justice, it's simply to destroy and eradicate.'[4] For the first time, the National Socialists make the astonishing discovery that a harsh crackdown directed against minorities can command the support of the masses. Dread of a communist-led coup haunts large sections of the populace. For most people, the fear of relapsing into political chaos is greater even than any trepidation about the unknown, about what's set to come.

Many Germans, perhaps even a majority, feel liberated from a parliamentary system with more than a dozen parties and from the fruitless debates that do nothing to alleviate people's suffering – in short, they're happy to be freed from the business of democracy. On 20 April, the forty-fourth birthday of the people's chancellor is celebrated throughout Germany. In the capital, the local authority for the Mitte district plants a Hitler lime tree in his honour in the Tiergarten, while in Westend, Reichskanzlerplatz is renamed Adolf-Hitler-Platz. In May 1933, the NSDAP registers sixty times more applications to join the party than in January.[5] Entire platoons of the Red Front Fighting League defect to the SA, complete with their marching bands.

And where people show no enthusiasm, terror is used to help them toe the line. 'Italian Fascism was a kindergarten next to it,' is Dorothy Thompson's verdict. During the period of the Reichstag fire, she is staying in Berlin and observing events as they unfold. Thompson witnesses SA stormtroopers cruelly abusing their victims, as they beat them with 'steel rods, knock their teeth out with revolver butts, break their arms or – a favorite trick – give them a liter of castor oil; bring them out of unconsciousness by throwing water in their faces, or mustard in their eyes, urinate on them, make them kneel and kiss the *Hakenkreuz* [the swastika]. Not a single newspaper dares to bring [out] anything of true events. The *Berliner Tageblatt* is unrecognizable. Three days ago the leading article was devoted to an account of conditions in Chile.'[6]

As head of the political division of the Prussian police in March 1933, it is Rudolf Diels's job to counter the worst excesses of the *Sturmabteilung*. The British newspaper correspondent Sefton Delmer describes him as a 'handsome young fellow of the modern managerial type, with a quick grasp and a superb gift of concentration'.[7] In command of a squad of a hundred Potsdam police, he surrounds a chaotically run internment camp that the SA has established in the town of Bornim near Potsdam. Without more ado, the SA men set up machine guns to repel the police. After the war, Diels recounts:

The camp commandant informed me that he would under no circumstances release his prisoners unless he received a direct order to that effect from the SA Group Leader Karl Ernst. He told me that the inmates of his camp included several well-known Communist terrorists, and that he wasn't about to let these men escape being 'worked over'. I was only able to form an impression of the terrible methods employed in these 'workings-over' a few hours later […] As I later learned, some of the detainees in this camp had been castrated by being forced to sit on the rapidly spinning wheels of a revved-up motorbike that had been bolted upside-down onto the floor.[8]

Soon after, in the first night of the spring of 1933, the Social Democrat Berlin city councillor Marie Jankowski, whose special area of concern is youth welfare and social services, is abducted from her apartment and taken to the SA meeting house on Elisabethstraße in Köpenick. In a barracks in the courtyard, the forty-six-year-old Jankowski is forced to strip and lie naked on a pallet covered with the black, red and gold flag of the Weimar Republic. For two hours, she is beaten by young men wielding clubs, steel bars and whips: 'They made me list the colours of the Republic, but instead of saying "Black, Red and Gold" I had to say "Black, Red and Shit. They asked me questions like: "Were you paid money by the Social Services Department?" "Did you take in Communists and feed them?" "Did you steal shoes from the unemployed?" and "Did you draw up a list of Nazi businesses to be boycotted?"'[9]

Eventually Marie Jankowski and two communist workers who were also being tortured at the SA house are forced to sing 'Deutschland, Deutschland über alles...' and she is made to sign a pledge that she will leave the SPD and renounce politics for good: 'Whereupon a remarkable change ensued in the way I was being treated. I was given a glass of water. My clothes were brushed down and handed back to me. The group leader ordered an SA man to "escort the lady out". The man supported me when I was about to keel over and closed the door behind me with a polite "Good night!"'. Marie Jankowski's husband lodges an official complaint but the police tell him that their hands are tied.

The main source of resistance at this time is the communists. Customers shopping in the atria of the big department stores are repeatedly subjected to showers of anti-Nazi leaflets from the upper floors. To evade capture, the activists employ so-called 'Flyer-Seesaws'. A board is placed on the balustrade of the atrium, weighed down at one end with a pile of leaflets and counterbalanced at the other with a leaky beach bucket half filled with water. Once enough water has drained from the bucket, the weight shifts to the pile of leaflets and the whole lot topples over into the atrium. Meanwhile, the culprit has had ample time to make a clean getaway.

Just three weeks and two days after rubber-stamping the 'Decree Concerning Safeguarding the People and the State', the German parliament – in the face of Social Democrat opposition and in the absence of the communist delegates, whose mandates have been 'annulled' – passes the Enabling Act. Under the impact of the ongoing Nazi campaign of terror and in the hope of still being able to bring some influence to bear on developments, even Brüning votes in favour of the bill, which retrospectively enshrines in law parliament's state of impotence. Now the action that has been foretold for years on campaign posters of the NSDAP actually comes to pass. In its last but one regular edition, *Die Weltbühne*, in an article entitled 'German for Germans', spells out the Nazi agenda: 'Our aim is to eradicate the vulture of Marxism root and branch!'[10] – an unintentionally comic mixed metaphor that only serves to heighten the grim seriousness of what is happening.

2

Three days after the parliamentary elections, in which almost five million voters still cast their ballots for the communists and over seven million back the Social Democrats, the following summary of the result appears in Hanussen's newspaper: 'So, the die is cast. From the top of the former bastion of the Communist terror regime, the Karl-Liebknecht-House in Berlin, the swastika flag now flies proudly as the symbol of Germany's final liberation from the Red pestilence. Cast to the four winds, wiped out and forced to their knees are the emissaries of Soviet Russia, the men of the KPD.'[11] Hanussen is cock-a-hoop: 'For years, I have been dreaming of the day that has finally dawned. Year after year, I found myself compelled to do battle with that rabble from the Münzenberg media […] And now they've all been swept aside and crushed! Whipped out of the country! The Soviet legionaries have been neutralized with a single swipe of the nation's mighty paw as it awakes. And Hitler will make sure that they never show their faces here again […].'

These are uncertain times; they hold great opportunities for some, but also unforeseeable risks. The clairvoyant is punch-drunk; Bruno Frei's sustained campaign against him, targeting his Jewish heritage, has caused irreparable damage. Still, Hanussen attempts to hit back, getting himself baptized in February 1933 and applying to join the Nazi Party in March. At the same time, he hopes to profit from the coming of the new age. Hanussen would dearly love to be in the mix when the media landscape of Berlin is reorganized; he has set his sights on acquiring the *Berliner Tageblatt*. He has half the leadership of the SA in his pocket, almost all of whom are in debt to him – the notorious gambler Count Helldorff, the head of the SA Ernst Röhm, his deputies Wilhelm Ohst and Karl Ernst, and in all likelihood Hermann Göring, too. He's lent them all money at some stage, and the IOUs are safely under lock and key. And haven't his friends from the SA also attended his 'weekend excursions' aboard his luxury motor yacht, *Ursel IV*, flying the swastika ensign, and gone skinny-dipping in Lake Scharmützel with 'willing women and boys'?[12] Won't all that play to the Jew Hermann Steinschneider's advantage now? Or will it prove his undoing?

In the event, the end comes very quickly. At around eight o'clock on the evening of 24 March 1933, a three-man death squad assembled earlier that evening by Karl Ernst and under the command of Wilhelm Ohst comes knocking at the 'Palace of the Occult'. Hanussen's secretary greets Ohst in 'a very friendly manner' and tells him: 'Go right on up, the boss is in his study.' Hanussen reacts with astonishment and anger when the man he thought was his friend tells him he's under arrest: 'Arrested!!??? And by you of all people, my dear Ohst? No, that can't be right – I ask you, don't play practical jokes like this on me after I've bailed you out so many times!' Ohst asks Hanussen to hand over all the outstanding IOUs. The other SA men present are not allowed to have sight of them. Ohst declares that it pains him to have to confront Hanussen like this, has a quick word with the ladies present and takes his leave of the clairvoyant's secretary.[13] The men drive off in Hanussen's red Bugatti, with Hanussen in the front passenger seat; their destination is the SA barracks on General-Pape-Straße. At around midnight, the detainee manages to call his wife, Elfriede Rühle, on the telephone and tells her: 'That swine Ohst has arrested me.'[14] The connection is abruptly terminated.

That same evening, Ohst informs his commanding officer Karl Ernst that he has carried out his orders. At the time, Ernst is enjoying an evening's socializing in the company of the senior civil servant Rudolf Diels and others. The next morning, the silver-grey Cadillac that the clairvoyant placed at the disposal of the regional NSDAP leadership is parked outside the door of the 'Palace of the Occult'. Inside the car are keys and documents. In a letter to the police, Karl Ernst maintains that he also handed back another car to Hanussen the day before, as he couldn't accept gifts 'for an SA department from a man who has in the meantime been exposed as a Jew'.[15] It is only a fortnight later, on the morning of 7 April, that the clairvoyant's body, which has by then started to decompose, is discovered by road menders in a small pine plantation next to the road running from Baruth to Neuhof, south of Berlin. The corpse exhibits injuries that are consistent with shots from a large-calibre revolver. One of the three bullets entered the skull behind the left ear and exited through the forehead. The face has been gnawed by wild animals and is badly disfigured.

3

'That's our man!'[16] the commander of the police squad is said to have exclaimed – clearly amazed at the rapid success of his search operation – when, at around 3.30 on the afternoon of 3 March, he surprises Ernst Thälmann while he is packing a suitcase at his carelessly chosen hideout, the Kluczynskis' house at Lützowstraße 9. An indictment is duly drawn up against Thälmann for having allegedly planned a coup. In January 1934 the Gestapo attempt to extract a confession from him. Eight Gestapo operatives, their fists raised in the customary Red Front salute, are there to receive him when he is led into the interrogation room on the fourth floor of the Gestapo headquarters on Prinz-Albrecht-Straße.[17] To begin with, they adopt the 'good cop' routine to try and get him to talk. When that fails, they move on to hypnosis: the prisoner is made to kneel in front of a hypnotist, who spends three-quarters of an hour, as Thälmann later recalls, 'magnetizing around me'. When this, too, yields no positive result, they resort to torture. He is struck in the face, knocking out four of his teeth, given a brutal kicking, and then lashed with a hippopotamus-hide whip, first on his back and buttocks and then full in the face. Stricken with 'severe angina' and foaming at the mouth, Thälmann lies prone on the floor of the interrogation room. It is only in the late evening, when the cleaning ladies arrive and the Gestapo men start worrying that they will be able to hear the tortured man's screams of pain, that they bring the torture session to an end.[18] It has lasted for more than four hours.

At this time, Hermann Göring is fond of playing the role of the well-fed tomcat who enjoys playing with a mouse. At the Nuremberg Trials in 1946, as the former head of the Prussian police, he is questioned about abuses that took place during the first weeks of the National Socialist regime, during the course of which he touches upon the mistreatment of Ernst Thälmann: 'I could not say today who it was who hinted to me that Thälmann had been beaten. I had him called to me in my room directly without informing the higher authorities and questioned him very closely. He told me that he had been beaten during, and especially at the beginning, of the interrogations. Thereupon […] I told Thälmann that I regretted that. At the same time I told him: "Dear Thälmann, if you had come to power, I probably would not have been beaten, but you would have chopped my head off immediately." And he agreed.' As Thälmann noted in 1944, Rudolf Diels was also present at this interview.[19] Seemingly oblivious to quite how cynical the advice was that he gave at the time to the maltreated communist, Göring went on to tell the Nuremberg tribunal: 'Then I told him that in future, he must feel free to let me know if anything of this sort should happen to him or to others. I could not always be there, but it was not my wish that any act of brutality should be committed against them.'[20]

Thälmann bravely withstands the physical abuse and does not betray a single one of his comrades. In his cell, he makes notes in preparation for his trial: 'I stand before you as a representative of the working class, as a guardian of the interests of socialist and also national-socialist workers […].'[21] He ponders whether he should call on Stalin to appear as a character witness: '[…] that would be the greatest sensation of the twentieth century.'[22] After the Nazis abandon the idea of a trial for tactical reasons, Thälmann is placed in permanent protective custody from the autumn of 1935 onwards. Fritz Ludwig is appointed as his official defence attorney, and a relationship of mutual respect develops between the lawyer and his client. Ludwig, a member of the Nazi Party, is offered payments by KPD couriers. He turns them down: 'I want to have a clear conscience. Just for once, Thälmann should learn that there's an honest person in the ranks of the bourgeoisie too.'[23] Members of the Politburo, meeting in Moscow, are incapable of imputing anything but underhand motives to Ludwig, decrying him as a 'scoundrel'.[24] All the while, the German Communist Party leader keeps hoping for a prisoner exchange or for the Soviet Union to make diplomatic representations on his behalf. Attempts to secure his release come to nothing or are broken off at the last minute on instructions from Moscow. 'Why are you behaving like such shitheads and letting me stew here?' Thälmann complains in one of his secret communications.[25]

His wife and children are allowed to visit him once a fortnight. It's not long before he comes to realize that his own side finds it more expedient to know that he's locked up in prison, not least for propaganda purposes. The show trials held in Moscow in 1937 anger him. Then again, he considers executions 'perfectly all right'.[26] In 1938 his daughter notes: 'Papa also says that Göring is a pretty decent bloke, on a personal level'.[27] After four years' imprisonment in Berlin's Moabit Gaol, the prominent detainee is transferred to Hanover. Here he is comparatively privileged; he is given a double cell and there's even a chaise longue in one of the rooms. He reads a lot, in particular Goethe, Schiller, Hölderlin, Nietzsche and Shakespeare, but also the works of Karl May and Edwin Erich Dwinger, the speeches and essays of Alfred Rosenberg and Kurt Plischke's *Der Jude als Rassenschänder* ('The Jew As Miscegenator').[28] He receives copies of the *Berliner Tageblatt* and the *Berliner Börsen-Zeitung* and later is even allowed to listen to the radio. But for years on end, there's no one to share his thoughts with.

Periods of dejection alternate with others in which, echoing his attitude when he headed the party, he gets carried away with an inflated impression of his own importance. On one occasion he says of his own early letters that they were 'clever in their content, extraordinarily interesting and masterfully written' and 'committed to paper with a passionate energy and a Teutonic spirit. In particular, the four letters I wrote to my daughter on the occasion of her birthday were select masterpieces by someone who was already a genius letter-writer'.[29] The KPD leadership keeps in contact with its chairman via Rosa Thälmann, who gives information to a courier and receives instructions back from him. The party's solicitude extends to even the most intimate aspects of the Thälmanns' lives. After Rosa pays Ernst a visit in his Hanover cell at Christmas 1937, the Politburo begins to worry about a possible pregnancy.[30] The Gestapo becomes alarmed, too, fearing that Thälmann might develop prison psychosis as a result of the psychological pressure he is under. They even weigh up the possibility of transferring him to a psychiatric ward, but eventually abandon this idea over concerns that it might provide 'the international gutter press with more ammunition for its propaganda campaign of horror stories and lies directed against the Reich'.[31]

In 1939 contact with the courier is broken off and even the deliveries of money dry up. In her desperation, Rosa turns to the Soviet Embassy on Unter den Linden.[32] On at least eleven occasions, she travels from Hamburg to Berlin and tries to hand over the letters that her husband has personally written to Stalin ('To you and your closest friends…'). In these letters, which run to several pages, Thälmann analyses the current political situation on the basis of his reading of the daily press, magazines and books. In February 1939, he observes: 'The campaign of World Jewry against Germany has had a major impact on the German people in as much as, prior to this, it failed to recognize how influential the Jewish lobby was in global affairs. Even key elements of the NSDAP have been completely taken aback by the quite significant power wielded by World Jewry.'[33] Having said this, he finds it necessary to deny that many of the key players of the communist movement come from a Jewish background.

Sometimes Thälmann can be extraordinarily perspicacious in his political analyses, while on other occasions he is grotesquely wide of the mark. 'Hitler and Ribbentrop are honest and upright in their desire to maintain and further strengthen the friendship between Germany and the Soviet Union,'[34] he notes in March 1940 and adds: 'The congratulatory telegram that Hitler sent to Stalin on his sixtieth birthday was without question a major sensation.' Thälmann's attempts to force his ideas to conform to the meandering party line, rather than using it to sharpen his mind, clearly indicate that he is living in a double prison: just as thick as the walls of the gaol that separate him from the world outside are the self-imposed walls of ideology. The workers' leader hopes that he will be released through Soviet intercession. At the embassy in Berlin, officials at first refuse to take the letters from Rosa Thälmann. The tender flower of German–Soviet friendship is to be allowed to grow undisturbed. 'Frau Thälmann left in a very embittered mood,' reports a telegram sent to Stalin from the Berlin embassy.[35]

October 1939 finds Thälmann hoping that the Hitler–Stalin pact will bring the release of political prisoners in Germany: 'I'm sure of it, my gut instinct tells me that the hour of my release can't be far off now.'[36] And indeed, some prisoners are freed, though in the Soviet Union rather than in Germany. If they are German communists or Jews, they are released from NKVD-run gaols or the gulags straight into the hands of the Gestapo.[37] The fact that Thälmann is allowed to write letters to Stalin, that the letters can reach Moscow from the gaol without hindrance, and that Stalin, after briefly acknowledging receipt, consigns the letters straight to the archives, speaks volumes about Thälmann's significance in the bigger political picture. The Gestapo urges the prominent German communist to buy his release by sending a 'detailed plea' to Himmler, but he steadfastly refuses. Two years later, when the German Wehrmacht is camped outside the gates of Moscow and the Soviets are making plans to evacuate the city, Stalin has some harsh words to say about the German communist leader in a conversation with Georgi Dimitrov: 'They've clearly been working on Thälmann over there in all kinds of ways. He's not a Marxist who sticks to his principles, and his letters suggest he's been influenced by Fascist ideology [...] They won't kill him because they clearly want to be able to make use of him as and when the need arises as a 'sensible' Communist…'[38]

In August 1943, Thälmann is sent to a prison in Bautzen, where the Gestapo offer the married couple the opportunity to move into a small house with a garden in the vicinity of an internment camp. Ernst and Rosa refuse to surrender themselves into the hands of the secret police in such a tame way. Almost all of his comrades-in-arms who were arrested with him are now dead, some murdered in Nazi Germany but more often executed in Soviet exile.[39] Is there any safe place for Thälmann at this time? From the close circle of friends around the KPD leader, only Herbert Wehner manages to escape the Moscow snake pit. The fact that he only does so by informing on his comrades by the dozen dogs him throughout his life and forms the basis of his later political activity, which is characterized by a bitterness and severity that colleagues from later generations find irksome. Thälmann liked and trusted Wehner, whereas he viewed the devious bureaucrat Walter Ulbricht (the future leader of the communist-run German Democratic Republic) with suspicion. After the war, Wehner, who renounces communism, is instrumental in ensuring that the SPD in West Germany turns its back on Marxism (in the Godesberg Programme of 1959) and becomes electable. In the same year, Johannes R. Becher – the 'poet laureate' of the GDR – writes a laudatory poem to Ulbricht to mark his sixty-fifth birthday, which contains a whole series of misconceived images, including the line: 'Thälmann's eye looks through your face' (*Das Auge Thälmanns blickt durch dein Gesicht*).

For Thälmann socialism is a 'powerful [...] movement of conviction made up of idealistic campaigners and people ready to sacrifice themselves'.[40] He finds something comforting in the thought that his suffering has been preordained: 'Now and then, driven by my woes or by a sudden flash of spiritual enlightenment, I will try and stand up to the blows of fate.'[41] After eleven years in gaol, Thälmann takes stock of things in a letter to a young fellow prisoner: 'When I think of all the things that have passed me by during my time in gaol, I have to close my eyes. It's quite something to simply stay focused and not lose direction or die inwardly before you actually pass away.'[42] To this same fellow inmate – a man convicted of being an accessory to a robbery with murder, whom Thälmann thinks shares his socialist beliefs – he reveals how he sees himself:

I'm not some gypsy type who shuns the world. I am a German with experience both of my own country and of the world at large. My people, whom I am part of and whom I love dearly, are the German people and my nation, which I regard with immense pride, is the German nation, a chivalrous, proud, and strong country. Sprung from Nordic lineage, I am of the very same flesh and blood as the working class of Germany, and as their revolutionary offspring I later became their revolutionary leader.[43]

A few months after writing this, in August 1944, after more than 4,000 days and nights in solitary confinement, Thälmann is shot dead on the orders of Heinrich Himmler.[44]

4

Brüning no longer feels safe in Germany either. When the National Socialists stage-manage the opening of the newly elected parliament by putting on the 'Day of Potsdam' on 21 March 1933, in which they proclaim the joining of 'old grandeur with new power', the Centre politician agrees to attend, albeit with some degree of apprehension. The only people absent from this pageant are the Social Democrats and the communists. As the new interior minister of the Reich Wilhelm Frick cynically puts it, their 'valuable work in the concentration camps' prevents the latter from putting in an appearance. And even as late as 16 May, Brüning is still discussing foreign policy matters with Hitler. The two men have known one another since the early 1920s.[45] What Brüning says to a French journalist at this time can only be construed as a tactical manoeuvre, a mixture of circumspection and wishful thinking: 'Hitler is a decent person, moderate and reasonable, and far more receptive to rational arguments than the tone of his language and the actions of his subordinates might lead one to believe. He is not lacking in a religious conscience.'[46] In their personal dealings, Hitler gives the ex-Chancellor the feeling that he values his advice as an elder statesman. Yet behind his back he is contemptuous of Brüning, calling him a 'lackey of Rome'[47] and a 'characterless individual'. They meet for a second time on 30 May. The Reich

Chancellor denies that any mistreatment of opposition politicians has been going on; Brüning invites him to pay a visit to some of the wounded and mutilated patients in St Hedwig's Hospital, where Brüning has been occupying a two-room cell for some time.[48] By this stage, it seems to have become increasingly clear to him that Hitler is playing by his own rules, following the law of the jungle.

By the autumn of 1933, the role of the Centre in German politics is all played out. SA units turn up intermittently outside the hospital and chant 'Down with Brüning'. In October the management of the hospital comes under pressure from the Interior Ministry to serve notice on Brüning to quit his rooms. In the event, Brüning himself volunteers to give up his place of refuge. From now on, his life becomes a deadly game of hide-and-seek. In January 1934, Göring and Rudolf Diels are summoned by Hitler to the Berghof on the Obersalzberg. Hitler complains about 'traitors' and the missed opportunities of the National Socialist revolution: 'It beggars belief that this Strasser and Schleicher, these arch-traitors, have managed to survive this long,'[49] he argues and, in an accusatory tone, turns to Göring and says: 'The whole lot of them are all still alive – Brüning and Treviranus and Westarp too!'

The Gestapo hunt Brüning for seven months. There are times when he doesn't sleep in the same bed two nights running. When word gets around about his desperate plight, he starts to receive letters, many of them from ordinary citizens, some of them communists even, offering to take him in. He is put up by priests and university professors, some of whom ultimately pay a high price for their common decency.[50] Apparently the former Reich Chancellor still has his contacts. In May 1934 growing rumours begin to swirl that a major 'round-up' is imminent. Brüning is finally persuaded to flee the country and go into exile. Before he does so, he makes sure he passes on an urgent warning to numerous friends and former political adversaries alike. Fortunately, he manages to get away to Holland.

Via Great Britain and Switzerland, Brüning arrives in the

United States in 1935, where he takes up teaching posts at various universities. On a visit to Switzerland in 1936, two Gestapo agents are put on his tail, with orders to kill him. They are instructed to win the confidence of the ex-Chancellor and then poison him with specially doctored cigars. One of them is a former communist, who voluntarily offered his services to the Gestapo immediately after being released from gaol. After the assassination had failed, he maintained that he had been supposed to kill Otto Braun in Ascona rather than Brüning.[51] In the USA, Brüning refrains from making any political statements in public, but does advise American government agencies about the inner workings of the German political scene. In September 1945, in a briefing session with the US Judge Advocate General's Office, he recalled that during the Weimar years, Stalin had asked several German politicians via intermediaries: 'Why don't you shoot the leader of your Communist Party?'[52]

Brüning first goes back to Germany in 1948. He is struck by the energy of his compatriots. It is as if they were moving about the streets half as fast again as people in neighbouring countries. Even the old people walked like they were fleeing a bombing raid.[53] In 1951, Brüning takes up a chair in politics at the University of Cologne, but returns to the United States for good four years later. Looking back at the Nazi years, it would never have crossed Brüning's mind to gloss over their atrocities – or, as the poet Günter Eich once put it, 'to decorate the abattoir with geraniums' – but at the same time, he warns people against thinking that the Nazi dictatorship encapsulates the whole of German history: 'No nation that has had it dinned into it on a daily basis how utterly depraved and immoral it has been can hope to survive.'[54]

Part of the tragedy of this political life is that the former Reich Chancellor starts to show growing symptoms of a persecution complex. During his time in Cologne, he feels that he is 'under constant surveillance by Adenauer; he refused to use the telephone in his flat and became convinced that his mail was being read'.[55]

Eventually, he ends up leaving the small, book-lined study of his wooden house in Norwich, Vermont, only on rare occasions. At the end of a life that has had more than its share of disappointments, he concludes: 'At least I achieved one thing: I never despised anyone.'[56] After his death in 1970, the former Chancellor's companion, Claire Nix, continues to live at the property. In October 2014, she dies at the age of ninety-six in a nursing home in New Hampshire. For the last seventeen years of her life, she has received an honorarium of 700 euros a month from the President of the Federal Republic of Germany.

5

Following his arrest, Carl von Ossietzky is brought to the police detention centre on Alexanderplatz, which by now is bursting at the seams. In mid-March, Rudolf Diels invites representatives of the foreign press to come and inspect the facility and, as proof that prisoners are being treated humanely, presents Ernst Torgler, Carl von Ossietzky and Ludwig Renn.[57] The National Socialists regard Torgler as the instigator of the Reichstag fire. At the press briefing, the three men are photographed alongside Rudolf Diels. The picture appears in the *Berliner Illustrierte Zeitung* soon after.[58] Is the photo staged? Whatever the case, Ossietzky and Renn now come under suspicion of being involved in the arson attack. It is claimed that the two of them were seen in a bar with Torgler on the evening in question. However, the publican who is prepared to testify to this entangles himself in glaring contradictions, with the result that the state prosecutor – albeit only after more than fifty days of testimonies – is forced to drop the case.[59]

Maud finds it hard coming to terms with the situation after Carl's arrest. In order to spare their daughter, who by this time has returned to Berlin, the hostility of her classmates and teachers, she sends her to school in England. A circle of women – mostly long-serving colleagues from *Die Weltbühne* like Hilde Walter, a close friend of Christa Winsloe – looks after Rosalinde and maintains contact with the imprisoned Carl. In April 1934 he is transferred to the Sonnenburg concentration camp in East Brandenburg. The Charlottenburg SA unit number 33 – the so-called 'murder squad', which Hanussen had engaged to provide security at his performances – has taken over the running of this camp, which is notorious for the particularly inhumane treatment it metes out to those in its 'protective custody'.

Now the guards at Sonnenburg exact their revenge on the journalist, who recently called Hitler a 'cowardly, effete milksop'[60] and Goebbels a 'hysterical cheese-mite'.[61] Ossietzky is roused from his sleep in the middle of the night, and driven outside to exercise in his nightshirt and bare feet. He is forced to march endlessly to and fro at the double and on the blast of a whistle to drop down and support himself on his fingertips and the tips of his toes. In this position he has to try and keep his balance while his tormentors lay into him. A unit commander delivers vicious kicks while yelling: 'Just die, will you, you Polish pig!'[62] While this is happening, his bed is doused with cold water. He and the Jewish anarchist writer Erich Mühsam are forced to dig their own graves. Rosalinde writes him a postcard from England: she tells him she's glad to be in England, where things are nicer than in Germany. The thirteen-year-old can have no inkling that this will lead to further brutal mistreatment of her father.[63]

Friends urge Maud to follow her daughter into exile abroad, but she's adamant that under no circumstances will she leave her husband behind in Germany. Initially she is kept under constant surveillance by the police, with searches of the house and interrogations almost a daily occurrence. Her drinking problem grows even worse and she starts to 'hallucinate about house searches that had clearly never happened'.[64] She suffers a nervous breakdown and is admitted to a sanatorium on the shores of the Schlachtensee. She writes to her daughter: 'There's something dead inside of me – cold, so cold, that I can sometimes feel a cold hand running all over my body at night.'[65] In addition, there are money worries. Maud is unable to keep hold of the house that she has only recently moved into, and so she moves to Hamburg to live with her father-in-law.

She receives support from the group around Hilde Walter. Maud's alcoholism poses a serious risk to Hilde and her helpers: on the one hand, Maud is the most important person who is in contact with Carl von Ossietzky, but on the other hand it's by no means certain how secure the knowledge of this clandestine support network is in her hands.[66] In the meantime, Carl has been moved to the Esterwegen concentration camp. His wife visits him there and is shocked by the condition she finds him in. At around the same time, the Swiss diplomat Carl Jacob Burckhardt also comes to see the detainee. He reports encountering a 'trembling, deathly white presence… a being that appeared to have lost all sensation, with one eye puffed up, its teeth apparently knocked out and dragging a broken, badly healed leg.'[67] Since 1934, there has been a campaign running abroad to award Carl von Ossietzky the Nobel Peace Prize. The driving force behind it in Norway is a young German student and journalist named Willy Brandt.[68] This touches a raw nerve with Goebbels: 'There was a time when treason was considered socially acceptable, even fashionable,' he declares on the radio.[69] 'And even today, there are people who lobby for traitors to be awarded prizes. But all we see in a person who betrays his country is a criminal.' Goebbels is in no doubt how things should proceed in the case of Ossietzky: 'It's better for a traitor to lose his head in peacetime than for many hundreds of his fellow countrymen to lose their lives in war because of him. So I say: off with his head!'

Pressure grows on the National Socialist regime in 1936, the year the Olympic Games are held in Berlin. Göring orders that the terminally ill Ossietzky should be transferred to a Berlin hospital.[70] Whether, as the rumours claim, he really was injected with the tuberculosis pathogen while interned in the Esterwegen camp can never be determined. Maud tries to visit him as often as she can: 'I think about you the whole day, and when it's visiting time, I could scream for sheer longing! It's awful, so unbelievably awful, to be separated from you like this,'[71] she writes to Carl. 'I have so much I want to say to you but cannot find the words, because I'm all choked up inside and my throat is constricted. But enough of me, my love; don't lose hope, things will and must get better, and a change of air and surroundings will surely do you some good.'

Göring questions the prisoner at Gestapo headquarters.[72] In November 1936, Ossietzky is officially released from custody and moved to the Westend Hospital. A few days later, the Norwegian committee award him the Nobel Prize for Peace. Hitler responds by issuing a 'Führer Directive' prohibiting citizens of the German Reich from 'accepting the Nobel Prize for all time' in order to 'prevent any shameful scenes'.[73] The Nazis also expect Carl von Ossietzky to turn down the prize, but he refuses to do so. The prize money is paid into a Norwegian account. Maud takes a room in the Budapester Straße and cares for her husband in the months that remain to him despite the danger of contracting TB herself. One evening, she gets talking to a man in a restaurant. He is a lawyer and offers her his help in transferring the Nobel Prize money to Germany. However, the man turns out to be a fraudster who embezzles 80 per cent of the funds.

Maud and Carl von Ossietzky spend his final months in a hospital in Niederschönhausen, with the Gestapo always lurking in the wings. Their daughter Rosalinde, who has since moved to Sweden, is a constant subject of discussion whenever Carl and Maud talk. At the end, Carl weighs just 36 kilograms, and the male nurse assigned to care for him carries him round in his arms like a child.[74] He dies on 4 May 1938. Maud secretly has a death mask made. The authorities ban any funeral ceremony for Carl von Ossietzky, no name can be inscribed on the urn containing his ashes and people are even prohibited from laying flowers. After her husband's death, Maud is drained of all vitality. She suffers another nervous breakdown and is sent to a sanatorium for four months. Over the following years, she moves from one home to the next. She ekes out an existence on welfare and supplements her meagre funds, including what remains of the Nobel Prize money, by giving illegal English lessons.[75]

With the demise of the Nazi regime, a memorial plaque is mounted on Ossietzky's grave. In post-war Berlin, Maud tries to obtain a licence from the British military authorities to resume publication of *Die Weltbühne*, but eventually decides to publish the magazine from 1946 under a Soviet licence instead. In February 1946, the original share capital for the new Ossietzky Verlag publishing house is provided by the Communist Party.[76] Outwardly the new *Weltbühne* resembles its predecessor, but in spirit it is now no longer an independent enterprise. In 1966 Maud publishes a book in which she eulogizes her Anglo-Indian family and her relationship with Carl; many of her rose-tinted reminiscences do not withstand the scrutiny of later biographical research. Maud von Ossietzky dies in East Berlin in 1974. On her deathbed, she confesses to her daughter: 'You know, Rosalinde, I have been afraid my whole life.'[77]

6

On 1 March 1933, Otto Braun receives a call from the office of the Reich President. A few days after the Reichstag fire he is told by 'an old hunting pal'[78] that his arrest is imminent. This telephone call sets in motion the 'Red Czar's' passage into exile in Switzerland. A little while before, advertising pillars right across Berlin were plastered with posters bearing the legend, in large letters: 'Two Million Stolen'. Berliners were given two days to puzzle over its meaning before the blank white space underneath was filled in, in equally bold capitals, with the propaganda lie: 'By Braun and Severing'. By various tortuous routes, Otto Braun takes flight across Germany and on 4 March, the day before the election, boards a ferry across Lake Constance. What he cannot know is that the German border officials lose no time in telephoning Berlin to inform the authorities that the prominent Social Democrat politician has left the country.

On the Sunday of the election, Joseph Goebbels has the news read out over the radio every hour, and lards it with his own mocking commentary.[79] Many people take it to be just another Nazi lie. It is an even bitterer pill to swallow when it turns out to be true. Emilie dies in 1934 and Braun withdraws even further from public life. In his memoirs, which are published in 1938, he takes stock of his life in politics. At the same time, he hopes that sales of the book will help him out of the straitened financial circumstances he has fallen into in the meantime. Ferdinand Sauerbruch, who once treated Braun, is a frequent visitor to Ascona. The surgeon's patients include Generals Hammerstein and Beck and Colonel Stauffenberg – all prominent anti-Nazis in the upper echelons of the army; Stauffenberg will lead the failed plot to assassinate Hitler in July 1944. Sauerbruch consults with the former prime minister of Prussia about the ongoing illegal work of the SPD in Germany.[80] In 1944, he tries to recruit Braun for a government to take over after the Nazis are toppled from power.

During his exile, Braun is energized by the thought of playing an active role in the revival of Germany after the fall of the Nazi regime. He reactivates old contacts, writes memoranda and sets up a clandestine working group. But by the time the war comes to an end, he is tired and worn out: 'Prussia is Russian. What use would a Prussian prime minister be there?'[81] he writes to a friend in June 1945. In the post-war SPD, Braun is seen as a relic of the Weimar years, and his love for Prussia strikes many of his party colleagues as suspect. He lives a modest life in Switzerland. 'I bet you'd never have imagined,' he writes to his former liaison officer, 'that the "Czar of Prussia" would end up having to cook his own potato pancakes in his dotage.'[82] Braun only ever returns to Germany on the occasional visit. When he dies in December 1955, just a small circle of acquaintances attends his funeral in Lugano. 'It was a very sad burial,' reports a friend. 'But as far as the world of today was concerned, he'd already been dead a long time.'[83]

From the window of her house in March 1933, Bella Fromm watches SA men dragging the black, red and gold flags of the republic that they have seized through the mud: 'Passers-by – most of them women, who are easily given to outbursts of hysteria anyway – have a gay old time of it trampling up and down on the flags.'[84] When she throws a cocktail party for her high-society friends, SA stormtroopers gather outside the house from the early hours in order to disrupt the reception. 'Shortly before my guests arrived, an SA unit had discovered a particularly large example of a Weimar Republic flag that had been forgotten about on the roof of a nearby hospital. They tore it down and dragged it through the streets.'[85] Fromm's telephone call to complain about the SA men who are intent on 'smoking out the dump' reaches Vice-Chancellor Papen, who dispatches a mounted protection squad. But by this time her guests, who include André François-Poncet, have lost their appetite for partying and start to disperse. Shortly afterwards, Fromm goes to pick up her daughter, who has just returned from a skiing trip, at Anhalter Station. She notices an SA unit marching towards the platform and wonders what bigwig they've been assigned to meet. But the men are yelling slogans like 'Jews out!' and 'Death to the Jews!' and simply move on to the next platform to greet the next train that's pulling in there in the same manner.[86]

The journalist is also encountering increasing difficulties in her career. The Red and White Tennis Club files a formal complaint against 'this lady' and insists that future reports of their activities be written 'by Aryan journalists'.[87] The ranks of her allies are steadily thinning out. A friend who joins the NSDAP justifies his action by saying that he has a mother, a wife and two children to support. 'If newspaper people keep getting laid off at the rate they are now,' he prophesies, 'then next spring all the "leaves" [the German word *Blätter* also means 'newspapers'] will be brown instead of green.'[88]

The pressure is growing on foreign correspondents, too. In June 1934 Bella Fromm reports: 'The Führer needs someone to vent his anger on now. Maybe it'll be Dorothy Thompson.'[89] Despite being in great danger herself, Bella Fromm uses her extensive contacts to try and save others' skins.[90] Leo Baeck, president of the Reich Deputation for German Jews, later gratefully acknowledges her help. In September 1938, she manages at the eleventh hour to emigrate to the United States. She is forty-seven years old and destitute. For the first few years there, she muddles through by working as a waitress and taking on piecework sewing gloves. Later she turns her attention to the diaries and notes she kept in Germany, which she fleshes out with some new entries and compiles into a book with the support of two American publishers. In the autumn of 1942, *Blood and Banquets* becomes a bestseller. A PR campaign accompanies the book launch. Apparently the New York police receive a tip-off that four Nazi agents in Mexico have been instructed to travel to New York and assassinate Bella Fromm.[91] After the war Fromm, by now a naturalized American, appears as a material witness in one of the trials resulting from the Nuremberg War Crimes tribunal. Right up to her death in 1972, she tirelessly devotes her efforts to bringing about reconciliation between America and Germany.

In the meantime, Dorothy Thompson's fame has outstripped that of her husband, the Nobel Literature Laureate of 1930. Over these years, her marriage is put to a stern test. Dorothy buries herself in her work and in her love affair with Christa Winsloe to try and escape Sinclair Lewis's alcoholism. In January 1933, she senses in herself 'a gentle languor'; she is pregnant and wants to have a 'long-legged, red-headed girl'.[92] In the days after the Reichstag fire, she is 'on the move from nine in the morning until twelve at night'[93] and suffers a miscarriage. From the Italian resort of Portofino, where she spends time recuperating at Christa Winsloe's villa, she writes to her husband: 'Have no fears, I ain't thata way.'[94] Over time, Christa and Dorothy also grow apart. Christa moves to France and ends up living at Cluny in Burgundy. There, in June 1944 she and her new female companion come under suspicion of having spied for the Germans and are shot dead by the French Resistance.

It can often happen that mistakes and setbacks occur in life which in retrospect turn out to be blessings in disguise. And this is exactly what happens to Dorothy Thompson. When, after many years of fruitless effort, she finally gets a chance to interview the leader of the NSDAP, she prophesies: 'Oh, Adolph! Adolph! [sic] You will be out of luck!'[95] For over three years, she has the opportunity both to observe how grave her misjudgement was and to deepen her aversion towards Hitler and his 'movement', until finally, in August 1934, she becomes the first American to be ordered to leave the country, within twenty-four hours.

The initial setback of her expulsion proves to be an important milestone in the reporter's life. As the writer Klaus Mann puts it: 'No sooner does stupid Adolf finally get into power than he expels the American reporter from the country, thereby ensuring her fame. And only then did this gifted polemicist really let rip and show what she was capable of. The emotive, feminine pathos and the intelligent, well-founded basis of her loathing were largely instrumental in opening the American public's eyes to the seriousness of the Nazi threat.'[96]

Dorothy Thompson's expulsion from Germany makes international headlines; the story even appears on the front page of the *New York Times*. Thompson is given her own column in the *New York Herald Tribune*, one of the country's most influential newspapers. From March 1936 onwards, her byline appears three times a week under the heading 'On the Record'. She is increasingly fêted as a journalistic authority. Her radio broadcasts for NBC, in which she reports on conditions under the National Socialist regime or presses for the liberalization of US immigration policy, reach some six million of her fellow Americans, while her newspaper reports are syndicated to over 180 outlets.[97] As a confidante of the President's wife Eleanor Roosevelt, she campaigns for émigrés from Europe to be let into the USA. She eventually ends up meeting many of her German friends again in the States. She works to support those who have fled from the Nazis; even Heinrich Brüning is able to count on her assistance. She comments clear-sightedly on the Western powers' policy of appeasement towards Hitler. On the 1938 Munich Peace Accord, she writes: 'This is not peace without victory, for the victory goes to Mr Hitler. This is peace without virtue. Therefore it is not peace – but the initiation of a terrific world crisis.'[98]

Sinclair Lewis used to joke in former years that he would cite Hitler as a co-respondent if he and Dorothy ever filed for divorce. By 1942, it has indeed come to that; their marriage, which has been on the rocks for a long time, is finally annulled. Thompson continues to wage her journalistic crusade against the Nazis. As an official war correspondent, sporting the uniform of the American armed forces, she spends her time shuttling between Brussels, Paris and London as Allied troops advance across occupied Europe. Her radio broadcasts even reach German listeners via the CBS shortwave network. In April 1942, Goebbels notes: 'Dorothy Thompson has delivered an absolutely crazy speech against Hitler. It is shameful and maddening that silly little women whose brains are made of nothing but straw even have the right to speak out against giants of history like the Führer.'[99]

Listen, Hans is the title of the series of radio programmes that Dorothy Thompson broadcasts every Friday from March to October 1942. They are aimed at German listeners in general but specifically at her German friend 'Hans'– that is, Helmuth James von Moltke. She appeals to his conscience, trying to get him to undertake some action from within Germany against the regime, which has in the meantime become a menace to the whole of civilization. At the same time, on von Moltke's estate in Kreisau, which Dorothy Thompson and Sinclair Lewis know from a visit in 1928, a group of opponents of the Nazi regime meet to discuss the new order that will emerge after the end of the dictatorship. This group dissolves after the failure of the Stauffenberg plot to assassinate Hitler on 20 July 1944. In January 1945, Helmuth James Count von Moltke is sentenced to death and hanged in the prison at Plötzensee. In a farewell letter to his children, he writes: 'Throughout my life, even at school, I have fought against the spirit of narrow-mindedness, restriction, arrogance, lack of respect for others, intolerance, absolutism and unforgiving strictness that inhabits the German character and which has really come to the fore in the National Socialist state.'[100]

Even before the Second World War draws to a close, Winston Churchill and Franklin D. Roosevelt send personal letters of thanks to Dorothy Thompson in recognition of her work as a journalist against Hitler.[101] As early as 1945 she visits war-shattered Germany, where she organizes relief efforts, meets old friends and takes an early stance against any idea that the German people bear collective responsibility for the conflict. Her warnings about the rise of a second totalitarian regime, in the shape of the Soviet Union under Stalin, finds far less of a hearing in the United States than her journalistic crusade against the Nazis. She now turns her hand to writing articles on gardening, animal welfare and child-raising for women's magazines. In 1943 Dorothy Thompson finally finds happiness, late in the day, with the Czech-born painter and sculptor Maxim Kopf. 'He's the man I ought to have married in the first place,'[102] is her postscript on her love life. She increasingly withdraws into her private life. By the time she dies in 1961, she has long since ceased to be a public figure.

And what of Franz von Papen? In his role as vice-chancellor to Hitler, he finds things slipping away from him. In the highly foreseeable event of Hindenburg's death, he makes plans for the restoration of the monarchy in Germany. But who is Papen? The only thing he has going for him is that he is the Reich President's favourite. Hindenburg, however, ensconced in his far-off estate in Neudeck in East Prussia, has in the interim come to see eye to eye with the once-despised 'Bohemian corporal'. Papen causes a political stir just one more time: in a speech he gives in June 1934 in Marburg, written for him by the lawyer Edgar Jung, he speaks out against the excesses of the National Socialist regime during its first few months in power, against the 'enforced conformity' imposed on the press, against the idea of a 'permanent revolution' as practised above all by the SA: 'It would be utterly repellent to think that a nation can be unified through terror, which is invariably the product of a bad conscience [...] Have we gone through an anti-Marxist revolution merely just in order to implement a Marxist programme? [...] No nation wishing to make its mark on history can afford permanent insurrection from below.'[103]

Hindenburg sends a telegram of congratulation. Goebbels ensures that the speech is not reported within Germany and hits back during a summer solstice celebration in Berlin: 'A small band of critics is mobilizing itself in the country with the aim of disrupting our great reconstruction programme from its hiding place in the shadows. They are laughable little pipsqueaks! The people haven't forgotten the days when these men used to rule the country from their club armchairs. [...] These people won't be able to halt this century's onward march. We'll ride roughshod over them.'[104] Now it's time to sweep away these 'laughable little pipsqueaks' for good. Hitler, Göring and Goebbels are also keen to halt the 'permanent insurrection from below' and to use this opportunity to get rid not only of their chief adversaries Ernst Röhm and his SA sidekicks but also a few hundred other opponents as well. Two days after the vice-chancellor's address, speechwriter Edgar Jung, author of a much-discussed critique of democracy entitled 'Rule of the Inferior' (*Herrschaft der Minderwertigen*) is arrested. The day after the 'Night of the Long Knives' (30 June 1934), his body is found in a roadside ditch in Oranienburg, north of Berlin.[105] Papen's chief press officer

Herbert von Bose is called out of a meeting and summarily shot dead. His body is left lying in the vice-chancellor's front parlour.

Papen himself is placed under house arrest. He and his son are watched around the clock in their private apartment in Lennéstraße on the fringes of the Tiergarten by SS men. In Neudeck, Hindenburg, alerted to what is going on by a colleague of Papen's who makes it through to East Prussia with the news, intervenes and, via the minister for the Reichswehr, manages to secure his former favourite's release.[106] When Papen's phone line starts working again after three days, Göring calls up and enquires hypocritically why the vice-chancellor hasn't been attending cabinet meetings.[107] This spells the end of Papen's involvement in public affairs – the same Papen who was going to squeeze Hitler 'into a corner within two months… so hard he'll squeal'.[108] His parting shots are to write a number of letters of complaint and finally to request that he be put to work in the diplomatic service.

Over the coming years, with half the world ablaze and in ruins, Franz von Papen spends his time shaking innumerable hands at diplomatic gatherings. After the long nightmare is over, a photograph in an American illustrated news magazine shows him during a lunch pause at the Nuremberg War Tribunal in 1946, flanked by other major figures of the Nazi regime and scraping his food from a Wehrmacht mess tin. In 1952 Papen publishes his memoirs: *Der Wahrheit eine Gasse* ('The Narrow Path of Truth'). The title alone should be enough to place the reader on his or her guard. There are some people who remain unchanged by even the greatest upheavals in life. Everything that happens to them, all the knowledge they amass, is put through a filter so that it always results in the same design. And the sole purpose of this is to confirm a worldview that they have held from early on. As Kurt von Schleicher once said disparagingly of Papen, he was 'a hat with no head in it'.[109] And the historian Golo Mann believes it should give us pause for thought 'that a man of so little substance should for a brief moment have decided the fate of nations and shaped world history'.[110]

7

Kurt von Schleicher has found happiness only late in life with Elisabeth. A private photograph from the year they get married, 1931, shows the youthful-looking couple in a tender, natural pose, both with open, intelligent faces. The family is completed by the eleven-year-old Lonny, Elisabeth's daughter from her first marriage. But what hardly anyone outside the close family circle knows is that Schleicher is suffering from anaemia. Symptoms of his condition are a propensity to quickly grow tired, a raised heart rate, a pallid complexion and sensations of numbness and pins and needles in his hands and feet. Events up to February 1933, in which Schleicher plays a central role, often push him to the edge of his endurance.

Thereafter, things calm down around Schleicher. There is a reconciliation not just with Brüning but also with Wilhelm Groener, his fatherly friend and erstwhile patron. The ex-army minister and ex-Chancellor Schleicher withdraws from public life to a villa that he has found for his family in Neubabelsberg near Potsdam, with grounds fronting Lake Griebnitz. The household comprises Kurt and Elisabeth, Lonny, Schleicher's aged mother, his widowed sister, the housekeeper Marie Güntel and the parlourmaid Ottilie. The Schleichers now acquire their own car. The chauffeur who is hired to drive them around also doubles as their gardener. The family often rents a motorboat, too. Their waterborne excursions – up the chain of lakes as far as the Great Wannsee, then back via the River Havel past Peacock Island and the Church of the Redeemer in Sacrow and passing under Glienicke Bridge to Lake Griebnitz – can sometimes take the entire day.

During those months, Kurt von Schleicher feels secure, and he speaks openly, critically and rarely with much caution about the prominent figures of the day and current affairs in National Socialist Germany. Presumably he also guesses that his private telephone line is being bugged by Göring's 'Air Ministry Research

Department', since he did exactly the same thing when he was in charge.[111] Warnings come his way with increasing frequency from the spring of 1934 onwards, along with offers to travel abroad for extended spells, to Japan for instance, in order to keep him out of the firing line. At the beginning of January 1934, the French ambassador in Berlin, André François-Poncet, intimates to Schleicher that he is being too indiscreet in his public utterances. The lady who is tasked with passing this message to Schleicher reports back to the ambassador that Schleicher knows how to defend himself should he be called to account. To which François-Poncet replies prophetically: 'In these overheated times, one usually doesn't even get the chance to respond.'[112]

On Saturday 30 June 1934, at around midday, Marie Güntel is sitting in her master's study doing the household accounts.[113] After adding up the bills, she finds that they are one hundred Marks in the black. At the same time, just before 12.30 p.m., an auburn-coloured Mercedes-Benz Nürnberg cabriolet with Berlin number plates pulls up outside the house on Griebnitzstraße 4. Its occupants are six young men, all aged between twenty-five and thirty. Five of them get out of the car, while the driver waits behind the wheel. One of the men is wearing a black suit, while the rest are dressed in light casual clothes. In response to their frenetic ringing on the doorbell, Marie Güntel goes to the front door, peers through the spyhole and asks the men who they are and what their business is. 'We need to see the General!' comes the curt reply, whereupon Marie presses the electronic switch that activates the garden gate while at the same time opening the front door. Seeing the men standing menacingly in front of her, the housekeeper reacts instinctively by telling them that 'the General' has gone out for a walk. The man in the dark suit snaps back at her not to lie to him.

Marie Güntel notices that the men all have one hand behind their backs. Realizing she won't be able to stop them pushing past her, she takes to her heels with the words: 'I'll just go and look.'

She rushes down the hallway to the study. The man in the dark suit enters the vestibule and orders his companions: 'After her!' The housekeeper makes it to the study ahead of her five pursuers. Kurt von Schleicher is still sitting there at his desk with his back to the door, while his wife Elisabeth is in an adjoining room listening to the radio and busy with some needlework. Before Marie can say anything, she hears a voice behind her ask: 'Are you General von Schleicher?' Half turning round to his right, Schleicher rises to his feet and replies: 'Yes, I am.' In almost the same instant, shots ring out. Seven bullets strike the former Chancellor in the torso. In a matter of seconds, all the endeavours of decades are extinguished and all the carefully crafted networks of connections that have been built up through a combination of shrewdness, tenacity and sheer luck, together with all the hopes for a future that might still be within reach, are swept away. In panic, Marie Güntel flees into the garden. After barely two minutes the men are gone. When the housekeeper re-enters the study she finds Kurt von Schleicher dead and his wife Elisabeth lying seriously wounded on the floor.

A little later on this lovely early summer's day – there is light cloud, but at 30 °C it's very warm – Lonny von Schleicher, who is on her way back from school, gets off the bus at the Enver Pasha Bridge stop and walks up Griebnitzstraße. She's looking forward to showing her mother and stepfather her annual school report. But on arriving home, she finds the house and grounds cordoned off. The local policeman recognizes her as the family's daughter and allows her access to the house, where she learns what has happened from her aunt and the housekeeper: 'Your mother's still alive, they've taken her to hospital in an ambulance.' In a taxi, Lonny does the rounds of the hospitals in Potsdam first and, drawing a blank there, moves on to the clinic in Nowawes. There she is met by the head surgeon Fritz Schulze, who has shouldered the difficult task of breaking the terrible news: 'I'm afraid your mother died on the way here.'[114]

8

In Neubabelsberg, a familiar figure appears on the scene: Count Helldorff. In the interim, he has been appointed police chief of Potsdam. Like the discovery of Hanussen's body the previous year, the murder of Schleicher and his wife falls under his jurisdiction. Helldorff instructs his officers not to keep a written record of witness statements but simply to prepare a report about the scene of the crime. At around four o'clock in the afternoon, the Gestapo arrive and take charge of the case. At the same time, Hindenburg receives news of Schleicher's death. He is told the lie that the general attempted to resist arrest by drawing a weapon. In the early evening, Brüning's childhood friend and former minister Gottfried Treviranus turns up in Neubabelsberg, looking for a place to take refuge. He is on the run from an SS death squad, which had tried and failed to seize him earlier that day while he was playing tennis at a friend's house in Dahlem. Treviranus later recounted what happened next: '[…] as I was approaching Schleicher's house I encountered a crowd of people. I asked the nearest person: "What's going on here, then?" "They shot the general and his wife this lunchtime," came the reply. "Who did?" I asked. "No idea. The cops are in the house."'[115]

Despite having been a protégé of Ernst Röhm, Helldorff emerges from the National Socialist 'purges' even stronger. Although an investigation is launched into the IOUs found at Hanussen's, with the highest party court of the NSDAP examining the allegation that Count Helldorff accepted loans from a Jew, Achim von Arnim, who himself took money from the clairvoyant as recently as the beginning of March 1933, testifies in writing that his then boss Helldorff knew nothing about Hanussen's Jewish background.[116] A public notice is posted at the town hall in Potsdam in July 1934, calling for the town's police chief to swear an oath of disclosure.[117] In the summer of 1935, Helldorff spends a brief holiday on the

Baltic Sea coast with Goebbels and Hitler, after which the party's proceedings against him are dropped.[118] The 'old fighter' manages to discharge his outstanding debts, which amount to some twenty to twenty-five thousand Reichsmarks, thanks to a handout from the Reich Chancellery, personally approved by Hitler.[*] Thus freed of all his financial burdens, the police chief of Potsdam is at liberty to take up the same position in Berlin.[119] Yet in no time he finds himself saddled with money problems again, mainly thanks to his ruinous fondness for the turf. For a while Helldorff finds a pragmatic solution to this, by helping German Jews persecuted by National Socialist terror to emigrate – in return for a so-called 'Helldorff contribution', supposedly in order to build a fund to alleviate Jewish hardship. In 1938, he plans to have a Jewish ghetto created in Berlin, paid for by the very victims of persecution themselves.

Things ultimately do not turn out well for Helldorff, who over the coming years becomes increasingly distanced from his former comrades. He speaks out against the mass shootings in Poland and finds himself drawn into the plot to assassinate Hitler. In 1944, Helldorff appears in the dock at the People's Court, where due process is nothing but a sham. For a long time now a person's political attitude, hardly an objective yardstick of justice, has been the key determinant here. Not that the defendant in this case is wholly without blame for letting things come to such a pass. When Hitler was shown the record of Helldorff's interrogation and his signed confession, he is said to have remarked: 'I really wouldn't have imagined Helldorff could be such a villain. He's always been foolish, that's for sure. At least four or five times I've had to bail him out by settling his debts […]. I feel sorry for his wife and his lovely children, but this Augean stable really must be cleared out once and for all.'[120] Helldorff's former defence counsel, Roland

---

[*] In the Third Reich, the term 'old fighter' (*alter Kämpfer*) described a person who had joined the Nazi Party at an early stage. It became an official designation in October 1933 and was generally applied to anyone with a party membership number from 1 to 300,000. [Translator's note]

Freisler, now sits in judgement on him. Hitler issues an order that Wolf-Heinrich von Helldorff must witness the slow and agonizing death of at least three of his co-conspirators before he himself is also hanged on 15 August 1944.

And what of Gregor Strasser, the 'almost-vice-chancellor', who was latterly the Reich Organisation Leader of the NSDAP and Hitler's most dangerous rival? The trained chemist Strasser retires from politics to private life, secures a directorship at the Schering drug and chemical concern, and with Hitler's blessing becomes chairman of the Reich Pharmaceutical Industry Association. In return, he has to promise not to engage in any political or social activism. However, Göring wants rid of Strasser and is keen to stage a fake suicide, or a hunting or automobile accident, to do away with his old rival. In October 1933, both Criminal Counsellor Arthur Nebe and Gestapo chief Rudolf Diels turn down their employer's request to put this plan into action.[121] But not long after, in the spring of 1934, the time comes to settle accounts. Strasser senses that he is under threat and sends a letter appealing to the 'Deputy Führer' Rudolf Hess: 'I am writing to you today to ask you what, in the view of the Party, I need to do in order to make my political abstinence – which I have sworn to adhere to in several declarations and have scrupulously observed – clear to any outside observers. In this regard, I am ready to meet any demand or requirement that the Party makes of me […] I would never do anything to harm the Party.'[122]

The ex-politician has been advised several times, most recently by Heinrich Brüning, to get out of the country. But Strasser turns a deaf ear to all the warnings. Quite simply, he is exhausted. In January 1931, he broke a vertebra in a skiing accident and for a while his life hung in the balance. Ever since, his mobility has been seriously impaired, he suffers constant acute pain and requires a walking stick. On Sunday 30 June 1934 he and his family are having lunch in their Berlin apartment at Müllerstraße 170–171 when the doorbell rings and five Gestapo men inform the head of the household they have a search warrant and ask him to accompany them to his office at Schering's. There, he is handed over to an SS unit, who take him to Prinz-Albrecht-Straße and put him in a holding cell. That afternoon, he is moved and taken down, past several fellow prisoners, to an individual cell in the basement. There, just hours after his arrest, he is killed by a volley of pistol shots fired through the inspection hatch of his cell. In common with many victims of the 1934 Nazi 'purge', his cause of death is recorded as 'suicide'.[123]

Karl Ernst, the man responsible for assembling the death squad that murdered Hanussen, likewise finds himself caught up in the orgy of bloodletting that has gone down in history as the 'Night of the Long Knives'. At midday on 30 June 1934, as he and his wife are about to board a ship in Bremen taking them on their honeymoon cruise to Madeira, he is arrested by a special detachment of the SS and flown back to Berlin. News of his execution is announced on the radio while the plane is still in the air. From Tempelhof airfield, he is driven to the barracks of Adolf Hitler's SS bodyguard in Lichterfelde, where Ernst, who still believes he is the victim of a misunderstanding, is summarily shot dead. His body is 'dismembered on the spot and carried away in several bloody sacks'.[124] During a house search conducted at the apartment of the murdered man, an envelope full of the signed receipts that Hanussen demanded from his debtors is found tucked away behind a bookshelf. Karl Ernst evidently planned on using them to blackmail his comrade Count Helldorff.

9

On the day after the great bloodbath in the summer of 1934, Secretary of State Roland Freisler, whose glittering career will take him to the presidency of the National Socialist 'People's Court', issues an order that all investigations in the Schleicher murder case are to be shelved. A hastily passed law grants immunity from prosecution to all those involved in crimes committed during the 'purges'.[125] Hindenburg sends a telegram to the Reich Chancellor: 'You have saved the German people from a great danger.'[126] Without delay, Hitler travels to the Reich President's estate at Neudeck to inform him of the events that took place during the alleged 'coup attempt' by Röhm. He can count on the President's approval. Röhm's claim that he could supplant the Reichswehr with a three-million-strong 'People's Army' of SA stormtroopers, the unchecked outrages carried out by his men and his call for a 'second revolution' involving socialist plans to dispossess the rich – from Hindenburg's point of view, all this poses such a serious threat that the Chancellor's decisive move to nip it in the bud has his full support. After Hitler's visit to Neudeck, Goebbels notes in his diary: 'Hindenburg was just great. The old man's a class act.'[127] At the meeting, the Reich President airily dismisses the appalling violence that accompanied the 'Night of the Long Knives' by observing: 'Quite right – it couldn't be done without spilling some blood.'[128]

A few days later the Reich Chancellor justifies his actions in a speech to the now irrelevant Reichstag.[129] In his address, Hitler accuses his predecessor Schleicher of having had treacherous contacts with Röhm and several foreign diplomats, and states ambiguously that Schleicher planned to 'get rid' of Papen. The fact that an anonymous gang of murderers did away with one of their own meets with not a single word of protest from the generals of the Reichswehr. Goebbels sums up the events surrounding the slaughter of the Nazis' opponents: 'Everything went according to plan in Berlin. The only hitch was that Elisabeth Schleicher was killed too. A shame, but there's no helping that now.'[130] French ambassador André François-Poncet takes a very different view: *Les boches ont vaincu les Allemands* ('The *Boches* have triumphed over the Germans'). In the summer of 1934, the Reich President's health takes a decided turn for the worse. At the end of July, Hindenburg asks Professor Sauerbruch, who comes to examine him in Neudeck: 'Is Friend Hein in the house yet?'[131] 'No,' the doctor replies, 'not yet. But he's prowling round the garden.' Hindenburg dies on 2 August. Just the day before, Hitler enacts a law making himself Reich Chancellor and Reich President combined. This effectively robs opponents of the Nazis of all hope that the regime will be toppled any time soon.

Now the country is unified once more, under the sign of the crooked cross. Things are noticeably on the up. Germany makes preparations to host the Olympic Games in Berlin. 'Peoples! Come and be our people's guest / Come in through our open gate! / Peace to the People's Festivities! / Let Honour be our rallying cry' ran the ditty of an amateur poet, which in September 1934 wins an open competition to become the official 1936 Olympic Anthem and is set to music by Richard Strauss.* In March 1935, the world's first regular television programme is broadcast from Berlin, and shortly afterwards the 'Reichsautobahn' between Frankfurt and Darmstadt is inaugurated. Now it's no longer six million Germans who are seeking work, but just two million. In June of that year, hundreds of thousands of people throughout the country take part in a state-sponsored ceremony to celebrate the summer solstice. Marie Güntel, though, who until recently was the Schleicher family's housekeeper, cannot bear to live in this world any longer. She falls prey to terminal melancholy. In July 1935 she puts an end to her life by drowning herself in Heiliger See in Potsdam.[132]

---

* In the original, the 'Olympische Hymne' runs: *Völker! Seid des Volkes Gäste, / Kommt durchs offne Tor herein! / Friede sei dem Völkerfeste! / Ehre soll der Kampfspruch sein.* The poet was Robert Lubahn, an unemployed Berlin actor. Richard Strauss was less than complimentary about his commission, writing to Stefan Zweig: 'I am whiling away the boredom of the advent season by composing an Olympic Hymn for the plebs – I of all people, who hate and despise sports.' [Translator's note]

Endnotes

The Straight Shooter:
Heinrich Brüning

1 Hömig 2005, p. 568.

2 Ibid., p. 584.

3 'Well done, this is your handiwork. You've got your man into office' (*Ihr Werk, Ihr Mann*) ibid., p. 147.

4 Up to 1931, Hitler and his entourage frequented the Sansscouci on Potsdamer Platz, and, from February 1931 onwards, the Kaiserhof (Friedrich 2007, p. 291).

5 'slowly tortured to death by his own party' (*von der eigenen Partei langsam zu Tode gequält*) Brüning 1972, Vol. I, p. 170.

6 'It's your turn to take the helm, Heinrich' (*Heinrich, du musst ans Ruder*) *Der Spiegel*, 14/1969, p. 68.

7 Hömig 2000, p. 29.

8 Treviranus 1968, p. 16.

9 'Father Filucius with the Iron Cross, First Class, hanging from his rosary' (*Pater Filucius mit dem E. K. I am Rosenkranz*) *Die Weltbühne*, 23. 9. 1930, p. 465. Father Filucius was an anti-Jesuit caricature created by the popular satirical illustrator Wilhelm Busch (1832–1908).

10 Beer 1931, p. 8.

11 'If the world should break in pieces around him, the ruins would leave him undaunted!' (*Selbst wenn der Weltbau krachend einstürzt, treffen die Trümmer noch einen Helden!*) Treviranus 1968, p. 17.

12 'anyone who dedicates his life to serving mankind and the common good ought not to give himself solely to another person or start a family' (*wer sich dem Dienst an der Menschheit, dem Gemeinwohl verschreibt, der sollte sich keinem anderen allein zuwenden, keine Familie gründen*) Hömig 2000, p. 211.

13 Ibid., p. 210.

14 'They taught their laws, hymns and encomia – in other words jurisprudence, religion, and history – through the act of singing' (*Gesetze, Hymnen und Enkomien – also das Recht, die Religion und die Geschichte, lernte man bei ihnen singend*) Treviranus 1968, p. 22.

15 He was held in high esteem by his comrades…' (*Unter den Kameraden war er hochgeehrt…*) ibid., p. 31.

16 'gypsy of welfare' (*Zigeuner der Wohltätigkeit*) Tucholsky 1998, p. 12.

17 'How would he react when under fire, or after the fighting has ended, or in the absence of any orders?' (*Wie würde er unter Feuer, nach Gefechtsende, ohne Befehl handeln?*) Treviranus 1968, p. 30.

18 Höhne 1983, p. 83.

19 'I will stand by you, and you must stand by me' (*Ich verlasse Euch nicht, und ihr sollt mich nicht verlassen*) Beer 1931, p. 56.

20 Ibid., p. 69 f.

21 'People who find themselves in only temporary financial embarrassment are to be given the opportunity to have a good and cheap lunchtime meal...' (*Leuten, die sich in einer nur vorübergehenden Geldverlegenheit befinden, soll Gelegenheit gegeben werden... Mittag essen zu können*) Treue 1976, p. 139.

22 'I am taking on a challenge that's already nine-tenths a lost cause!' (*Ich übernehme eine Aufgabe, die zu neun Zehnteln verloren ist*) Hömig 2000, p. 657.

23 'the uneasy feeling of being an outsider in most people's company' (*das beklemmende Gefühl, unter den meisten Menschen ein fremder zu sein*) ibid., p. 48.

The Dodgy Dealer:
Eric Jan Hanussen

1 'Germany's First Negro Bar' (*Deutschlands erste Negerbar*) advertisement in: Erik Jan Hanussen's *Berliner Wochenschau*, 1.4.1932.

2 Delmer 1961, p. 122.

3 Herbert 1972, p. 38.

4 'On the newsstands at Friedrichstraße railway station, titles like the *Berliner Morgenpost*, *Vorwärts* and *Die Rote Fahne* vie for space...' Cf. the 1926 photograph reproduced in Beachy 2014 of a newsstand at the station openly displaying the gay newspaper *Die Freundschaft* and the lesbian journal *Frauen Liebe* (Landesarchiv Berlin A. Pr. Br. Rep. 030, No. 16935–2).

5 'with their enormously rich stock of illustrations tell you more than an entire library' (*mit ihrem enorm reichen Bildmaterial eine ganze Bibilothek ersetzt*) advertisement by the publishing house of A. Möller in: *Die Jugend*, No. 7, 10. 2. 1931, p. 111.

6 'Only you know what torments you go through...' (*Nur Sie allein wissen, welchen Kummer Sie empfinden...*) advertisement in: Erik Jan Hanussen's *Berliner Wochenschau*, 1.4.1932.

7 'learned to fashion his own clothing and hats with tremendous expertise' (*eine außerordentliche Gewandheit... namentlich im Garnieren von Damenhüten*) *Berliner Tageblatt*, 27.2.1912, quoted in: Beachy 2014, p. 172.

8 'She gets herself invited to all the receptions...' (*Sie ist eingeladen zu den Empfängen...*) Nea Matzen: 'Selten ein Mensch, Bella Fromm und die verführerische Nähe zur Politik',

in: *epd medien*, No. 77, 2.10. 2010, pp. 3–6.

9 'slender and shy girl' (*schlankes und scheues'girl'*) Mann 1993, p. 490.

10 Delmer 1961, p. 239.

11 Ibid., p. 147.

12 Ibid., p. 167.

13 Ibid., p. 129.

14 The following account is based on a contemporary newspaper article by 'Kuka' entitled 'Skandal um Weißenberg. Religiöser Irrsinn in Berlin', in: *Hamburger Echo*, 22.7.1930.

15 'Under the strictest of supervision...' *Zeitschrift für kritischen Okkultismus und Grenzfragen des Seelenlebens*, Vol. 3, 1928, p. 160.

16 Zuckmayer 1976, p. 325.

17 'In actual fact, there is no future, no time, no space!' (*Eigentlich gibt es gar keine Zukunft, es gibt keine Zeit, keinen Raum!*) interview with Hanussen, in: *Göttinger Zeitung*, 26.3.1930, quoted in: Kugel 1998, p. 19.

18 'the experiences of a person who always sailed pretty close to the wind where plausibility was concerned' (*die Erlebnisse eines Menschen, der immer hart an der Grenze des Wahrscheinlichen stand*) Hanussen 1988, p. 13.

19 'If anyone had business to attend to at night there...' (*Wenn jemand nachts dort zu tun hat...*) ibid., p. 22.

20 'a cross between a jackal and a grizzly bear' (*eine Kreuzung zwischen Schakal und Grizzlybär*) ibid., p. 39 f.

21 'Regent, you fine grey beast...' (*Regent, du weißes gutes Tier...*)

ibid., p. 50.

22 'Is this what life is all about, then?' (*Wie? Sollte das Leben nur dazu gelebt werden*) Juhn 1930, p. 10.

23 'a crude device made of wires and wood' (*ein aus Drähten und Holz verfertigter plumper Apparat*) ibid., p. 16 f.

24 Ibid., p. 25.

25 'This was written by a man...' (*Dies ist die Schrift eines Mannes...*) ibid., p. 29.

26 From the memoirs of Albert Hellwig, quoted in Kugel 1998, p. 94.

27 'A genuine prophet is *seized* by an idea...' (*Den Propheten erfasst die Idee...*) Juhn 1930, p. 40.

28 'Anyone who claims to be showing people something miraculous' (*Wer den Menschen das Wunder...*) ibid., p. 89.

29 'how to eat glass, ingest fire and gravel...' Hanussen 1988, p. 52.

30 'For every ten revolutions, they were given a free ride' ibid., p. 56.

31 A citation with an address (Komitatsgasse) appears in: *Illustrierte Kronen-Zeitung*, 7.8.1911, p. 4.

32 Quoted in Kugel 1998, p. 27.

33 *Mährisches Tagblatt*, 28.6.1915, p. 6.

34 'trench theatre, louse-racing contests, and games of tombola' (*Schützengrabentheater, Läusewettrennen, Tombolaspiele*) Hanussen 1988, p. 127.

35 *Mährisch-Schlesische Presse*, 8.12.1917, p. 4.

36 'This experiment was likewise a complete success' (*Auch dieses Experiment gelang*

vollkommen). Zentralblatt für Okkultismus: Monatsschrift zur Erforschung der gesamten Geheimwissenschaften, 13, 1919/20, p. 431.

37 Juhn 1930, p. 73.

38 Kugel 1998, p. 66.

39 'You're no medium! Don't ever volunteer for these experiments again!' (*Sie sind kein Medium! Melden Sie sich nie mehr zu solchen Experimenten!*) Juhn 1930, p. 58.

40 'Nothing is more merciless or cruel…' (*Nichts ist unbarmherziger und grausamer…*) Hanussen 1988, p. 114.

41 'of all cities in the world' (*von allen Städten der Welt*) ibid., p. 249 f.

42 Kugel 1998, p. 129.

43 'When, shortly thereafter, his twelve-year-old son came home from school, he shot him too' (*Als kurz darauf sein zwölfjähriger Sohn von der Schule heimkam, tötete er auch diesen*) *Göttinger Tageblatt*, 22.10.1930, quoted in: Treue 1976, p. 143.

44 'What is magic, though?' (*Aber was ist Magie?*) quoted in: Kugel 1998, p. 48.

The Pig-headed Proletarian: Ernst Thälmann

1 Testimony by Hans Ziesemer, who worked in a print works opposite the Thälmanns' greengrocer's shop, quoted in: Fuhrer 2011, p. 18.

2 Börrnert 2001, p. 31.

3 'But what I was reading' (*Aber was ich las…*) Thälmann 1994, p. 15.

4 Testimony by his sister Frieda, quoted in: Fuhrer 2011, p. 27.

5 'Your life is about to take a more serious turn…' (*Euer Leben beginnt…*) quoted in: Fuhrer 2011, p. 26.

6 'Over these weeks, I often fell to thinking…' (*Wie so oft habe ich in diesen Wochen gedacht…*) Thälmann 1994, p. 21.

7 Regina Scheer: 'Ich bin kein weltflüchtiger Zigeuner' – Legende und Wirklichkeit einer Jugend. Über die frühen Prägungen Ernst Thälmanns, in: Monteath 2000, pp. 41–58.

8 'I really used to love dancing' (*Ich tanzte doch so gern*) quoted in: Fuhrer 2011, p. 31.

9 'Up and down steps all day long…' (*Den ganzen Tag treppauf…*) quoted in ibid., p. 32.

10 'So, you reckon I ought to volunteer, do you?' (*Sie denken vielleicht, ich soll mich freiwillig melden?*) reminiscences of Rosa Thälmann, quoted in: ibid., p. 44.

11 Thälmann 1994, p. 63 (diary, 24.11.1916).

12 'Two o'clock in the afternoon: deserted from the front…' (*Mittags 2 Uhr abgehauen…*) diary of Ernst Thälmann, quoted in: Fuhrer 2011, p. 60.

13 'Anyone who stands in the way of the Socialist juggernaut…' (*Wer sich dem Sturmwagen der sozialistischen Revoliurtion entgegenstellt…*) Rosa Luxemburg: 'Ein gewagtes Spiel', in: *Die Rote Fahne* (Berlin),

24.11.1918.

14 Around this same time, she writes to Luise Kautsky: 'The atrocities perpetrated by the Bolsheviks give me sleepless nights' (*Die Greuel der Bolshewiki lassen mich nicht schlafen*) quoted in: *Vorwärts*, 15.1.1929.

15 'Anyone who suggests that the Social Democrats and the Communists…' (*Wer heute vorschlägt, daß sich Sozialdemokraten und Kommunisten…*) *Die Weltbühne*, 7.1.1930, p. 42.

16 'so that she'll make my life easier' (*damit sie mir das Leben leichter macht*) reminiscences of Rosa Thälmann, quoted in: Fuhrer 2011, p. 70 f.

17 'You have to admit, Rosa, that I often struggle to formulate my thoughts clearly' (*Du wirst doch zugeben, Rosa, dass ich meine Gedanken oft nicht so klar darlegen kann*) reminiscences of Rosa Thälmann, quoted in: ibid., p. 208.

18 'Every worker should defy the law…' (*Ein jeder Arbeiter pfeift auf das Gesetz…*) Winkler 2001, p. 516.

19 'talking shop' (*Quasselbude*) speech in the Hamburg Parliament, 30. 3. 1921, in: Thälmann 1956, p. 19.

20 Figures from: Gumbel, E. J.: Vom Fememord zur Reichskanzlei, Heidelberg 1962, p. 46, quoted in: Weber 2015, Part 1, p. 385.

21 'postmen with great sacks full of banknotes…' (*Postboten sehen, die große Säcke voller Banknoten…*) reminiscences of Erna von Pustau, quoted in: Fergusson 2011, p. 255.

22 Friedrich 1998, p. 175.

23 Weber 2014, p. 169.

24 'The coming revolution in Germany…' (*Die kommende Revolution…*) *Die Rote Fahne*, 10.10.1923, quoted in: ibid., p. 169.

25 Besymenski 2006, p. 41.

26 'it will be to our advantage if they attack first' (*für uns ist es von Vorteil, wenn sie als erste angreifen*) Stalin to Zinoviev, 7.8.1923, in: ibid., p. 42.

27 Ernst Wollenberg, Der Hamburger Aufstand und die Thälmann-Legende, in: *Schwarze Protokolle*, No. 6, October 1973, Berlin.

28 'I won't give a single inch' (*Keine, aber auch keine Konzessionen*) letter to Iwan Katz, 1924, quoted in: Weber 2003, p. 17.

29 'the German party's best and most valuable asset…' (*das Beste und Kostbarste, was die deutsche Partei besitzt…*) Weber 2015, Part 1, p. 688.

30 Montefiore 2005, p. 226.

31 'He looked exactly like you'd imagine a Hamburg dock worker…' (*Er sah genauso aus wie man sich den Hamburger Hafenarbeiter vorstellte…*) Margarethe Buber-Neumann, life companion of KPD Politburo member Heinz Neumann since 1929, on Thälmann, quoted in: Börrnert 2002, p. 34.

32 Weber 2014, p. 58.

33 'Rather ominously, it is starting

to become apparent that Teddy...' (*Verhängnisvoll macht sich geltend, dass Teddy...*) Clara Zetkin to Nikolai Bukharin, 11.9.1927, in: Weber 2015, Part 1, p. 580 (Doc. 173).

34 'His closing address...' (*Seine abschließende Rede...*) report of the Comintern emissary Vissarion Lominadze on a KPD rally in the Sportpalast in Berlin, 11.4. 927, in: ibid., p. 559 (Doc. 169).

35 'These are the kind of people...' (*Das sind solche Leute...*) Ernst Thälmann: *Der revolutionäre Ausweg und die KPD* ('The revolutionary way forward and the KPD') speech at the plenary session of the central committee of the Communist Party of Germany on 19 February 1932 in Berlin, p. 64.

36 Weber 2015, Part 1, p. 602 (Doc. 178).

37 'we carry on this serious ideological struggle...' (*diesen ernsten ideologischen Kampf...*) Thälmann 1956, p. 178 (from his speech on the report of the German commission, 15.3.1926).

38 'is unfit to remain at the head of the party...' (*dass er geeignet ist...*) quoted in: Weber 2003, p. 29.

39 'Comrade Thälmann, you'd be doing the workers' movement a great service...' (*Genosse Thälmann, tun Sie der Arbeiterbewegung...*) quoted in: Fuhrer 2011, p. 189.

40 Weber 2003, p. 133.

41 'Reich President' Thälmann Toppled! (*'Reichspräsident' Thälmann gestürzt!*') 27.9.1928.

Facsimile in: ibid., p. 130.

42 'dead mechanism' (*todten Mechanismus*) Clara Zetkin in March 1929 to Jules Humbert-Droz, quoted in: ibid., p. 60.

43 Heinrich Brandler to Isaak Deutscher, 4.2.1959, quoted in: Weber 2014, p. 50.

44 Rudolf Diels: 'Die Nacht der langen Messer ... fand nicht statt', in: *Der Spiegel*, 19.5.1949, p. 18.

45 Zarusky 1992, p. 191.

46 'organized revenge' (*organisierter Rachedienst*). Hans Kippenberger in a confidential report on the work of the 'military–political apparatus' of the KPD, 2.2.1936, in: Weber 2015, Part 1, p. 1160 (Doc. 375 a)

47 'Over the passage of time, with its shifting dynamic, the woman always remains grounded...' (*So steht die Frau lebensverbunden...*) Ernst to Rosa Thälmann, 22.3.1937, quoted in: Monteath 2000, p. 54.

48 'modest, quiet, loyal to her mother and well-behaved' (*bescheiden, ruhig, muttertreu und brav*) Ernst to Rosa Thälmann, 24.10.1934, quoted in ibid.

49 Ronald Sassning: Thälmann, Wehner, Kattner, Mielke. Schwierige Wahrheiten, in: UTOPIE kreativ, H. 114 (April 2000), pp. 362–75, here p. 365.

50 Ernst Thälmann's voice and his style of oratory were captured for posterity in the recording of a speech he delivered in Moscow on 15.2.1928.

51 'What pitifully thin wrists you

have!' (*Was hast du bloß für jämmerlich dünne Gelenke!*) Buber-Neumann 2002, p. 338.

52 See Italiaander 1982, p. 79, also: Buber-Neumann 2002, p. 338.

53 'Left-wing social democracy...' (*Die linke Sozialdemokratie...*) Thälmann at the KPD Party Conference, quoted in: Weber 2003, p. 292.

54 'Calls of "Bravo!", sustained bursts of applause' (*Bravorufe, langanhaltender Beifall*) quoted in: Podewin 1995, p. 94.

55 'Today Our Leader [*Führer*] Speaks.' (*Heute spricht unser Führer*) facsimile in: Weber 2003, p. 303.

The Devoted Lover:
Maud von Ossietzky

1 'She spoke Persian and wrote poetry' (*Sie sprach persisch und schrieb Gedichte*) Suhr 1988, p. 258.

2 'water contaminated with typhus bacteria' (*Typhuswasser*) ibid., p. 257.

3 In her autobiography, Maud claims to have attended the prestigious Cheltenham Ladies' College. However, her name does not appear anywhere in that school's records (Brinson/ Malet, p. 119, note 503).

4 Suhr 1988, p. 253.

5 'He appeared transformed when he spoke' (*Er schien sich zu verwandeln, wenn er sprach*) Ossietzky 1988, p. 18.

6 'Never before had I felt such delight in "putting on my glad rags"' (*Nie zuvor hatte ich mich mit so viel Freude 'feingemacht'*)

ibid., p. 19.

7 'All of a sudden, a figure appeared by my side...' (*Plötzlich tauchte an meiner Seite eine Gestalt auf...*) ibid., p. 23.

8 'Only now that you're absent do I realize...' (*Jetzt, wo Du mir fehlst... halfen beim Aussuchen*) ibid., p. 28.

9 'The bride wore an ivory silk dress...' (*Die Braut trug ein elfenbeinfabrebenes Seidenkleid...*) ibid., p. 31.

10 'If you want to see my ancestors...' (*Wenn du meine Ahnen sehen willst...*) ibid., p. 32.

11 'If you don't mend your ways...' (*Wenn Sie Ihr Verhalten nicht ändern...*) ibid., p. 40.

12 'Free thinkers, atheists, sectarians...' (*Freidenker, Atheisten, Sektierer...*) ibid., p. 41.

13 'I had grown vain...' (*Ich war eitel geworden...*) ibid., pp. 43 and 45.

14 'on a bright and sunny morning' (*an einem sonnenhellen Vormittag*) ibid., p. 52.

15 'In all honesty, we just don't have enough to eat' (*Eigentlich haben wir nicht genug zu essen*) ibid., p. 55.

16 'There are now three of us...' (*Wir sind jetzt drei... gesund machen wie früher*) ibid., p. 60.

17 'Ossietzky will never be a writer!' (*Ossietzky wird nie ein Schriftsteller!*) ibid., p. 61.

18 'Because the men had business to discuss...' (*Da es sich um ein Gespräch unter Männern handelte...*) Ossietzky 1988, p. 69.

19 Specifically, the issue published

on 18.10.1927.

20 Source: Records of the legal division of the Foreign Ministry, confidential documents relating to Kreiser und Ossietzky, vols 1–3, 23.11.1931, K 2027/K 520 469–97.

21 'I still have some business to attend to here in Copenhagen…' (*Ich habe hier in Kopenhagen noch einiges zu erledigen…*) 27.10.1930, in: Ossietzky 1988, p. 74.

22 'I've no idea what lies in store' (*Was kommen wird, weiß ich nicht*) Ossietzky 1988, p. 77 (1.1.1931).

23 'to do his utmost to resist and protect against acts of treachery' (*wirksamste Abweh… gegen das Verrätertum*) letter from Kurt von Schleicher to Bernhard Wilhelm von Bülow, 9.7.1931, quoted in: Kraiker/Suhr 1994, p. 85.

24 'motivated by a noble and ardent love of country' (*aus hoher und glühender Vaterlandsliebe*) opinion of the court at the trial held in Ulm of army officers charged with high treason for having engaged in National Socialist activities within the Reichswehr, quoted in: Berkholz 1988, p. 25.

25 Source: Records of the legal division of the Foreign Ministry, confidential documents relating to Kreiser und Ossietzky, Vols 1–3, 23.11.1931, K 2027/K 520 469–97.

26 *Die Weltbühne*, 24.11.1931 (unpaginated).

27 'The gagging of public criticism…' (*Man sollte die Mundtotmachung…*) letter of Thomas Mann to Alfred Apfel, 10.1.1932, quoted in: Berkholz 1988, p. 30.

28 'Political journalism isn't life assurance…' *Der politische Journalismus ist keine Lebensversicherung…*) *Die Weltbühne*, 10.5.1932, p. 691.

The Red Czar:
Otto Braun

1 Schulze 1981, p. 120.

2 'He was born into the wrong class' (*Der hat in der falschen Wiege gelegen*) Hermann Pünder, secretary of state in the Reich Chancellery, quoted in: Schulze 1981, p. 35.

3 'pretty down-to-earth' (*ganz nüchtern*) ibid., p. 302.

4 'genuine leadership personality' (*eine wirkliche Führerpersönlichkeit*) *Vossische Zeitung*, 28.1.1932; *Vorwärts*, 28.1.1932; *Königsberger Volkszeitung*, 28.1.1932, quoted in: Schulze 1981, p. 708.

5 'a real fighter, worthy of the respect of even the most implacable political adversary' (*Kämpfer, vor dem auch der schärfste innenpolitische Gegner*) *DAZ*, 28.1.1932, quoted in: Schulze 1981, p. 708.

6 'There are already signs that I'm beginning to come apart at the seams…' (*Bei mir knistert es schon bedrohlich…*) letter to Karl Kautsky, 19.2.1932, quoted in: Schulze 1981, p. 711.

7 'Otto Braun's a solid chap…' (*Der Otto Braun ist ein Kerl…*) quoted in: Schulze 1981, p. 664.

8 'overanxious solicitude'
(*überängstliche Fürsorge*) ibid.,
p. 40.

9 'thoroughly dispelling any
belief in God for my entire
life' (*gründlich für das ganze
Leben...*) ibid., p. 41.

10 'It was the *Arbeiter-Chronik*,
published in Nuremberg'
(*Es war die in Nürnberg
herausgegebene 'Arbeiter-
Chronik'*) ibid., p. 43.

11 'Before long we were holding
meetings with a few like-
minded workers...' (*Bald saßen
wir mit wenigen gleichgesinnten
Arbeitern...*) ibid., p. 52.

12 'bourgeois nonsense'
(*bürgerlichen Klumpatsch*) ibid.,
p. 53.

13 Ibid., p. 64.

14 'in all likelihood within
the foreseeable future'
(*höchstwahrscheinlich bereits in
absehbarer Zeit*) ibid., p. 129.

15 'All theoreticians should be
locked up together until they've
devoured one another' (*Man
sollte einfach alle Theoretiker
gemeinsam einsperren, bis sie
sich gegenseitig aufgefressen
haben*) ibid., p. 124.

16 Ibid., p. 118.

17 'Anything that's against nature
is ungodly' (*Was gegen die
Natur ist, das ist gegen Gott*)
ibid., p. 75.

18 'Even the most superficial
observer...' (*Dem oberflächlichen
Beobachter...*) Otto Braun:
'Landarbeiterflucht', in: *Der
Neue Weltkalender für 1911*,
Hamburg 1911, p. 33, quoted in:
Schulze 1981, p. 75.

19 'Even the weak find strength

within a community' (*In der
Gemeinschaft ist auch der
Schwache stark*) Schulze 1981,
p. 146.

20 'Rye is, and will remain, a
German crop' (*Der Roggen ist
und bleibt eine deutsche Frucht*)
ibid., p. 166.

21 'lying dead on the grass with
a bullet in the chest within a
few weeks' (*nach Wochen mit
durchschossener Brust den Rasen
decken*) ibid., p. 177.

22 'a vain, ambitious political
poseur' (*ein eitler ehrgeiziger
politischer Poseur*) ibid., p. 183.

23 'I was racked with indescribable
pain...' (*Unsägliche Schmerzen
peinigten mich...*) ibid., p. 188.

24 'All the pain would be over
and done with...' (*Vorbei aller
Schmerz...*) ibid., p. 189.

25 'I often envy those people...'
(*Oft beneide ich die Menschen...*)
ibid., p. 191.

26 'It must be stated openly and
quite unequivocally...' (*Es
muß aber auch offen und ganz
unzweideutig ausgesprochen
werden...*) leader article in
Vorwärts, 15.2.1918, quoted in:
Schulze 1981, p. 217.

27 'Oh, what the hell...just say
"yes"!' (*Ach was... sag einfach
ja!*) Schulze 1981, p. 223.

28 'There they all were, standing
in a conspiratorial huddle in
the conference room...' (*Im
Konferenzsaal standen sie Kopf
an Kopf...*) Braun 1979, p. 43.

29 'whose highly polished uniform
buttons reflected the majesty of
the Crown' (*in deren blanken
Uniformknöpfe sich der Glanz
der Krone widerspiegelte*) ibid.,

p. 41.

30 Ibid., p. 45.

31 'An old bureaucrats' trick' (*Ein alter Bürokratentrick*) ibid., p. 49.

32 'I had a pair of galoshes made from them' (*Davon habe ich mir Gummischuhe machen lassen*) Schulze 1981, p. 266.

33 'the Prussian spirit is the mortal enemy of all democracy' (*preußischer Geist ist der Todfeind aller Demokratie*) ibid., p. 225.

34 'If Germany is to live, then Prussia in the form it has taken hitherto must die!' (*Wenn Deutschland leben soll, muß Preußen in der bisherigen Gestalt sterben*) ibid., p. 252.

35 'The empire was so to speak a guest of Prussia's in Berlin' (*Das Reich war sozusagen in Berlin bei Preußen zu Gast*) Papen 1952, p. 126.

36 'fundamental problem facing the future internal configuration of Germany' (*Kernproblem der künftigen inneren Gestaltung Deutschlands*) Schulze 1981, p. 252.

37 'The new, democratic Prussia should not be destroyed' (*Das neue, das demokratische Preußen soll man nicht zerschlagen*) ibid., p. 254.

38 'Truly, we haven't fought against the dictatorship...' (*Dazu haben wir wahrlich nicht gegen die Diktatur...*) ibid., p. 239.

39 'old military blowhard who meddles in politics' (*politisierender alter Gamaschenknopf*) ibid., p. 292.

40 'has become the de facto dictator of Prussia...' (*zum tatsächlichen Diktator Preußens...*) *Kreuzzeitung*, 18.9.1920, quoted in: Braun 1979, p. 236.

41 'adept at taking on board and accepting different opinions...' (*abweichende Meinungen aufzunehmen und gelten zu lassen...*) Walther Schreiber, quoted in: Schulze 1981, p. 342.

42 'The whole apparatus can only function properly...' (*Der ganze Apparat funktioniert erst...*) ibid., p. 345.

43 'If someone had the choice of becoming a director...' (*Wenn jemand die Wahl hätte, den Posten eines Direktors...*) ibid., p. 498.

44 'natural governing type' (*regierende Natur*) ibid., p. 490.

45 'My friends in Hanover...' (*Meine Freunde in Hannover...*) ibid., p. 489.

46 'It's outrageous the way Prussia is being governed!' (*Das ist ja unerhört, wie in Preußen regiert wird!*) ibid., p. 492.

47 'I got the feeling...' (*Ich hatte das Gefühl...*) Severing 1950, vol. 2, p. 56.

48 'The democratic rubber truncheon...' (*Der demokratische Gummiknüppel...*) Braun 1979, p. 320.

49 'So, are you telling me that Herr Braun can dispatch a couple of policemen...?' (*Wenn er will, kann Herr Braun ein paar Polizisten über die Straße schicken...?*) ibid., p. 492.

50 'All this fuss over crises and resignations...' (*Mit Krisenlärm und Demission...*) quoted in: ibid., p. 496.

The Nazi Monster:
Graf von Helldorff

1 'electric horse' (*elektrisches Pferd*) Kugel 1998, p. 133.
2 Ibid., p. 181.
3 'The visit by the undersigned…' (*Der Besuch des Gefertigten…*) ibid., p. 134.
4 Ibid., p. 209 f.
5 'for insomnia, agoraphobia, disinclination to work…' (*gegen Schlaflosigkeit, Platzangst, Arbeitsunlust…*) ibid., p. 173.
6 'Erik Jan Hanussen prophesies the future…' (*Erik Jan Hanussen prophezeit die Zukunft…*) ibid., p. 159.
7 Ibid., p. 170 f.
8 *Kölner Volkszeitung*, 2.10.1931, quoted in: ibid., p. 187.
9 'An enduring political scene without Brüning…' (*Eine dauernde Politik ohne Brüning…*) quoted in: Frei 1980, p. 85.
10 'The world is not going to become Bolshevist…' (*Die Welt wird nicht bolschewistisch…*) preview of the year 1932, in: *Querschnitt*, XI, 12, Berlin, December 1931, pp. 829–32, quoted in: Kugel 1998, p. 187.
11 'tireless in his devising of erotic games' (*unerschöpflich in der Erfindung von Liebesspielen*) quoted in: ibid., p. 181.
12 Ibid., p. 182.
13 Bruno Frei: *Hanussen*, Strasbourg 1934, pp. 141–5, quoted in: ibid., p. 182.
14 'a chancer and mercenary of the worst kind, a drunken, vainglorious lout' (*Abenteurer und Landsknecht übelster Sorte… versoffener ruhmseliger Lümmel*) Konrad Heiden 1944 and Klemens von Klemperer, quoted in: Ted Harrison: 'Count Helldorff and the German Resistance to Hitler': *Working Papers in Contemporary History and Politics*, No. 8, European Studies Research Institute, University of Salford, January 1996, p. 22. The spelling of the name 'Helldorff' varies – in contemporary references and in older secondary literature on the subject, he often appears as 'Helldorf', though 'Helldorff' is correct.
15 Delmer 1961, p. 166.
16 'curious mix of daredevil mercenary and nonchalant aristocrat' (*seltsame Mischung von draufgängerischem Landsknecht und nonchalantem Grafen*) Gisevius 1982, p. 332.
17 'My position […] is one of extreme nationalism and extreme socialism' (*Meine Einstellung… ist eine extrem nationale und eine extrem soziale*) Ted Harrison: 'Count Helldorff and the German Resistance to Hitler': *Working Papers in Contemporary History and Politics*, No. 8, European Studies Research Institute, University of Salford, January 1996.
18 'the need of sterilising all Negroes in the United States. If you do not do this, the Negroes will one day own the country' William E. Dodd/Martha Dodd: *Ambassador Dodd's Diary*, London 1941, p. 141 f.
19 Oehme/Caro 1930, p. 18.
20 'Berlin needs stirring up!'

(*Berlin braucht Klamauk*) ibid., p. 108.

21 'what his Jewish and Marxist advisers instruct him to do' (*was seine jüdischen und marxistischen Ratgeber…*) *Der Angriff*, 29.12.1929.

22 'The old goat should clear off, or at least not forever be standing in the way of the young generation' (*Der alte Bock soll abhauen, und wenn nicht, so doch nicht ewig der Jugend im Wege stehen*) Goebbels 1998–2006, Part I, Vol. 1, p. 55 (4.1.1930).

23 'a Galician Jew' (*einem galizischen Juden*) Reuth 1990, p. 169.

24 'Marching forward across graves!' (*Über Gräber vorwärts*) quoted in: Bernhard Sauer: 'Goebbels "Rabauken". Zur Geschichte der SA in Berlin-Brandenburg,' in: *Berlin in Geschichte und Gegenwart, Jahrbuch des Landesarchivs Berlin* 2006, p. 115.

25 'Chairs were smashed to pieces…' (*Stühle zerkrachten…*) Julek Karl von Engelbrechten: *Eine braune Armee entsteht. Die Geschichte der Berlin-Brandenburger SA*, Munich and Berlin 1937, quoted in 'Goebbels "Rabauken". Zur Geschichte der SA in Berlin-Brandenburg,' in: *Berlin in Geschichte und Gegenwart, Jahrbuch des Landesarchivs Berlin* 2006, pp. 107–64, here p. 114.

26 Bernhard Sauer: 'Goebbels "Rabauken". Zur Geschichte der SA in Berlin-Brandenburg,' in: *Berlin in Geschichte und*

Gegenwart, Jahrbuch des Landesarchivs Berlin 2006, p. 118 f., see also Becker 1992, p. 24.

27 Cf. Hentschel 1978, pp. 108–17. Hentschel comes to the conclusion that a 'marked preponderance' of the NSDAP's funds came from self-financing initiatives as opposed to sporadic donations from German industrialists. In the case of heavy industry, it was primarily the steel baron Fritz Thyssen and Emil Kirdorf (chairman of the giant GBAG coal-mining concern) who began making donations to the National Socialists from the early 1920s on.

28 Oehme/Caro 1930, p. 91.

29 Ibid., p. 46.

30 'Take a look at these parasites on the Party…' (*Da seht euch die Parteischädlinge an…*) Walter Bergmann to Karl Ernst, quoted in: Bernhard Sauer: 'Goebbels "Rabauken". Zur Geschichte der SA in Berlin-Brandenburg,' in: *Berlin in Geschichte und Gegenwart, Jahrbuch des Landesarchivs Berlin* 2006, p. 129.

31 'Really quite passable' (*Ganz passabel*) Goebbels 1998–2006, Part I, Vol. 2, p. 61.

32 Delmer 1961, p. 129.

The Dogged Newshound: Dorothy Thompson

1 Sheean 1964, p. 23.

2 Ibid., p. 52.

3 Ibid., p. 26.

4 Ibid., p. 22.

5 Ibid., pp. 306–7.

6 Ibid., p. 20.
7 Ibid., p. 286.
8 Ibid.
9 From the diary of Dorothy
   Thompson, quoted in: Sheean
   1964, p. 45.
10 Ibid.
11 Sheean 1964, p. 45.
12 Ibid., p. 46.
13 Ibid., p. 47.
14 Ibid., p. 59.
15 Thompson 1928, p. 24.
16 Letter of Dorothy Thompson
   to Sinclair Lewis, 31.10.1927, in:
   Sheean 1964, p. 59.
17 Ibid., p. 87
18 Ibid., p. 88.
19 Ibid., p. 85.
20 Ibid., p. 91.
21 From the diary of Dorothy
   Thompson, in: Sheean 1964,
   p. 115.
22 Ibid.
23 Ibid.
24 Ibid., p. 193.

The Gentleman Jockey:
Franz von Papen

1 'Ah, I've got something really
   special for you. You'll be
   amazed' (*Ich habe da ganz was
   Feines, Sie werden staunen*)
   quoted in: Petzold 1995, p. 61.
2 'He was thought of as
   superficial...' (*On le dit
   superficiel, brouillon, faux,
   ambitieux, vaniteux, rusé,
   intrigant. Il a, en tout cas, une
   qualité: l'aplomb, l'audace,
   une audace aimable et comme
   inconsciente*) François-Poncet
   2016, p. 77.
3 'extenuating circumstances...
   due to his extreme parochialism'
   (*immer mildernde Umstände...
   wegen seiner enormen
   Beschränktheit*) quoted in:
   Petzold 1995, p. 8.
4 'guardian and bastion' (*Wächter
   und Sturmblock*) Papen 1952,
   p. 133.
5 'Growing up with merry
   siblings' (*Aufgewachsen mit
   lustigen Geschwistern...*) ibid.,
   p. 18.
6 Ibid., p. 21.
7 'a brief waltz with a pretty
   princess in a hidden corner of
   one of the great staterooms'
   (*in der verstohlenen Ecke
   eines der großen Prunkräume
   einen kurzen Walzer mit
   einer hübschen Prinzessin zu
   absolvieren*) ibid., p. 23.
8 'He was extremely gracious...'
   (*Er war sehr gnädig...*) ibid.,
   p. 37.
9 'easily beat off several attacks by
   the Zapatistas' (*mit Leichtigkeit
   einige Überfälle der Zapatisten
   zurückgeschlagen*) ibid., p. 40.
10 On the so-called 'German
   Corpse Factory', a notorious
   example of anti-German
   propaganda in the First
   World War, cf. Hermann
   Kellermann: *Der Krieg der
   Geister. Eine Auslese deutscher
   und ausländischer Stimmen
   zum Weltkrieg 1914*, Dresden
   1915, as well as the afterword
   in: Peter Walther (ed.): *Endzeit
   Europa. Ein kollektives Tagebuch
   deutschsprachiger Schriftsteller,
   Künstler und Gelehrter im Ersten
   Weltkrieg*, Göttingen 2008.
11 'failed because the target was
   heavily guarded' (*scheiterte an
   der Bewachung des Objekts*)

Papen 1952, p. 58.

12 'The plan was relatively simple' (*der Plan war relativ einfach*) ibid., p. 61.

13 'We got into the habit of going into one of the large department stores en masse...' (*Wir pflegten, gemeinsam in eines der großen Warenhäuser zu gehen...*) ibid., p. 60.

14 Jeffreys-Jones 2013, p. 33.

15 'Master Spy' (*Meisterspion*) Petzold 1995, p. 22.

16 'idiotic Yankees' (*die idiotischen Yankees*) Papen 1952, p. 73.

17 Ibid., p. 75.

18 'The German press should refrain from commenting...' (*Die deutsche Presse soll über diese Angelegenheit...*) quoted in: Hellmut von Gerlach: 'Herr von Papen', in: *Die Weltbühne*, 7.6.1932, p. 842.

19 'The debts the Western Powers incurred...' (*Die Verschuldung der Westmächte...*) Papen 1952, p. 67.

20 'You can be sure that the American people and their Congress...' (*Sie können sicher sein, das amerikanische Volk und sein Kongreß...*) ibid., p. 82.

21 'to report to the Western Front within the next twenty-four hours' (*sich innerhalb der nächsten vierundzwanzig Stunden an die Westfront zu begeben*) ibid., p. 84.

22 'An indescribable feeling of despair' (*ein unbeschreibliches Gefühl der Hoffnungslosigkeit*) ibid., p. 111.

23 'Consider the matter closed' (*Betrachten Sie die Sache als erledigt*) ibid., p. 111.

24 'The world that I had known and loved...' (*Die Welt, die ich gekannt und geliebt hatte...*) bid., p. 116.

25 'I thus experienced at close quarters...' (*Aus nächster Nähe erlebte ich so...*) ibid., p. 122.

26 'own party line' (*die eigene politische Linie*) letter from Papen to Graf Paschma, 4.5. 924, quoted in: Petzold 1995, p. 32.

27 Ibid., p. 33.

28 '... les catholiques, furieux de voir le gouvernement aux mains d'un homme qu'ils considèrent comme un faux frère' François-Poncet 2016, pp. 87–8.

29 'the gentleman and his press organ...' (*daß der Herr und sein Organ...*) Max Schlenker to Friedrich Springorum, 21.5.1929, quoted in: Petzold 1995, p. 46.

30 'I do not believe I am overselling myself...' (*Ich glaube, nicht zu viel zu versprechen...*) Franz von Papen to Heinrich Brüning, 24.1.1930, quoted in: ibid., p. 54.

31 Ibid., p. 52.

32 'how to handle, look after and love horses' (*Behandlung, Pflege und liebe zum Pferde*) Papen 1952, p. 149.

33 'signs of moral decline... chic to cultivate a radical champagne socialism' (*moralische Verfallserscheinungen... schöngeistig, einen Salonbolschewismus zu pflegen*) ibid., p. 155.

34 German League for the Protection of Western Civilisation (*Deutscher Bund zum Schutz abendländischer Kultur*) the chairman of this organization was Werner von

Alvensleben (1875–1947), who in various political constellations acted as an intermediary to prominent figures in the NSDAP.

35 *Papen leur sert un peu de tête de Turc; ils le plaisantent et le taquinent volontiers, sans qu'il s'en offusque. C'est lui, d'ailleurs, qui est le préféré, le favori du maréchal; il distrait le vieillard par sa vivacité, son enjouement; il le flatte par le respect, la dévotion qu'il lui manifeste; il le séduit par sa hardiesse; il est, à ses yeux, le type accompli du gentilhomme,* François-Poncet 2016, p. 79.

36 'Is political life any different to horsemanship…?' (*Ist es etwa im politischen Leben anders als im reiterlichen…?*) Papen 1952, p. 29.

37 'whereas the race jockey has to overcome obstacles in order to stay in contention, to those same ends, the statesman must often circumvent them' (*Während der Rennreiter die Hindernisse überwinden muss…*) Theodor Eschenburg: 'Franz von Papen', in: *Vierteljahrshefte für Zeitgeschichte*, Jahrgang 1 (1953), Heft 2, pp. 153–69, here p. 157.

38 Communication by Ambassador Horace Rumbold to British Foreign Secretary Sir John Simon, 19 November 1932, from the Foreign Office Papers in the National Archives, Kew, FO 371/15947/C 9793.

39 'a grumpy billy goat…' (*ein verbiesterter Ziegenbock…*) Kessler 2010, p. 434 (11.6.1932).

40 'He had […] all the characteristic traits of a trained General Staffer…' (*Er hatte… die Eigenschaften eines geschulten Generalstäblers…*) Tschirschky 1972, p. 135 f.

41 *Bien élevé, au surplus, de manières parfaites, très homme du monde, fortuné, assidu au club des Seigneurs et au club de l'Union, le Jockey de Berlin, il parle couramment l'anglais et le français. Sa vie de famille est irréprochable* François-Poncet 2016, p. 78.

The String-Puller:
Kurt von Schleicher

1 'The cadet detailed to look after us…' (*Der uns zugeteilte Kadett…*) Vogelsang 1965, p. 10.

2 *'Immer tönt sein breites Lachen / Nimmer tat der Strom versiegen. / Als er einmal stillgeschwiegen / Ganze fünf Minuten lang, / Hiess es: "Schleicher, sind Sie krank?"'* quoted in: Plehwe 1983, p. 16.

3 'nerves of steel' (*Eiserne Nerven*) Vogelsang 1965, p. 15.

4 'Knight's Cross with Swords of the Royal House Order of Hohenzollern' (*Kreuz der Ritter des Königlichen Hausordens*) Plehwe 1983, p. 19.

5 'a law unto himself, a real one-off…' (*ein Kapitel für sich, ein ganz eigenartiger Mensch…*) Tagebuch Oberst von Thaer, late April 1918, quoted in: Vogelsang 1965, p. 17.

6 'I predict a great future for him…(*Ich prophezeie ihm eine große Zukunft…*) diary of Colonel von Thaer, July 1918, quoted in: ibid., p. 18.

7 'The Field Marshal [Hindenburg] and I want to support Ebert…'(*Der Feldmarschall und ich wollen Ebert… stützen*) Groener-Geyer 1955, p. 117.

8 'The Army regards the Ebert administration as legal…' (*Das Feldheer hält die Regierung Ebert für legal…*) quoted in: Vogelsang 1965, p. 21.

9 Ibid., p. 34.

10 'set the whole city ablaze…' (*die ganze Stadt anzünden…*) a facsimile of Hoelz's pamphlet is reproduced in: Plehwe 1983, Plate 5 (plate section from p. 80 onwards).

11 'through a sea of blood' (*durch ein Meer von Blut*) quoted in: Plehwe 1983, p. 72.

12 Ibid., p. 57.

13 Helm Speidel: 'Reichswehr und Rote Armee', in: *Vierteljahrshefte für Zeitgeschichte*, Jahrgang 1 (1953), Heft 1, pp. 9–45, here p. 20.

14 Ibid., p. 33.

15 'German Workers Killed by Soviet Shells' (*Deutsche Proletarier durch Sowjetgranaten getötet*) ibid., p. 7.

16 Meissner 1983, p. 113.

17 Plehwe 1983, p. 54.

18 *Glabre, le crâne rasé, plus que blême, blafard, son masque, où brillent deus yeux aigus, ses traits, noyés dans une mauvaise graisse, ses lèvres minces à peine marquées, ne plaident pas en sa faveur* François-Poncet 2016, p. 85.

19 *il a de fort belles mains* ibid.

20 Plehwe 1983, p. 53 f.

21 Rheinbaben 1968, p. 253.

22 'cardinal in political matters'(*Kardinal in politicis*) Theodor Eschenburg: 'Die Rolle der Persönlichkeit in der Krise der Weimarer Republik: Hindenburg, Brüning, Groener, Schleicher', in: *Vierteljahrshefte für Zeitgeschichte* 9 (1961), Heft 1, p. 10.

23 Hentschel 1990, p. 50.

24 'This new family idyll…' (*Das neue Familienidyll…*) Letter to Gerold von Gleich, 26.4.1931, quoted in: Vogelsang 1965, p. 72.

25 Rheinbaben 1968, p. 252.

26 'He was never at a loss for an argument or a solution…'(*Um ein Argument oder eine Lösung war er nie verlegen…*) Theodor Eschenburg: 'Die Rolle der Persönlichkeit in der Krise der Weimarer Republik: Hindenburg, Brüning, Groener, Schleicher', in: *Vierteljahrshefte für Zeitgeschichte* 9 (1961), Heft 1, p. 10.

The Destruction of New York

1 Demps 2010, p. 152.

2 Beer 1931, p. 67.

3 'Even in the heyday of the Prussian government…' (*Es wird selbst in den besten Zeiten…*) Schulze 1981, p. 644.

4 'The people have been shaken to the core by the restructuring that has gone on within Brüning's cabinet' (*Das Volk ist eben durch die Sanierungsarbeit des Kabinetts bis in seine Tiefen aufgerüttelt worden*) Pünder 1961, p. 59 (16.9.1930).

5 Schulze 1981, p. 639.

6 'while they are still too weak…' (*solange sie noch zu schwach sind…*) Braun 1979, p. 309.

7 'becoming increasingly difficult…' (*wird immer schwieriger…*) Schulze 1981, p. 653.

8 'Quite by chance, while in conversation with someone who is close to the circle around Max Hölz…' (*Von einer dem Max Hölz Kreise nahestehenden Person zufällig gesprächsweise gehört…*) Kessler 2010, p. 389 (26.10.1930).

9 'National Socialism is a feverish spasm…' (*Der Nationalsozialismus ist eine Fiebererscheinung…*) ibid., p. 377 (15.9.1930).

10 'I have nothing against decent Jews…' (*Gegen anständige Juden habe ich nichts einzuwenden…*) 15.10.1930, quoted in: Oehme/Caro 1930, p. 86.

11 'I can assure you…' (*Ich darf Ihnen versichern…*) quoted in: Hilke Dening: *Chronik 1930. Tag für Tag in Wort und Bild*, Dortmund 1989, p. 160.

12 'The system will have to pay us…' (*Das System muß uns bezahlen…*) quoted in: Brüning 1972, p. 198.

13 'We are fighting against this state…' (*Wir bekämpfen diesen Staat…*) quoted in: Bernhard Sauer: 'Goebbels "Rabauken". Zur Geschichte der SA in Berlin-Brandenburg', in: *Berlin in Geschichte und Gegenwart, Jahrbuch des Landesarchivs Berlin* 2006, p. 155.

14 'The head of a prominent Jew will be impaled on every telegraph pole from Berlin to Munich' (*Auf jeder Telegraphenstange von München bis Berlin wird das Haupt eines prominenten Juden aufgespießt werden*) quoted in: Oehme/Caro 1930, p. 49.

15 'Where New York once stood…' (*Wo New York war…*) quoted in: Kugel 1998, p. 144.

16 According to the testimony of Christoph Schröder: Erik Jan Hanussen, in: *Zeitschrift für metaphysische Forschung* 4, 6, Berlin, 24.1.1934, p. 176 f., quoted in: Kugel 1998, p. 153.

17 'It's not a city…' (*Es ist doch keine Stadt…*) quoted in: ibid., p. 146.

18 'In every conversation you have…' (*Die Stimmung, die dir… aus jedem Gespräch… entgenschlägt…*) from Leopold Schwarzschild's diary, 23.8.1930, quoted in: Schulze 1998, p. 326.

19 According to the testimony of Gertrud Schuch, in: Kugel 1998, p. 184.

20 'I must say I've taken a very close look at Hanussen…' (*Ich muß sagen, daß ich Hanussen genau geprüft habe…*) quoted in: ibid., p. 195.

21 'I must admit…' (*Ich muß zugeben…*) ibid., p. 155.

22 'together with a long handwritten note…' (*versehen mit einem langen Handschreiben…*) Beer 1931, p. 54, and Brüning 1972, p. 260.

23 'didn't even bat an eyelid' (*zuckte nicht mit der Wimper*) ibid., p. 58.

24 'experience has taught me that the first car…' (*erfahrungsgemäß*

der erste Wagen...) Brüning 1972, p. 255.

25 Thompson 1932, p. 104.

26 'use his tail like a fox...' (*wie der Fuchs mit dem Schwanz...*) Beer 1931, p. 39.

27 'silent partnership with the SPD' (*Stille Partnerschaft mit der SPD*) Treviranus 1968, p. 288.

28 According to the testimony of Arnold Brecht, in: Arnold Brecht: 'Gedanken über Brünings Memoiren', in: *Politische Vierteljahrsschrift*, Vol. 12, No. 4 (December 1971), pp. 607–40, here p. 626.

29 Delmer 1961, p. 129.

30 'worthwhile elements of the population' (*wertvolle Teile der Bevölkerung*) Jasper 1986, p. 78.

31 'I had to marvel at Dr Brüning's self-restraint' (*Ich mußte Dr Brünings Selbstbeherrschung bewundern*) Fromm 1994, p. 39 (10.2.1931).

32 'let Germany work its way to freedom through hunger' (*Deutschland sich zur Freiheit emporhungern zu lassen*) Hoegner 1989, p. 19.

33 'I can't sit by and watch this anymore' (*Das kann man nicht mehr mit ansehen*) Treviranus 1968, p. 323.

34 'For many years I'd had in mind the possibility...' (*Mir hatte seit Jahren die Möglichkeit vorgeschwebt...*) Van Bergh 1983, p. 8.

35 'welter of missives from the cream of German society' (*eine große Anzahl von Briefen der besten deutschen Männer*) Brüning 1972, vol. II, p. 441.

36 'brown waistcoats, so-called 'climbing vests'... (*braune Westen, sogenannte Kletterwesten...*) Friedrich 2007, p. 319 f.

37 A KPD-led 'hunger demonstration' was held, for instance, on 30.6.1931 on Frankfurter Allee in Berlin, see also Schulze 1981, p. 666.

38 'Jews are strolling up and down the pavements...' (*Juden flanieren die Trottoirs herauf...*) *Der Angriff*, 28.11.1927.

39 'a single place on my body that wasn't cut or bruised...' (*am ganzen Körper keine heile Stelle...*) Dirk Walter: *Antisemitische Kriminalität und Gewalt. Judenfeindschaft in der Weimarer Republik*, Bonn 1999, p. 211, quoted in: Friedrich 2007, p. 319 f.

40 'refuge in the entrance to the Siegfried Levy department store' (*Zuflucht vor dem Geschäft von Siegfried Levy*) eyewitness account quoted in: Reiner Zilkenat: 'Der "Kurfürstendamm-Krawall" am 12. September 1931', in: Yves Müller/Reiner Zilkenat (eds): *Bürgerkriegsarmee. Forschungen zur nationalsozialistischen Sturmabteilung (SA)*, Frankfurt am Main and elsewhere, 2013, pp. 45–62.

41 Quoted in: Bernhard Sauer: 'Goebbels "Rabauken". Zur Geschichte der SA in Berlin-Brandenburg', in: *Berlin in Geschichte und Gegenwart, Jahrbuch des Landesarchivs Berlin* 2006, p. 130.

42 Ted Harrison: 'Count Helldorff and the German Resistance

to Hitler': *Working Papers in Contemporary History and Politics*, No. 8, European Studies Research Institute, University of Salford, January 1996.

43 Reiner Zilkenat: 'Der "Kurfürstendamm-Krawall" am 12. September 1931', in: Yves Müller/Reiner Zilkenat (eds): *Bürgerkriegsarmee. Forschungen zur nationalsozialistischen Sturmabteilung (SA)*, Frankfurt am Main and elsewhere, 2013, pp. 45–62.

44 'large leather whip, as used by the driver of a horse-drawn artillery limber' (*große lederne Artilleriefahrer-Peitsche*) Bahar/Kugel 2001, p. 568.

45 'Why do those fat Jewesses go around so provocatively wearing furs...?' (*Warum tragen die dicken Jüdinnen so aufreizend Pelzen...?*) Reiner Zilkenat: 'Der "Kurfürstendamm-Krawall" am 12. September 1931', in: Yves Müller/Reiner Zilkenat (eds): *Bürgerkriegsarmee. Forschungen zur nationalsozialistischen Sturmabteilung (SA)*, Frankfurt am Main and elsewhere, 2013, pp. 45–62.

46 'Laval's teeth, completely yellowed by nicotine...' (*Lavals Zähne, ganz gelb von Nikotin...*) Fromm 1994, p. 46.

47 *À bas le chancelier des Juifs!* François-Poncet 2016, pp. 50–1.

48 '*Le voyage a dû être bien fatigant pour ce vieux monsieur!*' ibid., p. 54.

49 '*Au milieu de la nuit, il avait été réveillé par une douloureuse indigestion, et pour secouer les vapeurs qui l'oppressaient, il avait dû sortir et faire les cent pas dans l'avenue des Tilleuls, à la stupeur des sentinelles, chargées de lui rendre les honneurs! Mauvais présage! pensai-je, tandis que le train s'éloignait*'. ibid., p. 57.

50 'What took place on the Kurfürstendamm...' (*Was am Kurfürstendamm geschehen sei...*) Ted Harrison: 'Count Helldorff and the German Resistance to Hitler': *Working Papers in Contemporary History and Politics*, No. 8, European Studies Research Institute, University of Salford, January 1996.

51 'District Judge Ohnesorge...' (*Landgerichtsdirektor Ohnesorge...*) *Die Weltbühne*, 16.2.1932, p. 270.

52 Over this period, membership of the SA grew from 3,557 to 9,923; see also Friedrich 2007, p. 325.

Halma

1 Thompson 1932, p. 107.
2 Ibid., p. 104.
3 Ibid.
4 Ibid.
5 Ibid.
6 Ibid.
7 Ibid., p. 107.
8 Hitler, *Mein Kampf* 1925–27; official English translation by James Murphy, London 1939, Vol. I, Chapter X, p. 134.
9 Thompson 1932, p. 106.
10 Suhr 1988, p. 255.
11 'being locked up would be the most uncomfortable position for me' (*als Eingesperrter am unbequemsten*) 8.5.1932, in:

Kraiker/Suhr 1994, p. 89.

12 'One of life's few satisfactions…
deserves the very best' (*Vor den
Drohungen irdischer Macht…
der das beste haben muß*)
Ossietzky 1988, p. 77 f. (6.3.1932).

13 'the generals' payback' (*Quittung
der Generale*) *Die Weltbühne*,
17.5.1932, p. 734.

14 Berkholz 1988, p. 61.

15 Ibid., pp. 104, 110.

16 'I'm sending you the *Weltspiegel*
picture…' (*Ich schicke dir
die Weltspiegel Bild von sein
Abschied…*) Maud to Rosalinde
von Ossietzky, 29.5.1932, in:
Berkholz 1988, p. 101.

17 Carl is to blame for the fact
that I don't speak German
perfectly…' (*Dass ich Deutsch
nicht perfekt kann, daran ist Carl
schuld…*) Brinson/Malet, p. 120
(15.11.1932).

18 'Neither your letters nor the way
you looked when you last came
to visit…' (*Ich habe weder aus
Deinen Briefen noch aus Deinem
Aussehen bei Deinem Besuch…*)
Carl to Maud von Ossietzky,
12.6.1932, in: Berkholz 1988,
p. 110.

19 'I bade […] my father farewell'
(*An einem Frühlingsabend des
Jahres 1859 sagte ich […] meinem
Vater Lebewohl*) Hindenburg
1920, p. 11.

20 Hindenburg 1920, p. 12.

21 Pyta 2009, p. 15.

22 'an independent, spirited
character of great ability'
(*Ein selbständiger schneidiger
Charakter von großer
Befähigung*) ibid., p. 15.

23 'When all is said and done, war
is the normal state of affairs for

a soldier' (*für einen Soldaten ist
ja der Krieg der Normalzustand*)
quoted in: ibid., p. 16.

24 'The best that I have to offer…'
(*Das Beste, was ich zu bieten
vermag…*) quoted in: ibid., p. 21.

25 Quoted in: ibid., p. 19.

26 'Petrol ruins the character'
(*Benzin verdirbt den Charakter*)
quoted in: Meissner 1988, p. 221.

27 Ibid., p. 198.

28 Ibid., p. 265.

29 'Well, that's a matter of opinion'
(*Das wäre so Ansichtssache*)
Berkholz 1988, p. 128 (recounted
by Rudolf Olden).

30 Meissner 1988, p. 224.

31 'The Reich President is eighty-
five…' (*Der Reichspräsident ist 85
Jahre alt…*) *Frankfurter Zeitung*,
9.9.1932 (national edition).

32 'All we have left is an old
general…' (*Ein alter General ist
uns geblieben…*) *Die Weltbühne*,
25.3.1930, p. 476.

33 'A deep gulf in ideology
and political understanding
separates me from Herr von
Hindenburg…' (*Mich trennt in
Weltanschauung ind politischer
Einsicht eine tiefe Kluft von
Herrn von Hindenburg…*)
quoted in: Schulze 1981, p. 719.

34 'Swallow your pride or you'll
get Hitler!' (*Schluckt es herunter,
sonst kommt Hitler!*) quoted in:
Plehwe 1983, p. 158.

35 'having clearly thrown in his
lot with Social Democracy'
(*eindeutig auf die Seite der
Sozialdemokratie gestellt*) quoted
in: Blasius 2006, p. 38.

36 'Who elected me, though?
(*Wer hat mich denn gewählt?*)
quoted in: Höhne 1983, p. 155.

See also two letters written by Hindenburg to the Conservative politician Elard von Oldenburg-Januschau on 17 and 22 February 1932 respectively, in which he strongly insists upon having a broad majority of support as a presidential candidate from parties that are not on the left, in: Vogelsang 1962, p. 442 f.

37 'I got the feeling that he'd dropped me' (*Ich hatte das Gefühl, er habe mich aufgegeben*) Brüning 1972, Vol. II, p. 442.

38 Delmer 1961, p. 162.

39 Höhne 1983, p. 166.

40 'will sit together over a bottle…' (*bei einer Pulle zusammen…*) Vogelsang 1965, p. 73.

41 'the right shoulder' (*die rechte Schulter*) quoted in: Petzold 1995, p. 58.

42 'Business knows full well…' (*Die Wirtschaft weiß gena…*) quoted in: Höhne 1983, p. 134.

43 'powerful forces…' (*starke Kräfte…*) Ernst Feder in the *Berliner Tageblatt*, quoted in: Höhne 1983, p. 134.

44 'I must finally turn to the right, then' (*Ich muß jetzt endlich nach rechts gehen…*) according to the testimony of Hermann Pünder, head of the Reich Chancellery, in: Pünder 1961, p. 128.

45 'We want to reel in the Nazis…' (*Die Nazis wollen wir einfangen…*) quoted in: Plehwe 1983, p. 141.

46 Vogelsang 1962, p. 456 (from the papers of Wilhelm Groener, October 1932). A recording of Groener's speech in the Reichstag is available for download from the historical sound archives of the Südwestrundfunk (SWR) radio station: https://www.swr.de/swr2/wissen/archivradio/der-reichstag-vor-hitler-1932-reichswehrminister-wilhelm-groener-rechtfertigt-verbot-der-sa/-/id=2847740/did=21202296/format=pdf/gp2=13598660/nid=2847740/6ysmyz/index.html

47 'towards responsibility…' (*in das Bett der Verantwortung…*) quoted in: Blasius 2006, p. 54.

48 'Brüning should fall in the next few days' (*Brüning soll in den nächsten Tagen schon fallen*) Goebbels 1998–2006, Part I, Vol. 2/2, p. 165 (8.5.1932).

49 'so wrapped up in confidential and hypothetical matters…' (*so sehr mit dem Geheimnisvollen und Hypothetischen beschäftigt…*) Brüning 1972, p. 685.

50 'A state cannot get back on its feet…' (*Ein Staat kann nicht hochkommen…*) ibid., p. 611.

51 'That's the really awkward thing…' (*Das ist ja das Fatale…*) ibid., p. 614.

52 'But I've already put your name forward to the old man' (*Aber ich habe Sie bereits dem Alten Herrn vorgeschlagen*) Papen 1952, p. 184.

53 'In a little sailing dinghy…' (*In einem kleinen Segelboot…*) ibid., p. 185.

54 'As always he received me with fatherly kindness' (*Wie immer empfing er mich mit väterlicher Güte*) ibid., p. 189.

55 Brüning 1972, p. 650.

56 Treviranus 1968, p. 333.

The Coup

1 'Have you noticed how alike the National Socialists and the Communists are?' (*Haben Sie schon die Ähnlichkeiten zwischen Nationalsozialisten und Kommunisten bemerkt?*) Fromm 1994, p. 35 (15.8.1930).

2 Ibid., p. 48.

3 'I have a genuine admiration for this great soldier' (*Ich verehre diesen großen Soldaten aufrichtig*) ibid., p. 20 (26.4.1925).

4 'The young Hindenburgs aren't terribly likeable' (*Die jungen Hindenburgs sind wenig anziehend*) ibid., p. 23 (10.2.1926).

5 'The whole room fell silent when he came in' (*Alles verstummte, als er eintrat*) ibid.

6 'having a love affair with Miss Lisa Abel...' (*mit Fräulein Lisa Abel ein Liebesverhältnis unterhalte...*) Nea Matzen: 'Bella Fromm – Viele Leben in einem: Societylady, Journalistin, Bestsellerautorin im Exil', in: *Medien & Zeit*, September 2009, pp. 28–56, here p. 39.

7 'I attended the same parties as before...' (*Ich besuchte die gleichen Partys wie vorher...*) Bella Fromm, radio interview 1944, in: Nea Matzen/Jan Ehlert: 'Bella Fromm. Von der Gesellschaftsreporterin in Berlin zur politischen Exilantin in New York', *Deutschlandfunk* radio programme 2006, corrected broadcast transcript, p. 9.

8 'The upper classes are moving closer to Hitler' (*Die Leute der Oberschicht nähern sich Hitler*) Fromm 1994, p. 51 (29.1.1932).

9 'It would be just too ghastly...' (*Es wäre doch zu unangenehm...*) ibid., p. 41 (17.6.1931).

10 'What would I want with that brown-hatter?' (*Was soll ich mit dem Hinterlader?*) ibid., p. 88 (23.1.1933).

11 'Whoever controls Prussia...' (*Wer Preußen hat...*) Bracher 1960, p. 581.

12 'Anyone who wants a Soviet Prussia...' (*Wer ein Sowjet-Preußen... will...*) quoted in: Schulze 1981, p. 667.

13 'I have the distinct feeling...' (*Ich habe das Gefühl...*) Fromm 1994, p. 5 (6.3.1932).

14 'I promise at all times to fight unceasingly for the Soviet Union...' (*Ich gelobe, stets und immer für die Sowjetunion... zu kämpfen*) quoted in: Plehwe 1983, p. 128 f.

15 'Resistance will as a matter of principle be punishable by death' (*Widerstand wird grundsätzlich mit dem Tode bestraft*) Die Boxheimer Dokumente, in: *Das Parlament*, 3. Jahrgang, Heft 3 (18.3.1953). These documents were drafted by a group under Werner Best, a lawyer from Darmstadt and legal adviser to the Nazi Party who played a leading part in the resistance to French occupation of the Rhineland in the 1920s, and named after the house where the group met, 'Boxheimer Hof'.

16 'I was supposed to instil the masses of people...'

(*Ich sollte die in gewaltigen Massenversammlungen…*) Braun 1979, p. 374.

17 'Something's got to happen now' (*Jetzt muß irgendetwas geschehen*) quoted in: Kissenkoetter 1978, p. 133.

18 'I'm pretty much at the end of my tether' (*Ich bin so ziemlich am Ende meiner Kraft*) letter to Raphael Friedeberg, 5.5.1932, in: Schulze 1981, p. 729.

19 Meissner 1983, p. 126.

20 *Vossische Zeitung*, 26.5.1932, morning edition.

21 Ibid.

22 '8 seriously injured…' (*8 Schwerverletzte…*) Goebbels 1998–2006, Part I, Vol. 2/2, p. 289 f. (28.5.1932).

23 'As long as these gentlemen…' (*Solange diese Herren…*) Braun 1979, p. 394 f.

24 'The fact that this election campaign…' (*Daß dieser Wahlkampf…*) *Vossische Zeitung*, 23.6.1932, evening edition, quoted in: Blasius 2006, p. 60.

25 'fight against the Swastika and the Red Star' (*im Kampf gegen Hakenkreuz und Sowjetstern*) quoted in: Franz Osterroth/ Dieter Schuster: *Chronik der deutschen Sozialdemokratie*, Vol. 2: Vom Beginn der Weimarer Republik bis zum Ende des Zweiten Weltkrieges, Bonn 1980.

26 'Smash Hitler, the village policeman…' (*Schlagt Hitler, den Gendarmen…*) Höhne 1983, p. 183.

27 Ibid., p. 171.

28 'As the first participants in the National Socialist Sports Day began to arrive in Ohlau…'

(*Als die ersten Teilnehmer des nationalsozialistischen Sportsfestes in Ohlau eintrafen…*) quoted in: Blasius 2006, p. 64.

29 Léon Schirmann: *Justizmanipulationen. Altonaer Blutsonntag und die Altonaer bzw. Hamburger Justiz 1932–1994*, Berlin 1995 (2nd edn).

30 The police report on the incident written at the time by the president of the region of Schleswig, Waldemar Abegg (a man with republican sympathies), states that there was suddenly 'a volley of gunfire from the dwellings, roofs and balconies of the houses on the corner […] After the National Socialists marched off, at around 18.45 the police officers came under heavy fire once more. Weapons of every calibre were used in this assault (revolvers, teschings [handguns of very small calibre – less than 6mm – named after their first place of manufacture, Teschen (now Cieszyn) in Silesia], carbines and rifles) and the police officers are quite certain that they even heard automatic weapons (machine pistols or sub-machine guns) being discharged. The commander of the Second Police Battalion was now tasked with restoring order to the whole of the riot area. He advanced with two snatch squads and a machine gun and after fifteen minutes succeeded in subduing the enemy's fire.' (Report of the Schleswig regional president

Abegg to Prussian interior minister Severing, 19 July 1932, BA, R 43 I/2283, Bl. 252). Léon Schirmann has shown that the evidence which was used to convict four communists was manipulated (Léon Schirmann, *Altonaer Blutsonntag, 17. Juli 1932. Dichtungen und Wahrheit*, Hamburg 1994). The author claims that no shots were fired from roofs or balconies, and that the sixteen innocent bystanders who lost their lives were 'in all probability' killed by rounds fired by the police, who were keen to hush this fact up. Schirmann, too, ascribes the killing of the two SA stormtroopers to a communist group. In 1992 his investigations led to a full exoneration of the four communists who had been convicted of murder, however.

31 'I am only submitting to this under duress' (*Ich weiche nur der Gewalt*) Winkler 2002, p. 179.

32 'We'll crush them like lice' (*Wir werden sie wie die Läuse zerdrücken*) Karl Höltermann, quoted in: Höhne 1983, p. 193.

33 'I saw Reichsbanner members in tears at that time…' (*Ich sah in jenen Tagen Reichsbannerleute weinen…*) Schulze 1981, p. 752.

34 'well organized… police officers and administrators' (*gut organisierte… Polizeioffiziere und Beamte*) report by the former Berlin police commander Magnus Heimannsberg, in: Bracher 1960, p. 735.

35 'it would have been positively childish to believe that the communists…' (*der Glaube, daß die Kommunisten…*) Severing 1950, p. 342.

36 The German Federal Archives contain a summary, presumably prepared by the Prussian Interior Ministry, of all the incidents of violent political disorder that took place in Prussia during the period from 1 June to 20 July 1932. According to this, the total number of clashes was 461, with 82 dead. The parties identified as being the 'aggressors' broke down as follows: the KPD in 281 cases, the Reichsbanner in 23 cases and the NSDAP in 108 cases, while the groups deemed to have been on the receiving end of the violence were: the KPD in 56 cases, the Reichsbanner in 41 cases, the NSDAP in 266 cases and the police in 45 cases (BA, R 43 I/2283, Bl. 274 f.).

37 'I must capture your head!… once it's over you're absolutely knackered!' (*Ich muß Ihren Kopf… is man schlapp*) Braun 1979, p. 398.

38 'If requests of any kind are received from the old Prussian government…' (*Wenn von seiten der alten Preußenregierung…*) Schulze 1981, p. 765.

39 Ibid., p. 766 f.

40 Ibid., p. 789.

41 The Braun government died an unlovely… death, far from the limelight…' (*Tief im Hintergrunde starb die Regierung Braun…*) *Die Weltbühne*, 14.2.1933, p. 236.

42 Schulze 1981, p. 785.

Balls of Destiny

1 'There's a mood of oppressive excitement…' (*Eine schwüle Erregung…*) quoted in: Kugel 1998, p. 208.

2 'Scanning the starting list and seeing the Count's name…' (*bei Durchsicht der Starterliste beim Namen des Fürsten…*) *12-Uhr Blatt*, Berlin, 23.5.1932, quoted in: ibid., p. 199.

3 'Count Lobkowicz must drive carefully…' (*Fürst Lobkowicz muß vorsichtig fahren…*) *Kriminalistische Monatshefte*, 7, 1, Berlin, January 1933, p. 20, quoted in: ibid., p. 199.

4 'Hitler and Hanussen are a good fit' (*Hitler und Hanussen passen zusammen*) *Berlin am Morgen*, 10.6.1932, quoted in: ibid., p. 197.

5 From the papers of Hermann Graf Keyserling held at the Darmstadt University and Provincial Library (correspondence A2-Z2, box 097).

6 'Hanussen is the Cagliostro of the German Starvation Republic…' (*Hanussen ist der Cagliostro der deutschen Hungerrepublik…*) Bruno Frei: *Hanussen. Ein Bericht*, Strasbourg 1934, p. 115 f., quoted in: Kugel 1998, p. 197. Count Alessandro di Cagliostro was the pseudonym of the magician and occultist Giuseppe Balsamo (1743–95) whose demonstrations of alchemy and psychic healing captured the imagination of the aristocracy of eighteenth-century Europe. After his death he came to be widely regarded as a charlatan.

7 'Berlin has been cleansed of the last remnants of this clairvoyance filth' (*als bis Berlin von dem letzten Rest des Hellseher-Schmutzes gereinigt ist*) *Berlin am Morgen*, 14.12.1932, p. 9, quoted in: ibid., p. 201.

8 Burkert 1982, p. 35.

9 Kugel 1998, p. 183.

10 'Hitler's future while in a trance' (*in Trance Hitlers Zukunft*) Erik Jan Hanussen's *Berliner Wochenschau*, 25.3.1932.

11 'The idea of National Socialism…' (*Die Idee des Nationalsozialismus…*) ibid., 8.9.1932.

12 'Death Horoscope for the Reichstag' (*Todeshoroskop des Reichstags*) ibid., 24.9.1932.

13 'attempt to launch a politically motivated attack…' (*Versuch eines politischen Attentats…*) ibid., 10. 11. 1932.

14 'We will acquire a leadership…' (*Wir bekommen eine Führung…*) ibid., 8.12.1932.

15 'Erik Jan Hanussen, or to give him his proper Jewish name, Hermann Steinschneider' (*Erik Jan Hanussen, der mit seinem ehrlichen jüdischen Namen Hermann Steinschneider heißt*) *Berlin am Morgen*, 14.8.1932, quoted in: Kugel 1998, p. 202.

16 'a well-known Jew' (*bekanntlich Jude*) *Der Angriff*, 12.12.1932, quoted in: ibid.

17 'is not a Jew' (*übrigens kein Jude*) *Der Angriff*, 13.12.1932, quoted in: ibid.

18 'descendant of Moravian rabbis…' (*mährischen Rabbinersprößling…*) *Berlin am Morgen*, 14.12.1932, quoted in:

ibid., p. 203.

19 'When I began hounding Hanussen…' (*Als ich die Verfolgung Hanussens aufnahm…*) Frei 1980, p. 9.

20 'If by a military dictatorship one means a regime…' (*Wenn man unter Militärdiktatur eine Regierung versteht…*) Vogelsang 1965, p. 81.

21 Plehwe 1983, p. 222.

22 Thompson 1932, p. 106.

23 The first meeting between Hitler and Hindenburg took place on 10.10.1931 (Meissner 1983, p. 63).

24 'So, he wants to become Reich Chancellor, does he?' (*Reichskanzler will der werden?*) ibid., p. 65.

25 'Then I'll have to shoot you, Herr Hitler!' (*Herr Hitler, ich schieße!*) Höhne 1983, p. 202.

26 Hohlfeld 1934, p. 496.

27 'could not justify before God, before his conscience or before the Fatherland…' (*vor Gott, seinem Gewissen und dem Vaterlande…*) Höhne 1983, p. 203.

28 'allow Hitler to turn Germany into his guinea pig' (*nicht Deutschland als Versuchskaninchen übergeben*) from a letter written by Hindenburg to Otto Fürst zu Salm-Horstmar, quoted in: ibid., p. 225.

29 The product of a 14-year-long Bolshevist education system…' (*Das Produkt einer 14-jährigen bolschewistischen Erziehungsmethode…*) Blasius 2006, p. 86.

30 Papen 1952, p. 226 f.

31 'A National Socialist emergency decree would have gone about things quite differently…' (*Eine nationalsozialistische Notverordnung würde hier ganz anders durchgegriffen haben…*) *Völkischer Beobachter*, 11.8.1932, quoted in: Paul Kluke: Der Fall Potempa, in: *Vierteljahrshefte zur Zeitgeschichte* 5 (1957), 3. Heft, pp. 279–96, here p. 281 f.

32 'it'd be just fine if he didn't go on living for even another day…' (*es sei recht, wenn dieser keine 24 Stunden mehr leben würde…*) From the ruling of the special court hearing on the Potempa outrage held in Beuthen, in: Paul Kluke: Der Fall Potempa, in: *Vierteljahrshefte zur Zeitgeschichte* 5 (1957), 3. Heft, pp. 279–96, here p. 288.

33 Blasius 2006, p. 89.

34 'The post-mortem reveals…' (*Die Obduktion ergibt…*) the account of Konrad Pietrzuch's murder is based on the Beuthen special court's explanation of its verdict in: ibid., pp. 286–96.

35 'My comrades!…' (*Meine Kameraden! …*) *Völkischer Beobachter*, 24.8.1932, quoted in: ibid., p. 283.

36 Reproduced on 24.9.1932 in the *Völkischer Beobachter*, quoted in: ibid., p. 285.

37 'For him [i.e. Hitler], one human soul is not on a par with any other…' (*Für ihn ist nicht Seele gleich Seele…*) ibid.

38 Sheean 1964, p. 207.

39 Ibid., p. 195.

40 Ibid., p. 199.

41 Ibid., p. 200.

42 Ibid., p. 198.

43 Ibid., p. 199.

44 Ibid., p. 205.
45 Ibid., p. 199.
46 Ibid., p. 201.
47 Ibid., p. 203.
48 Ibid., p. 205.
49 Ibid., p. 200.
50 Ibid.
51 Ibid., p. 205.
52 Ibid., p. 208.
53 Ibid., p. 211.
54 Ibid.
55 Ibid., pp. 205–6.

The Strike

1 'It was absolutely right not to appoint Hitler Chancellor' (*Ja, es war doch wohl richtig, Hitler nicht zum Kanzler zu berufen*) Rheinbaben 1968, p. 274.

2 'quiet intellectual' (*sanften Intellektuellen) Die Weltbühne*, 16.8.1932, p. 230 (under the pseudonym Thomas Murner).

3 'Adolf Hitler is unquestionably the leader of the party...' (*Adolf Hitler ist wohl der Führer der Partei...) Völkischer Beobachter*, 19.4.1932, quoted in: Höhne 1983, p. 196.

4 'right to work' (*Recht auf Arbeit*) Kissenkoetter 1978, p. 137.

5 Ibid., p. 130.

6 'Little Franz has found his feet' (*Fränzchen hat sich selbst entdeckt*) Meissner 1983, p. 156.

7 Italiaander 1982, p. 45 (from the memoirs of Johann Baptist Gradl).

8 *On peut tout faire avec des baïonnettes, sauf s'asseoir au-dessus!* François-Poncet 2016, p. 85.

9 'I hereby declare parliament open...' (*Ich eröffne den Reichstag...*) quoted in: Treue 1976, p. 323. A sound recording of Zetkin's speech has survived: https://www.youtube.com/watch?v= KlmsXuHArpI.

10 'This is the first time for many years...' (*Zum ersten Mal besitzt der Reichstag...*) https://www.youtube.com/watch?v= KlmsXuHArpI (from 5:34).

11 Ernst Rudolf Huber: *Verfassungsgeschichte*, Vol. VII, p. 1101, quoted in: Blasius 2006, p. 105.

12 These clashes often claimed lives. In the last three years before they came to power the National Socialists counted 143 dead as victims of the violence throughout Germany, while over the same period the 'Red Aid' organization (a socialist welfare body) mourned 171 fallen comrades, either communists or fellow-travellers (Rosenhaft 1983, p. 6).

13 'Very popular among both male and female gang members...' (*Sehr beliebt sind...*) Christine Fournier: Ringvereine der Jugend, in: *Die Weltbühne*, 20.1.1931, p. 92.

14 'performing coitus in public for a specified period...' (*coram publico in einem bestimmten Zeitraum...*) ibid., p. 93.

15 'it's absolutely necessary and also permitted for Nazis to be included...' (*die Hineinnahme von Nazis...*) speech on 24 April 1932, quoted in: Röhl 1994, p. 105 f.

16 'Communists and revolutionary workers...' (*Die Kommunisten und revolutionären Arbeiter...*)

ibid., p. 110.

17 'win the trust of the working masses on a grand scale' (*im großen Maße das Vertrauen der Arbeitermassen zu erringen*) ibid., p. 108.

18 Ibid., p. 137 and Document 2 on p. 304.

19 'things can't go on like this' (*So kann es nicht weitergehen*) *Die Weltbühne*, 7.6.1932, p. 872.

20 'From every window, the united front of hardship displayed its flags' (*Von allen Fenstern demonstrierte die Einheitsfront des Elends*) *Arbeiter-Illustrierte-Zeitung*, No. 41, 9. 10. 1932, quoted in: Kerbs 1992, p. 102.

21 The SPD had a majority on both the supervisory board and the management committee of the corporation. Similarly, the shop stewards were all members of the Socialist-donated Unity trade union (*Einheitsgewerkschaft*). It is this conflict of trying to simultaneously represent the interests of both workers and management that made the SPD vulnerable. Thälmann frankly admitted on several occasions that his strategy was to deliberately try and exacerbate the crisis in order to gain political capital from it, for example in the speech he gave to the plenary session of the central committee of the KPD (15.–17.1.1931): 'We've already seen from the clashes in the Ruhr how every wage dispute can, as a result of its current political significance, become a powerful factor in exacerbating the crisis, if the proletariat inflames the situation under proper leadership by the Reich Trade Union Congress. The key to this revolutionary situation lies in taking offensive action, in launching counteroffensives, and in the revolutionary mass struggle of the proletariat.' (Ernst Thälmann: *Reden und Aufsätze zur Geschichte der deutschen Arbeiterbewegung*, Vol. 3, [Selection from the period September 1930 to February 1932], Cologne 1975.)

22 Röhl 1994, p. 158.

23 According to its estimates, support for the strike only stood at 68 per cent (ibid., p. 143).

24 'keeps in touch with the Führer by telephone on an hourly basis' (*mit dem Führer in stündlicher, telefonischer Verbindung*) Joseph Goebbels: *Vom Kaiserhof zur Reichskanzlei*, Munich 1934, p. 268 f., quoted in: ibid., p. 187.

25 'The blood of the man who had been shot stained the asphalt red...' (*Sie stehen mitten auf dem blanken Asphalt...*) *Der Angriff*, 4.11.1932, quoted in: ibid., p. 202 f.

26 'This was an opportunity for us to show our true socialism' (*Wir durften jetzt unseren ehrlichen Sozialismu beweisen*) *Der Angriff*, 7.11.1932, quoted in: ibid., p. 204.

27 'In Schöneberg we carry the SA man Reppich...' (*In Schöneberg tragen wir den SA-Mann Reppich...*) Goebbels 1998–2006, Vol. 9, p. 277 (11.11.1932)

28 'Young Reuter is a brilliant and lucid thinker...' (*Der junge*

*Reuter ist ein brillanter und
klarer Kopf…*) letter written in
late 1918, to Clara Zetkin, quoted
in: Brandt/Loewenthal 1957,
p. 121.

29 Röhl 1994, p. 114.

30 'To find the real crooks…' (*Der
wahre Räuber…*) *Die Rote Fahne*,
10.11.1929, quoted in: Büsch 1987,
p. 231.

31 'If there was a proletarian
dictatorship…' (*Gäbe es eine
proletarische Diktatur…*)
6.11.1929, quoted in: Klein 2014,
p. 338.

32 Ibid., p. 326.

33 'so impressed the Communists
present…' (*begeisterte
die herumstehenden
Kommunisten…*) *Vossische
Zeitung* 5.11.1932, midday
edition, quoted in: Röhl 1994,
p. 208.

34 'When the police tried to
disperse the crowd…' (*Als die
Polizei die Menge zerstreuen
wollte…*) ibid., p. 210.

35 'Once again, we Berlin
Communists must lower our
flags…' (*Wieder senken wir
Berliner Kommunisten unsere
Fahnen…*) quoted in: Kerbs
1992, p. 175.

36 'We will do everything within
our power both intellectually
and materially to counter this
never-ending radicalization…'
(*Dieser grenzenlosen Verhetzung
unserere Jugend…*) quoted in:
Röhl 1994, p. 216.

37 'under the protection of the
police…' (*unter dem Schutz
der beim kleinsten Ereignis
schußbereiten Polizei…*)
Vossische Zeitung 5.11.1932,

evening edition, quoted in: ibid.,
p. 220.

38 Reported in the *Vossische
Zeitung* 7.11.1932, evening
edition.

39 'with tears in his eyes'
(*mit Tränen in den Augen*)
Kissenkoetter 1978, p. 169.

40 Ibid., p. 166 f.

41 'Papen means war…' (*Papen
bedeutet Krieg…*) *Vorwärts*,
28.11.1932, evening edition.

42 This 'war game' is extensively
documented in Wolfram
Pyta, 'Vorbereitungen für den
militärischen Ausnahmezustand
unter Papen/Schleicher,'
in: *Militärgeschichtliche
Mitteilungen* 51 (1992), pp. 385–
428.

43 '… difficulties that cannot be
overcome by force of arms' (…
*plastisch die mit Waffengewalt
nicht zu erledigenden
Schwierigkeiten*) quoted in:
Blasius 2006, p. 140.

44 'Then in God's name we must let
Herr von Schleicher try his luck'
(*Dann müssen wir in Gottes
Namen Herrn von Schleicher sein
Glück versuchen lassen*) quoted
in: Höhne 1983, p. 216.

Endgame

1 Circulation figures for the
respective magazines: *Das
Tage-Buch*: 14,000 (1930), *Die
Weltbühne*: 15,000 (1932), *Die
Tat*: 30,000 (1932).

2 Does Herr Zehrer really
believe…' (*Glaubt Herr Zehrer
wirklich…*) Ossietzky, under the
pseudonym Thomas Murner in:
Die Weltbühne, 22.11.1932, p. 772.

3 'Intellectually, these times are no longer comprehensible' (*Diese Zeit ist intellektuell nicht mehr zu verstehen*) quoted in: Kurt Sontheimer: Der Tatkreis, in: *Vierteljahrshefte für Zeitgeschichte* 7, Heft 3, 1959, p. 239.

4 'not there to protect outdated conditions of ownership' (*nicht dazu da, überlebte Besitzverhältnisse zu schützen*) quoted in: Hohlfeld 1934, p. 544.

5 'the spectre of Papen' (*das Gespenst Papen*) Kessler 2010, p. 531 (2.12.1932).

6 'not just a man of extraordinary ability...' (*nicht nur ein Mann ungewöhnlicher Befähigung...*) *Berliner Volksstimme*, 5.12.1932.

7 'Most people...' (*Die Mehrheit der Bevölkerung...*) Zuckmayer 1976, p. 448.

8 'The violent confrontation with Marxism...' (*Die brachiale Auseinandersetzung mit dem Marxismus...*) quoted in: Höhne 1983, p. 217.

9 See Kissenkoetter 1978, p. 174.

10 'If the party disintegrates...' (*Wenn die Partei einmal zerfällt...*) Goebbels 1934, p. 220.

11 Höhne 1983, p. 234 f.

12 'in recent times...' (*in der letzten Zeit...*) quoted in: ibid., p. 234.

13 Ibid., p. 221.

14 Barth/Friederichs 2018, p. 126.

15 Conversation between Ursula Madrasch-Groschopp and Rosalinde von Ossietzky-Palm, quoted in: Ossietzky 1988, p. 152.

16 'My dear children, you're not to worry about me...' (*Ihr solltet keine Sorgen um mich haben...*) Berkholz 1988, p. 161 (22.7.1932).

17 'I'm full of woes...' (*Ich habe viel Kummer...*) ibid., p. 226 (27.10.1932).

18 'Every morning the postbag of submissions...' (*Immer noch laufen allmorgendlich...*) Ossietzky 1988, p. 87.

19 Berkholz 1988, p. 201.

20 'As for my exercise regime in here...' (*Was meine Freiübungen hier angeht...*) 22.9.1932, in: ibid., p. 210.

21 'It's not Hindenburg's clemency...' (*Nicht die Gnade Hindenburgs...*) ibid., p. 84.

22 'It was only then that I noticed...' (*Mir fiel zum ersten Mal...*) ibid., p. 275.

23 'her husband's intimate friendship' (*von der engen Freundschaft ihres Mannes*) Brinson/Malet, p. 157 (Hilde Walter in a letter to Rudolf Olten, 24.8.1935).

24 Must We Get Divorced Straight Away? (*Muß man sich gleich scheiden lassen?*) Berkholz 1988, p. 117.

25 Letter to Kurt von Schuschnigg, quoted in: Höhne 1983, p. 231.

26 Meissner 1983, p. 193.

27 *Eins läßt sich sicher sagen, / Und das freut uns rundherum: / Hitler geht es an den Kragen. / Dieses 'Führers' Zeit ist um.* Simplicissimus, 1.1.1933.

28 'end his life with a bullet' (*sein Leben mit einer Kugel beenden*) quoted in: Höhne 1983, p. 241.

29 'I'm delighted to tell you...' (*Mit Freude drücke ich Ihnen...*) Treviranus 1968, p. 347.

30 'All best wishes for '33' (*Alles Gute für '33*) quoted in: Höhne 1983, p. 220 f.

31 'doesn't drink any alcohol'
   (*keinen Alkohol trinkt*) ibid.,
   p. 239.

32 Brüning 1972, Vol. II, p. 676.

33 'The man cuts quite a different
   figure...' (*Der Mann macht eine
   ganze andere Figur...*) Meissner
   1983, p. 216.

34 'Little Franz has betrayed you!'
   (*Fränzchen hat Sie verraten!*)
   Höhne 1983, p. 242.

35 *Faut-il le compter parmi ceux qui
   ne brillent qu'au second rang et
   s'éclipsent au premier... Mû par
   le désir de désarmer les préjugés
   de la gauche, il arme ceux de
   la droite. À gauche, il est peu
   probable [...] qu'il recrute des
   partisans. Il perd, en revanche,
   ceux qu'il avait à droite* François-
   Poncet 2016, pp. 106–7.

36 'bombarding a village with heavy
   artillery'(*Beschießung eines
   Dorfes mit schwerster Artillerie*)
   quoted in: Hentschel 1990,
   p. 402.

37 'If you don't keep your fingers
   out of politics...' (*Wenn du
   nicht die Finger aus der Politik
   läßt...*) Tschirschky 1972, p. 89
   (according to the testimony of
   Elbrechter).

38 'I'm afraid we're not goingto
   be able to get round this
   Hitler chap' (*Ich fürchte, wir
   werden um diesen Hitler nicht
   herumkommen*) Meissner 1988,
   p. 342.

39 'Red Hindenburg' (*der 'rote
   Hindenburg'*) Pyta 2009, p. 786.

40 In 1933 the Hindenburg estate in
   East Prussia received generous
   donations from Hitler and
   Göring following a visit by the
   Nazi leaders to Neudeck (Pyta

2009, p. 833).

41 'last night's hotpot was good'
   (*Hat gestern Nacht der Eintopf
   geschmeckt?*) Meissner 1988,
   p. 343.

42 'I think not' (*Nee, die kriegen Se
   nich*) Rheinbaben 1968, p. 284.

43 *Vossische Zeitung*, 24.1.1933,
   morning edition.

44 'The SA, the SS and the KPD
   must be proscribed...' (*Die SA,
   die SS und die KPD müssen
   verboten [...] werden*) Meissner
   1983, p. 250.

45 'The old man will be forced to
   reinstate me,...' (*Der Alte Herr
   muss mich wieder holen*) Ibid.,
   p. 250.

46 *Vossische Zeitung*, 29.1.1933,
   morning edition. Schleicher's
   presence at the ball is not
   mentioned in the article.

47 'Ladies and gentlemen, your very
   good health!' (*Na denn Prost*)
   Meissner 1983, p. 251.

48 'My dear sirs, you surely can't
   imagine...' (*Sie werden mir
   doch nicht zutrauen*) quoted in:
   Enzensberger 2008, p. 104.

49 Ibid., p. 104 f.

50 Meissner 1983, p. 259 f.

51 Höhne 1983, p. 256.

52 Kugel 1998, p. 193, and Meissner
   1983, p. 187.

53 'sealed cattle-truck' (*plombierten
   Viehwagen*) Hentschel 1990,
   p. 120.

54 Meissner 1991, p. 259f., and
   Höhne 1983, p. 256.

55 Vogelsang 1962, p. 397.

56 'I'm very sorry about the hateful
   insults... vital we stand shoulder
   to shoulder now!'(*Ich bedauere
   die Ihnen... müssen wir aber
   fest zusammenhalten!*) Meissner

1983, p. 270.

57 'We will become a bloc…' (*Wir werden ein Block sein*) Alfred Hugenberg: Block oder Brei, in: *Der Tag*, 28.8.1928.

58 Brüning 1972, Vol. II, p. 684.

59 'Now we can go up at last!' (*Jetzt können wir endlich hinaufgehen*) Meissner 1983, p. 274.

60 Ibid., p. 275.

61 'And now, gentlemen, forward with God!' (*Und nun, meine Herren, vorwärts mit Gott!*) Höhne 1983, p. 260.

62 'We've done it! (*Wir haben es geschafft!*) ibid., p. 262.

63 'A few minutes later…' (*Einige Minuten später…*) ibid., p. 262 f.

64 'Grandmother is dead!' (*Großmutter ist tot!*) Fromm 1994, p. 90.

65 'Young men, nothing but young men' (*Jugend, nichts als Jugend*) Hoegner 1977, p. 56.

66 'Tight formations of men…' (*Dichte Kolonnen…*) quoted in: Friedrich 1998, p. 399

67 '*Et de ces hommes en chemises brunes, bottés, disciplinés, alignés, dont les voix bien réglées chantent à pleine gorge des airs martiaux, se dégage un enthousiasme, un dynamisme extraordinaires. Les spectateurs qui font la haie se sentent gagnés par une contagion chaleureuse*' François-Poncet 2016, p. 114.

68 'I cannot possibly eat as much as I'd like to puke' (*Ich kann nicht so viel fressen, wie ich kotzen möchte*) quoted in Bernd Küster: *Max Liebermann – ein Malerleben*. Hamburg 1988, p. 216.

69 Communiqué from the British ambassador to Germany Sir Horace Rumbold to Foreign Secretary Viscount Simon, 1.2.1933, quoted in: Becker 1992, p. 39, see also the report in the *Berliner Morgenpost*, 31.1.1933.

70 'the cheering swells to the force of a hurricane…' (*schwillt der Jubel zum Orkan…*) *Völkischer Beobachter*, 31.1.1933, quoted in: Friedrich 2007, p. 420.

71 'This Doctor is a sorcerer' (*Dieser Doktor ist ein Hexenmeister*) Hitler to Heinrich Hoffmann, quoted in: ibid., p. 419.

72 'What an enormous task lies ahead of us…' (*Welche ungeheure Aufgabe…*) quoted in: Höhne 1983, p. 265.

73 'Here was history in the making, not written on parchment…' (*Geschichte, nicht in Pergament…*) *Völkischer Beobachter*, 31.1.1933, quoted in: Friedrich 2007, p. 421.

74 *Hanussen-Zeitung*, 8.2.1933, quoted in: Kugel 1998, p. 213.

75 'When the facts contradict one another…' (*Mit dem Widerspruch der Tatsachen…*) *Vossische Zeitung*, 31.1.1933, morning edition.

Red Circles

1 'Hey there! Long live Moscow! (*He! Heil Moskau!*) quoted in: Karasek 1980, p. 73.

2 Ibid., p. 90.

3 This account of van der Lubbe's movements is taken from the police record of his interrogation on 28.2.1933, quoted in: *Der Spiegel*,

28.10.1959, pp. 44–7.

4 Frei 1980, p. 107, Kugel 1998,
   p. 217.

5 A full description of the interior
   decor of Hanussen's 'Palace of
   the Occult' is given in Kugel
   1998, p. 217 and Frei 1980,
   p. 106 ff.

6 'Germany will take
   great strides towards its
   resurrection...' (*Deutschland
   geht seiner Wiederaufrichtung
   in Riesenschritten entegegen...*)
   Izmet Aga Dzino, *Hanussen-
   Zeitung*, 8.3.1933, quoted in:
   Kugel 1998, p. 226.

7 Hermann Hacker: Privat-Séance
   bei Hanussen, *12 Uhr Blatt*,
   27.2.1933, quoted in: ibid., p. 225.

8 'with an enthusiastic show of
   support...' (*mit begeisterten
   Kundgebungen...*) Izmet Aga
   Dzino, *Hanussen-Zeitung*,
   8.3.1933, quoted in: Ibid., p. 226.

9 'I pulled my head back...' (*Ich
   zog meinen Kopf zurück...*)
   Paudler 1978, p. 122 f.

10 Pyra 2009, p. 814.

11 Papen 1952, p. 302. Cf. also
   Meissner 1983, p. 302.

12 'at 100 kilometres per hour' (*Im
   100-km-Tempo*) Goebbels 1998–
   2006, Vol. 2, p. 383 (27.2.1933).

13 'You are now witnessing the
   beginning of a great new
   epoch in German history,
   Herr Delmer...' (*Sie sind Zeuge
   einer großen neuen Epoche in
   der deutschen Geschichte, Herr
   Delmer...*) See *Braunbuch* 1933,
   p. 100 and Delmer 1961, p. 189.

14 Sworn deposition by Frank
   Höllering quoted in: *Braunbuch*
   1933, p. 106.

15 'silent for minutes on end...'

(*minutenlang wortlos...*)
Kaufmann 1993, p. 276.

16 'I was staring at the dome of
   the building, eerily lit from
   the inside...' (*Ich starrte auf
   die gespenstisch von innen
   beleuchtete Kuppel...*) Frei 1972,
   p. 162.

17 'Now I saw that his face was
   purple...' (*Nun sah ich, daß
   sein Gesicht flammend rot
   war...*) Rudolf Diels: 'Die
   Nacht der langen Messer...
   fand nicht statt', in: *Der Spiegel*,
   9.6.1949, p. 18. It is clearly an
   understatement to describe
   Diels's role in the Nazi regime
   as in any way shadowy, since
   much of what he wrote after
   the war was clearly designed to
   exculpate himself. Nonetheless,
   his statements remain valuable
   as first-hand accounts of the
   inner workings of the Nazi state-
   terror apparatus.

18 'Hitler is in a towering rage'
   (*Hitler ist in Rage*) Goebbels
   1998–2006, Vol. 2/III, p. 137
   (28.2.1933).

19 'As we have now learned...' (*Wie
   wir jetzt erfahren haben...*) Ernst
   Thälmann to the leadership of
   the Comintern, 25.2.1933, in:
   Weber 2015, Part 1, p. 941 (Doc.
   308). His report only reached
   Moscow in April.

20 Ronald Sassning: Zur NS-
   Haftzeit Ernst Thälmann.
   Legende und Wirklichkeit, in:
   Pankower Vorträge. Helle Panke,
   Heft 6, Berlin 1997, p. 20.

21 Suhr 1988, p. 200.

22 'What are we going to do
   now?... I'll just give it three
   days' (*Was machen wir nun?*

... *Ich warte noch drei Tage*)
Ossietzky 1988, p. 89.

23 Brinson/Malet 1990, p. 18 f.

24 'Chin up! I'll be back soon' (*Kopf hoch! Ich komme bald wieder*)
Ossietzky 1988, p. 89.

25 'I was put into a car...' (*Ich wurde in ein Auto gebracht...*)
Brüning 1972, Vol. II, p. 688.

26 'So, are those of us who have served the Reich President, and who voted for him in February and April, now seen as outlaws...?' (*Sind wir vogelfrei, die dem Herrn Reichspräsidenten gedient, ihn im Februar und April gewählt haben...*) quoted in: Hömig 2005, p. 90.

27 Hitler 1980, p. 161 (29.12.1941).

28 'I only hope that our people had nothing to do with it...' (*Ich hoffe nur, unsere Leute haben damit nichts zu tun...*) Delmer 1961, p. 186.

29 This is a prime example of a so-called *Flüsterwitz* ('whispered joke'), a surreptitious popular witticism that dared to poke fun at the National Socialist terror regime. Another joke at the time of the Reichstag fire, pointing to Nazi complicity in the blaze ran thus: 'A Nazi stormtrooper whispers to his mate: "The Reichstag's on fire!" "Shh!" answers his friend, putting his finger to his lips and glancing round nervously, "that's only supposed to happen tomorrow!"' (Cited in: Philip Gooden and Peter Lewis: *The Word at War: World War Two in 100 Phrases*, London 2014).

30 'degenerate and perverted aristocrat' (*degenerierte*

und pervertierte Aristokrat)
Braunbuch 1933, p. 114 f.

31 Koestler 2011, p. 241.

32 See Ted Harrison: 'Count Helldorff and the German Resistance to Hitler': *Working Papers in Contemporary History and Politics*, No. 8, European Studies Research Institute, University of Salford, January 1996.

33 'rogue elements...' (*ein 'wildes Kommando'...*) Meissner 1991, p. 275.

34 Hermann Göring under cross-examination by Robert H. Jackson at the Nuremberg Tribunal, in: *Trial of the Major War Criminals Before the International Military Tribunal*. Vol. IX. *Proceedings: 3/8/1946–3/23/1946*. Nuremberg: International Military Tribunal, 1947 (Eighty-Fourth Day, Monday, 3/18/1946, Part 16).

Finale furioso

1 Meissner 1983, p. 302 f.

2 'the electricity and transport networks' (*das Lichtnetz und den Verkehr*) minutes of the Reich cabinet meeting held on 28.2.1933, quoted in: Kellerhoff 2008, p. 56.

3 Meissner 1991, p. 273.

4 'The measures I'm planning to institute won't be hampered...' (*Meine Maßnahmen werden nicht angekränkelt sein...*) Quoted in: Becker 1992, p. 117.

5 Jürgen W. Falter: Die 'Märzgefallenen' von 1933: neue Forschungsergebnisse zum sozialen Wandel innerhalb der

NSDAP-Mitgliedschaft während der Machtergreifungsphase. *Historical Social Research, Supplement*, 25 (1998), p. 280–302 (Diagram, p. 287).

6 Dorothy Thompson, letter to Harriet Cohen 18 March 1933. Quoted in Kurth 1991, p. 187.

7 Delmer 1961, p. 182.

8 'The camp commandant informed me…' (*Der Kommandant des Lagers erklärte mir…*) Rudolf Diels: Die Nacht der langen Messer… fand nicht statt, in: *Der Spiegel*, 23.6.1949, p. 19.

9 'They made me list the colours of the Republic…' (*Ich musste die Farben der Republik aufzählen…*) *Braunbuch* 1933, p. 201.

10 'Our aim is to eradicate the vulture of Marxism…' (*Wir wollen den Aasgeier des Marxismus… ausrotten*) *Die Weltbühne*, No. 9, 28.2.1933, p. 342.

11 'So, the die is cast' (*Die Würfel sind gefallen*) quoted in: Kugel 1998, p. 242 f.

12 Ibid., p. 181.

13 In the course of an SA internal investigation ('Honour Court) conducted in connection with the so-called 'Röhm Putsch' of 1934 ('Night of the Long Knives') one of Hanussen's murderers, Rudolf Steinle, described the circumstances of his detention. Quoted in: ibid., p. 250.

14 'That swine Ohst has arrested me' (*Das Schwein Ohst hat mich festgenommen*) testimony of Elfriede Mandt, 9.3.1967, quoted in: ibid.

15 '… from a man who has in the meantime been exposed as a Jew' (*… inzwischen als Juden bekanntgewordenen Herrn*) quoted in: ibid., p. 252.

16 'That's our man!' (*Da ist er ja!*) testimony of Martha Kluczynski, 27.10.1947, quoted in: Fuhrer 2012, p. 273. On the circumstances of Thälmann's arrest, see also: Ronald Sassning: Thälmann, Dünow, Wehner, Mewis. Bilder mit Radierungen. Vom Kippenberger-Apparat zum IM-System Mielkes, in: UTOPIE kreativ, H. 115/116 (May/June 2000, p. 558–83).

17 Thälmann 1994, p. 37.

18 Ibid., p. 38.

19 Ibid., p. 39 f.

20 Göring during questioning by his defence attorney Otto Stahmer on 13.3.1946, in: *Trial of the Major War Criminals Before the International Military Tribunal*. Vol. IX. *Proceedings: 3/8/1946–3/23/1946*. Nuremberg: International Military Tribunal, 1947. A film clip of Göring's testimony that day can be seen on YouTube: www.youtube.com/watch?v=AeqGANa7xRU (From 01:19 on). After the war Rudolf Diels claimed to have been the one who alerted Göring to Thälmann's situation and to have taken him to the communist leader's cell (*Der Spiegel*, 16.6.1949, p. 21 f.). See also Thälmann 1994, p. 39 f.

21 'I stand before you as a representative of the working class' (*Ich stehe hier als Vertreter der Arbeiter…*) Gabelmann 1996,

p. 128.

22 '...that would be the greatest sensation of the twentieth century' (... *das wäre die größte Weltsensation*) ibid., p. 130.

23 'I want to have a clear conscience...' (*Ich will ein reines Gewissen haben...*) ibid., p. 119.

24 'scoundrel' (*Halunke*) ibid., p. 120.

25 'Why are you behaving like such shitheads?...' (*Warum seid ihr solche Scheißkerle? ...*) ibid., p. 155.

26 'perfectly all right' (*ganz in Ordnung*) quoted in: Ronald Sassning: Zur NS-Haftzeit Ernst Thälmanns. Legende und Wirklichkeit, in: Pankower Vorträge. Helle Panke, Heft 6, Berlin 1997, p. 45.

27 'Papa also says that Göring...' (*Papa sagt auch, dass der Göring...*) Gabelmann 1996, p. 294.

28 Ibid., p. 214.

29 '... committed to paper with a passionate energy and a Teutonic spirit' (... *mit glühender Kraft und teutonischem Geist*) ibid., p. 215 f.

30 Ronald Sassning: Zur NS-Haftzeit Ernst Thälmanns. Legende und Wirklichkeit, in: Pankower Vorträge. Helle Panke, Heft 6, Berlin 1997, p. 46.

31 'the international gutter press...' (*der internationalen Hetzpresse...*) Gabelmann 1996, p. 216.

32 In the spring of 1939 the courier Walter Trautzsch was arrested with a false passport. See also Ronald Sassning: Zur

NS-Haftzeit Ernst Thälmanns. Legende und Wirklichkeit, in: Pankower Vorträge. Helle Panke, Heft 6, Berlin 1997, p. 50.

33 'The campaign of World Jewry...' (*Die Weltkampagne des Judentums...*) Adolphi 1996, p. 19 f.

34 Ibid., p. 54 (5.3.1940).

35 'Frau Thälmann left in a very embittered mood' (*Frau Thälmann ist sehr verbittert gegangen*) Ronald Sassning: Zur NS-Haftzeit Ernst Thälmanns. Legende und Wirklichkeit, in: Pankower Vorträge. Helle Panke, Heft 6, Berlin 1997, p. 52.

36 'I'm sure of it, my gut instinct tells me...' (*Ich weiß es, mein Innerstes sagt es mir...*) Adolphi 1996, p. 41.

37 See: Wilhelm Mensing: 'Eine 'Morgengabe' Stalins an den Paktfreund Hitler? Die Auslieferung deutscher Emigranten an das NS-Regime nach Abschluss des Hitler-Stalin- Pakts – eine zwischen den Diktatoren arrangierte Preisgabe von 'Antifaschisten'?', in: *Zeitschrift des Forschungsverbundes SED-Staat*, No. 20/2006, pp. 57–84.

38 'They've clearly been working on Thälmann...' (*Offensichtlich wird Thälmann...*) diary entry by Dimitroff on 15.10.1941, quoted in: Weber 2003, p. 63.

39 Ronald Sassning: Zur NS-Haftzeit Ernst Thälmanns. Legende und Wirklichkeit, in: Pankower Vorträge. Helle Panke, Heft 6, Berlin 1997, p. 46.

40 'powerful [...] movement of

conviction' (*gewaltige [...] Glaubensbewegung*) Gabelmann 1996, p. 212.

41 'Now and then, driven by my woes...' (*Manchmal getrieben durch Heimsuchungen...*) ibid., p. 213.

42 'When I think of all the things...' (*Wenn ich bedenke...*) Thälmann 1994, p. 34.

43 'I'm not some gypsy type who shuns the world' (*Ich bin kein weltflüchtiger Zigeuner*) ibid., p. 56.

44 The decision to execute Thälmann was taken at a meeting held by Hitler and his inner circle at the 'Wolf's Lair' bunker on 14.8.1944. A note to this effect made by Himmler on that same day has survived. The precise time, location and circumstances of Thälmann's murder remain unclear to this day. This has to do on the one hand with a deliberate practice of hushing-up by the National Socialist authorities, and on the other with the KPD and SED's policy of mythologizing Thälmann in the post-war period. See: Gabelmann 1996, pp. 220–73.

45 Hömig 2005, p. 34.

46 'Hitler is a decent person...' (*Hitler ist ein anständiger Mensch...*) quoted in: ibid., p. 100.

47 'lackey of Rome' (*Römling*) quoted in: Ibid., p. 23.

48 Treviranus 1968, p. 333.

49 'It beggars belief...' (*Es ist gar nicht zu verstehen...*) Rudolf Diels: Die Nacht der langen Messer... fand nicht statt, in:

Der Spiegel, 7. 7. 1949, p. 19.

50 Brüning 1972, Vol. II, p. 716 f.

51 See Hömig 2005, pp. 181–7.

52 Brüning 1974, p. 539.

53 Hömig 2005, p. 429.

54 'No nation that has had it dinned into it...' (*Kein Volk, dem täglich eingehämmert wird...*) ibid., p. 411.

55 'under constant surveillance by Adenauer' (*von Adenauer überwacht*) Andreas Rödder: Reflexionen über das Ende der Weimarer Republik. Die Präsidialkabinette 1930–1932/33. Krisenmanagement oder Restaurationsstrategie?, in: *Vierteljahrshefte für Zeitgeschichte* 47 (1999), 1. Heft, p. 88.

56 'At least I achieved one thing...' (*Etwas habe ich erreicht...*) quoted in: Hömig 2005, p. 583.

57 Ernst Torgler: 'Der Reichstagsbrand und was nachher geschah', in: *Die Zeit*, 28.10.1948.

58 The image, from the edition of 31.3.1933, is reproduced in Suhr 1988, p. 202.

59 Frei 1978, p. 209.

60 'cowardly, effete milksop' (*feige, verweichlichte Pyjamaexistenz*) *Die Weltbühne*, 3.2.1931, p. 157.

61 'hysterical cheese-mite' (*hysterische Käsemilbe*) *Die Weltbühne*, 3.1.1933, p. 3.

62 'You Polish Pig!' (*Du polnische Sau*) Ossietzky 1988, p. 99.

63 Suhr 1988, p. 205.

64 'hallucinate about house searches...' (*Haussuchungen zu halluzinieren...*) Hilde Walter, who maintained contact with Ossietzky, in a letter to Ika

Olden, 11.6.1934, in: Brinson/
Malet 1990, p. 20.

65 'There's something dead inside of me…' (*Innerlich ist in mir etwas tot…*) Suhr 1988, p. 221 (20.7.1933).

66 Brinson/Malet 1990, p. 163.

67 'trembling, deathly white presence:' (*zitterndes, totenblasses Etwas …*) Burckhardt 1960, p. 60 f.

68 Brandt 1988.

69 'There was a time when treason was considered socially acceptable, even fashionable…' (*Landesverrat war einmal eine salonfähige Sache…*) radio broadcast on 12.3.1936, quoted in: Ossietzky 1988, p. 111.

70 Frei 1978, p. 268.

71 'I think about you the whole day…' (*Ich denke an dich den ganzen Tag…*) 20.11.1936, in: Suhr 1988, p. 223.

72 Brinson/Malet 1990, p. 50 f.

73 'prevent any shameful scenes' (*um beschämenden Vorgängen vorzubeugen*) quoted in: Ossietzky 1988, p. 116.

74 Ossietzky 1988, p. 132.

75 Brinson/Malet 1990, p. 27 f.

76 I am grateful to Dr Peter Böthig, head of the Kurt Tucholsky Literature Museum in Rheinsberg, for providing me with this information.

77 'You know, Rosalinde…' (*Weißt du, Rosalinde…*) Suhr 1988, p. 253.

78 'an old hunting pal' (*einem alten Jagdfreund*) Burghard Ciesla: 'Bei meiner Liebe zum Walde und zur Jagd …' Anmerkungen zur privaten Gegenwelt des Otto Braun, in: Görtemaker 2014,

pp. 85–101

79 Ibid., p. 148.

80 Schulze 1981, p. 812.

81 'Prussia is Russian' (*Preußen ist russisch*) letter to Heinrich Georg Ritzel, 6.6.1945, quoted in: Schulze 1981, p. 821.

82 'I bet you'd never have imagined…' (*Das hätten Sie sich wohl auch nicht gedacht…*) letter to Herbert Weichmann, 23.3.1948, quoted in: ibid., p. 837.

83 'It was a very sad burial' (*Es war eine sehr traurige Beerdigung*) Herbert Weichmann to Fritz Corsing, 22.12.1955, quoted in: ibid., p. 849.

84 'Passers-by – most of them women…' (*Passanten, vor allem Frauen…*) Fromm 1994, p. 98 (10.3.1933).

85 'Shortly before my guests arrived…' (*Kurz vor Ankunft meiner Gäste…*) ibid., p. 98 (10.3.1933).

86 Ibid., p. 118 (1.4.1933).

87 'by Aryan journalists' (*durch arische Journalisten*) Nea Matzen/Jan Ehlert: Bella Fromm. 'Von der Gesellschaftsreporterin in Berlin zur politischen Exilantin in New York', Deutschlandfunk-Feature 2006, edited broadcast transcript, p. 19 f.

88 'If newspaper people keep getting laid off…' (*Wenn das mit den Entlassungen…*) Fromm 1994, p. 121 (4.4.1933).

89 'The Führer needs someone…' (*Der Führer braucht jetzt jemanden…*) ibid., p. 194 (28.6.1934).

90 Nea Matzen: 'Bella Fromm – Viele Leben in einem:

Societylady, Journalistin, Bestsellerautorin im Exil', in: Medien & Zeit, September 2009, pp. 28–56, here p. 42.

91 Article in the magazine *True Detective*, November 1942, quoted in: Nea Matzen/Jan Ehlert: Bella Fromm. 'Von der Gesellschaftsreporterin in Berlin zur politischen Exilantin in New York', Deutschlandfunk-Feature 2006, edited broadcast transcript, p. 36.

92 Sheean 1963, pp. 210–11.

93 Ibid., p. 223.

94 Ibid., p. 233.

95 Thompson 1932, p. 104.

96 'No sooner does stupid Adolf finally get into power...' (*Der dumme Adolf, schließlich also doch zur Macht gekommen...*) Mann 1993, p. 490.

97 Schad 2010, p. 74.

98 Dorothy Thompson: 'Peace – And the Crisis Begins', NBC broadcast, 1.10.1938.

99 'Dorothy Thompson has delivered an absolutely crazy speech...' (*Dorothy Thompson hält eine absolut verrückte Rede...*) Goebbels 1998–2006, Part II, Diktate, vol. 4, p. 51 (5.4.1942).

100 'Throughout my life, even at school...' (*Ich habe mein ganzes Leben, schon in der Schule...*) Moltke 1991, p. 50 (11.10.1944).

101 Sheean 1963, pp. 257–8.

102 Ibid., p. 289.

103 'It would be utterly repellent to think...' (*Verwerflich wäre der Glaube...*) quoted in: Petzold 1995, p. 215 f.

104 'A small band of critics is mobilizing itself...' (*Im Lande*

macht sich ein kleiner Kreis von Kritikern auf den Weg...*) 21 June 1934, quoted in: Gisevius 1982, p. 58.

105 Ibid., p. 90.

106 Pyra 2009, p. 851.

107 Papen 1952, p. 356.

108 '... so hard he'll squeal' (*... dass er quietscht*) Schulze 1998, p. 410.

109 'a hat with no head in it' (*Ein Hut... aber kein Kopf*) Treviranus 1968, p. 334.

110 'that a man of so little substance...' (*Dass ein Mensch von solchem Federgewicht...*) Mann 2009, p. 794.

111 Memorandum by Undersecretary Dr Grützner, 18.1.1952, quoted in: Theodor Eschenburg: Zur Ermordung des Generals Schleicher, in: *Vierteljahrsheft zur Zeitgeschichte* (1) 1953, p. 95; see also Rudolf Diels: 'Die Nacht der langen Messer... fand nicht statt', in: *Der Spiegel*, 16.7.1949, p. 20.

112 Rheinbaben 1968, p. 285.

113 This account of the events of 30 June 1934 is based on the contemporary documents that Theodor Eschenburg has appended to his article on the murder of General Schleicher, in: *Vierteljahrsheft zur Zeitgeschichte* (1) 1953, pp. 71–95.

114 Based on an interview conducted in 2011 with Lonny von Schleicher, who died in 2014: https://www.youtube.com/watch?v=9-YVtxrq8N4.

115 Hömig 2005, p. 148, also Ohrt 2012, p. 47.

116 Ted Harrison: 'Count Helldorff

and the German Resistance to Hitler': *Working Papers in Contemporary History and Politics*, No. 8, European Studies Research Institute, University of Salford, January 1996. See also BA R2–03/D, A 210 Helldorf, Wolf Graf von, p. 25 (3.3.1933).

117 Bundesarchiv, R2–03/D, A 210 Helldorff, Wolf Graf von, p. 55.

118 Ted Harrison: 'Count Helldorff and the German Resistance to Hitler': *Working Papers in Contemporary History and Politics*, No. 8, European Studies Research Institute, University of Salford, January 1996.

119 Kugel 1998, p. 261.

120 I really wouldn't have imagined...' (*Ja, ich hätte nicht gedacht...*) Ted Harrison: 'Count Helldorff and the German Resistance to Hitler': *Working Papers in Contemporary History and Politics*, No. 8, European Studies Research Institute, University of Salford, January 1996.

121 Gisevius 1982, pp. 47–51.

122 'I am writing to you today to ask you...' (*Heute bitte ich Sie um Auskunft...*) Gregor Strasser, letter to Rudolf Hess, 18.6.1934, quoted in: Kissenkoetter 1978, p. 193.

123 Ibid., p. 194 f.

124 'dismembered on the spot...' (*an Ort und Stelle... zerstückelt*) ibid., p. 194.

125 Plehwe 1983, p. 297.

126 'You have saved the German people...' (*Sie haben das deutsche Volk... gerettet*) quoted in: Pyra 2009, p. 850. According to the testimony of Otto Meissner, this telegram was actually the work of the Nazi chief press officer Walther Funk (Meissner 1991, p. 355 f.).

127 'Hindenburg was just great...' (*Hindenburg war knorke...*) Goebbels 1998–2006, Vol. 3/I, p. 76 (6.6.1934).

128 'Quite right...' (*Das ist richtig so...*) quoted in: Pyra 2009, p. 849.

129 On 13.7.1934. Cf. Theodor Eschenburg: Zur Ermordung des Generals Schleicher, in: *Vierteljahrsheft zur Zeitgeschichte* (1) 1953, p. 71 f.

130 'Everything went according to plan in Berlin' (*In Berlin programmgemäß*) Goebbels 1998–2006, Vol. 3/I, p. 72 (1.7.1934).

131 'Is Friend Hein in the house yet?' (*l'ami Heinz, est-il déjà dans la maison?*) François-Poncet 2016, pp. 307–8. *Freund Hein* is a (now archaic) German euphemism for death.

132 Plehwe 1983, p. 294.

Bibliography

Adolphi, Wolfram, and Schütrumpf, Jörn (eds), *Ernst Thälmann: An Stalin. Briefe aus dem Zuchthaus 1939 bis 1941* (Berlin, 1996).

Bahar, Alexander/Kugel, Wilfried, *Der Reichstagsbrand. Wie Geschichte gemacht wird* (Berlin, 2001).

Ballhause, Walter, *Zwischen Weimar und Hitler. Sozialdokumentarische Fotografie 1930–1933* (Munich, 1981).

Barth, Rüdiger, and Friederichs, Hauke, *Die Totengräber: Der letzte Winter der Weimarer Republik* (Frankfurt am Main, 2018).

Beachy, Robert, *Gay Berlin: Birthplace of a Modern Identity* (New York, 2014).

Becker, Josef and Ruth (eds), *Hitlers Machtergreifung. Dokumente vom Machtantritt Hitlers 30. Januar 1933 bis zur Besiegelung des Einparteienstaates am 14. Juli 1933*, 2nd revised edn (Munich, 1992).

Beer, Rüdiger Robert, *Heinrich Brüning*, 2nd edn (Berlin, 1931).

Bergh, Hendrik van, *Wie Weimar starb. Gründe und Hintergründe zum Sturz der ersten Republik* (Exklusiv-Interview mit Franz von Papen, Reichskanzler a. D.,

über die Vorgeschichte und die letzten Monate der Republik von Weimar) (Hamburg, 1983).

Berkholz, Stefan (ed.), *Carl von Ossietzky. 227 Tage im Gefängnis. Briefe, Texte, Dokumente* (Darmstadt, 1988).

Besymenski, Lew, *Stalin und Hitler. Das Pokerspiel der Diktatoren.* Translated from the Russian by Hilde and Helmut Ettinger, 2nd edn (Berlin, 2006).

Blasius, Dirk, *Weimars Ende. Bürgerkrieg und Politik 1930–1933*, 2nd edn (Göttingen, 2006).

Boegel, Nathalie, *Berlin – Hauptstadt des Verbrechens: Die dunkle Seite der Goldenen Zwanziger* (Munich, 2018).

Börrnert, René, *Ernst Thälmann als Leitfigur der kommunistischen Erziehung in der DDR. Dissertation am Erziehungswissenschaftlichen Fachbereich der Technischen Universität Braunschweig* (Braunschweig, 2002).

Bracher, Karl Dietrich, *Die Auflösung der Weimarer Republik. Eine Studie zum Problem des Machtzerfalls in der Demokratie*, 3rd edn (Stuttgart/Villingen,

1960).

Brandt, Willy, *Die Nobelpreiskampagne für Carl von Ossietzky* (Oldenburg, 1988).

Brandt, Willy, and Löwenthal, Richard, *Ernst Reuter. Eine politische Biographie* (Munich, 1957).

Braun, Otto, *Von Weimar zu Hitler* (Hildesheim, 1979), reprint of 2nd edn (New York, 1940).

Braunbuch über Reichstagsbrand und Hitlerterror (Paris, 1933).

Brecht, Arnold, *Vorspiel zum Schweigen. Das Ende der deutschen Republik* (Vienna, 1948).

Brinson, Charmian, and Malet, Marian (eds), *Rettet Ossietzky! Dokumente aus dem Nachlaß von Rudolf Olden* (Oldenburg, 1990).

Bronder, Dietrich, *Bevor Hitler kam. Eine historische Studie*, 2nd expanded edn (Geneva, 1975).

Broszat, Martin, *Die Machtergreifung. Der Aufstieg der NSDAP und die Zerstörung der Weimarer Republik* (Munich, 1990).

Brüning, Heinrich, *Memoiren 1918–1934*, 2 vols (Munich, 1972).

Brüning, Heinrich, *Briefe und Gespräche 1934–1945*, ed. Claire Nix in collaboration with Reginald Phelbs and George Pettee (Stuttgart, 1974).

Buber-Neumann, Margarete, *Von Potsdam nach Moskau. Stationen eines Irrwegs* (Berlin, 2002).

Burckhardt, Carl Jacob, *Meine Danziger Mission 1927 bis 1939* (Munich, 1960).

Burkert, Hans-Norbert, Matußek, Klaus and Wippermann, Wolfgang, '*Machtergreifung*'

(Berlin, 1933, 1982).

Büsch, Otto and Haus, Wolfgang, *Berliner Demokratie 1919–1985: Berlin als Hauptstadt der Weimarer Republik* (Berlin, 1987).

Caro, Kurt, and Oehme, Walter, *Schleichers Aufstieg. Ein Beitrag zur Geschichte der Gegenrevolution* (Berlin, 1933).

Cziffra, Géza von, *Hanussen. Hellseher des Teufels. Die Wahrheit über den Reichstagsbrand* (Munich/Berlin, 1978).

Delmer, Sefton, *Trail Sinister* (London, 1961).

Delmer, Sefton, *Black Boomerang* (London, 1962).

Demps, Leurenz, *Berlin-Wilhelmstraße. Eine Topographie der preußisch-deutschen Macht*, 4th edn (Berlin, 2010).

Diels, Rudolf, *Lucifer ante portas* (Zurich, 1949).

Duerr, Hans Peter, and Souchy, Augustin, *Stalinismus und Anarchie in der spanischen Revolution oder Bruno Frei und die Methode Denunziation* (Berlin, 1973).

Enzensberger, Hans Magnus, *Hammerstein oder Der Eigensinn* (Frankfurt am Main, 2008).

Fergusson, Adam, *When Money Dies: The Nightmare of the Weimar Hyper-Inflation* (London, 2010).

Flechtheim, Ossip K., *Die KPD in der Weimarer Republik* (Frankfurt am Main, 1971).

François-Poncet, André, *Souvenirs d'une Ambassade à Berlin 1931–1938* (Paris, 2016).

Frei, Bruno, *Der Papiersäbel. Autobiographie* (Frankfurt am Main, 1972).

Frei, Bruno, *Carl von Ossietzky. Eine politische Biographie*, 2nd edn (Berlin, 1978).

Frei, Bruno, *Der Hellseher. Leben und Sterben des Erik Jan Hanussen* (Cologne, 1980).

Friedensburg, Ferdinand, *Die Weimarer Republik* (Berlin, 1946).

Friedrich, Otto, *Morgen ist Weltuntergang. Berlin in den Zwanziger Jahren* (Berlin, 1998).

Friedrich, Thomas, *Die missbrauchte Hauptstadt. Hitler und Berlin* (Berlin, 2007).

Fromm, Bella, *Blood and Banquets: A Berlin Social Diary* (New York, 1942).

Fuhrer, Armin, *Ernst Thälmann. Soldat des Proletariats* (Munich, 2011).

Gabelmann, Thilo (pen name of Egon Grübel), *Thälmann ist niemals gefallen? Eine Legende stirbt* (Berlin, 1996).

Giebel, Wieland (ed.), *Goebbels' Propaganda. 'Das erwachende Berlin' – Ein Fotoband des NS-Agitators* (annotated edition of the original work of 1933) (Berlin, 2012).

Gisevius, Hans Bernd, *Bis zum bitteren Ende. Bericht eines Augenzeugen aus dem Machtzentrum des Dritten Reiches* (Munich/Zurich, 1982).

Goebbels, Joseph, *Vom Kaiserhof zur Reichskanzlei* (Munich, 1934).

Goebbels, Joseph, *Die Tagebücher des Joseph Goebbels*, ed. Elke Fröhlich, 9 vols (Munich, 1998–2006).

Görtemaker, Manfred (ed.), *Otto Braun. Ein preußischer Demokrat* (Berlin, 2014).

Groener-Geyer, Dorothea, *General Groener. Soldat und Staatsmann* (Frankfurt am Main, 1955).

Gunther, John, *So sehe ich Europa* (Amsterdam, 1937).

Gutjahr, Wolf-Dietrich, *Revolution muss sein. Karl Radek – die Biographie* (Cologne, 2012).

Hanussen, Erik Jan, *Meine Lebenslinie* (Munich, 1988).

Heiber, Helmut (ed.), *Joseph Goebbels, Reden 1932–1945* (Bindlach, 1991).

Hentschel, Volker, *Weimars letzte Monate. Hitler und der Untergang der Republik* (Düsseldorf, 1978).

Hentschel, Volker, *So kam Hitler. Schicksalsjahre 1932–1933. Eine Bild/Text-Reportage* (Düsseldorf, 1990).

Herbert, David, *Second Son: An Autobiography* (London, 1972).

Hett, Benjamin Carter, *The Death of Democracy. Hitler's Rise to Power and the Downfall of the Weimar Republic* (London, 2018).

Hindenburg, Bernhard von, *Paul von Hindenburg. Ein Lebensbild* (Berlin, 1915).

Hindenburg, Paul von, *Aus meinem Leben* (Leipzig, 1920).

Hitler, Adolf, *Monologe im Führerhauptquartier 1941–1944. Die Aufzeichnungen Heinrich Heims*, ed. von Werner Jochmann (Hamburg, 1980).

Hoegner, Wilhelm, *Flucht vor Hitler. Erinnerungen an die Kapitulation der ersten deutschen Republik 1933* (Frankfurt am Main/Berlin, 1989).

Hohlfeld, Johannes (ed.), *Deutsche Reichsgeschichte in Dokumenten 1849–1934*, vol. IV (Berlin, 1934).

Höhne, Heinz, *Die Machtergreifung. Deutschlands Weg in die Hitler-*

Diktatur (Reinbek, 1983).

Hömig, Herber, *Brüning – Kanzler in der Krise der Republik. Eine Weimarer Biographie* (Paderborn/ Munich and elsewhere, 2000).

Hömig, Herbert, *Brüning – Politiker ohne Auftrag. Zwischen Weimarer und Bonner Republik* (Paderborn/ Munich and elsewhere, 2005).

Horsley, Joey, and Pusch, Luise F. (eds), *Frauengeschichte. Berühmte Frauen und ihre Freundinnen*, 2nd edn (Göttingen, 2010).

Italiaander, Rolf (ed.), *Wir erlebten das Ende der Weimarer Republik. Zeitgenossen berichten* (Düsseldorf, 1982).

Jasper, Gotthard, *Die gescheiterte Zähmung. Wege zur Machtergreifung Hitlers 1930–1934* (Frankfurt am Main, 1986).

Jeffreys-Jones, Rhodri, *In Spies We Trust: The Story of Western Intelligence* (Oxford, 2013).

Juhn, Erich, *Leben und Taten des Hellsehers Henrik Magnus* (Vienna, 1930).

Karasek, Horst, *Der Brandstifter. Lehr- und Wanderjahre des Maurergesellen Marinus van der Lubbe, der 1933 auszog, den Reichstag anzuzünden* (Berlin, 1980).

Kaufmann, Bernd, Reisener, Eckhard, Schwips, Dieter, and Henri, Walther, *Der Nachrichtendienst der KPD 1919–1937* (Berlin, 1993).

Kellerhoff, Sven Felix, *Der Reichstagsbrand. Die Karriere eines Kriminalfalls* (Berlin, 2008).

Kerbs, Diethart, *Berlin 1932 – das letzte Jahr der ersten deutschen Republik* (Berlin, 1992).

Kerbs, Diethart and Uka,

Walter (eds), *Fotografie und Bildpublizistik in der Weimarer Republik* (Bönen/Westfalen, 2004).

Kessler, Harry Graf, *Das Tagebuch*, vol. 7, *1918–1923*, ed. Angela Reinthal with the assistance of Janna Brechmacher and Christoph Hilse (Stuttgart, 2007).

Kessler, Harry Graf, *Das Tagebuch*, vol. 9, *1926–1937*, ed. Sabine Gruber und Ulrich Ott with the assistance of Christoph Hilse (Stuttgart, 2010).

Kiaulehn, Walther, *Mein Freund, der Verleger. Ernst Rowohlt und seine Zeit* (Reinbek, 1967).

Kissenkoetter, Udo, *Gregor Strasser und die NSDAP (= Schriftenreihe der Vierteljahrshefte für Zeitgeschichte*, vol. 37) (Stuttgart, 1978).

Klein, Annika, *Korruption und Korruptionsskandale in der Weimarer Republik* (Göttingen, 2014).

Knickerbocker, Hubert Renfro, *Deutschland so oder so?* (Berlin, 1923).

Koestler, Arthur, *The Invisible Writing: The Second Volume of an Autobiography* (London, 2011, 1st edn, 1954).

Köhler, Henning, *Geschichte der Weimarer Republik* (Berlin, 1981).

Kolb, Eberhard, *Die Weimarer Republik* (Munich, 1984).

Köster, Barbara, 'Die Junge Garde des Proletariats', *Untersuchungen zum Kommunistischen Jugendverband Deutschlands in der Weimarer Republik*, o. O. (Bielefeld, 2005).

Kraiker, Gerhard, and Suhr, Elke, *Carl von Ossietzky* (Reinbek,

1994).

Kugel, Wilfried, *Hanussen, Die wahre Geschichte des Hermann Steinschneider* (Düsseldorf, 1998).

Kurth, Peter, *American Cassandra: The Life of Dorothy Thompson* (Boston, 1991).

Longerich, Peter, *Joseph Goebbels. Biographie* (Munich, 2010).

Löwenstein, Hubertus Prinz zu, *Die Tragödie eines Volkes. Deutschland 1918–1934* (Amsterdam, 1934).

Magida, Arthur J., *The Nazi Séance: The Strange Story of the Jewish Psychic in Hitler's Circle* (London, 2011).

Mallmann, Klaus-Michael, *Kommunisten in der Weimarer Republik. Sozialgeschichte einer revolutionären Bewegung* (Darmstadt, 1996).

Malzacher, Werner M., *Berliner Gaunergeschichten. Aus der Unterwelt 1918–1933* (Berlin, 1970).

Mann, Golo, *Deutsche Geschichte des 19. und 20. Jahrhunderts* (Frankfurt am Main, 2009).

Mann, Klaus, *Der Wendepunkt* (Reinbek, 1993).

Mannes, Astrid Luise, *Heinrich Brüning. Leben, Wirken, Schicksal* (Munich, 1999).

Meissner, Hans-Otto, *Die Machtergreifung 30. Januar 1933* (Esslingen, 1983).

Meissner, Hans-Otto, *Junge Jahre im Reichspräsidentenpalais. Erinnerungen an Ebert und Hindenburg 1919–1934* (Esslingen/ Munich, 1988).

Meissner, Otto, *Ebert, Hindenburg, Hitler. Erinnerungen eines Staatssekretärs* (Esslingen/ Munich, 1991).

Mey-Leviné, Rosa, *Im inneren Kreis. Erinnerungen einer Kommunistin in Deutschland 1920–1933*, ed. Hermann Weber (Cologne, 1982).

Mierau, Fritz, *Russen in Berlin. Literatur, Malerei, Theater, Film 1918–1933* (Leipzig, 1987).

Möckelmann, Reiner, *Franz von Papen. Hitlers ewiger Vasall* (Darmstadt, 2016).

Mohler, Arnim, *Die Konservative Revolution in Deutschland 1918–1932. Ein Handbuch* (Graz/ Stuttgart, 1999).

Molderings, Herbert, *Fotografie in der Weimarer Republik* (Berlin, 1988).

Moltke, Helmuth James von, *Briefe an Freya 1939–1945*, ed. Beate Ruhm von Oppen, 2nd edn (Munich, 1991).

Mommsen, Hans, *Die verspielte Freiheit. Der Weg der Republik von Weimar in den Untergang 1918 bis 1933* (Berlin, 1989).

Monteath, Peter (ed.), *Ernst Thälmann. Mensch und Mythos* (Amsterdam/Atlanta, 2000).

Montefiore, Simon Sebag, *Stalin. The Court of the Red Tsar* (London, 2003).

Morsey, Rudolf, *Brüning und Adenauer* (Düsseldorf, 1972).

Noske, Gustav, *Erlebtes aus Aufstieg und Niedergang einer Demokratie* (Offenbach, 1947).

Oehme, Walter, and Caro, *Kurt, Kommt 'Das Dritte Reich'?* (Berlin, 1930).

Ohrt, Rainer, *Der SD-Mann Johannes Schmidt, der Mörder des Reichskanzlers Kurt von Schleicher?* (Münster, 2012).

Ossietzky, Maud von, *Maud von Ossietzky erzählt*, 2nd expanded edn (Berlin, 1988).

Palmer, Torsten, and Neubauer, Hendrik, *Die Weimarer Zeit in Pressefotosund Fotoreportagen* (Cologne, 2000).

Papen, Franz von, *Der Wahrheit eine Gasse* (Munich, 1952).

Papen, Franz von, *Vom Scheitern einer Demokratie* (Mainz, 1968).

Paudler, Maria, '... *auch Lachen will gelernt sein*' (Berlin, 1978).

Petzold, Joachim, *Franz von Papen. Ein deutsches Verhängnis* (Berlin/ Munich, 1995).

Peukert, Detlev J. K., *Die Weimarer Republik. Krisenjahre der Klassischen Moderne* (Frankfurt am Main, 1987).

Pförtner, Rudolf (ed.), *Alltag in der Weimarer Republik. Erinnerungen an eine unruhige Zeit* (Düsseldorf/ Vienna/New York, 1990).

Plehwe, Friedrich Karl von, *Reichskanzler Kurt von Schleicher. Weimars letzte Chance gegen Hitler* (Esslingen, 1983).

Podewin, Norbert, *Walter Ulbricht. Eine neue Biographie* (Berlin, 1995).

Pünder, Hermann, Politik in der Reichskanzlei. Aufzeichnungen aus den Jahren 1929-1932, ed. Thilo Vogelsang (*Schriftenreihe der Vierteljahrshefte für Zeitgeschichte*, Nr 3) (Stuttgart, 1961).

Pyra, Wolfram, *Hindenburg. Herrschaft zwischen Hohenzollern und Hitler* (Munich, 2009).

Reuth, Ralf Georg, *Goebbels* (Munich/Zurich, 1990).

Rheinbaben, Werner von, *Viermal Deutschland. Aus dem Erlebten eines Seemanns, Diplomaten, Politikers 1895-1954* (Berlin, 1954).

Rheinbaben, Werner von, *Kaiser, Kanzler, Präsidenten. 'Wie ich sie erlebte' 1895/1934* (Mainz, 1968).

Röhl, Klaus R., *Die letzten Tage der Republik von Weimar. Kommunisten und Nationalsozialisten im Berliner BVG-Streik von 1932* (Munich, 2008).

Röhm, Ernst, *Die Geschichte eines Hochverräters*, 2nd edn (Munich, 1930).

Rosenhaft, Eve, *Beating the Fascists? The German Communists and Political Violence 1929-1933* (Cambridge, 1983).

Schacht, Hjalmar, *1933. Wie eine Demokratie stirbt*, 2nd edn (Düsseldorf/Vienna, 1969).

Schad, Martha, *Frauen gegen Hitler. Vergessene Widerstandskämpferinnen im Nationalsozialismus*, 2nd edn (Munich, 2010).

Schebera, Jürgen, *Damals im Romanischen Café...* (Braunschweig, 1988).

Schirmann, Léon, *Altonaer Blutsonntag, 17. Juli 1932. Dichtungen und Wahrheit* (Hamburg, 1994).

Schirmann, Léon, *Justizmanipulationen. Altonaer Blutsonntag und die Altonaer bzw. Hamburger Justiz 1932-1994*, 2nd edn (Berlin, 1995).

Schüddelkopf, Otto-Ernst, *Nationalbolschewismus in Deutschland 1918-1933* (Frankfurt am Main/Berlin/Vienna, 1983).

Schulz, Gerhard, *Zwischen Demokratie und Diktatur*. vol. 3: *Von Brüning zu Hitler* (Berlin, 1992).

Schulze, Hagen, *Otto Braun oder Preußens demokratische Sendung*

(Frankfurt am Main/Berlin/Vienna, 1981).

Schulze, Hagen, *Weimar. Deutschland 1917–1933* (Munich, 1998).

Schuster, Martin, Die SA in der nationalsozialistischen 'Machtergreifung', in *Berlin und Brandenburg 1926–1934* (Berlin, 2005).

Severing, Carl, Mein Lebensweg. Band I: *Vom Schlosser zum Minister*, vol. II: *Im Auf und Ab der Republik* (Cologne, 1950).

Sheean, Vincent, *Dorothy and Red* (New York, 1963).

Stampfer, Friedrich, *Die vierzehn Jahre der ersten deutschen Republik*, 4th edn (Cologne, 1953).

Sternberg, Wilhelm von, *Carl von Ossietzky. Es ist eine unheimliche Stimmung in Deutschland. Ein biographischer Bericht* (Berlin, 2000).

Suhr, Elke, *Carl von Ossietzky. Eine Biographie* (Cologne, 1988).

Thälmann, Ernst, *Reden und Aufsätze zur Geschichte der deutschen Arbeiterbewegung, vol. 1: Auswahl aus den Jahren Juni 1919 bis November 1928* (Berlin (Ost), 1956).

Thälmann, Ernst, *Zwischen Erinnerung und Erwartung. Autobiographische Aufzeichnungen, geschrieben in faschistischer Haft* (Hamburg, 1994).

Thompson, Dorothy, *The New Russia* (New York, 1928).

Thompson, Dorothy, *Kassandra spricht. Antifaschistische Publizistik 1932–1942*, ed. Jürgen Schebera (Leipzig, 1986).

Treue, Wilhelm (ed.), *Deutschland in der Weltwirtschaftskrise in Augenzeugenberichten* (Munich, 1976).

Treviranus, Gottfried, *Das Ende von Weimar. Heinrich Brüning und seine Zeit* (Düsseldorf, 1968).

Tschirschky, Fritz Günther von, *Erinnerungen eines Hochverräters* (Stuttgart, 1972).

Tucholsky, Kurt, *Gesamtausgabe Texte und Briefe*, Bd. 14 (Reinbek, 1998).

Turner, Henry Ashby, *German Big Business and the Rise of Hitler* (New York, 1985).

Ullstein, Hermann, *The House of Ullstein* (London, 2016).

Usadel, Georg, *Zeitgeschichte in Wort und Bild. Vom Alten zum Neuen Reich*, 4 vols (Oldenburg, Berlin, 1936–1939).

Vernekohl, Wilhelm, *Heinrich Brüning. Ein deutscher Staatsmann im Urteil der Zeit* (Münster, 1961).

Vogelsang, Thilo, *Reichswehr, Staat und NSDAP. Beiträge zur Deutschen Geschichte 1930–1932* (Stuttgart, 1962).

Vogelsang, Thilo, *Kurt von Schleicher. Ein General als Politiker* (Göttingen/Frankfurt/Zurich, 1965).

Wallbaum, Klaus, *Der Überläufer. Rudolf Diels (1900–1957) – der erste Gestapo-Chef des Hitler-Regimes* (Frankfurt am Main, 2010).

Weber, Hermann, *Ulbricht fälscht Geschichte. Ein Kommentar mit Dokumenten zum 'Grundriß der Geschichte der deutschen Arbeiterbewegung'* (Cologne, 1964).

Weber, Hermann, *Die Gründung der KPD. Protokoll und Materialien des Gründungsparteitages der KPD 1918/1919* (Berlin, 1993).

Weber, Hermann and Bayerlein, Bernhard H., *Der Thälmann-Skandal. Geheime Korrespondenzen mit Stalin* (Berlin, 2003).

Weber, Hermann, Drabkin, Jakov, Bayerlein, Bernhard H., and Galkin, Aleksandr, *Deutschland, Russland, Komintern*, vol. 1: *Überblicke, Analysen, Diskussionen* (Berlin/Boston, 2014).

Weber, Hermann, Drabkin, Jakov, Bayerlein, Bernhard H., and Galkin, Aleksandr, *Deutschland, Russland, Komintern*, vol. 2: *Dokumente, Part 1–5* (Berlin/Boston, 2015).

Weka (pen name of Willi Pröger), *Stätten der Berliner Prostitution: von den Elends-Absteigequartieren am Schlesischen Bahnhof und Alexanderplatz zur Luxus-Prostitution der Friedrichstraße und des Kurfürstendamms: eine Reportage* (Berlin, 1930).

Winkler, Heinrich August, *Arbeiter und Arbeiterbewegung in der Weimarer Republik, Der Weg in die Katastrophe. 1930 bis 1933* (Berlin, 1987).

Winkler, Heinrich August (ed.), *Die deutsche Staatskrise 1930–1933. Handlungsspielräume und Alternativen* (Munich, 1992).

Winkler, Heinrich August, *Von Weimar zu Hitler. Die Arbeiterbewegung und das Scheitern der ersten deutschen Demokratie. Antrittsvorlesung an der Humboldt-Universität am 28.* April 1992 (Berlin, 1993).

Winkler, Heinrich August, *Von der Revolution zur Stabilisierung. Arbeiter und Arbeiterbewegung in der Weimarer Republik 1918 bis 1924* (Berlin/Bonn, 2001).

Winkler, Heinrich August, *Weimar im Widerstreit. Deutungen der ersten deutschen Republik im geteilten Deutschland* (Munich, 2002).

Winkler, Heinrich August, *Weimar 1918–1933. Die Geschichte der ersten deutschen Demokratie* (Munich, 2018).

Wohlfromm, Hans J., and Wohlfromm, Gisela, *Und morgen gibt es Hitlerwetter! Alltägliches und Kurioses aus dem Dritten Reich* (Cologne, 2017).

Zarnow, Gottfried, *Gefesselte Justiz. Politische Bilder aus Deutscher Gegenwart*, 5th edn, vol. 1 (Munich, 1931).

Zarusky, Jürgen, *Die deutschen Sozialdemokraten und das sowjetische Modell. Ideologische Auseinandersetzungen und außenpolitische Konzeptionen 1917–1933* (Munich, 1992).

Zuckmayer, Carl, *Als wär's ein Stück von mir* (Frankfurt am Main, 1976).

Zuckmayer, Carl, *Aufruf zum Leben. Porträts und Zeugnisse aus bewegten Zeiten* (Frankfurt am Main, 1982).

Picture List

of Count Lobkowicz's Bugatti T 54 following the high-speed crash on the AVUS in Berlin on 22 May 1932 that killed the aristocratic Czech racing driver (Imagno/Getty).

pp. 214–15 The Berlin transport strike, November 1932. In many parts of the city (seen here, the high street in the district of Schöneberg), strikers laid heavy wooden beams, pieces of concrete and other debris across the tracks to prevent the passage of trams driven by strike-breakers (Bundesarchiv, Ohne Angaben).

pp. 232–3 An enthusiastic crowd, many with their right arms raised in a 'Hitler-greeting', hails the arrival of the Nazi leader at the presidential palace shortly after his appointment as German Chancellor on 30 January 1933 (bpk).

pp. 256–7 The plenary chamber of the burned-out Reichstag building. In the foreground is the name plaque of the NSDAP delegate Ludwig Münchmeyer (bpk).

pp. 272–3 Black-clad Gestapo men training German shepherd dogs at the Röntgental police dog-training facility north-east of Berlin in 1934 (Popperfoto via Getty Images).

Index